WARD ACTIVITIES FOR THE CLUELESS

WARD ACTIVITIES FOR THE CLUELESS

Clark L. and Kathryn H. Kidd

Kent D. and Shannon Pugmire

BOOKCRAFT

Visit us at www.deseretbook.com

Library of Congress Cataloging-in-Publication Data

Ward activities for the clueless / Clark L. Kidd . . . [et al.].
    p.   cm.
    Includes indexes.
    ISBN 1-57345-946-1 (pbk.)
    1. Mormons—Religious life. 2. Mormons—Recreation. I. Kidd, Clark.
BX8656 .W37 2001
254'.09332—dc21

2001002715

Printed in the United States of America   54459-6799

10 9 8 7 6 5 4 3 2 1

Contents

Acknowledgments

Although it's hard to admit, not all of the great ideas in this book originated in the tiny brains of the four coauthors. So it is only fair that we acknowledge the help and ideas we received from many others while writing this book:

Donna Kneeland, who provided several ideas for great service activities that she had helped plan;

Brenda Moran, for giving Shannon some of her terrific ideas, and then having the guts to tell Shannon when the write-ups were nowhere near as good as the original concepts. Brenda also held Shannon's sweaty hand when she was feeling a little unsure of herself, and is therefore deserving of eternal gratitude;

Nikki Pugmire, a wonderful daughter and best friend, for taking time to listen when Shannon needed to talk ideas through, and for her creative suggestions and interest in this project;

Charee Peck, stake Young Women president, South Salt Lake Stake, for allowing us to include her unique missionary activity;

Debra Woods, a friend of Shannon's since college, for allowing us to include a few ideas from her Primary, Etc., Web site;

Missy Hooper, Rona Scott, and JoAnn York for offering suggestions for activities that women enjoy;

Mike Mitchell, who stayed awake through his second stake conference in one day by coming up with activity ideas to enliven chapter 2;

Judy Willis, whose "Welcome Neighbor" packet was a brilliant idea, even though it was thwarted in the distribution;

Jane D. Brady, for enriching the enrichment section (bless your face!);

The humorous Emily Watts and the most excellent Cory Maxwell, for reasons they well understand;

Janna DeVore, for her contributions to the Primary section, and Aaron Taylor, the cartoonist whose work we so enjoy;

Scott and Kristine Card, who created the most brilliant rules for road shows we've ever seen—even though we promptly lost them and had to use an adaptation in this text;

And to all those dedicated and creative church leaders who plan wonderful activities and then share their ideas with others via the Internet. We have adapted (and hopefully improved) a good number of your ideas here, although we have not included any material that was copyrighted or that we suspected had been taken from a copyrighted source.

Introduction

Not Another Activity!

Once upon a time a casual acquaintance, unaware of our religious affiliation, made the following statement: "The people in my office are so boring. Every night at five they lock up their desks and go home. They don't want to go out for pizza or for a drink; they just want to get home to their families. The way they act, you would think they were a bunch of *Mormons* or something!"

Although members of The Church of Jesus Christ of Latter-day Saints do shun the types of worldly socializing embraced by many, it's just plain wrong to classify us as a humorless or rigid people. From the early days of the Church, social and cultural activities have been integral to the practice of the LDS faith. The Prophet Joseph Smith often taught that singing and dancing were acceptable ways of showing our appreciation to God for the blessings and joys of life. Joseph was known to be an accomplished dancer, and he and Emma would often host dances in their own home.

The journals of many Saints from the Nauvoo era depict the temple as being both the spiritual and cultural center of the town. During the day, it would be used for the performing of sacred temple ordinances. But at night the same Saints would gather to the temple to participate in feasting, praying, singing, and dancing. On at least one occasion, Brigham Young and other members of the Quorum of the Twelve danced late into the night to the music of a small orchestra. This was a radical concept at a time when many other Christian sects were condemning such activities as worldly and unholy.

The concept of worship through celebration was not a minor theme to the early Saints, but was just as indispensable a part of the gospel as were the principles of faith and repentance. You do not have to look far in latter-day scriptures for the justification of such beliefs. Any Primary child can probably quote you the Book of Mormon scripture "men are, that they might have joy" (2 Nephi 2:25). Even after the Saints were driven out of Nauvoo and were organizing at Winter Quarters before heading west, the Lord counseled them, "If thou art merry, praise the Lord with singing, with music, with dancing, and with a prayer of praise and thanksgiving" (D&C 136:28). The Saints followed this counsel, and would often conclude a long day's journey by gathering around the campfires to sing, dance, play music, and tell stories.

These activities did not cease when the Saints arrived in the Salt Lake valley. They proceeded to build tabernacles, theaters, music halls, and other structures that could be used for both spiritual and cultural growth.

But times have changed. In an age when we have the distraction of television and soccer games, do ward activities continue to have a place in the lives of Saints living in the twenty-first century?

Sadly, it seems to be a growing trend in these days of "too much to do in too little time" for people to ignore the social aspects of the LDS culture. In every ward, we run into active Church members who seem to have no interest in participating in social activities, and who view social interaction as an optional part of living the gospel. Even if they can be enticed to participate in a ward activity, they will be involved as little as possible—all the while resenting the imposition on their time. Some will even use the Church to rationalize their antisocial behavior, arguing that it's more important to cocoon themselves away with their families than to waste time at yet another ward activity.

We know that you, our discriminating reader, have no such mistaken attitudes. You fully understand and appreciate the need for balance in your life, and you realize that participating in the social aspects of Church membership is important for a number of reasons. In fact, you are probably in charge of planning some of these activities, or you would not be reading this book. But how do you deal with scoffers who just don't understand why you want to plan yet another activity? Unfortunately, these scoffers may not be just a few miscellaneous naysayers. In rare cases, even the bishop isn't keen on having ward social functions. If so, you've got a double workload ahead of you. Not only do you have to plan your activities, but you also have to convince your ward leaders that social outlets are important, and that you'll need their support in order for those activities to succeed.

If you need a little ammunition for converting the unconverted to the value of ward activities, here are the things we wish we could convey to every Church member:

Activities Teach Us to Serve

One of the major themes of the Savior's life was service to others. Members of The Church of Jesus Christ of Latter-day Saints are expected to follow that example, and to learn to serve others both inside and outside the Church.

Although many types of service activities can and should be done on a small scale, either as individuals or as families, service activities that can be done by large groups of people are also important. Organized service activities provide those who are new in the Church, or those just learning to serve, with a comfortable introduction to what service is all about. There is a good spirit that descends upon a group of Saints who are engaged in a worthwhile cause. Not only does service make the participants feel closer to God but it also helps them develop ties to one another because they are rendering service together.

Each year our ward participates in a community project that involves making major improvements and repairs to some of the older homes in our area. The men do most of the heavy work, while the women take over the cleaning and painting tasks. The youth are responsible for providing food and drinks to the workers. Even the children are involved as they wield a broom or carry supplies to the work site.

Although this project requires some sacrifice on the part of ward members, it also brings them closer together as a ward family. They get no pay for this donated Saturday, other than the grateful thanks and occasional tears of the homeowners they help.

Activities Promote Understanding

We're sure the homeowners helped by our ward's annual spring project have a much different impression of Latter-day Saints than they did before we arrived. Service-oriented activities help dispel false beliefs and open the doors to understanding and cooperation with those who are not of our faith.

Probably one of the best examples of this occurred during 1997, when the Church celebrated the 150th anniversary of the arrival of the pioneers in the Salt Lake valley. As part of the sesquicentennial celebration, each ward was asked to perform some type of service project that would benefit its community. Many wards responded, and hundreds of thousands of hours were donated to thousands of service projects throughout the world. This resulted in a flood of favorable publicity, as hundreds of governments and organizations praised the service that was rendered and the many good works that were performed throughout the year. Many comments were made about how our members had accomplished in one day what would have taken years to accomplish through normal channels. These comments did not cease in 1997, but continue to be made daily by organizations grateful for ongoing efforts of LDS people to improve their neighborhoods.

There are many ways that wards can reach out to their communities. In addition to service projects, they can plan and promote programs that educate and entertain their neighbors. Wards will quite often promote family history, food storage, or employment fairs, where members of the community can come and learn something new. When our stake dedicated a new stake center, it made arrangements for a noted time management expert to come and give a seminar. This event attracted a large crowd, many of whom were not members of the Church.

Activities Build Ward Unity

We have already noted that doing service projects promotes a good feeling among the members of a ward. This feeling of unity can arise from any ward activity—even those that are designed just to provide an evening of fun for ward members. You can sit next to someone in church for years, but you see a whole new side of that person when you are standing side by side washing dishes, with soapsuds up to your elbows. As your conversation turns to topics that are not typically discussed in a Sunday setting, you develop new appreciation for people. As you open your ears, you will invariably learn something new and interesting about everyone who crosses your path.

The scriptures tell us that the people in Enoch's day were taken into heaven because "they were of one heart and one mind, and dwelt in righteousness; and there was no poor among them" (Moses 7:18). If we are ever to reach that level of perfection, we will first need to develop absolute unity with our fellow worshippers. Developing a strong sense of kinship probably won't happen with one activity, but it certainly won't happen at all unless there are opportunities for ward members to socialize and work together. If there were no other reason to hold a ward activity than to strengthen ward unity, that would be reason enough.

Activities Provide Missionary Opportunities

Many who are outside the LDS faith have a deep curiosity about the programs and members of the Church. They may have Mormon friends or coworkers, they may have seen some of the LDS public service commercials on television, or they may be curious about the temples or meetinghouses located in their communities. Although many outsiders would be interested in learning more about our faith, most of them are probably not ready to get into a doctrinal discussion with a pair of missionaries. Thus ward activities provide the perfect setting for a nonthreatening introduction to the Church. The non-member doesn't feel threatened because nobody will be pushing a sales pitch in his face, and the member doesn't feel threatened because it is a lot easier to invite someone to a party than it is to challenge him to baptism. Ward activities provide a perfect opportunity for the curious outsider to learn more about the Church without making a major commitment.

Anyone who has done any missionary work will confirm that it is the Spirit that really does the conversion, rather than anyone involved in the actual teaching. If your ward activities are planned and executed correctly, those nonmembers who come will be able to feel that Spirit. This Spirit may uncover a longing for the feeling of love and family found in Mormon homes and wards—a feeling that may not be present in their own churches and families. An investigator who attends ward activities may start to realize that the Church could provide something that is missing in his life, and the recognition of this need will open the door to more traditional missionary discussions.

One recent activity in our ward was a Hawaiian luau. After a delicious dinner, those who attended were treated to a program of ethnic dances. Other than opening and closing prayers, and a few comments from some of the speakers, there was nothing that would connect this activity to a religious organization. Yet a good spirit was present, and it provided a great opportunity for ward members to invite those outside the Church for an evening of food and entertainment.

Even if you're one of those unbelievers who hate ward activities, your attendance at such activities is worthwhile because you are providing a good environment in which missionary work may be performed. You may be so shy that you don't say a single word to outsiders; but that doesn't matter. What does matter is that the nonmembers who attend see the spirit of love and fellowship that are found in the LDS community.

Activities Build Friendships

Just as ward activities provide a low-key introduction to the Church for those of other faiths, they can also provide a similar opportunity to reach those members whose testimonies and commitment have faded over time. If you home teach and visit teach part-member families or members who rarely attend church, you should consider inviting them to ward activities that would be of interest to them. If they accept your invitation and attend, this provides them an opportunity to be touched by the Spirit of the Lord and the spirit of ward members.

Perhaps you know such a person who has a talent or skill that could be shared with other ward members. Such people will often agree—and in fact will often be honored—if they are asked to participate in an activity where they can demonstrate and share their talents. This will often open the door to friendships and feelings of belonging that will lead to increased involvement with the ward.

The four contributors to this book have lived in many different states and nations, and have probably been members of two dozen different wards and branches. Even for active members of the Church, moving into a new ward is difficult, and it often takes a period of time to adjust and to make friends. But involvement in ward activities can help accelerate this process, as it helps you locate kindred spirits and find those who would be good additions to your circle of friends. It has also been our experience that those who accuse ward members of being unfriendly are the same people who never seem to make it to ward activities.

Activities Strengthen Testimonies

If you take the broad view that ward activities encompass any activity outside of the typical Sunday meeting block, then many activities will be planned that are designed to spiritually build and strengthen the testimonies of those who attend.

Just about every ward provides regular youth firesides where the young people of the ward can meet with the bishopric to hear a variety of guest speakers. Many wards will also offer similar programs to all ward members, where they can occasionally come together for an inspirational program, followed by the traditional punch and cookies.

As with other activities, those with a spiritual theme tend to be more informal than the regular meetings of the Church. Those attending are still receiving spiritual food, but they are doing so in a setting that is a little more casual, and perhaps a little more comfortable for members and investigators who are not ready to start attending each Sunday on a regular basis.

Activities Provide a Social Connection

So maybe you're the world's biggest social butterfly, and perhaps your little daily planner is so full of activities that you won't have a free night for three months. But consider that not everyone is as popular as you. Perhaps for someone else, that ward potluck dinner that you consider to be so dull will be the social highlight of the month.

Here's another scary thought. Even if you are the most popular kid on the block, consider that your luck will probably not hold out forever. You don't believe that? Just take an honest look at the members of your ward. While the stereotypical Mormon family (Mom, Dad, and a gaggle of kids) will be found in great abundance, you will also see a lot of families that don't fit that mold. You will find single kids away from home for the first time, newly-married couples fresh off the farm and with no kids yet, older people with no spouse for one reason or another, married couples with no children at home, single moms struggling to provide a foundation for their children, and many other combinations of nontraditional families. In some wards, nontraditional families are becoming so numerous that the nontraditional is becoming traditional, and the traditional is becoming an oddity.

We live in a ward that is about twenty-five miles outside of Washington, D.C. Many ward members are temporary transplants from the West who are only here a few years on military assignments, or while they attend school or serve in government internships. One of the nice traditions started by our ward is a yearly Thanksgiving leftovers dinner. This is just an opportunity to get together with other ward members and share some leftovers on the Saturday after Thanksgiving. While this type of activity would probably never be popular in Utah, it fills a need for those who may be temporarily away from home and feeling a little homesick around the holidays.

As pathetic as you might consider some of your ward activities, those ward members feeling isolated and lonely may actually look forward to them as one of the few events on their social calendar. So if you can't derive any value or enjoyment for yourself from a particular activity, take consolation from the fact that you might be doing a great service to someone else by providing them an evening of much-needed social interaction.

Activities Educate

Clark once taught a class at a Relief Society meeting that involved making little stained-glass butterflies. It was only about a ninety-

minute project, and Clark had done most of the work ahead of time. All the ladies needed to do was select the glass pieces they wanted, connect them together, and then clean the glass. Everyone seemed to enjoy the evening, and some of the butterflies were almost good enough to have been sold commercially. The next time Clark went to buy supplies at the stained glass store, the employee who waited on him was none other than one of the women who had attended the class. She said she had enjoyed the evening so much that she had taken some classes, and had been doing some projects and working at the store ever since. It was certainly a world-class example of how something learned at an activity could drastically alter the course of a person's life.

While there will probably be few such life-changing experiences associated with your activities, ward members can still derive much enjoyment from learning new things and developing new talents. We probably have all caught ourselves saying "One day I would really like to learn how to (fill in the blank), if only I had a little more (fill in the blank)." As someone in charge of activities for your ward, this is your great opportunity to fulfill these kinds of wishes on a small scale.

There are probably dozens of people in your ward who have knowledge or talents that would be of great interest to others. With just a small effort on your part, you can organize educational activities that can bring these people together with those who would benefit from their abilities. Like Clark, you might assist someone in uncovering a hidden talent or interest. But even if the person decides they have no interest or aptitude in the subject being presented, you have not failed. You have allowed them to explore something new with a minimal investment of time and money—and that could not be considered a failure by any standard.

Activities Motivate

We've all had the experience of setting a goal for ourselves, only to see that goal be forgotten after a short time. Our resolve to lose weight, read the scriptures more often, eat better foods, and get more exercise will often last only as long as that tempting homemade pie or that next distraction on the television. But a ward that implements goal-oriented activities can often motivate its members to succeed where they would have failed if left to their own devices.

Our ward is currently in the middle of a program designed to encourage members to read the Book of Mormon in ninety days. At the start of the program, bookmarks were distributed to remind members of the reading assignment for each week. As part of each Sunday's printed bulletin, a section reminds readers of the reading program for the coming week, and provides interesting facts about that portion of the scripture. At the end of the ninety-day period, a ward Book of Mormon party will be held, and members who achieved the reading goal will be encouraged to share their experiences at the next fast and testimony meeting. Those who have participated in similar programs in other wards claim that reading the entire Book of Mormon in a short period will give you new perspectives that escape the reader who reads a chapter or two per day.

Sometimes members will be more motivated to accomplish a goal if it can be done as part of a group, rather than individually. Those who plan ward activities should consider the power they have to motivate people for good.

If we still haven't convinced you that activities can be fun, perhaps you did notice another theme that passed through just about all of the reasons listed for supporting ward activities. Let us give you another hint by summarizing those reasons. When you support ward activities, you educate, motivate, provide social connections, strengthen testimonies, build friendships and understanding, promote missionary work, build ward unity, and help others. That's quite a list!

Did you catch it this time—that common theme of service? Here you thought all along that such activities were just for your enjoyment, when the real benefit has always been to provide opportunities for you to serve others in many different ways. So even if we couldn't convince you that you really are allowed to have fun at such activities, perhaps we have convinced you that you can look at your participation in ward activities as a type of service opportunity.

How This Book Can Help

As noted in the previous section, the authors take a pretty broad interpretation of the term "ward activity." We do not take it to mean the handful of ward socials held throughout the year. Instead, we cast the net wide enough to include any activity connected with your ward that is held outside of the traditional meeting block on Sunday. Thus, activities can include firesides, family history fairs, talent shows, plays, service projects, and basically any activity that brings the members of the ward together for some common purpose. We mustn't overlook those activities designed for a subset of the ward, such as youth activities or Primary activities. We should also include things that are not really activities (such as ward newsletters and Sunday bulletins), but which perform the same function of bringing people together and making them feel a part of the ward family. In short, the authors consider all of the above mentioned to be "ward activities," and, somewhere between the covers of this book, we will try to give you good ideas related to all of them.

If you stop to think about it, just about every calling in a ward invokes some responsibility for planning and sponsoring activities. It is certainly a big part of callings involving the youth. Experienced Young Men and Young Women presidents will probably tell you that a large portion of their callings involves the creation of new activities that will be exciting to the youth, and still teach them something.

There are many parables in which the Savior emphasizes the need of a good foundation before building a house (or a family, church, testimony, or anything worthwhile). Similarly, there are some basic principles that can help you in the planning of any kind of activity. A successful activity does not just happen, and does not plan itself. Rather, it is the result of many hours of planning, organizing and publicizing. In chapter 1 we will teach you many of these principles that will lead to successful activities that bring members together and foster feelings of joy and belonging. In addition to producing worthwhile activities, understanding these same principles will save you work because it will show you how to involve others in the process. You have probably heard the saying, "Many hands make light work." Having many ward members involved will lighten the load; it will also make for more successful activities because of their involvement and their contributions.

Don't let the first chapter give you the impression that this will be a scholarly book; the authors couldn't write one of those if they tried. Once we get you through the basic principles of planning, we just want to give you lots of good ideas for activities that have proved successful for the authors and for others. Members of the LDS community have always been willing to share their successful ideas, and we have tried to collect and summarize the best of those ideas, improving and fine-tuning them where necessary, and then presenting them in a manner flexible enough to work in many different ward settings. Thanks to all of those who have shared their ideas so freely (see acknowledgments) with no motive except that of helping others magnify their callings.

For most LDS members, hearing the words "ward activity" will bring to mind those traditional gatherings where everyone in the ward is invited. These are the kinds of activities we will highlight in chapter 2. Whether your motive is to build testimonies, find hidden talents, or just feed the starving hoards, you will hopefully find everything you need in this chapter.

Chapter 3 will narrow our focus just a bit, and concentrate on activities to which adults only will be invited. While most activities involve entire families, many wards will often sponsor some events designed just for grown-ups. This could be something like a "Date Night," where you bring your spouse or your latest friend-of-the-opposite-sex for a quiet dinner out. It could also be a fireside or educational workshop that would not be of interest to the younger set. Organizations such as the Relief Society will often sponsor events to which just the women are invited. If those involved with the Single Adults program are doing their jobs, your ward should also be having regular activities targeted towards them. We will try to present some ideas in this chapter that work especially well when your target audience does not include the kiddies.

In chapter 4, we will address activities designed for the youth. If you have ever served in the Young Men or Young Women organizations, you know that coming up with meaningful activities for these young charges will consume much of your time and many of your brain cells. Probably more than any of the other auxiliaries, these organizations have an unquenchable thirst for good activities that will entertain while teaching correct principles. This is partly because the youth have so many activities, but also because participants are at the age where any principle taught is better taught as part of an activity. A serious religious discussion that may be fascinating to the high priests quorum will never work for a bunch of energetic teenagers full of excess adrenaline and other youthful hormones. Holding the attention of any teenager for more than ten minutes is a major accomplishment, but hopefully this chapter will help.

Those who have burned themselves out in the youth programs are often given a peaceful hiatus by being reassigned to the Primary organization. They soon discover they have truly reached the celestial kingdom when they find that a simple toy or piece of candy can motivate, and that activities need not be every week. But while they may occur less often, Primary activities are no less important. In chapter 5 we will give you some ideas that work especially well for these tender children.

While all activities involve service to one degree or another, sometimes you will want to plan activities that are based solidly on the theme of service. These are obviously much different from the typical ward dinner or talent show, and must also be planned differently. We will try to help you do this in chapter 6, as we present ideas for many different service activities. Your opportunities for service will vary greatly depending on your circumstance, but the ideas presented in this chapter should be flexible enough that they can be adapted to just about any situation.

By the time we reach chapter 7, we will have covered all of the activities targeted toward specific groups within the ward. So we will then turn our attention back to some specific topics of interest to anyone planning activities. Most people called to serve on the ward activities committee will soon learn that the one activity they *must* produce is the ward Christmas party. Clark and Kathy once lived in a ward where this was so important that being assigned to oversee the ward Christmas party was a *calling*—bestowed annually upon some hapless couple or individual. While this may seem strange at first, those involved in planning activities soon learn that the calendar is your friend, rather than your foe. You are tasked with planning a certain number of activities per year or per month, and you soon learn that one of the challenges of that goal is coming up with themes for those activities. Having the event occur during a certain season or around a certain holiday will give you the perfect theme for the activity. Adult activities in February can center on Valentine's Day or President's Day. Any activity held during the autumn months can have a harvest theme. In chapter 7 we will exploit this idea, and try to give you enough theme ideas to cover just about every day of the year.

An experienced activity planner will also quickly learn the importance of having a few spare warm-up activities to save the day when the main activity begins to drag. These activities typically last only five to twenty minutes, and are done just for fun or to keep the crowd amused while waiting for something else to happen. We devote an entire chapter to these little warm-up activities (chapter 8), and classify them into Icebreakers (something to get the crowd warmed up while waiting for everyone to arrive) and Lifesavers (something to kill the time when transitioning from one part of an activity to another). With a little bit of imagination, you might even be able to turn some of these tiny activities into full-grown ones.

We have reserved the last chapter (chapter 9) for nontraditional activities (such as dinners provided for the family at funerals), and for those things that strengthen the bonds of communication and friendship within the ward without truly being activities. Examples of the latter include ward newsletters and the Sunday ward bulletin distributed by many wards in their sacrament meetings. Kent and Shannon are currently the chairmen of their ward's activities committee, and they also produce the Sunday bulletin. While this may seem odd to some, they have found that these callings really fit well together, as the bulletin is often used to promote activities ahead of time, and then report on their success after the fact. Having both of these callings has made them realize the greater purpose of activities—to increase communication, love, and friendship among the members of the ward.

At the end of most chapters you will find a section called "Questions from the Clueless." We included this section to address topics that applied to the chapter but don't really fit in any of the previous sections. We also used it as a place to answer those questions that weren't answered previously, or to give further information on something that may have already been presented but needed more detail. Sometimes using a question and answer format makes it easier to convey an idea, so we hope these sections will be as fun for you to read as they were for us to write.

As you read through the book, you will often see an arrow to the left of a paragraph. This is a sign that important information, usually in the form of a list, follows. Scattered throughout the book you will also find some little shaded boxes with the label "Sneaky Secret." These are reserved for those ideas that seem simple but can make the difference between an average activity and one that will be remembered. We also had fun writing these secrets, and hope they prove useful.

One other thing you'll notice is that we've set up a little guideline before each activity in this book, giving you a few hints that will help you with the preparation and planning. "Materials" will give you an idea of what props or other items you'll need to have on hand. "Effort quotient" refers to the effort your group will have to expend once they reach the activity. "Time" refers to the actual time spent participating in the event—excluding setup and cleanup. "Planning" refers to the work you'll be doing behind the scenes, with some activities requiring only minimal preparation, others needing extensive preparation, and a select few requiring a massive effort.

Icons have been used to define the estimated level of effort, planning, and time required for each activity. Here is a key to those icons.

Effort Quotient	Planning	Time
Passive 🖐	Minimal ★	Less than 30 minutes ⧖
Moderate 🖐🖐	Moderate ★★	Less than 1 hour ⧖⧖
Active 🖐🖐🖐	Extensive ★★★	1-2 hours ⧖⧖⧖
	Massive ★★★★	More than 2 hours ⧖⧖⧖⧖

About the Authors

The four authors of this book are all extremely talented at planning and executing just about any type of ward activity. Either that, or their bishops have just never figured out any other place to put them. Regardless of the reason, the authors have all served for many years on their respective ward activities committees, and have also been involved in planning activities for every ward auxiliary. Kathy has had the dubious claim of being the ward newsletter editor in just about every ward where she has resided. She either does a good job, or they are waiting for her to get it right. Kent and Shannon have had activity-related callings in many wards across the United States, and in other countries of the world. This has given them the vision of the Church as a worldwide church, and the perspective of how activities must be adapted for their audience.

But the authors realize they are not the source of all good activities, so they have tried to collect, categorize, and improve those activities designed by others in similar ward callings. These people have been kind enough to share their ideas anonymously, or without hope of compensation other than a simple acknowledgment. These ideas have been contributed by personal friends of the authors, and have also been gleaned from Internet Web sites, discussion groups, and mailing lists designed for the open sharing of such ideas. While all the good ideas from these sources could fill five hundred books, the authors hope that they have succeeded in summarizing and improving the best of these ideas.

Well, that's enough of an introduction. Let's start planning some fun and worthwhile activities. The people in your ward are just waiting to be entertained, taught, uplifted, and served. Your calling may not have the high profile of being a bishop, but you can gain as much satisfaction as you strive to make your ward members of one heart and one mind.

CHAPTER 1

Planning the Perfect Activity

There are many levels of involvement when organizing a ward activity. If you are a ward activities chairman, the entire question of when to have activities and what activities to have may be dumped in your lap, giving you the freedom—and the responsibility—to make all the decisions and plan all the details. But even if you chair your ward activities committee, this freedom isn't something you can take for granted. Some bishops and ward auxiliary leaders are micro-managers who plan every detail of each ward function, right down to the menu of a ward dinner and the color of the napkins. It may be hard to work under a bishop or an auxiliary leader who wants only your strong back and not your creativity, but your job is to do what is asked of you with a minimum amount of kicking and screaming. Remember (and you may have to keep reminding yourself of this)—what doesn't kill us only makes us stronger.

For the purpose of this book, however, we're going to assume you have a certain degree of authority as far as planning a ward activity is concerned. Whether you're planning the sit-down Christmas dinner or a costume parade for your Sunbeam class, you are the one making the decisions. This chapter will help you make the right choices—choices that will allow your activity to succeed in ways you may not have realized were possible. You'll find that success can be measured in more ways than simply counting the number of participants in attendance, and we'll show you what those ways are.

Whose Ward Is It, Anyway?

Before you begin to plan a ward activity, you should understand that you are planning the activity for *your* ward or *your* auxiliary or *your* tiny group within a ward or auxiliary. Wards are not made with cookie cutters. Some wards have a mix of ages, but others are composed almost exclusively of young and old people who have no middle ground (the "newly wed and nearly dead" wards). Still, other wards are composed solely of single people under age thirty—there are no children or old people to add to the mix.

Some wards have a wide range of ethnic groups; but others are composed of people from a single race and culture. Some wards are affluent, while others contain members who are counting their pennies between each paycheck. Some wards feature an entire population of university-educated people, and others are composed almost exclusively of people who work in the trades.

Even if your ward has the same age and ethnic mix as the ward(s) with which you share a building, the wards could have widely different personalities. Wards tend to reflect the traits of their leaders, so that one ward could be friendly and outgoing even as the neighboring ward is quiet and restrained. And other factors—mystery factors—may determine that your ward is quite different from the ward next door. One ward may be spiritually attuned, while its neighboring ward could suffer from a lack of spiritual commitment. One ward may reach out to the community, while its sister ward tends to focus inwardly and ignore the rest of the world.

In fact, your own ward may be entirely different from the ward it was ten years ago.

THIS WORKED WELL IN CALIFORNIA...

People move in. They move out. They die. Even people who stay change their focus over the years, so they may be different than they were a decade ago. New leaders take the reins from old ones. Neighborhoods change, and this affects the complexion of a ward too. And times change, so that activities that appealed to one generation may seem foreign to the next.

All this should tell you that when you're planning a party, you cannot import an idea from another ward and expect it to succeed in your ward or auxiliary. Your best friend's ward's Young Women program may traditionally make a spaghetti dinner for the young men, but if the young women in your own ward aren't even speaking to the young men, a spaghetti dinner may not be the best activity you can plan. Unless you know your ward before you plan your activity, you may be surprised to see that only three women show up for the women's overnight retreat that was such a huge success when it was held in a neighboring stake.

You also shouldn't use the same ward idea year after year in your own ward without examining it carefully to make sure it still works. For example, our own ward has a traditional Fourth of July pancake breakfast at a regional park. This has gone on for more years than any of us can count. Originally, a big patriotic program kicked off the event at sunrise. But over the years, people began to value their sleep more than they valued sitting through the patriotic stuff. Several years ago, the program was scuttled in favor of a quick flag-raising ceremony before the food was served, but people didn't even show up for that. This year the flag-raising ceremony wasn't even announced. Yes, it's pathetic when people prefer sleep to a show of patriotism, but times change. The patriotic breakfast that was so popular in years past may now be just a breakfast, but it's just as popular today as it was fifteen years ago. And because the organizers have had the vision to change the activity to fit the times, at least the holiday is still being observed.

Asking the Right Questions

There are as many different ways to organize a ward activity as there are people to do the organizing. Some may sit down with a Franklin® planner and treat the whole concept of having a party as seriously as they'd plot a military campaign, leaving no detail unorganized. Others may plan a party in such a haphazard way that they might as well be throwing darts at a dartboard, seemingly choosing menus and activities at random.

When you are organizing a ward activity, the final result is more important than how the decisions are made. If you're a dart-thrower, go ahead and throw the darts. If a military campaign is more your style, pull out the planner and get to work. But if you've never planned an event before, we have some suggestions that will help you organize your activity. No matter how big or how small your event, the best way to have a successful activity is to start by asking yourself the right questions. Here they are.

Who Is the Activity For?

This question may seem like a no-brainer. If you've been assigned to plan an activity for the Primary, you're obviously going to focus on the Primary children. If you've been assigned to plan an enrichment activity for your ward Relief Society members, you're obviously going to plan an event that appeals to women ages eighteen and up.

However, things are rarely as easy as they seem. "One size fits all" never fits everyone, and an event that appeals to eleven-year-old Primary children is going to be far too advanced for their four-year-old brothers and sisters unless you're careful to plan different activities for different age groups. By the same token, all Relief Society sisters were not created equal. An activity that focuses exclusively on young mothers is going to exclude people who have never been mothers, or who haven't been mothers for so many years that mother-related activities are no longer of interest. Your job as an event planner is to know your audience. If you can appeal to the interests of the people you're serving, you're going to have a successful activity. If you can't find a focus that will offer something to everyone on your potential

Sneaky Secret

The best way to attract participants is to make sure your event doesn't exclude large segments of people in your target audience. If you're planning an event such as a dance or a sports night or a poetry reading, people who don't dance or who aren't athletic or who don't like poetry are going to find excuses to stay home. You can't please everyone all the time, but you can make an effort to find themes that don't exclude vast numbers of your potential participants. For example, a Nephi's Shipbuilding Party may appeal to a broader base of potential guests than a softball game, simply because everyone who attends the shipbuilding party is at an equal disadvantage, and it presumes very little athletic ability.

guest list, you're going to have an uphill climb.

Finally, you're going to need to decide early on whether children should be welcomed to your activity. Clark and Kathy once lived in a ward where large groups of people boycotted every activity that did not include children. New families who moved into the ward were told about the boycotts and encouraged to participate in it. Liking children is one thing, but being held hostage to them is another. Ours is a family-centered church, and there are many ward activities—perhaps the majority—where children should be welcome. But there are some situations where adults should be allowed to interact with one another without having children as a buffer. When you're planning ward activities, use your common sense and determine whether the event would be enhanced if the children stayed home, and plan accordingly. Even in the face of opposition.

Sneaky Secret

When you're planning your event, don't forget to include people from non-traditional situations in the planning process. Single church members can be great resources, and you're overlooking a great asset to your committee if you leave them out. Even if you don't put a single on your committee for each activity, making your activity enjoyable for single and childless members should always be a consideration. People who aren't members of traditional families have a hard enough challenge without also being expected to attend ward activities that are designed exclusively for members who are part of a traditional family unit.

What Is the Purpose of the Activity?

If you read the introduction, you know there are legitimate reasons why we have ward activities. Those reasons are important to you as a person who plans an activity because the motivation behind an activity will make a big difference in the event you plan. Whether you're organizing a party for seven Beehives or a harvest dinner for the entire ward, you can't plan the best activity for your group unless you know why you're having the party in the first place. You may think the reason you're having an activity is no more complex than, "We're having it because we're supposed to have an activity in February." But do yourself a favor and ask the question anyway, because if you scratch down below the surface the answer may surprise you.

For example, let's say you're the ward activities committee chairman, and you're thinking it's about time to have another get-together. You ask yourself who the party is for and why you're having it, and you come up with the obvious answers. The activity is for the ward, you say, and the reason you're having the party is that the ward hasn't had an activity in a month or two. That sounds reasonable.

Using those answers as a springboard, you think a ward dinner might be a good idea. After all, everybody likes food. An informal dinner is more fun than a formal affair, and because it's summertime, a barbecue sounds like a great suggestion.

Naturally, your first reaction is that since the barbecue is for the ward, all ward members should be invited. If you think no farther than that, you may go right ahead and plan a party that will be successful, and that everyone who attends will enjoy. But as you're busily planning your barbecue, you may remember hearing a complaint that new ward members don't feel at home in your ward, and that old ward members don't make the effort to make new ones feel needed and welcome. You realize the ward could benefit from an activity where new ward members could interact with old ones, building bridges between the old members and the new.

Suddenly, the complexion of the ward activity has changed. When you were planning a party just to have a party, it was fine to have a barbecue and invite the entire ward. But when children are there, families tend to sit in family groupings so Mom and Dad can feed the children and keep them out of trouble. By the end of the evening, it's possible to have eaten the food and participated in the merriment without ever interacting with people outside the immediate family circle. This party may be a lot of fun, but it won't help new ward members get to know the old ones.

If you organize your activity around the goal of making new ward members feel more comfortable, the party you plan may be quite different. Perhaps you'll decide to have a barbecue without children, or maybe you'll give up on the barbecue idea altogether and come up with an event that calls for more active participation than sitting down and eating. Maybe you'll design a progressive dinner, where participants are asked to move to a different table for each course of the meal—forcing them to interact with many different people throughout the evening.

This doesn't mean a barbecue is a bad activity. In fact, under different circumstances a barbecue could be a great idea. Perhaps your ward does a good job of welcoming new members, but the parents in your ward have a hard time finding opportunities to spend time with their children. If that's the situation in your area, a family-oriented barbecue could be just the ticket. But unless the organization planner takes a few moments ahead of time and seriously determines what purpose the party should fulfill, you might find yourself having a barbecue when what your ward needs is a temple excursion or a romantic dinner-dance.

When Should the Activity Be Scheduled?

You'll soon find that choosing a date for your activity is far more complex than simply pointing to an open spot on your calendar. Every family in your ward uses a different calendar, and the success of your activity will depend on whether the date you choose is open on calendars other than yours. More than one ward activity has been ruined because the planners didn't realize parents would be tied up with a back-to-school night during the particular event in question, or that the local high school prom would strip the ward of any available baby-sitters. If your ward covers an area that is served by more than one high school, you may have to take several school schedules into account.

Other things to consider are school vacations, local holidays, possible weather complications, upcoming weddings that could involve large numbers of ward members, stake or regional activities, and community celebrations. We can't give you a list of these, because they vary from area to area. For example, ward activities in our area come to a standstill during the month of August, because so many breadwinners work for the government, and August is the traditional vacation month for government workers. When August comes, half the people in our area aren't available because they've left on vacation. Anyone who plans an August activity for a large group is doomed to failure, because the numbers aren't there to support a successful event. You can avoid such surprises by having an informal panel of "activity consultants" through which you pass the dates of any proposed activity. These should be other ward leaders, and those familiar with upcoming school, community, and ward events.

When you're doing your scheduling, make sure you take the hours of the event into account. More than one ward activity has been cut short because the planners scheduled an event to last until 10 P.M., never considering that baby-sitters needed to be home no later than 9 P.M. on a school night. Try to look at your time frame from all perspectives, and you'll be less likely to end up with unhappy surprises on the day of your event.

Where Will the Event Be Held?

The location of your event will be determined by how many people you're planning to involve. An activity that is planned for ten people can be held almost anywhere. On the other hand, if your activity is open to the whole ward membership, you may be limited to holding that activity in the meetinghouse or in the great outdoors. If you use any part of the ward meetinghouse, you'll need to schedule the building to make sure you don't conflict with others who are also planning on using the building. The more wards that share a building, the greater the potential for conflict. But even if your ward doesn't share a meetinghouse, you'll have to schedule the building anyway. Otherwise you may have several groups vying for the same facilities at the same time: the Relief Society claiming the kitchen for an enrichment meeting, the Young Women learning how to bake bread, and the missionaries trying to organize refreshments for a baptism.

If you don't know the name of the person who is in charge of scheduling events in your building, the ward executive secretary should be able to tell you. If several wards share a building, your activities may be limited to a specific ward activity night. It doesn't do any good to complain if the day you want isn't available to you. Don't even think about asking for exceptions unless the atmosphere between your wards is extremely congenial, because messing around with a building's schedule is a common cause of bad feelings between the members of sister wards.

If you use your ward meetinghouse for activities, it should go without saying that the building should be treated with respect. People should remember the sanctity of the chapel and shouldn't use the chapel in a way that will disrespect its purpose. That includes having people dress appropriately for activities that are held in the chapel.

Take other meetinghouse guidelines into consideration, too. Candles shouldn't be lit; use of ovens should be restricted; electricity shouldn't be used inappropriately. Your ward meetinghouse is used by many people, and tithing dollars are used to maintain it. Don't do anything that would endanger the building or restrict the future use of the facility.

If you decide to hold a ward activity outdoors, contingency plans should be made in case the weather intervenes. You may think of the ward meetinghouse as being a back-up site in case there's a thunderstorm, but you can't use that meetinghouse if someone else has scheduled it first. When you're trying to decide where an event should be held, never take anything for granted. You can't have the meetinghouse just because you want it, and you can't have the activity outside without taking the weather into account. And don't expect that someone who has a nice house or a great weekend cabin should just give you the keys for an activity you're planning. Using someone's home for a ward activity is a privilege, not a right.

How Much Will the Activity Cost?

Back in the good old days, many wards seemed to have an unlimited budget for their activities. If you wanted to serve stuffed Cornish hens at the ward dinner, all you had to do was write a check and spend the money. But those days are as extinct as the passenger pigeon. Ward budgets have been stripped to the barest essentials, and the bishop will probably determine that paying this month's utility bills is more important than giving you a lavish budget for your ward party. In most wards, it is probably typical for an auxiliary to get a fifty- to two hundred and fifty-dollar activity budget for the entire *year*. So don't plan to have caviar and prime rib at every activity.

When you're assigned to organize an event for your group or for the ward as a whole, the first thing to do is go to your auxiliary leader or to the bishop and ask what your budget will be. You may be appalled to learn you've only got a twenty-five-dollar budget for a ward dinner, but this isn't an insurmountable obstacle. Celebrations can be planned on a shoestring. It takes a little more creativity to work within a budget than it does to spend money as if there's no tomorrow, but there are ways to work around the lack of funds. Just be careful not to overwork your ward members, who already spend a lot of time and money as members of the ward. We'll explore this subject in greater detail in chapter 9, so you might want to jump there right now if you have an event to plan and no funds to spend.

HURRY AND FINISH YOUR SUSHI... THE LONDON SYMPHONY IS ABOUT TO START!

How Can You Involve Many People in the Event?

In order to have a successful activity, you'll need to involve as many people as possible. A party with 200 participants may be a wild success in a ward with 250 active members, but it's not as big a triumph in a ward with 450 active members on the roster.

Here's a tip for you to remember: *No matter how well you've planned your activity, people are inherently lazy.* Our lives are so busy that by the time we've gotten home from work or school, or have spent the day dragging children from one soccer game to another, even the most exciting ward activity may not sound as appealing as a nap in front of the television. You can, however, combat this human tendency toward inertia. One thing to keep in mind is that people tend to support events if their participation is crucial to the success of the event in question. Even if you can organize the entire party yourself, you'll get a wider base of support if other people are involved in the process. Delegate, delegate, delegate . . . and then delegate some more. If some people are bringing food and others are setting up the decorations and others are helping with the entertainment and still others are ready to clean up afterwards, those people will probably be attending your activity.

There's one other way to guarantee that ward members will support your activity, and it is something that is largely overlooked. In order to have a successful ward activity, your bishopric must be supportive to the point that they attend the event and bring their families. (If you're planning an activity just for a ward auxiliary, you'll need the same type of support from the auxiliary leaders.) *It is impossible to have a successful ward activity, no matter how well you plan it or how excited you are about it, if your bishopric doesn't support you.*

The members of your ward tend to follow the lead of the bishopric in determining which activities are important. This places an unfair burden on bishopric members, but it's a burden that cannot be avoided. And the vast majority of bishoprics will be supportive. They, too, know that if the bishopric doesn't attend ward activities, it sends a signal to everyone else in the ward that the activities aren't worthy of being supported . . . and ward members will not attend.

In the rare case that you find yourself with an unsupportive bishopric but have to host ward activities anyway, try issuing personal, handwritten invitations to your bishop and his wife. Or you can delegate a small but crucial part on the program to the bishop or one of his family members. After all, if the bishop's nine-year-old daughter is singing on the program, the bishop is far more likely to rearrange his schedule to attend the event.

How Should the Event Be Publicized?

No matter what event you're planning, the answer to that question is, "As vigorously as possible." A wise man once said that people forget the things they subconsciously want to forget. This may be true, but people also forget a lot of things they want to remember. If your activity has been publicized so extensively that people can't forget it even if they want to, your event will be far more successful.

Some of the avenues you can use include the ward newsletter, a meetinghouse bulletin board, flyers or invitations, a ward calendar, "telephone trees," the Sunday bulletin, the Relief Society newsletter, or a ward Web site. Word of mouth is another effective means of publicity. If someone has been personally invited to your event, or was called on the day of the event with a gentle reminder, they're far more likely to attend.

Remember—people tend to go where they're needed and wanted. If you let individuals know that they, specifically, are both wanted and needed at your ward activity, they're far more likely to attend the event you've so carefully put together than they would be if they believed their absence would never be noticed.

We'll tell you this again later on, but you should know right away that one thing that will sabotage even the best of activities is to schedule it on a week following a Sunday when your ward does not meet—for example, the week after general or stake conference. People need that reminder on the Sunday before the event, and if they don't have that, a good percentage of them will forget. You can avoid these problems by not scheduling events on those weeks, or by using tools such as "telephone trees" or postcards to remind people a couple of days before the event.

Organizing Your Committee

You may believe you can put together an entire ward activity on your own, and in fact you may be the person in your ward who is best qualified to do so. But because ward members are more likely to support an event if they're responsible for the success of that event, your best bet is to involve as many people as possible.

Here are some of the people you may want to have on the committee for your ward activity, along with the responsibilities of each one.

Obviously, not all activities need all these people—and some activities need even more people than we'll list here. (After all, a costume committee may be an integral part of a road show, but it isn't on the agenda of most other ward activities.) For smaller events, it is also common to have one person filling several of the roles mentioned here.

Event Chairman

In case you haven't figured it out, that's you. You may have a committee just to help you chair the event, but more than likely you're acting alone. The buck has to stop with somebody, and that person is going to be you. It's your job to decide what kind of activity you'll have, when and where the activity will be held, who will be invited, and how the money will be distributed. You will also be the person who chooses your committee members, and that's a big responsibility in and of itself.

Choosing the proper committee is vital because one important function of the event chairman is to let committee chairmen make their own decisions—within reason. Your food chairman may be grateful for your ideas, but don't offer those ideas unless she asks for them, and don't insist your ideas be followed. Just as you enjoyed choosing the theme of the party, the food chairman will enjoy choosing a menu and recipes, the decorations chairman will enjoy deciding how to beautify the surroundings, and the program chairman will enjoy figuring out how people will be entertained. You do have veto power, but you shouldn't exercise that veto power unless you have a deep and compelling reason to do so. For example, if the food chairman wants to serve ostrich filets and peppered kangaroo at the dinner, you may have a legitimate question as to how she can serve these items and stay within her budget. And if the program chairman decides on entertainment that is too risqué for tender Mormon eyes, you may have to step in and offer a voice of reason. But before you step in and veto the plans that others have made, make sure that your interference is absolutely necessary. If you learn that peanut butter pie is going to be served as dessert and you hate peanut butter, live with it. Your veto power should be used only for blatant violations of budget or ethics or good taste.

On the rare occasions when you as event chairman have to steer a committee chairman in a different direction, it is vital that you do so diplomatically. You may even have to enlist the bishop to help you by "playing the heavy" and vetoing a plan that could be detrimental to the people of the ward. (Be sure you counsel with the bishop before you do this!) But always remember that others' feelings are as tender as your own. There are ways to enforce your authority that won't make enemies in the process, and these ways should be used at all costs. You and your committee chairmen may be working together and living together in the same ward for many years to come. No ward event is so important that it justifies making enemies.

If you have never served in a calling before that allows you to delegate responsibility, you'll soon learn that delegation is a two-edged sword. It does ease your burden by adding additional bodies to share the work, but it will also introduce people with new ideas who will approach things differently, and will steer your activity in a different direction from what you may have planned. Perhaps your original idea for "A Night on Broadway" did not include macaroni salad and children singing Primary songs. A truly wise leader will understand that people do not expect a perfect activity, and that promoting ward harmony is more important than having absolute

Sneaky Secret

In order to be free to step in and help when someone else drops the ball, the event chairman should not have any assignments of his own on the day of the activity. If you've already committed to help with the program or to set up chairs, you're not going to be available if the kitchen crew doesn't show up. Making sure you don't have an assignment on the day of the activity isn't a sign of laziness—it's an indicator of common sense. Besides, by the day of the activity you will already have put in enough work that, on those rare occasions when everything goes right, you shouldn't feel guilty about sitting back and enjoying the party you've put together. But you should definitely plan on being the first person to arrive at the event and the last person to leave, just so you'll be available to lend a hand where one is needed.

control. These leaders will "not sweat the small stuff," but will choose their battles and get involved only when necessary, and will then do it in a manner where there will be no hard feelings.

In an ideal situation, you're going to pick a group of committee members who are so talented and reliable that all you'll have to do is make assignments and then sit back and admire everyone else's work. In reality, this isn't always the case. All too often, you're going to be working with people who have more enthusiasm than inspiration, or who have great ideas but can't be counted on to actually show up the day of the event. Sometimes you'll even have a person foisted on you who never darkens the door of a ward meetinghouse, but who is given an assignment by a bishop or ward auxiliary leader in the hope that it will inspire that person to want to return to church. Because you cannot predict human behavior, the best course of action for you as the event chairman is to know enough about each committee's job that you can step in and help at a moment's notice. If all goes well, you won't have to fill in at the last minute. The day of the event your work will be done, and you can step back and watch everybody else fulfill their assignments. But if your food committee chairman just doesn't bother to arrive on time—or at all—you'll be prepared to step in and do the work you need to do.

Food Chairman

In these days of minimal budgets, the food chairman is the person who is most responsible for pulling rabbits out of hats. The people who attend your party will want to eat the best quality food, and if youth are involved they're going to want to eat mass quantities of whatever you serve.

Chapter 9 will show you how to feed large numbers of people on a minimal budget. As food chairman, however, it will be up to you to decide how much food will be prepared by your committee, and how much will be provided by volunteer ward members. You'll also need to know how many committee workers you'll want in the kitchen on the day of the event, and what each of them should be doing.

As you make your preparations, don't neglect the things that are easily overlooked. Chief among these are salt and pepper, butter, and ice. Napkins, dishes, cups, and cutlery may also come out of your budget and be your responsibility to provide. You may also need to have utensils brought from home, because most ward kitchens don't come equipped with exotic items such as a melon-baller, unlimited rubber spatulas, or muffin tins. (If utensils are brought from home, make sure they go home with the people who brought them.) Remember—everything that has anything to do with food is your responsibility. If you forget to provide something, that item will not be on hand when you need it the day of the event.

Another huge responsibility of the food chairman is to know your budget and stick to it scrupulously. You may think the amount you've been allotted is not nearly enough to do whatever you want to do, but you don't have the authority to override that decision. Any extra money you spend will be used at the expense of somebody else's ward activity. Don't even consider exceeding your budget unless you are willing to make up the difference from your own checkbook—and that is a practice usually frowned upon as well. You should also resist the temptation to ease your budget burden by asking ward members to bring expensive items. Asking for a salad or a plate of cookies is reasonable; don't make food assignments such as turkeys, steaks, or whole hams. Doing so will simply transfer the budget burden from your shoulders to the shoulders of ward members.

Decorations Chairman

Although the food chairman may complain that he or she doesn't have enough money to do a creditable job for your ward activity, your lot is even worse. People have to eat, but they don't have to be surrounded by decorations. (At least that's the viewpoint of the men, who know where the real priorities are.) When money is handed out for decorations, the decorations committee chairman may get a minimal amount or none at all. This means that creativity, rather than a checkbook, is going to have to be at the bottom of everything you plan.

When you're in the process of decorating, remember your audience. For example, you don't want to put cunning little Lladro figurines on the tables if children are going to be invited to the event. Frilly decorations may not be the most appropriate (or most durable) if men are part of the equation. Look at the theme, look at the participants, look at your budget, and then go from there. Much can be done with few resources, if you're willing to expend a little creativity.

We remember one ward dinner that had a nostalgia theme. The decorations committee got large sheets of professional-quality matting board and glued an arrangement of nostalgic items on each one. Old sheet music, phonograph records, ancient gloves, and other treasures were artfully arranged on each matting board, and the results were attractive enough that they should have been permanently framed. On another occasion, a "Through the Looking Glass" theme was carried out by an artist who painted life-sized figures that were also suitable for

Sneaky Secret
The food chairman should always come to an event prepared to mark the dishes and utensils brought by other ward members. Usually just a roll of masking tape and a marking pen will do. As people bring their food assignments, make sure their names are somewhere on each dish or utensil where it will not come off, and use your handy marking equipment if necessary. You don't want to make an enemy for life because Sister Jones never got her temple-shaped Jell-O® pan back after the last activity.

framing. You may not know you have professional-quality talent in your ward, but you do. Find it and use it.

Even though decorations aren't considered important enough to get the lion's share of an activity's budget, the overall enjoyment of that event will be greatly influenced by the decorations that are in place. You are an artist, and the location of your party is your palette. You can create a thing of beauty, even in a ward cultural hall. But work with the other committee chairmen to make sure your decorations enhance their plans rather than provide a logistical nightmare.

One other piece of advice is to make sure you know your budget and adhere strictly to it. Just as you wouldn't want somebody writing an unauthorized check off your personal checking account, the ward doesn't want you skimming money from its meager account in order to enhance your decorations.

Program Chairman

It is virtually impossible to predict how much work you'll be required to do as program or entertainment chairman for a ward. Sometimes a program chairman is asked to provide a small postscript to a sit-down dinner; other times the entertainment is the highlight of the event. But whatever the case, you're not going to have a lot of money to spend to entertain people. In most cases, your own ward members will provide the entertainment for your ward activity.

There are many different opinions about what constitutes "talent" in a ward population. We have all sat through ward talent shows where an earnest ward member performed his heart out while the audience bravely tried not to laugh or cry. There are times when people come to a ward activity to let their hair down; and in some cases a demonstration of Susie's musical knees may be a showstopper. But there are times when ward members should be able to come to an evening of entertainment with the expectation of being uplifted. As program chairman, you will be the person who sets the tone for the event.

As program chairman, it is your job to carefully plan the entertainment around people's expectations. In all likelihood you'll have a "cheat sheet" for doing this. That cheat sheet is the theme of your party, which was probably determined before you even came on the scene. Elsewhere in this book, we'll have many ideas for how to build a party around a theme. Don't limit yourself to those ideas; rather, see how you can work on them to make them your own.

When you're doing your job as program chairman, don't overlook the things that are always overlooked. One of these weak links often seems to be the sound system. The best play or road show in the world isn't worth the time it takes to put it together if nobody can understand the words that are spoken. Lighting is another thing you'll have to consider. And if you're using a stage, don't forget props and curtains—a few inexpensive props can go a long way toward making the results look more professional. And don't underestimate the enhancement you can make to a ward dinner by piping in classical music or having someone play classical selections on the piano as background music to people's conversations. Again, this is something that will cost you next to nothing, but will greatly contribute to the mood you are trying to set for the event.

As program chairman, everything involved in the entertainment falls under your jurisdiction. If there are any warm-up activities, they should be your responsibility. Contests (complete with rules, judges, and prizes) are up to you, too. If there are written programs or other printed materials, these are your responsibility—at least until you delegate them to somebody else. But no matter what you do, stick to your budget. Rely on donated materials and prizes, or give prizes that don't cost a lot of money. The most perfect evening of entertainment will not end well if the bishop realizes the ward has gone into debt over your extravaganza. Make sure you don't leave a bad aftertaste in the collective mouth of the ward by spending more money than you've been given for your part of the activity.

Diplomacy is also a talent that must be cultivated by those in charge of coordinating the entertainment for an event. While it should always

Sneaky Secret

Here's a piece of advice that program chairmen should engrave in stone: *Not all people want to be the center of attention.* Don't *ever* plan an activity where ward members are cajoled or otherwise forced into taking part on the program without their knowledge or consent. You may think it's hilarious to drag the gawky financial clerk out of the audience to hula with the Relief Society president, but the financial clerk may be so humiliated that he'll never return to church. There is absolutely no piece of entertainment that is worth the loss of a person's human dignity—unless, of course, that person volunteers to sacrifice that human dignity on the altar of the evening's entertainment. Make sure everyone has a chance to be the center of attention for a few moments if he wants to be, but don't force people to do things they are unwilling or unable to do.

be your goal to provide a professional level of entertainment at any event, you must also realize that most of your performers will be ward members who are probably amateurs. People also have different levels of commitment to an assignment—Sister Jones may practice all week for that song she is singing, while Brother Johnson may not even glance at the music until the night of the performance. The entertainment chairman must walk the fine line of trying to encourage the best performances possible without causing any offense in the participants. Although we would all hope the entertainment at ward events would be the best possible, it is more important that no one ends the evening feeling hurt, embarrassed, or unappreciated. Choose someone to fill this calling who is good at working with other people, and is sensitive to their feelings. Even the best activity will be forgotten within six months, but hurt feelings can last for decades.

Setup/Cleanup Chairman

As setup or cleanup chairman, all you'll need is a group of volunteers who have strong backs and willing hearts. You have no budget to squander and no appetites to satisfy. You won't have to get up on stage and sing and dance, either. All you have to do is either set up the area so the decorations committee can decorate it, or clean up the area so church meetings can be held in it the following day. Make no mistake about it—if you don't do your job right, people will be unhappy. But this is one of those unsung jobs. After all, people expect the party to be set up when they arrive, and they also expect to attend church the next Sunday without seeing any evidence of confetti or tripping over out-of-place furniture.

The setup committee has the responsibility of working with the chairman of the decorations committee to see how to set up tables and chairs, and working with the entertainment committee to coordinate anything they need before the event. The area must be set up before the decorations can be put in place, so it's important to do your work according to the needs of others. You are also responsible for the entire physical facility, in that you'll need to make sure the building is open and properly heated or air-conditioned, the parking lot is clear of snow, and the lights are turned on.

If your job is involved solely with cleanup, you won't need to make any advance preparations except to make sure you know where to get (and how to use) the cleaning supplies that may be needed. Find out ahead of time whether your job also involves cleaning the kitchen area (perhaps even washing the dishes). Somebody has to do it, and the food committee may be counting on you.

In many wards, it seems to be customary for the priesthood to provide cleanup of everything but the kitchen, leaving the women to clean the kitchen after the activity. If this is the way it's done in your ward, fine. But as cleanup chairman you'll need to make sure somebody does it, because you shouldn't leave the building until everything is as clean or cleaner than it was before the activity.

In these confusing times, there are some wards where women have determined that doing the cooking for ward activities is somehow demeaning. If this is the case in your ward, it is perfectly acceptable for you to expect men to spend time cooking and serving the food. But equality runs both ways. If women expect the men to cook, the men should expect the women to clean. And this includes heavy work such as setting up (or taking down) tables and chairs.

No matter how you organize the setup or cleanup, you may think it's a thankless task. That being the case, we're thanking you ahead of time. Maybe this ward activity would have been a success without the help of a good cleaning crew, but if the building isn't properly cleaned after this activity, there may not be another one.

As with many other aspects of an activity, your leaders can help set the tone for the importance of cleaning up after the event. Our stake president can always be found running the vacuum, washing the dishes, stacking the chairs, and locking the doors as we exit the building after the event. He does not assume the role of the honored guest, but realizes that all the attendees have an equal obligation to keep the building clean. If you are fortunate enough to have similar leaders, your ward and stake members will soon get the message that doing the post-activity cleaning is just as important as any other aspect of hosting a successful activity.

Publicity Chairman

As publicity chairman, it's your responsibility to make sure that every potential guest of your ward function is aware of exactly when and where the function will be held, what sort of function it is, and what he or she should bring to contribute to the event. This may include publicizing your event to people in the community who are not members of the Church, or to members who only come once or twice a year.

Use your creativity about getting the word out to people. Invitations don't have to be printed on a flat piece of paper in order to do the job.

We've seen invitations that were incorporated into necklaces, attached to candy bars, or made into paper airplanes. The sky's the limit—at least as far as creativity is concerned. But make sure to keep careful note of that looming budget. If you spend the entire activity's allotment on invitations, there won't be anything left for entertainment or food.

One of your functions as publicity chairman may or may not be to print programs for the activity itself. Check with the event chairman to see if this is your job. In fact, it's a good idea to keep in touch with the event chairman anyway, just to make sure everything that can be done to publicize the event is being done to the chairman's satisfaction.

Make sure you also take advantage of the free publicity that is probably available to you through other ward publications. Most wards have a Sunday bulletin where they provide the program for sacrament meeting and also announce upcoming ward activities. Your ward may also have a ward newspaper that is printed on occasion, or newsletters that are printed and distributed by the various auxiliaries.

As the event draws closer, you may also ask ward leaders to announce the event during ward meetings and the opening exercises of auxiliary meetings. This is often done in many wards, although some leaders would prefer to leave such announcements in the bulletins or newsletters.

Checklists for the Hopelessly Disorganized

If making a list and checking it twice is good enough for Santa Claus, it should be good enough for you. A checklist will help you determine what needs to be done, and in what order. Even more important, using a checklist will prevent you from forgetting little details that may escape your notice—minor things, such as sending someone to the meetinghouse to let the decorations committee inside on the night they intend to decorate the building.

Printed on the next few pages are sample checklists for each of the major committee chairmen described previously. Feel free to add or subtract from these lists, or to divide the list into things to do during every week prior to your activity. After all, these are *your* checklists. Adapt them so that they fit your needs based on the activity you are planning.

Event Chairman Checklist

☐ Determine the purpose of the activity and who will be invited.

☐ Choose a theme.

☐ Select a date and time.

☐ Coordinate that date with others to make sure there are no conflicts.

☐ Select a location, and schedule the facility with the proper authorities.

☐ Determine a budget, based on specifications from the bishop or auxiliary leader; break it down to a specific amount for each committee.

☐ Decide what committees you will need. If it is your responsibility, select committee chairmen and invite them to serve with you, or have the bishop issue callings.

☐ Have a meeting with all committee chairmen to make plans and discuss the budget.

☐ Follow up with committee chairmen, individually, to forestall any problems. *Do this often to make sure nothing is being overlooked!*

☐ If you feel the need (especially for elaborate events), you may want to schedule additional coordination meetings with some or all of the committee chairmen.

☐ Enjoy (or at least endure) the activity. Be aware of anything that is falling through the cracks, and do it. If everything is going smoothly, circulate and visit with the participants. Be aware of people who may not fit in, and make sure they're included.

☐ Thank each individual who needs thanking.

☐ Write your post-activity report (see next section) and place a copy in the ward binder.

Food Chairman Checklist

☐ Determine the general theme and food requirements of the activity, and come up with some proposals for the food that should be served.

☐ When you meet with the entire committee, present your ideas and get feedback.

☐ Reach an agreement with the other members as to what the menu will be.

☐ Determine which foods will be purchased, and which will be prepared by members.

☐ For purchased foods, comparison shop to make sure the quantities and prices you can get are acceptable and within your budget. If not, contact the event chairman.

☐ For member-donated food, determine if recipes will be provided. If so, select and test those recipes, and type them up for distribution to willing volunteers. Answer any questions the volunteers may have to ensure that the right type of food arrives on time and ready to be served.

☐ Decide how the food will be served (waiters, self-service tables, box lunches, and so on).

☐ Work with the decorations chairman and the setup chairman to make sure the room will be set up to accommodate your menu and serving needs.

☐ Contact the program chairman to determine when the various food courses should be served. You may wish to have dessert after the program.

☐ You may need to coordinate with the publicity chairman if you need publicity for any of the food assignments. For example, you may want to provide the dessert by having a pie-baking contest open to all of the men.

☐ At the proper time before the event, purchase and store the foods you will use.

☐ Remind each person who signed up to prepare and bring food.

☐ During the event, be available in the kitchen to provide general help and solve problems.

- [ ] Make sure dishes and utensils are returned to the person that brought them. You may wish to make sure each item is marked with the owner's name as it arrives.

- [ ] Either thank your helpers yourself, or pass along the names to the event chairman if he or she plans on taking care of the thank-you duties.

- [ ] Submit receipts promptly for purchased foods, and make sure anyone who has spent money is reimbursed in a reasonable amount of time.

- [ ] Write your activity report for the event chairman.

Decorations Chairman Checklist

- [ ] After the general theme and location of the activity are determined, come up with some proposals for the type of decorations that would be appropriate.

- [ ] When you meet with the entire committee, present your ideas and get feedback.

- [ ] Reach an agreement with the other members as to what decorations will be used.

- [ ] Determine which decorations have to be purchased, and which can be donated or loaned by ward members.

- [ ] For purchased materials, comparison shop to make sure the prices you can get are acceptable and within your budget. If not, contact the event chairman to make alternate arrangements.

- [ ] Make arrangements with ward members for any decoration items that will be borrowed. Determine how and when the items will be delivered to the activity location, and how and when they will be returned to the members.

- [ ] Work with the food chairman, the program chairman, and the setup chairman to coordinate your decorations with their activities and needs.

- [ ] Work with the facility scheduler to determine the best time for you to arrive and put your decorations in place.

- [ ] If others are going to help in the decorating process, make sure your volunteers will be available at the appropriate times.

Contact them shortly before your scheduled decoration time to remind them.

☐ Determine if your activity provides any opportunities to involve nonmember neighbors or less-active members to help with the decorating process. Often, such programs provide wonderful opportunities for reaching out to these people in a way that is not threatening.

☐ Attend and coordinate the decoration of the facility. Make sure to thank those who attend and participate, not only verbally but also with a liberal supply of food and snacks to keep their energy level high.

☐ On the day of the activity, arrive early to make sure there are no last minute tasks to complete, and to make sure the decorations are still in good shape. Make any emergency repairs before and even during the activity.

☐ After the event, coordinate with the cleanup crew to make sure the decorations are removed carefully and then either returned to the owners or stored for later collection.

☐ Coordinate with those who loaned you items to make sure everything was returned and in good repair.

☐ Either thank your helpers yourself, or pass along the names to the event chairman if he or she plans on taking care of the thank-you duties.

☐ Submit receipts promptly for purchased items, and make sure anyone who has spent money is reimbursed in a reasonable amount of time.

☐ Write your activity report for the event chairman.

Program Chairman Checklist

☐ After the general theme and location of the activity have been determined, come up with some proposals for the type of program that would be appropriate.

☐ When you meet with the entire committee, present your ideas and get feedback.

☐ Reach an agreement with the other members as to the content of the program.

☐ Determine the format of the program, and those tasks that need to be done immediately. For example, if you are presenting a short play, you may need someone to write the script and someone to make the costumes.

☐ Solicit volunteers to perform the tasks identified in the previous step. Provide deadlines, and meet with your volunteers regularly to make sure they are on schedule and are not having any problems. Resolve any issues that may arise, contacting other chairmen as needed.

☐ If you need to purchase supplies as part of the program, comparison shop to make sure the prices you can get are acceptable and within your budget. If not, contact the event chairman to make alternate arrangements.

☐ Work with the decorations chairman and the setup chairman to coordinate your program with their activities and needs.

☐ Once the program starts coming together, you may have the need for more ward members to be involved. For example, once your play is written, you will need to select people to play the various parts. Make arrangements to solicit, train, and encourage these other members as needed.

☐ Determine if your program provides any opportunities for involving nonmember neighbors or less-active members. Often, such programs provide wonderful opportunities for reaching out to these people in a way that is not threatening.

☐ Consider using the publicity chairman to help you solicit ward members for their participation in the program. This will not only cause more ward participation but will also help build general enthusiasm for the event.

☐ Contact all program participants shortly before the activity to remind them and give them any last-minute instructions.

☐ On the day of the activity, arrive early to make sure there are no last minute problems to correct. During the program, step in as necessary to help keep the program moving along. Don't let all your hard work be wasted because of equipment or lighting problems, because these things should be easy to correct.

☐ After the event, coordinate with the cleanup crew to make sure any items used in the program are removed carefully and then either returned to their owners or stored for later collection.

☐ Coordinate with those who loaned you items to make sure everything was returned and in good repair.

☐ Either thank your helpers yourself, or pass along the names to the event chairman if he or she plans on taking care of the thank-you duties.

☐ Submit receipts promptly for purchased items, and make sure anyone who has spent money is reimbursed in a reasonable amount of time.

☐ Write your activity report for the event chairman.

Setup/Cleanup Chairman Checklist

☐ Meet with the activities committee, and determine their needs. Present your ideas related to the setup of the facility and get feedback.

☐ Reach an agreement with the other members as to the setup and cleanup tasks that will be required.

☐ Work with the facility scheduler to determine the best time for you to arrive and set up the facility. Coordinate this with the other chairmen, as their activities may depend upon when your setup is completed.

☐ If you do not have access to the facility, make arrangements to gain access on the day you plan to set up.

☐ Solicit volunteers to assist you in performing your duties.

☐ Call those with assignments to remind them the day before you are scheduled to set up. If you have a separate cleanup crew, remind them the day before the activity.

☐ Coordinate the facility setup, and make sure everything is in place. Communicate any problems to the event chairman, or to the other chairmen, so that problems can be corrected before the event.

☐ After the event, supervise the cleanup crew and make sure everything is put away and cleaned thoroughly. You should probably be the last person out the door. Coordinate with the other chairmen to make sure any borrowed items are removed carefully and returned to their proper owners or stored for later collection.

☐ Either thank your helpers yourself, or pass along the names to the event chairman if he or she plans on taking care of the thank-you duties.

☐ If asked to do so, write your activity report for the event chairman.

Publicity Chairman Checklist

☐ After the general theme and location of the activity have been determined, come up with some proposals for the type of publicity that would be appropriate.

☐ When you meet with the entire committee, present your ideas and get feedback.

☐ Reach an agreement with the other members as to the publicity that will be provided.

☐ If you need to purchase supplies to be used as part of your publicity, comparison shop to make sure the prices you can get are acceptable and within your budget. If not, make arrangements that are within the budget.

☐ If others are to be involved in the publicity effort, solicit your volunteers. Meet with them as needed to make assignments and answer questions. Contact them on a regular basis to make sure everything is on schedule, and to solve any problems that may arise.

☐ As needed, contact other ward members who can help with publicity, such as the editor of the Sunday bulletin and the editor of the ward newsletter. You may also want to consider asking home teachers and visiting teachers to deliver invitations. If appropriate, ask auxiliary presidents to announce the event to their members.

☐ If you are planning an activity for an auxiliary, make sure to provide adequate publicity for those who may not regularly participate in that auxiliary because of other callings. For example, those planning Relief Society activities should make sure that those who work with the Primary or the Young Women will be notified.

☐ If you are planning an event to which the neighborhood and community will be invited, consider contacting the local media to get your event covered. You may want to do this as soon as possible, because some of these organizations require quite a bit of advance notice to meet their deadlines.

☐ Either thank your helpers yourself, or pass along the names to the event chairman if he or she plans on taking care of the thank-you duties.

☐ Submit receipts promptly for purchased items, and make sure anyone who has spent money is reimbursed in a reasonable amount of time.

☐ If invited to do so, write your activity report for the event chairman.

The detail level of the checklists will vary according to the type of person assigned to the task. Some people need only a short checklist to remind them of the major tasks, and then they keep track of everything else in their heads. Other people prefer to have a detailed checklist with every possible step listed, and then take great satisfaction in checking off items one by one. But don't forget to read the next section and keep those items on your checklist. You are the one who will need to thank your committee members for all the work they've done, and the activity report will not be complete without the information you have to share.

The Morning After

After the party is over, everyone is free to look forward to the next ward activity. But the event chairman's responsibilities don't end when the party does. There are things that should be done while the party is still fresh in the mind of the chairman, and no diligent organizer will let these things go overlooked.

First, people need to be thanked for the work they did. If at all possible, some acknowledgment to the committee chairmen and their committees should have been made at the time of the activity. Whether this consists of having the workers take a bow or printing their names in the program depends on you, but some acknowledgment should be made. And remember, please, that all of your workers are created equal. We once saw an activity where three large bouquets of flowers were presented to the event chairman, but the committee chairmen received nothing at all.

However, don't restrict your thank-yous to an acknowledgment on the scene. Each committee chairman should get some sort of personal acknowledgment from the event chairman after the event, whether it be in the form of a thank-you note or a plate of cookies, or even one of the centerpiece decorations. After all, these people volunteered their services for free to make you look good. The least you can do is spare them a thank-you note and a stamp.

Thank-you notes for services rendered should be handled promptly. Do not follow the example of Kathy, who wrote this paragraph even as she was three months late in sending a thank-you note to a Relief Society president in another ward. If you can't think of any other inspiration to thank people promptly, you may want to consider that as long as people remain unacknowledged for one act of service, you can't in good conscience ask them to do anything else.

But thank-you notes are not the only post-activity responsibility of the event chairman. It is equally important to record the activity for posterity, if only so the person planning the event next year (you or your replacement) will have a guideline for how much food to purchase and serve. These reports don't have to be long, but they should be thorough. They should cover such important items as how much money was spent, how much food was prepared, and how many people were served. It also helps if you add a section mentioning what things you'd do again, and what things need changing. If, for example, the dinner you prepared to feed 200 only served 175, you may want to mention portion control in your report.

Be sure to involve your committee chairmen in this process, because they have information you don't. You may want to have them submit their part of the report at the same time they submit bills for reimbursement. That way they won't get their money until you get your report. For elaborate meals, you may wish to have the food chairman include recipes for the foods served and a record of the quantities of food purchased. Similarly, for events that feature elaborate decorations or programs, you may wish to have the appropriate chairmen submit reports that include those details. All of these details will be fresh in your mind right now (although you will probably never wish to expend another brain cell thinking about the event), but we can guarantee you will forget most of the details by next year if it is not written down.

The post-activity report is so vital to the success of an activity that we're including a sample one on the next page for you to study. It may not include all of the items mentioned above, but it is a good general form for most activities. If you like the format and want to steal it for yourself, there's also a blank form for you to copy at no extra charge.

As long as you're going to the trouble to make this post-activity report, there should be at least two copies. One should go in a binder that contains reports on all activities held in the ward or in your auxiliary. (If your ward or auxiliary doesn't have a binder, you can be the person to start one.) As soon as word gets around that reports are available for event chairmen to study, this binder can be a valuable resource for future activities chairmen.

But face it—people are people. Just in case that binder gets lost, it would be to your advantage to have a copy of any reports for activities you've chaired, or that you plan to chair in the future. If you have a general idea of what has been done in the past, you won't have to reinvent indoor plumbing every time you're called to throw a party for the ward.

Questions from the Clueless

? *How do I get people there on time?*

Unfortunately, "Mormon Standard Time" is so pervasive in the United States that everyone knows exactly what the phrase means. But the seriousness of the problem is something that varies from ward to ward, with some wards barely afflicted by the problem and other wards being crippled by it.

Ultimately, your ward's adherence to or disregard of the clock depends on your bishopric. If meetings begin exactly on time, people will start arriving on time. But if people know the bishopric will wait to start a meeting until almost everyone gets there, they're going to sleep that extra five or ten minutes before they pile the family into the car.

ACTIVITY SUMMARY REPORT

Activity Title, Date, & Time:

Autumn Harvest Dinner; Friday, October 27, 2000; 7 P.M.

Description (theme, invited audience, food, decorations, entertainment, publicity):

This was the annual dinner held to celebrate the end of summer and the arrival of the cool autumn weather. All ward members were invited. As people arrived, they were offered a glass of cold apple cider or hot chocolate. Bishop Winters welcomed everyone at 7:30, and a blessing was pronounced on the food. Food was served from two different buffet tables, and included chili, chips and salsa, cornbread, tossed salad, and water to drink. The tables were decorated with ceramic pumpkins and turkeys, and there were dried corn stalks and bales of straw in the corners of the room and in front of the closed stage curtains. After dinner, people were invited to visit four different areas, where they could carve pumpkins, bob for apples, learn to square dance, or (for the children) make and color pictures of autumn scenes. At 9:00, homemade ice cream and cookies were served for dessert, and prizes were given for the best chili and ice cream. A closing prayer was given, and the event ended at 9:30. The event was publicized in the Sunday bulletin, and flyers were delivered by home and visiting teachers. Approximately 200 people attended.

Committee Assignments:

Event Chairman: Susan King	Program: Vicky Nicolaides	Food: Lynne Van Atta
Setup/Cleanup: Chad Clarke	Decorations: Angela Stradling	Publicity: Janece Ford

Budget (show amount budgeted first, and then amount spent; include totals):

Food:	$100.00	$89.76
Decorations:	$20.00	$22.17
Program:	$20.00	$23.43
Publicity:	$10.00	$8.91
(Total)	$150.00	**$144.27** ($5.73 under budget)

What Worked Well:

Having a contest for the best chili and ice cream created a spirit of competition among the men, and also kept us within the food budget. Walt Hedges was asked to present the square dancing instruction, and he seemed to enjoy that. It was good to see him at church again. Having the home and visiting teachers deliver promotional flyers worked well, because many members attended who would otherwise never have heard of the activity.

What Would You Do Differently?:

The chips and cornbread were good, but left lots of crumbs on the carpet for the unfortunate cleanup crew. We needed more newspapers and plastic tarps in the pumpkin carving area, as that tended to be a bit messy. Scheduling the party on the night of a BYU football game probably hurt our attendance, and we should avoid this in the future.

ACTIVITY SUMMARY REPORT

Activity Title, Date, & Time:

Description (theme, invited audience, food, decorations, entertainment, publicity):

Committee Assignments:

Budget (show amount budgeted first, and then amount spent; include totals):

What Worked Well:

What Would You Do Differently?:

You can't control your bishopric, but you can make an effort to inspire people to be at your activity on time. There are creative ways to entice people to be at your party from the beginning, but you'll have to determine what works for your specific ward or your individual activity.

When Kathy was a Relief Society homemaking leader, a wise friend suggested to her that the Relief Society provide an "early bird special" to women who arrived exactly on time for homemaking meeting. This could take the form of some chocolate, or a creative handout, or some other incentive that would get the women to homemaking meeting exactly when it was supposed to start. This worked like a charm as long as Kathy was willing to enforce it, but eventually she ruined it all. Always a pushover, she started feeling sorry for people who had missed the treat, and allowed the treat to be distributed even after "early bird" time was over. As soon as the women of our ward realized they didn't have to arrive early to get the treat, they stopped arriving early. Remember— people *can* be trained to arrive on time, but only if the person doing the training is strict about enforcement. Offer a good incentive, and then start your activity exactly when it's supposed to start. If Pavlov's dogs could be trained into civilized behavior, your ward members can be trained just as easily. Or, as Kathy sadly learned, they can be conditioned to forget their training and follow their own natural inclinations.

No matter what you do to lure participants to your activity on time, there are some people who are chronically late, and who will always be chronically late no matter what incentives you give for them to be there. Know who those people are. If you draft them to help you on the night of the activity, make sure you take their habits into consideration. Ask them to provide a dessert rather than an appetizer, and make sure you don't ask them to give the opening prayer. If they're going to be late anyway, there will be fewer hard feelings if you accept their lateness and work around it without making a big deal out of it.

? *How do I know if an activity would be appropriate for my ward?*

You are in an unenviable position if you are somewhat new to a ward, yet your first calling involves the planning of activities. If you read through this chapter carefully (and we *know* that you did), you will remember us telling you that every ward has its own personality, and activities that work well in one ward may fall flat in another.

So what do you do? You can start by talking with the other leaders in the ward. If you are planning an activity for the entire ward, talk to the bishop or one of his counselors. If you are planning an activity for a priesthood or auxiliary group, then talk to the leaders of that group.

If talking to the leaders still does not provide adequate clues, find those "old time" members of the ward who have lived there forever. If you cannot identify them by their appearance, ask around to determine those with long experience in that ward. When you reach those folks, they should be able to tell you the successes and failures of the past, and what they think would be successful given the current composition of the ward.

Another idea is to perform a random sampling of ward members and ask their opinions. To make it accurate, make sure to include all age groups, cultures, and family situations in the ward. If you can get a green light from all of your sample groups, it is pretty likely that your event will be a real winner.

? *How can I discard all of our stale activities and do something fresh?*

Sometimes a ward activity is so enjoyable that the "powers that be" decide to hold an identical activity the next year. If it is marginally successful the second year, it may then become a ward tradition that is repeated annually. After a while, it just becomes a yearly ritual that is done more out of habit than anything else, and no one takes the time to analyze whether it is still meeting the needs of the ward. Clark and Kathy were once in a ward where the summer party was so set in stone that you needed to get the bishop's permission to alter any detail, including the menu that was to be served.

For some wards, those in charge may not care about establishing any traditions. This makes it easy for you as an activities person to simply throw out the old and try something new. But you may be stuck in a situation such as the one described above, and any attempt to discard or change the activity will put your likeability ratings in peril. If that is the case, you must learn to use patience and diplomacy to get your changes made. You will need to alter just a few details each year, and may need several meetings with ward leaders to convince them that the changes you propose will result in a better event. If you have the skills and the time to do this, you may eventually transform the event into something completely different, without tampering with the tradition associated with the activity.

Even if you cannot change the ground rules of the event, you can encourage variety by getting different people on the event committee each year. Each person in the ward will bring different ideas to the same assignment, so some measure of creativity is almost certain if you have different bodies doing the work every time the activity is held.

CHAPTER 2
Bring the Whole Gang

★ **IN THIS CHAPTER**
- ✔ Building Unity through Activities
- ✔ Adapting Activities to Your Ward
- ✔ Entertaining the Ward
- ✔ Letting Talents Shine
- ✔ Putting on Road Shows
- ✔ Ending with a Bang
- ✔ Questions from the Clueless

No matter how hard you try to hide from the bishop, eventually he's going to find you and tell you it's time for another ward activity. *Do not panic.* At least, don't panic now. (You'll have plenty of time later.) Now that you've read chapter 1, you realize that planning a ward activity can be a cinch. Just don't forget that the bottom line for every ward activity is ward unity, regardless of what the stated purpose might be.

Arguably, the most challenging activities to plan are those that involve a whole spectrum of people. It's not easy to plan a celebration that pleases Primary children as well as people who are older than dirt. But don't worry. You are a party-planning professional. With a little careful planning, large-group activities can be the most fun and rewarding.

Unfortunately for the Clueless, planning a party for a diverse group can appear daunting. The good news is, it doesn't have to be. This chapter is dedicated, not to the "how-to" of an activity, since that was covered in chapter 1, but rather to successful activities themselves. This chapter includes: activities just for the halibut (fun), activities for the talented and not-so talented, how to build a better mouse trap section (educational kinds of activities), road shows, and, of course, more questions from the Clueless.

Sneaky Secret
The key to good activities is variety. By doing a variety of activities, you will eventually hit something for everyone. Equally important are the following three maxims of a successful activity:
• Choose activities you like or enjoy. If your activities are enjoyable, you'll have a good time even if you have a mediocre turnout.
• Get someone else to do all the actual work, leaving yourself available to help out where needed.
• Make sure that anyone who complains about a particular activity is included on the planning committee for the next activity. It's funny how this eliminates a lot of complaints.

Ready for the Main Event

Before planning the real meat-and-potatoes portion of the activity, check out chapter 8 to find some shorter activities that will help people get acquainted and ready to party. Consider those warm-up events to be the "appetizers" for your main event.

More often than not, we have a ward activity simply to get together and have a little fun and to socialize. Social activities are excellent for building ward unity as well as interacting with nonmembers in a non-threatening way. Look at these activities and determine which will work for your particular group. Choose an activity and make your own modifications. After all, the perfect activity for your group is one that is adapted to the personality of your own ward setting.

Here are some examples of how you can modify your ideas to suit the people in your congregation. If your youth group likes soccer, have them play "crab soccer" by playing a game as they walk upside down on their hands and feet and try to hit a beach ball toward the goal. If your elders enjoy the "Jeopardy" game show, devise a "Mormon Jeopardy" with church-related questions. Any idea can be adapted to create a party if only you'll think for a minute or two. If you enjoy the Academy Awards and decide to have an Academy Awards night, here are three ways to expand on that theme:

- Celebrate the Academy Awards concept, with participants coming as their favorite or invented actors or actresses. Be sure to roll out the red carpet, and have paparazzi take pictures of people as they arrive in their own "limousines." Young women can take the role of screaming teenagers, asking for autographs from the "stars." After everyone has arrived, have an Academy Awards trivia contest. At the end of the evening, make sure to give awards for the best costumes!

- Create your own ward version of the Academy Awards show, with such categories as "most creative costume at the Halloween party," "best performance by a bishop at the ward summer picnic," "most pathetic campaigning to win the chili cook-off competition," and so on. At the end of the evening, you could even present a surprise award for "best acceptance speech" at this year's award ceremony.

- Have a two-part video night. For the first half of the activity, divide your players into groups and assign them to make a five-minute "movie" on a particular subject during the allotted time frame. The second half of the activity will be showing the finished tapes and presenting "Academy Awards" to the winners.

Now that you know how to adapt activities for your own ward, here are some other possible activities that may act as a springboard for your imagination:

- Roaring Twenties Night. (Choose a different decade if another one appeals to you.)

- Elvis Night. (Impersonators, anyone?)

ELVIS HAS LEFT THE WARD BUILDING!

- Around the Campfire. (What about an *indoor* campfire, with everyone gathered around a fake fire in the cultural hall, telling ghost stories and singing camp songs and eating s'mores?)

- Pirate Night. (Walk the plank by blindfolding contestants and having them walk a marked line with shouted instructions from the audience. Step off the line three times, and you're eaten by a shark.)

- Cartoon Character Night. (This can be narrowed down to, say, a Flintstones night, or you can adapt it even more by scuttling the whole cartoon idea in favor of the caveman theme.)

- Harry Potter Night. (People are divided into teams by means of a sorting hat. Competitions might feature Hermione's logic puzzle and Harry's Quidditch paper airplane contest—each team has 15 minutes to prepare a fusillade of paper airplanes and must fly them toward a goal as a "bludger" tries to block the airplanes).

- Karaoke Night.

- Super Heroes Night. (Have everyone come as the super hero he'd be, based on his talents or characteristics. Don't forget the feats of strength!)

- Most Outrageous Clothes Night. (Give awards for best T-shirt or most dated prom dress.)

- Mardi Gras Night. (Have parades or costumes; serve a king cake for dessert.)

- Sports Hero Night.

- Backwards Night.

Now that you've seen some of the possibilities, here are some tried and true ideas for ward activities. You'll see that some of them are elaborate, but that others can be thrown together with very little preparation. You may want to try a mix of these. On some occasions, it's great to bowl people over with your creativity. But sometimes the focus should be getting a party together on the spur of the moment to enhance ward unity. Figure out what kind of party you need, and go from there.

By the way, these are by no means the only suggestions for parties in this book. Other party ideas will be found throughout the text, categorized as youth or service activities, or tied to a specific holiday or season. Chapter 7 will be an invaluable resource as you plan your parties, because it takes you through the calendar and gives you a reason to celebrate every day of the year.

Circus Night

Materials: Booths where participants can "purchase" food or play midway games; tickets to distribute to ward members for

"buying" their treats; prizes for midway games; circus decorations; refreshments (see below).
Effort Quotient: ♆♆♆
Time: ⌛⌛⌛
Planning: ★★★★

Although this activity takes a lot of planning, no one has to do all the work because you can delegate each booth or part on the program to a different person and let him be responsible for everything pertaining to it.

This activity can be a great hit with young and old ward members alike. Set up carnival booths around the periphery of the cultural hall, and start your event with the sort of attractions you'd see at a carnival. Distribute tickets to everyone, so people can decide where to spend their "money." There can be face-painting or "go fish" for the kids, together with throwing contests, pie-eating contests, watermelon seed-spitting contests, or feats of strength for the adults. Booths can be set up where people can "buy" circus food such as hot dogs (or corn dogs), candy apples, bags of peanuts, and cotton candy. You may even want to have a sideshow, where ward members with unusual talents can entertain the gawkers by touching their noses with their tongues, demonstrating their double joints, or doing other tricks. End the evening with a big-top circus consisting of acts that are put on by your ward members. Use your imagination and your humor to come up with these acts, and use a charismatic ringmaster to add to the fun. Don't forget the clowns!

Magic Talent Show

Materials: Magician's props and standard decorations; extra props for magic classes; microphones as needed
Effort Quotient: ♆♆
Time: ⌛⌛⌛
Planning: ★★

This activity depends entirely on local talent. Canvass your ward to see if you have any aspiring magicians in your group. (Hint: Boys and men are fascinated from a young age with the idea of performing sleights of hand.) If you don't have an amateur magician in your ward, there's

Sneaky Secret

Having a magic show is a great way to involve people who don't have traditional talents they can share in a ward talent show. People aren't as embarrassed by performing a trick as they would be to bare their souls singing a love song in front of an audience. Find people who are personable but who aren't always onstage and give them each a magic trick to learn and perform. In the process of entertaining your audience, you'll be giving people who don't usually spend time in the spotlight a chance to shine.

bound to be one in your community—hopefully, a magician who will do a show for free. If not, there are many books on the market that teach people how to perform magic tricks. Find volunteers to each learn a trick and perform it as part of the show.

Begin the evening by having someone teach the audience how to perform specific tricks. You may want to have separate classes for young children and adults, letting people gather around their teachers and practice a few sleights of hand for a half hour or so. Then progress to the magic show, which should last about forty minutes. If you've opted for having a series of ward members each perform one magic trick, the program chairman should coordinate the tricks to make sure there are no duplicates, and to plan the agenda so that it ends with the most spectacular feats. It goes without saying that no humans or animals should be harmed in the course of the show. Make sure to have a charismatic master of ceremonies, because a good emcee can add excitement to the most pedestrian feats of magic.

Human Board Game Night

Materials: Giant game board, large enough for human beings to serve as playing tokens
Effort Quotient: ♥♥
Time: ▨▨▨▨
Planning: ★★★

This is an activity that takes a whole lot of preparation for the people who have to put the game board together. Pick a game, such as Life® or Clue®, that doesn't go on forever. Have ward members create a giant board game so that people can serve as playing tokens, or use rooms in the building to represent rooms on the playing board. You may need a giant spinner or giant money, too. On the night of the game, choose people to serve as the tokens, and others to serve as the players. Everyone else can cheer on his or her favorite teams.

One way to adapt this game for children would be to have a human checkers game. Kids love the idea of leap-frogging over other players.

For a more active human board game, try a game of human foosball. Use PVC pipes (which are really very cheap), and set up the cultural hall with masking tape markings. Four or five people hold one long, connected together PVC pipe and form five or six rows on each side of the cultural hall. The teams face each other and work together to block a Nerf® ball from making it to the other end of the cultural hall. It's a blast, especially for the younger set. Older ward members might not like all the ruckus, but could make a good audience.

UnTalent Show

Materials: None, with the exception of appropriate decorations
Effort Quotient: ✦
Time: ✖✖✖
Planning: ★★

This is a unique spin-off of a typical ward talent night. The object is to have everyone come prepared with unique, not-so-unique, bizarre, weird, and totally useless talents. Here are some sample untalents that participants can demonstrate:

- Prepare grass seeds in a pot and then watch grass grow
- Explain the art of setting a table
- Touch one's own nose with his tongue or kiss his own elbow
- Show how to fold common household towels or napkins
- Sing a song without any singing ability
- Read a poem that was written by somebody else
- Show how to scratch the middle of one's own back

Sneaky Secret

When you're planning this activity—or any ward activity where success depends on people being heard—never assume that people's voices are loud enough to carry across a crowded room. *Always* use a microphone, or several of them. Make sure you have someone on hand who is well equipped to work the microphone, and to correct any audio problems that may crop up. Remember—long hours of practice may result in a perfect performance, but it won't be appreciated if nobody can hear what is being said or sung.

If members use their imaginations, they can come up with all kinds of unique untalents. This is a riot for the whole congregation, and it's the only place in a church setting where jeers from the audience are acceptable.

Book of Mormon Olympics

Materials: Depending on events, some of the following: name tags, sashes, stickers, plastic straws with paper covers, paper plates, balloons, butcher paper, marshmallows, baking pans, and refreshments

Effort Quotient: ✋✋✋

Time: ⌛⌛⌛⌛

Planning: ★★★★

As they enter the cultural hall, divide up ward members into teams, ensuring that no family members are on the same team. Give each team a Book of Mormon name (Nephites, Lamanites, Jaredites, Jacobites, and so on) that can be indicated by the color of a player's sash or the design on his name sticker. Each team participates in all of the following events:

Cimiter Throw: Each team member is given a straw still in its paper. The object is to see how far each team member can blow the paper off the straw. Record the individual distances and the team aggregate.

Land of Many Waters Relay: Each team member is given a large marshmallow (don't eat it!). The object is to place the marshmallow in a 9x13-inch cake pan with one inch of water and record how long it takes each member to blow his marshmallow from one end to the other. Record the individual times and team aggregate.

Manti to Zarahemla Relay: Each team member is to place a straw in his mouth. The team captain is given a Lifesaver® candy. The object is to see how long it takes the team to pass the Lifesaver® from teammate to teammate and back again. Using your hands is prohibited. Record the team time. Note: Before you start this activity, make sure you're using a straw that's small enough for a Lifesaver® to move freely along it. Don't use fruit-flavored Lifesavers,® either; they have smaller holes than the mint flavors, and they get sticky.

Rameumptom Tower Jump: One by one, each team member stands against a wall (already covered with butcher paper) in the cultural hall. The person raises his hand as high as possible against the paper. A judge jots down where the fingertips hit the paper. The person then jumps, with hand raised, as high as he can. The judge measures the height of each member's jump. Record the individual and team aggregate heights. *Note: You may want to put charcoal on a player's fingertips to get accurate measurements.*

Seine Toss: Each team stands behind a line. The first member is given a balloon. The object is to toss, overhand or underhand—but no thumping or pulling the end and letting go—the balloon as far as he can. Record individual distances and aggregate team distance.

Curelom Pie Throw: Each team stands behind a line. The first member is given a paper plate. The paper plate is placed in the palm of the hand. The object is to toss, overhand like a baseball—not fling like a Frisbee!—the paper plate. Record the distance for each team member, as well as the team aggregate distance.

Sidon River Dash: Each team stands behind a line. Each team member is given a paper plate. The team captain is given an extra paper plate. The object is to move from the starting line to another line (approximately 10 to 15 yards away) by stepping only on your paper plates. The captain places his extra plate in front of him and moves forward to it. Each team member moves up. The last person moves up and grabs the end paper plate and passes it forward. Repeat action until each member has crossed the line and returned to and passed the starting line. Record the team time.

Award gold, silver, and bronze stickers to the individual and team winners in each game category. Serve fruit and vegetables at intermission and homemade (or store bought) ice cream at the completion of the events. This is a great activity for the whole family.

Cruise to Nowhere

Materials: "Boarding Passes" (tickets) for ward members, to be passed out ahead of time and taken at the door; shipboard decorations that can be as simple or elaborate as you want; shuffleboard and ping pong equipment; materials for craft projects;

Sneaky Secret

Using admission tickets such as the "boarding passes" issued for the Cruise to Nowhere is a good tactic for reminding people of your party. The tickets are free, and you don't need to tell people they aren't required for admission. (In fact, you can put a telephone number on the ticket, telling people they can get additional tickets by calling that number.) But as ward members ask for tickets, you'll get a rough estimate of the number of people you can expect at your party. The tickets serve as an extra reminder of the party, too, because people will keep them in a prominent place so they won't get lost. Every time a family member sees those tickets on the refrigerator door, it will be a subtle reminder that a ward activity is fast approaching.

microphone; fancy fruit drinks, complete with the little umbrellas; lavish refreshments as the budget allows

Effort Quotient: ✋✋
Time: ⧗⧗⧗
Planning: ★★★★

Everyone wants to go on a cruise, but it's easier to bring the cruise to your ward members. A cruise could be a theme for a formal ward dinner, but it could just as easily apply to a less formal occasion. Decorate your cultural hall to resemble the SS (name of ward) and go from there. It doesn't matter whether the ward members have ever been on a cruise. It's more important to play on people's perceptions of cruises. The stereotypical cruise would feature shuffleboard games and cruise crafts, so you may want to include those activities. A lifeboat drill may make for an interesting few minutes. Make sure to have bad singing by lounge lizards who croon to loud groans from the audience, and open the floor to dancing while the "entertainers" are singing. The bishop will be your captain, and your master of ceremonies will be the cruise director. Don't forget to have a ship's photographer taking pictures of participants as they go aboard. You may be able to have them developed as the activity is in progress and give them out as souvenirs of the evening when the ship docks.

Black Light Volleyball

Materials: Volleyball, net, black lights
Effort Quotient: ✋✋✋
Time: ⧗⧗⧗⧗
Planning: ★★

Black light volleyball is a new spin on an old activity. Kent and Shannon have used it with spectacular results. You will need to set up the volleyball net in the cultural hall prior to everyone's arrival. Place between six to eight black lights strategically throughout the cultural hall. It's important to place the lights somewhat away from the actual playing area so they don't get hit during play, yet close enough to provide adequate light. It's also important to place reflective tape around the perimeter of the court and across the net. Have everyone wear white and, if needed, put reflective tape on the ball itself, to make it easier to see. You don't have to be very good at volleyball to really enjoy this game.

New Move-In, Move-Out Party

Materials: Varies
Effort Quotient: ✮✮✮
Time: ⧖⧖⧖
Planning: ★★

This is a great way to meet and highlight new members or families of your ward or to say farewell to members of your congregation who are moving from the area. If it's a new move-in party, a couple of warm-up activities (see chapter 8) can be used to get things started off. After the ice has been broken, spend the rest of the time mingling and getting to know the new move-ins. To add a special touch, prepare a short spotlight on each new move-in family.

If it's a move-out party, start with a warm-up activity or two to loosen everyone up. Then mingle and say your final farewells to your departing friends. A mini roast can also be loads of fun. As a farewell gift, you may want to collect recipes from ward members and then put them in a recipe box or recipe binder to give to the women who are moving away. This is a memorable way to send off those members of your ward who have affected your lives. Incorporating a potluck meal is also a nice touch, since no one has to spend tons of time doing a lot of planning.

Hillbilly Hoedown

Materials: Down-home decorations like you'd find in a log cabin
(bales of hay make great benches and chairs)
Effort Quotient: ✮✮✮

Time: ☒☒☒
Planning: ★★★

If you ever wanted to go barefooted to a party, here is your chance. Everyone should wear their bib overalls or jeans, and let their hair down for this casual party. Here are some ideas to enhance the event:

- Have a watermelon seed-spitting competition.

- Have a hog-calling contest.

- Make sure to have a hitching post. Have a Marryin' Judge on hand to hitch people who want to be hitched. This can be a Sadie Hawkins event where the girls ask the boys. Just make sure to give a marriage license to everyone who participates, being sure to misspell the appropriate words.

- Have a whittling contest or soap-carving contest for adults. *Don't allow any sharp implements to get into the hands of children.*

- Have a square dance.

- Make lovely fashions out of newspaper and masking tape. Have people model their creations.

- This may be a great opportunity for demonstrations of the home arts. Food canning or drying classes could be held, along with other aspects of food storage in a setting that doesn't induce guilt.

- Play fiddle music. You may want to have washboards on hand so people can provide their own musical accompaniment.

- Serve lots of "vittles," none of them healthy. Anything fried or barbecued, accompanied by cornbread, should do the trick.

- Have a "still" dispensing home-brewed root beer.

- Have a pie-baking contest to provide dessert.

Outdoor Park Activity

Materials: Outdoor game equipment (kickball, volleyball, softball, Frisbee) and watermelon
Effort Quotient: ♥♥♥

Time: ⌛⌛⌛⌛
Planning: ★

This is an excellent venue for getting the whole ward together for an afternoon at the park. This is best done in the spring or summer and can be done on a holiday or Saturday afternoon. With enough varied activities, there will be something for everyone, even for those who just want to socialize. Each family can bring a picnic meal and the ward can provide the ice-cold watermelon during and after the games. This is a great activity because it requires little planning, is relatively inexpensive, and is held outside so cleanup is minimized.

Swiss Family Robinson Party

Materials: A huge assortment of junk items that can be used as prizes in the island exploration; props to make the cultural hall (and other rooms) look like a desert island
Effort Quotient: 🖐🖐🖐
Time: ⌛⌛⌛⌛
Planning: ★★★

This is a great opportunity for your ward members to show what they're made of. Have participants explore the island by going in groups from room to room in the building and finding different activities in each area. Activities should be in the form of quick contests or trivia questions that people can win. Prizes should be in the form of a household item or piece of junk to signify something that washed up on the beach. These can include a piece of wood, a flashlight, a cardboard box, a roll of masking tape, a screwdriver, a ball of yarn, a lampshade, or any one of a number of other items. Let everyone who attends win one item, but nobody should win more than one. (Make sure to have some contests that young children can win, so everyone gets a prize.) As each person wins a prize, have him return to the cultural hall and form teams as individuals arrive. Give the teams a set amount of time to construct some sort of invention with the items they've collected. Have each team demonstrate their inventions to the assembled group, and give prizes for the team with the most original, most functional, and most unusual creations. Then move on to a few feats of strength and ingenuity that will allow castaways to test their skills in several areas. Be sure to serve a dinner that castaways can assemble themselves. A salad bar or potato bar will allow people to use their creativity to customize their own meals. Or serve clam chowder and coconut cake to simulate island cuisine.

Moonlight Hike

Materials: Flashlights, sack lunches, a moonlit trail for walking
Effort Quotient: ✋✋✋
Time: ⌛⌛⌛
Planning: ★

Consult your almanac for a night with a full moon, and find an easy trail for a moonlight hike. Everyone should carry a flashlight to guard against stumbles on the path; and if you're walking in a place that allows campfires, you may want to roast marshmallows when you reach your destination. If everyone packs a picnic lunch, this is a virtually free activity—unless, of course, the ward provides marshmallows for toasting. If you want to have a program, campfire songs, or a lesson on constellations at the end of the hike, go ahead and do it. It's your activity. Just remember to allow enough time for everyone to walk home again.

Family Feud

Materials: Poster board, marking pens, scoring device, fabulous prizes
Effort Quotient: ✋✋
Time: ⌛⌛⌛
Planning: ★★

This activity is patterned after the popular television game show, "Family Feud." This version requires preparing a list of questions in advance, asking those questions to your ward members, and then tabulating the answers. Sample questions can include the following: What is the first thing you do when you get home from church? What is your favorite church meeting? How many minutes do you typically spend in the shower? What is the distance (miles) between your house and the church? What is your favorite Sunday dinner? What is your favorite after-church activity? What is the size, in number of people, of the average family in your ward? What is the average height, in feet and inches, of your bishopric? How many boxes of breakfast cereal do you have in your house? How many houses are on your street? How many cars are parked in the church parking lot during an average sacrament meeting? In which temple were most ward members married? What is your favorite ward activity?

Come up with as many questions related to your ward as you can. After the answers are compiled, choose the top five answers to each question (together with the number of votes each answer got). Keep those answers secret from potential players!

Most ward members who attend will serve as the audience, with "families" being created for the purpose of the game. You may want to hand-pick people to be on the teams who will provide a lot of laughs for the audience. This will make the game as fun for those who watch as for those who play. Share the wealth by only having one person from a real ward family on stage at a time. Also ensure that there are roughly equal numbers of adults and youth/Primary children on each team, so as not to give either team an unfair advantage. (Or even better, play two games— one with adult participants and one with "families" composed of youth.)

Line up each "family" so it will be easier to question them. The emcee starts out with the first "family" and asks the first question on the list to the first person on the team. He then moves down the line of members, until all the top five answers are given or until the family gets three strikes. If the team gets all five answers, they get the points associated with the answers. If a family gets three strikes, then the question is passed to the next family. Continue until all questions have been asked and the points to the answers have been recorded. The first place family gets a big award, but make sure to pass out some sort of award to each family. Conclude the activity with light refreshments.

Knight Night

Materials: Long banquet tables, banners, armor, other medieval accoutrements, dinner

Effort Quotient: ♛♛♛ (for the young men), ♛ for everyone else

Time: ⚔⚔⚔

Planning: ★★★★ Remember that work can be delegated (see below)

If you ever wanted a ward dinner but didn't want to wash the silverware, this is the event for you. It is also a great opportunity to let your young men be the stars of the evening, with the center of activity being focused on them.

Set up tables around the periphery of the cultural hall. Serve a dinner around the tables before the festivities begin. Remember that this was a pre-silverware era. Serve big hunks of bread to mop up the gravy, chicken legs for the kiddies, and turkey legs for the adults, and other food that can be eaten with the hands. Apple juice is a good drink to accompany the dinner. Play Elizabethan music in the background during the meal to enhance the mood. After the meal, have the young men engage in a medieval tournament consisting of a half dozen different contests. Each knight should be wearing his own colors, with banners in those colors placed strategically in the hall. Young women may want to make the banners before the event, and one or more of them can serve as each knight's champion and cheerleader. (Young men can make their own shields ahead of time, to add to the authenticity.) There should be a whole lot of friendly competition as ward members cheer on their favorite knights. Be sure to award medals or other prizes to the winner of each competition, and other prizes to the knights so that every competitor gets some sort of award. Be sure to have a good master of ceremonies (perhaps attired as a

Sneaky Secret

Quite often, the key to the success of a ward activity is to get a good master of ceremonies. Find somebody with a booming voice and an outgoing personality, and then give that person a microphone so everyone can hear him. It always helps to have an emcee who is a quick thinker, ready to improvise as improvisation is needed. If a good emcee is excited about the activity, his enthusiasm will be contagious. Don't just choose the first person who comes to mind; put a little thought into choosing the best master of ceremonies for the job. And yes, your master of ceremonies can be a woman. What's important is the stage presence of the person in question—not the gender.

court jester or a king of the realm) to inspire enthusiasm in the competitors and crowd alike.

Game Night/Game Competition Night

Materials: Air hockey table, Ping-Pong table, foosball table, indoor bowling set, various board games
Effort Quotient: ♉♉
Time: ▨▨▨
Planning: ★

This is an activity that is usually quite successful and elicits a reasonable turnout. Because you can plan a little something for everyone in an activity like this, no one really gets bored. Game nights can be a little costly if you have to rent the air hockey, Ping-Pong, and foosball tables, but can cost very little if ward members have the equipment and are willing to donate it to the ward for an evening. Have everyone bring a little something to munch on, and the evening is bound to be a success. You can top off the evening with a ward breakfast or something similar. This one's fun for the whole gang.

For a variation on the game night, try a game competition night where all members play only one or two games, and an eventual winner is crowned in each game. For example, you can offer a choice between Scrabble® and Balderdash®, with everybody playing the same game. Set up the cultural hall with lines of tables. Divide the group according to age and experience levels into small groups of four or more people (depending on the game being played). Game winners move up, while the losers move down. For the younger crowd, children's games can be played by using the same procedures, with winners moving up and losers moving down. The idea is to get a champion in each game. You can break up the different rounds of the competition with mini activities from chapter 8. Snacks can be served throughout the competition. Inexpensive prizes can be awarded for the winners, runners-up, and the other participants.

Although this is listed as a whole-ward activity, children under the age of about ten would be bored out of their minds at this sort of party, and would be such a distraction for their parents that the whole event could fail. Make sure to have some sort of activity to entertain the younger crowd while their older siblings and their parents are enjoying their board games. Standard birthday party games such as pin the tail on the donkey might be appropriate, augmented by prizes from the trusty old Oriental Trading Company.

Alice in Wonderland

Materials: Looking-glass entryway; costumes for Queen of Hearts, Mad Hatter, and White Rabbit; decorations specific to the book; croquet set
Effort Quotient: ♥♥
Time: ⧗⧗⧗
Planning: ★★★★

The *Alice in Wonderland* books are so full of bizarre images and scenes that the ideas for a party based on the story are limitless. Consider having the Mad Hatter award fabulous prizes to the first person who steps through the looking glass and enters the party—and the last. The White Rabbit, who introduced Alice to Wonderland, is your emcee. The imperious Queen of Hearts reigns over the event. You may want to have a Mad Hatter's Party, where those who dine eat one bite of finger food and then move to the next seat. Another option is Queen of Hearts croquet. Any sort of backwards activity is appropriate for this party, as is a race where contestants run around in circles, going nowhere. If you want to have a contest, try having a Knave of Hearts Tart (cookie) Judging event. Or read the books and come up with your own activities—the stranger the better.

Sneaky Secret

You can get huge assortments of prizes for pennies by calling and requesting a catalog from Oriental Trading Company. (U.S. residents call 1/800/875–8480.) This remarkable outlet sells the sort of cheap toys found in gum machines. It also sells bulk candies such as wax lips and teeth. You can buy these treasures by the dozen or by the gross if you like, and you'll be paying a mere pittance for your order. Oriental Trading Company is also an excellent source for Primary teachers, who may benefit from having occasional incentives to give their students.

Arabian Nights

Materials: An entryway that can "open sesame"; a cave with prizes for the children; pillows for seating on the floor; decorations with a Middle Eastern flavor
Effort Quotient: ♥♥♥
Time: ⧗⧗⧗
Planning: ★★★

The entrance to your party should be a door that "magically" opens when people say the magic word. You may also have a treasure cave where children can go to pick out a treasure. This can be in the form of a cookie or some other valuable prize.

One good activity for an Arabian Nights experience would be a "Sinbad's Voyage," which may be in the form of a treasure hunt or some other puzzle-solving adventure. You may even want to have Scheherazade on hand for some storytelling. Play musical chairs without the music by having Scheherazade read a tale and stop reading in odd places. Or forget the musical chairs and have Scheherazade read a story to the kiddies while the parents are taking Sinbad's Voyage.

Square Dance

Materials: Square dance caller, music, decorations, refreshments
Effort Quotient: ♥♥♥
Time: ⧓⧓⧓⧓
Planning: ★★

This is an absolutely fabulous activity for the whole family. Even teenagers enjoy it, once they get dancing and laughing. This activity can be a little expensive if you have to hire a square dance caller, but you can probably get him to reduce his rates for a church function. Of course, if you have a square dance caller in your ward, then you might be able to waive the caller fees altogether. Kent and Shannon tried this activity in their ward with much success. Most ward members had long forgotten how to allemande left, so they spent the first forty minutes learning a few basic moves. (It is especially helpful if the caller can bring a few members of his square dance club to mingle and help everyone out.) After everyone learned the basics, they square danced their little hearts out. Western decorations can also really add to the atmosphere and the festivities—and be sure to have a lot of cold water or punch on hand to quench the thirst of the dancers.

Latin Dance

Materials: Latin dance band and caller, decorations, refreshments
Effort Quotient: ♥♥♥
Time: ⧓⧓⧓⧓
Planning: ★★

This activity is similar to the ward square dance since you don't really have to know much about dancing to have fun. The downside to this activity is, that unless you have ward members that perform Latin music, it can be a little costly to hire a band. Start the evening with some dance instruction, and then dance for an hour or so.

If you're looking for dance instructors, you may want to look no farther than the young women in your ward. Many wards may have girls that are on dance teams at their high schools and would get a kick out of teaching the ward how to do this. Other girls may not know how to dance today, but they can learn by tomorrow in order to fulfill the assignment. Remember—always look for opportunities to spotlight members of your ward. This may be a good opportunity to do so.

Charlie and the Chocolate Factory

Materials: Chocolate factory decorations; chocolaty treats; a chocolate tree; golden tickets
Effort Quotient: ♥♥♥
Time: ▨▨▨
Planning: ★★★★

This is another party idea that comes from such a rich source (the book *Charlie and the Chocolate Factory* by Roald Dahl, or the movie *Willie Wonka and the Chocolate Factory*) that the possibilities for entertainment are endless. Be sure to issue golden tickets that invite people to the party, and that people will use to enter the premises. Also keep in mind that the story had a definite theme, which is that honesty and integrity are rewarded. Any activities that bring these points to mind for the younger members of the congregation are good. Some activities might include Augustus' Jell-O®-Eating Contest; an Ooompa-Loompa Race (you decide what that entails!); Violet's Steamroller Race (have children roll to the finish line, giving them prizes for how many balloons they flatten and pop along the way); a chocolate-dipping class for women; a men's cooking contest featuring chocolate treats; and Charlie's Three-Legged Race (teaming children with adults). One activity for children could center on the chocolate tree. Make up a list of Primary-related questions. These could be questions about Primary songs, the Primary theme, scripture stories, or the Articles of Faith. Whenever a child gets a correct answer, he's allowed to choose a piece of candy from the chocolate tree.

One piece of candy may have a coupon inside for a big prize. Come up with other games and prizes by reading the book or seeing the movie.

Ward Breakfast

Materials: Breakfast foods (pancake mix, eggs, bacon, sausage, milk, juice, and so on); camping stoves or grills; plates; plastic utensils; and so on
Effort Quotient: ♨♨
Time: ⌛⌛⌛⌛
Planning: ★★★★

A lot of effort goes into planning any type of ward meal. The wards that meet in our building hold an annual ward breakfast at a local park. This is nice for the ambiance and saves on cleanup and wear and tear of your cultural hall. If you don't have a park nearby, your ward's parking lot is a good substitute. Set up tables on one side of the building and serve the food outside.

To share the burden of planning this breakfast, we alternate planning it with the other ward that shares our building. This annual breakfast takes place on the morning of July 4. If the breakfast starts at 7 A.M., start cooking by 6:30. Make sure that you have adequate cooking stoves, either gas or electric. If you use electric stoves, make sure the facility at the park can handle the workload. (Kent learned this from sad experience.) After the breakfast, you can play outdoor games, go swimming, or do some other activity available at the site. Just be sure you reserve your site ahead of time. Some places take reservations a year in advance.

Mission to Mars

Materials: Appropriate decorations to simulate a spaceship or a planetary landscape
Effort Quotient: ♨♨
Time: ⌛⌛⌛
Planning: ★★★

Children of all ages are fascinated by space, and a space party can provide numerous opportunities for fun activities. You can have a space trivia contest for adults or a moonwalk for the children. Try having a "Cooking with Tang" competition or demonstration to honor our astronauts' favorite beverage. Have a contest where people identify constellations, or sit around a fake campfire and point out shiny simulated constellations that have been affixed to the walls. You may want to have an alien design contest, where teams create aliens as they might have developed in different environments. (For example, aliens that live on planets with low gravity might be tall and spindly, while aliens who call a bright planet home might have very small, shaded eyes.) Have people explain their design decisions, and award prizes for the winners in various categories. And don't forget to serve MoonPies® for your astronauts to eat!

Ice Cream and Dessert Social

Materials: Homemade ice cream and desserts
Effort Quotient: ♥♥
Time: ⌛⌛⌛
Planning: ★★

This is a perfect activity for a hot summer night. Assign various members to make and bring homemade ice cream. (You may want to make a contest out of it and award prizes, but that isn't necessary unless you're in a competitive mood.) Another group of members can bring a variety of toppings. Assign other members to make and bring their favorite desserts. Have everyone gather in the cultural hall for a couple of warm-up activities. Play games for approximately thirty to fifty minutes. After everyone is loosened up, serve the ice cream, toppings, and desserts. Socialize and maybe play another game or two.

Activities for the Talented

This section includes those ward activities that fall into the category of talent—talent to plan and pull off an activity or talent to participate in an activity. There is not a ward in the Church that doesn't have a few incredibly talented members or at least members with talented friends. Some talents are known to one and all. Someone with an incredible singing voice or who plays a musical instrument is probably accustomed to performing in front of others, and it is pretty easy to get him to participate. The real trick is uncovering people who keep their talents hidden from public view and coaxing them to share their talents with the rest of the ward. Keep the environment nonthreatening, and you'll usually get a good response.

Here are some ward activities that revolve around the area of talent. And for those who don't want to display their talents, there's always a need for a good audience.

Talent Show/Collections Night

Materials: Tables to exhibit collections, stage decorations or other props
Effort Quotient: ♨♨
Time: ▨▨▨
Planning: ★★★

Announce your intent to have a talent show at least six weeks to two months in advance. Send sign-up sheets around to all the organizations. Try to make sure each organization provides at least five participants. And don't forget family participation. Some families can do some really cool stuff, such as playing Jingle Bells with pop bottles.

Narrow your list down to no more than twenty acts or demonstrations. Try to get a variety of acts to interest all age groups. Acts can include singing, playing musical instruments, dancing, martial arts demonstrations, storytelling, poetry reading, gymnastics, juggling, painting, or whatever else comes to mind. You can even throw in a couple of funny acts or gag acts. The key to a successful talent show is to have a good, entertaining master of ceremonies. There is inevitably some slack time between acts, so the emcee needs to have several good jokes or short stories to hold things together. There are thousands of books you can use as sources for short stories and jokes. Look at Amazon.com, or browse your local bookstore. Nice decorations can also add to the ambiance. Decorators also show real talent, so make sure the emcee mentions them.

Don't forget talents that never appear on a stage. If people do artwork or make pottery or create stained glass or produce jewelry, or even do home arts such as canning and sewing, these talents can go on display before the show. If you start the party an hour before the talent show begins, ward members can go from room to room and view the talent displays, or even see demonstrations of how things are made.

An alternative to a talent display is to have members or nonmembers bring some of the things they collect. People collect everything, from baseball caps to Monopoly games, cookie cutters to nativity scenes, and so on. Set aside an intermission about halfway through the acts so the audience can view the collections and eat some light refreshments, making sure that the collections are protected from food spills or from children's inquisitive hands. End the evening with the remainder of the refreshments. A little simple planning can go a long way in making this a really enjoyable evening for the whole family. The clueless can do this!

Luau

Materials: Grass skirts, gourd drums, roast pig, decorations, and whatever else comes to mind
Effort Quotient: ♆♆♆
Time: ▨▨▨
Planning: ★★

The key to a good luau is planning. Divide the planning up between the meal and the entertainment. You can also do these activities separately, depending on time and resources. Most ward dinners are challenging in and of themselves, and roasting a pig only adds to the challenge. Most of us are not able to bury a pig on the church grounds and have it slow roast all day. As an alternative, go to a local restaurant or grocery store (preferably one that roasts turkeys for Thanksgiving) and see if you can get them to do your pig roasting. You should be able to accomplish this, especially if they know it's for a church or some other worthy cause. Side dishes can be pretty simple, including a vegetable, maybe a salad, and bread. For dessert, have cake with coconut frosting. And don't forget the Polynesian dancing. If you can get authentic dancers, great. If not, ask yourself how likely it is that most ward members can differentiate between authentic Polynesian dancing and pure creativity. If you don't have any South Seas natives in your ward, fake it and enjoy yourselves. Books can serve as a good resource for learning about Pacific culture and dancing. Include the audience in some of the dancing, and you'll be sure to have a rousing success. Encourage people to wear their loudest Hawaiian attire. Pass out leis as people enter. There aren't any rules: you can have a luau that consists of dancing and light refreshments, or go "whole hog" with the pork meal and massive entertainment. If all you can do is pass out plastic leis and play recorded Hawaiian music throughout the meal, that will work fine.

Health Fair

Materials: Demonstrations for CPR, aerobics, martial arts, and nutrition; brochures; some decorations; and light refreshments
Effort Quotient: ✹✹
Time: ▨▨▨
Planning: ★★

This can be an excellent activity for involving some of your ward "experts" in the presentations, skits, and demos. You can choose to present almost anything as long as it pertains to health, wellness, or a related topic. A key to the success of the activity is to make sure that at least several of the presentations are interactive. Have a nurse give a refresher on first aid and pick a few folks from the audience to participate in a CPR demo. Have an aerobics instructor talk about the importance of daily exercise and then lead the entire group in some sort of *very* light workout. Have a family martial arts demo and then lead the entire group in a few brief and simple moves. Have a nutritionist lead the group in a lively discussion of eating for good health. A short video on a health-related topic could also be inserted into the evening. This activity can be fun, instructive, and informational for the whole family—especially if you make sure to set up classes that appeal to children. A children's aerobics class or first aid class or even a child's nutrition class could appeal to the younger set and help them lean toward a healthy lifestyle. Remember to keep your classes—for adults as well as children—simple, lively, and informative.

Personal and Family Finance Night

Materials: Banking demo, investment counselor, stock broker/ trader, grocery store manager, local business leader, employment specialist, brochures and literature, light refreshments
Effort Quotient: ✹
Time: ▨▨▨
Planning: ★★

It's never too early to get started on good financial habits, so think about hosting a family finance seminar that involves the whole family. Using moneysaving and investing tricks is easy, once we know what those tricks are. You'll be surprised how much and how quickly kids can learn financial tricks. Start the evening out with a brief look into the workings of a bank and what banks do with our money. (How early should kids start saving?) Next move to a discussion about family investing and how families can work together. Move to a discussion on food purchasing and what to look for at the grocery store. Have someone talk about employment in your area, including such topics as what's hot and what's not. Listen to a local business leader discuss his/her business and its plans for the future. Have a couple of kids talk about jobs they've held and what they liked and didn't like about them. Spice up the evening with a game or two related to the subject matter. Financial seminars don't have to be boring. The key to a successful activity is to look for ways that people of all ages can participate—not just listen—and learn.

Family Preparedness Night

Materials: Canning demo, food storage tips, 72-hour kits, education counselor, emergency preparedness expert, informational brochures, light refreshments
Effort Quotient: ✹
Time: ⧖⧖⧖
Planning: ★★

Family preparedness isn't just an adult activity, and it doesn't just involve cooking food that no human being would want to eat. With a little creativity, you can fascinate even young children and convince their parents that being prepared is possible and even fun. Use your ward welfare and employment specialist in planning this activity. Start out with a demo on proper procedures for canning and other canning related tips. Move to a discussion on the bare necessities of home storage and short-term emergency kits. Have someone talk about the importance of continued education and what to look for in that area. Have someone from your local government tell the group what plans are in place for emergency preparedness in your area. The key is to keep the discussions short, lively, and interactive. End the evening with some light refreshments, preferably taken only from members' food storage stashes.

Craft Fair

Materials: Depends on the crafts you choose
Effort Quotient: ✹✹

Time: ▧▧▧
Planning: ★★★★

Craft days aren't just for the Relief Society. When properly planned, craft days can be fun for the whole family. The key to a successful craft day is to make sure anyone can succeed—even people who aren't artistically talented. If you have a variety of crafts that appeal to people with different skill levels, you should be able to perform that rare miracle of pleasing all the people all the time. There are other factors, too. Your crafts can't be too expensive. Keep in mind that some families are quite large, and may not have a lot of money to throw around. If this is a true family activity, with children invited, there should be some very easy— and free—crafts that appeal to children of all ages. Select crafts that can be finished during the allotted time. People who don't finish their crafts on site are not going to finish them when they get home, so time is of the essence. Your ward craft day can take place on a Friday afternoon, Saturday morning, or Saturday afternoon. The time of year will determine the theme and the types of crafts you'll work on. Christmas crafts can range from simple tree ornaments to some more complex etched nativity sets. Spring can inspire flowerpots and picture frames. Regardless of when you hold your craft activity, it is best to have experienced crafters lead the various classes. And make sure to have people sign up and pay for their craft projects ahead of time, so you won't be stuck with leftover supplies on the day of the event.

Road Shows

Some members of the Church, who remember the hard work involved in these activities, think of the words *road show* as one four-letter word. But before you write off the idea of doing a road show, at least hear us out and read the next few pages. Road shows used to be quite popular in the Church, but have become almost extinct due to budget constraints and the lack of free time in the lives of the members. Nevertheless, it is possible for road show activities to overcome these limitations and provide a terrific activity for those involved.

The idea behind a road show is to have each ward in the stake (or each auxiliary within a ward) produce a short dramatic production that lasts about fifteen minutes, and have all the shows presented on the same night to the members of the ward or stake. Back when road shows were popular in the Church, they required the sacrifice of much time and money to write a script, cast the parts, hold rehearsals, create scenery, and craft costumes. On the night of the performance, each ward would pack its cast and scenery into trucks, drive around to the various meetinghouses in the stake, and present their production at each location. The idea was for each congregation to meet in its own building, and have the different productions go on the road (thus the name of the event) and bring the show to them. Each show was judged on the quality of the script and the performances, and based on the ability of the crew to get in and out within the time limit. Prizes were often given for the best shows.

The intent of our modified road show activity is to keep the same basic idea, but to remove those elements that caused cutthroat competition and the waste of excessive amounts of time and money. Here are some considerations for sponsoring one of these "road show light" activities for your group:

▶ Location

All of the shows should be presented in the same building. Do not require groups to travel around to the different buildings in the stake and present their show numerous times. It is not unreasonable to ask members to come to the stake center for an activity.

▶ Script

You may want to give each group a general title, and let them do their own interpretation. For example, the title might be "A Typical Saturday Evening on Noah's Ark." Scripts may be authored by one member of the ward or by committee. The advantage of the committee is that more ward members will get to participate, but the disadvantage is that it's virtually impossible to get a great script through a committee effort. Weigh your priorities and decide which is more important to you. If you choose the committee approach, make sure to do it as part of a regular class activity so that extra time on the part of the members is not required. Regardless of who writes the script, establish a script committee (maybe just the bishop and yourself) who must approve the script before the road show is produced.

▶ Music

Most traditional road shows have two or three musical numbers interspersed with the plotline. You may choose to make this part of the activity or leave it up to the individual groups as to how much music will be included in their production. If music is to be included, you may or may not wish to provide the melodies and require each group to write lyrics that fit with those tunes. As with the script, all musical content should first be approved by the script committee.

▶ Participants

Road shows have always been designed primarily for the youth, with adults and younger children taking parts as needed. Determine your target participants, but don't exclude anyone who has an interest.

▶ Rehearsals

Enforce strict limits on the amount of time that can be spent rehearsing the production. You may wish to schedule one activity night to write the script, a second activity night to do the rehearsing, and then have the presentation of the road shows on the next Friday or Saturday. No one expects these to be professional productions, and limiting the rehearsals will not require extra time commitments except for the night of the performances. Another option would be to plan this as a Saturday activity where each group writes, rehearses, and presents the production all on the same day.

▶ Scenery and Props

Identify some basic props and items of scenery and provide them to any group that wants to use them in their production. In fact, you may require groups to use specific props in their production—thus giving them an extra challenge as they create their road shows. For example, you might provide a couch, four folding chairs, a floor lamp, a rusty hammer, and some old travel posters. Having the groups use your scenery will not only save them time and money, but will test their creativity as they have to write a script that incorporates one or more of your provided items. As an alternative, allow the groups to provide their own scenery, but restrict them to only household items (no money can be spent) and limit the number allowed. Another option is to provide a number of abstract props (such as boxes of different sizes and colors), and allow each group to arrange them as needed.

▶ Costumes

No money should be spent on costumes, nor should the costume take more than sixty minutes to make. Encourage participants to make costumes using the normal items they should already have around the house. For example, you could specify dark pants, a white shirt, and a colorful bandanna around the neck. These are items that just about everyone should already have or should be able to borrow from another member of the group.

▶ Time Limits

Not only should there be a time limit on the length of each production but (as already noted) you should also limit all aspects of the preparation so that little time, if any, is required outside of the normal activity times of the groups.

▶ Budget

In no circumstances should any money that will not be reimbursed be spent by individual participants in the activity, and a limited budget should be approved from the budget of the groups involved. If you follow the previous rules, your expenses for costumes and scenery should be minimal, and you might need only a few dollars for items such as the copying of scripts. In most cases, a budget of twenty dollars per group should be more than sufficient. To increase the challenge, you might even make it a "zero budget" activity, so that participants have to be creative to produce something with no expenses at all.

▶ Awards

It is nice to recognize the efforts of people, but you want to make sure there are no hurt feelings caused by any of the awards you present. Consider choosing judges from outside your ward or stake, so there will be no real or perceived favoritism toward any group. Also, avoid giving "best" awards, or any kind of award that ranks one performance above another. One stake solved this problem by asking the judges to award three or four different awards to each group. These were awards such as "Most Enthusiastic Performer," or "Excellence in Script Writing." Because a similar number of awards were given to each production, it allowed each group to be honored for the things they did well, without implying any kind of comparison between the productions.

Ending with a Bang

We've already established that warm-up events are the appetizers of a ward party, and that the activity itself constitutes the meat and potatoes. But almost everybody's favorite part of dinner is the dessert. When you're planning a ward activity, don't overlook the dessert of your party—which is the grand finale of any event.

Most of the time, the grand finale presents itself as the literal dessert. American members of the Church know the party isn't over until the food (most of it sugary and caloric) has been trotted out and consumed. But event planners who stop with food are overlooking something that is far more memorable than mere cakes and cookies. When properly planned, the dessert of your ward activity may be everyone's favorite part of the party.

If you are giving awards, don't just throw the winner a candy bar. Go to a little effort ahead of time and make creative certificates that can be filled in on the spot and presented with flourish to the winners (and to the spectacular losers). If your master of ceremonies is as personable and spontaneous as he should be, he can come up with some hilarious ways to present these awards—and the awards themselves can be just as funny. Be on the lookout for spontaneous things that happen throughout the course of the event, and be sure to award certificates with a lot of fanfare.

Another way to add appeal to the awards process is to present awards that are worth winning. Unless you live in an area where there's a meetinghouse on every street corner, local businesses are often glad to donate a free dinner for two or a free gift from their store to churches in exchange for that all-important free publicity. And even if you live in an area where there are hundreds of award-seeking congregations, you can probably track down ward members who have connections to various local businesses that may be willing to help you out. When you get prizes from local businesses, be sure to write thank-you notes afterwards, describing with great enthusiasm your gratitude for the award and the delight with which the prize was received. Enclose a copy of a program or ward bulletin where the company's name was mentioned in a thank you, or say something in the text of your note to indicate that everyone at the event knew who the donor was.

Another way to keep people interested until the end of the party is to award door prizes. These can be donated from local businesses, or they can be natural by-products of the party. For example, a lot of effort often goes into table centerpieces or other decorations. These may be awarded to randomly selected participants at the end of the evening.

An always-popular cap to an event is a white elephant gift exchange. This is successful only for parties of about forty persons or fewer, and it needs to be planned ahead of time because participants must each contribute a wrapped white elephant gift. The exchange is simple. Everyone sits in a circle, with the attractively wrapped "gifts" in the center. Somehow it is determined that a particular member of the group goes first. (Perhaps you can single out the winner of a warm-up activity for that honor.) That person chooses an item from the center of the floor and holds it, still in the wrapping paper, on his lap. Then go left around the circle, with each person having a choice of taking any item from the center or stealing an item that was selected by someone who went before. If someone's white elephant is stolen, he must take another item from the center of the circle or from somebody else's lap. (A player can't steal back something that was just stolen away, but he can reclaim a cherished treasure if the opportunity presents itself later.) Swapping and stealing goes on until all the presents have been distributed. Only then are the presents opened, so the combatants can see exactly who got the treasures and who got the trash.

But not all extravagant desserts involve prizes. In these days of digital cameras and camcorders, a ward event can be photographed in process—and the video can be shown or the pictures prominently displayed by the end of the evening. This is a good way to spotlight individual members, especially if you have a photographer who chooses subjects who aren't always on stage getting recognition. Using photography is also a good way to spotlight the photographer's handiwork and show a little appreciation for an often-unappreciated skill.

No matter what method you choose to end your activity, try to do something memorable at the end of each event. Not only will this bring people back to your next activity, but it will also keep people on hand until your activity ends. People who stick around until the closing prayer are likely to help the cleaning committee restore order to the building, so it's to everyone's advantage if you serve the proper dessert at the end of every ward activity.

Questions from the Clueless

? *What do I do if I put my heart and soul into preparing for an activity and no one shows up?*

If people don't show up for your activities, there's a reason. Go back to chapter 1 and scan through the questions you should be asking yourself to see what you've missed. Maybe the activity was targeted to the wrong audience, or perhaps you had the right audience in mind but chose the wrong activity. Maybe a scheduling conflict kept people away. Perhaps you didn't have the support of your ward leaders, so nobody else felt inspired to attend. Maybe there weren't enough follow-ups to the publicity. These are questions that should be addressed after the event. But as the event proceeds, keep a smile on your face and never show disappointment at the low turnout. Keep a couple of warm-up activities in your back pocket for appropriate times (you'll find those in chapter 8). And always go into an activity with a few ways you can modify that event to succeed even if there are only a few participants.

? *What happens if someone gets hurt during an activity?*

Few people who plan for a ward event take the possibility of injury into account. But people can be injured in any activity. They can be seriously burned with glue guns when they're assembling crafts, or can be scalded in a kitchen accident. They can even miss a chair in musical chairs and land on the floor, injuring themselves in the process. That being the case, there should always be a first-aid kit on hand at any ward activity. Make sure you know where the first-aid kit is, and how to use the supplies that are found in that kit. You may also want to come to each activity with the phone number of an emergency medical center or ambulance. And it only makes sense that if you're enjoying activities that take you away from civilization, you should make every effort to have a ward member who is a health care professional attend that event, fully equipped to deal with emergencies. Ninety-nine times out of a hundred, all these precautions will be unnecessary. But when you need medical help, the situation could be critical.

CHAPTER 3

Leave the Little Darlings at Home

★ **IN THIS CHAPTER**
- ✔ Planning Adult-Only Activities
- ✔ Activities for Mom and Dad
- ✔ Small Group Activities
- ✔ Activities Just for the Guys
- ✔ Ladies' Night Out
- ✔ Home, Family, and Personal Enrichment Meetings
- ✔ Questions from the Clueless

You are not evil if you dream of having an afternoon or evening away from home without your precious offspring. A child-free activity is not only acceptable, but even preferable in some situations. Children are wonderful creatures, but they can command a lot of attention. If their parents aren't looking at them, children tend to seek activities that will focus Mom and Dad's attention squarely on themselves, even if it means braining another child in the process. It can be difficult to have a conversation with other adults if children are running around underfoot. Thus, the best way to have an activity where adults can focus on each other is to leave the children at home.

As you have probably experienced, the dynamics of child-free activities are different for those that include an entire ward congregation. The menu can be more exotic, the decorations can be more fragile, and the program can be more sophisticated if children aren't present—but they don't have to be. The purpose of activities that do not include children is not so much to indulge in activities that children wouldn't appreciate, as to enjoy interacting with other adults.

This chapter is dedicated to activities that are sponsored by adults, for adults. It includes activities for couples, men only, women only, and thoughts on the Relief Society's home, family, and personal enrichment night—in addition to the regular Questions from the Clueless.

Just Mom and Dad

It may be a scary concept to realize that Mom and Dad have permission to spend an evening away from the kids. But unless you make plans for something to do, you're likely to find yourselves all dressed up with no place to go. Ward activities can provide that "some place." Being with other couples from the ward will give you a good chance to get to know the people who sit next to you at church fifty-two weeks out of the year in, perhaps, slightly less formal surroundings. After all, people tend to make friends from the people around them. If you're going to make friends as a couple, what better pool of people to choose from than the ones with whom you share the gospel?

Picking a theme for your party is easier than you may think. All you have to do is pick a noun and build a party around it. Pincushion night? Flamingo night? Stinky feet night? It can be done. If you find yourself at a loss for picking a party theme, look at chapter 7 for ideas you can use every day of the year.

The location of your activity will depend on the size of your group. Choose a ward member's house for intimacy, or gather at the ward meetinghouse if you're expecting a lot of participants. In addition to accommodating a much larger group, using the meetinghouse gives you ample room to move around and do different things. Decorations are important, especially for setting whatever mood you are after, but they don't need to be too elaborate or expensive. The key to a good adult get-together is to have it well planned out and have some fun and interesting things for everyone to do. Make sure to leave some time at the end so participants can socialize and get to know one another a little better. Throw in some light refreshments and you'll have the fixings for a relaxing activity that everyone will long remember.

Adult Firesides

Materials: Varies depending on theme, but normally minimal; light refreshments

Effort Quotient: ✋✋

Time: ☒☒☒
Planning: ★

Firesides can be a great way to get away from the kids for an hour or so on a Sunday evening. Although the Church continues to stress that Sundays are family days, an hour or two out of a Sunday evening, maybe every other month or on a quarterly basis, can be refreshing and spiritually uplifting for Mom and Dad. Firesides can take on any number of themes or topics. Here are a few to get you started: time management, food storage, marriage relations, financial management, continuing education, stress management, job searching, family unity, scripture topics, church history topics, holiday themes. The key to any fireside is to find speakers who are both knowledgeable and entertaining. People can sleep at home; they're certainly not going to go to an optional activity that is boring enough to put them to sleep. Depending on your theme, there's no rule against having a panel discussion instead of a single speaker. It really depends on how much time, effort, and inclination you have and want to expend on this type of activity.

If you're planning a fireside, make sure to leave some time at the end for mingling. Our three-hour Sunday meeting schedule doesn't give us the opportunity to visit with other ward members—and once Sunday meetings end, everyone scatters for meals and sleep. The end of an uplifting fireside is the perfect time to just sit or stand around and socialize or discuss the fireside topic with your fellow ward members. It may be the speaker that gets people to come out on a Sunday night, but visiting after the fireside may be the most therapeutic part of the activity. Insert a couple of adult firesides into your planning calendar and you'll be surprised at how quickly your ward members start to come together.

As you're planning your program, keep in mind that firesides don't have to be elaborate to be good. The key is to have an entertaining and worthwhile topic, a few moments to socialize, and some light refreshments. The simpler it is, the less stress it will be on everyone.

A final hint is to ask the young men and young women to "volunteer" to watch the young ones who can't be left at home with an older sibling. This way you'll be able to capture some of the folks who wouldn't otherwise have a chance to come out.

Temple Excursions

Materials: Transportation, food
Effort Quotient: ♥♥

Time: ⚅⚅⚅⚅
Planning: ★ or ★★★★, depending on proximity to a temple

We all know we should attend the temple, but we often don't get around to making the effort unless we're inspired to do so by being invited to go in a group. A temple excursion presents the ideal opportunity to do this important work.

If you live far from a temple, you undoubtedly know exactly what is involved in getting a temple excursion together. Buses have to be rented or other transportation provided. Children have to be cared for—and it isn't easy to find people who will tend your children for days at a time. Time must be taken off work. Money must be saved and, in some cases, passports have to be obtained. Organizing a temple excursion may require months or even years of concentrated effort.

If you live close to a temple, the logistics are easier. In fact, local temple trips are so easy that Saints may take the temple for granted as they get caught up in the business of daily life. But temple excursions can represent significant and successful ward activities if planned correctly. Here are a few tips to help you do so.

- Temple excursions are more successful if they occur at regular intervals. If ward members know a temple excursion is going to be held on the last Thursday of the month, and that ward members will be attending the 7:30 P.M. session, they'll be more likely to make the necessary arrangements.

- You may have better success if you have two regular temple excursion trips—one for people who can only go at night, and another for people who attend during the day. The Relief Society may want to organize the daytime trip, with one of the priesthood quorums coordinating the nighttime excursions.

- As you plan your temple excursions, don't leave anybody out. Elderly church members may be particularly interested in attending the temple, but may be hesitant to go on a ward excursion because they can't provide their own transportation or are less mobile than other ward members. New members should also be considered. Even if they can't do regular endowment sessions, they can certainly participate in baptisms for the dead. Issue personal invitations to these and others who may want to attend, but who may not feel welcome to do so.

- Don't forget that other temple ordinances can be performed in addition to endowment sessions. Ward members can work in the baptistry or do initiatory work or sealings. Be sure to make appointments to do this work—or to attend the endowment session, if you attend a temple where appointments for endowment sessions are necessary. Remember that temple workers will be waiting for your group to arrive, and if you cannot attend, a cancellation phone call is appreciated.

Child care should be taken into consideration. Teenagers may be available to offer baby-sitting services, or parents can alternate temple trips with other parents as families take turns baby-sitting for each other. In some wards, members who are unable to attend the temple are glad to perform the service of watching children while endowed members go to the temple. Don't abuse the situation, however. Offer to do family temple names for people who are taking care of your children, or give your sitters an occasional gift in gratitude for their service.

Personalize your temple excursions by doing work for the families of ward members. Avid genealogists often find themselves with thousands of family names and no opportunity to do the temple work for them. If family names are available in your ward, take advantage of them.

Temple attendance is one area that is greatly enhanced by the presence of ward leaders. If your bishopric and auxiliary leaders are present at temple excursions, they'll inspire other ward members to be present also.

Although temple service should be reward enough, attendance at temple excursions is boosted by the promise of a shared meal afterwards. Smaller groups can make arrangements to visit a restaurant or, if you're planning a larger temple excursion, you may want to have soup and salad waiting at a ward member's home on your return.

Adult Activity Night

Materials: Depends on your activity; light refreshments
Effort Quotient: ♥♥
Time: ▩▩▩
Planning: ★★

The sky's the limit with an adult activity night. It can take the form of a potluck dinner and some type of sing-along, or it can consist of a bowling night or miniature golf night out on the town. How about an evening featuring volleyball, an easy meal, and maybe some light refreshments? If that doesn't inspire you, maybe you'd prefer an afternoon craft fair, or even a white elephant exchange to help you get rid of some of those "treasures" you've been keeping around the house. You don't need to do much planning to get away for an evening that consists of a light meal, some sort of activity, and some socializing with friends. If you have a ward with a lot of young marrieds, an adult activity night could be a monthly event. Try setting aside the same night every month for your activity, so people will remember to make room for it on their calendars. A First Friday Activity Night may be a real hit in your ward—especially if you can draft young men and young women to help you with the baby-sitting responsibilities.

Oldlywed Game

Materials: Poster board, marking pens, scoring device, fabulous prizes
Effort Quotient: ✸
Time: ✕✕✕
Planning: ★★

This activity for adults is a G-rated version of the classic television game show, *The Newlywed Game*. This version requires preparing a list of questions in advance. You'll need nine questions per game, although you'll probably be able to fit several games into an evening. Sample questions might include these: Who is your spouse's hero? Who is your spouse's favorite author? What is your spouse's favorite all-time movie? What was your spouse's all-time favorite church calling? What was your spouse's favorite vacation? What is your spouse's favorite meal? On a scale of one to five, with five being terrific, where does your spouse rate his in-laws?

Once you have the questions, you'll need four couples per game. These can be chosen from names drawn from a hat or by some other means of random selection. First seat the wives on the stage, sending the husbands to a "sound-proof booth" so they can't hear the wives' answers. Ask the wives four questions (one at a time), and have them write their answers on individual pieces of poster board. Then bring the husbands back to guess the wives' answers. Give each husband-wife team five points for each correct answer. Then send out the wives to the soundproof booth and ask five questions to the husbands. The first four questions will be ten-point questions, and the last question will be a twenty-five-point bonus question. The team scoring the highest gets a fabulous prize, and everyone in the group will enjoy an evening of laughter. This is a great way for people to get to know other couples in the ward, and it's a game that even new ward members can enjoy without knowing anyone else or having any particular talent.

Treasure Hunt

Materials: Clues as prepared by the activity planner, fabulous prizes, dessert
Effort Quotient: ♆♆♆
Time: ▨▨▨
Planning: ★★★

It has been many years since Clark was a Boy Scout, but he still fondly remembers the yearly treasure hunts organized by his long-suffering Scoutmaster. The troop was divided into teams, and each team would compete against the others to be the first one to find the treasure. As the activity began, each team was given a clue as to where the next clue would be found. Clues were written in such a way as to tap into the knowledge that every Scout was supposed to know. Team members might have to locate a particular plant or type of tree, or they might have to walk twenty paces toward a constellation in the night sky. Some of the clues were even written in Morse code. Once the team deciphered the clue, they would be off to find the next clue. This was good exercise because vehicles were not allowed, and teams would sometimes run for miles as they went from one corner of the ward boundaries to another. As they followed the chain of clues, they would finally find a clue that would direct them back to the Scout room in the meetinghouse. The first team back (with all their clues in hand) would be the winners, and would receive some kind of small prize. When everyone was back, ice cream would be served.

Although a treasure hunt is an ideal activity for youth, there aren't any activity police to stop adults from having a treasure hunt of their own. The clues can be written to test for any kind of knowledge, such as understanding the scriptures or knowing what is in the headlines of yesterday's newspaper. If you're playing with coed teams, make sure to have clues that would be more readily answered by women as well as clues that would draw on stereotypical male knowledge. Make sure the clues rotate so that different teams visit clue locations at different times. This will prevent a team from locating a clue location just by following another team. The distance covered by the hunt can also vary, depending on the stamina of the adults in your ward.

Road Rally

Materials: Clues as prepared by the activity planner, automobiles, fabulous prizes, dessert
Effort Quotient: ♦♦♦
Time: ✕✕✕
Planning: ★★★

This is similar to the treasure hunt activity, with the difference being that teams travel by automobile rather than on foot. Set a time limit for everyone to be back, so that those who get lost will not be wandering around the neighborhood forever. Select teams small enough that they can easily fit into one car. Each car will represent a team. If the youth are involved, make sure that adult leaders are the ones actually doing the driving.

One way to make this activity safer and more fun is to divide the participants into teams, and then assign one team member from each team to ride in the car of another team. Each "spy" will have the assignment of making sure the driver in his car does not exceed the speed limit.

You may want to make the spy's role even more intriguing by announcing ahead of time that each spy can help the team members in his car as they work to solve their clues. The caveat is that nobody will know whether the spy is really helping, or is actually leading the rival team astray. It can go either way, because some spies will switch allegiance to their adoptive teams, but others will retain their loyalty to the original group. When prizes are awarded at the end of the evening, there should be a prize given to the team member who was forced to ride shotgun in a rival team's vehicle . . . unless, of course, the spy switched loyalties and actively helped his adoptive team.

Small Group Activities

Not every activity you coordinate has to involve the entire ward. Sometimes the best activities are small parties that take place in the ward and are organized by the ward but held in members' homes. If your ward hosts game nights or dinner nights, for example, you could find yourself coordinating ten or more parties that are being held on the same night throughout the ward, each of them limited to no more than eight participants.

No matter what sort of small-group activity you organize, they all follow a similar pattern. Small groups should be limited to no more than eight participants per group. Participation is entirely voluntary, and activities coordinators can solicit members ahead of time with sign-up sheets or personal invitations. If this is a ward activity, however, it is vital that every couple or single who wants to participate is welcome to do so. Church functions are no place to limit your participants to people whom you'd like to be part of your own personal circle of friends.

Once you have a list of ward members who wish to participate, the next step is to divide them up into different groups. Try to place three to four couples or singles in each group, choosing couples that you believe would be compatible with one another. Select a reliable couple or single to host the first event. The host is responsible for contacting each person in the group, selecting a workable date and time for the activity, providing the meeting place, and making any other decisions that are related to the particular event. Providing each host with written instructions and a listing of those in his group will be helpful.

In subsequent months, each group continues to meet together once a month, but the duties of the host rotate through the group until all members have had a chance to host the group once. After that, organize new groups with different people. If the groups work as planned, you will have one activity per month for three or four months, after which you will be assigned to a different group of people.

As the organizer of the groups, you will have more success if you contact each host after about two weeks to make sure plans are underway to hold the first activity. You may want to do this each month with each new set of hosts, because scheduling these small-home activities seems to get postponed forever unless there is someone to follow up. Each time you reorganize the groups, you should also allow for new people to become involved and for existing members to leave the groups.

The hardest part of coordinating a successful small-group activity is making sure the hosts of your events follow through. One option to get better participation is to set aside a certain day each month when all the groups in your ward will meet. If you choose the second Saturday of the month and name your group "The Second Saturday Dinner Group," or "The Second Saturday Game Group," people will know ahead of time when the events should be held, and will plan their schedules accordingly. That way you'll have fewer scheduling conflicts, and your groups will have a greater chance of success. People who have other plans on a particular month will be able to cancel without making the hosts feel as though they have to reschedule the entire event for a more convenient time.

Dinner or Restaurant Groups

Materials: Dinner and a place to eat it
Effort Quotient: ↡
Time: ✕✕✕
Planning: ★

The idea behind dinner groups is to help people meet other ward members by gathering in their homes for small informal potluck dinners. We have participated in these groups in several wards, and they are always fun if the program gets off the ground. In our experience, this seems to work better as an "adults only" activity, although you may want to experiment with a family dinner group.

The host should provide some food (such as the main course), and the other invitees should also bring a food item or beverage as coordinated by the host. Food may be coordinated around a particular theme, with each participant bringing ingredients for a Chinese dinner or a Texas barbecue, or you may do away with a theme and just have people bring whatever they enjoy cooking. The format of the dinner is usually just to gather the food together and eat. After dinner, you can either play games or just visit and get to know each other.

Although it is more expensive, another option for dinner groups is to have them eat at a different restaurant each month, rather than to bring potluck to the host's home. This gives you the same opportunity to meet new people, plus you may also find some new places to eat.

Groups should decide before they go out what the limits of the meals should be. Cost is a big consideration, as are distance from home and the particular cuisine. Having guidelines in place ahead of time will eliminate the embarrassment of going to a fine restaurant, only to have one couple order nothing more than a glass of water. You may also want to check out the likes and dislikes of members of your group, as well as their physical restrictions. If most of your members love seafood but you have a group member who is violently allergic to it, you may want to postpone your trip to the seafood restaurant until you're part of a different group.

Game Groups

Materials: Various board games, appetizers or light refreshments
Effort Quotient: ♥
Time: ☒☒☒☒
Planning: ★

As the name implies, the object of game groups is for members to get together to play board games. The host is responsible for selecting a board game or two for playing that evening. There are literally hundreds of games available; in fact, most of us have several still in our basements that haven't been used or played in ages. Don't make the games too intense, since the idea is not to win or lose but to socialize and get to know each other in small, unthreatening situations. Some games that are wildly successful are Pit®, Beyond Balderdash®, and Ultimate Outburst®, because nobody really cares who wins or loses. Games such as Trivial Pursuit® that require specialized knowledge may be less successful, because somebody is invariably better at the game than everyone else, and this causes embarrassment all around. Take into account that most games provide for a limited number of players, so it is vital to have groups of no more than eight participants.

Even though the idea of game groups is for members to come together to play games, food is always part of the equation. The host can provide the snacks, or can ask each participant to bring an appetizer or a treat. If your group consists of people who are not familiar with the others, take a few moments for everyone to get to know everyone else. Gathering around the refreshments provides a great opportunity to get to know others in the group.

Puzzle Groups

Materials: Various puzzles, light refreshments
Effort Quotient: ♥
Time: ☒☒☒
Planning: ★

A puzzle group is a perfect activity for socializing and getting to know other members of your group because solving a puzzle doesn't take all your concentration. There's plenty of time to visit with one another as well.

Make sure you pick puzzles that can be put together in an evening or, if your group chooses, you can work on the same puzzle for several meetings (you just have to worry about storing it until the next scheduled meeting). End the evening with some light refreshments or snack on them throughout the activity.

Mystery Dinner Party

Materials: Mystery dinner games and light refreshments
Effort: ♣♣
Time: ▨▨▨
Planning: ★★

Mystery dinners are also played and hosted in small groups and can be a real scream, especially if they are planned out ahead of time and everyone has had a chance to read and practice his part. Dressing the part also adds greatly to this activity. One of the downsides to a mystery dinner is the cost of the game itself. One alternative is to have a few couples contribute to the cost of the game. Alternatively, if you have some creative folks in your congregation, have them write a couple of short, simple scripts and use those instead of the costly ones that are available to purchase. Set a time limit to each scene or scenario. Don't be too hard on people if they don't do or say all the things they are supposed to say, but keep the scenes moving. As soon as the scene starts to bog down, that's your cue to move on. Have your guests bring refreshments following the same theme as the mystery dinner; this can also add to the overall atmosphere of the evening. Remember, you don't have to be a great actor or actress to have a ball at a mystery dinner. Just be yourself and ham it up a bit. Fun can be had by all. End the evening with your light refreshments and some good-natured reminiscing over the evening's performances. Some of your fellow ward members will really surprise you.

Movie Night

Materials: None
Effort Quotient: ♣
Time: ▨▨▨
Planning: ★

Movies are a great date for small groups, and cheap movies are even better because they fulfill our interest in thrift as well as our need for a good time. The downside to a movie night is that you can't do too much socializing during a movie. However, if you combine the movie with a small dinner or ice cream afterwards, you can do your socializing over your meal. Movies can be fun in any size group. It is especially fun comparing notes after the movie to see if others saw some of the same things that you did or didn't.

If it's too difficult or too expensive to go to a movie en masse, it's easy to rent one from a local video store. You'll have to do a little judicious planning to choose movies that are entertaining but also conform to church decency standards. That being the case, you may want to consider an old mystery or comedy that many of the group may have seen, but which is so good that people can watch it again and again. *What's Up, Doc?* and *Take the Money and Run* are two oldies that fit into this category, but there are hundreds of others.

If you choose the option of going to a theater, you may want to keep ticket availability in mind. One option is to designate somebody to purchase all the tickets for the group—especially if you're going to see a first-run film. Designating someone the official ticket person can eliminate an embarrassing moment if the showing is sold out when you arrive.

Congregate afterwards for a light meal or refreshments. This can be done at a local restaurant or at someone's home. Keep it simple, and fun will be had by all.

UM, YES...
276 TICKETS
TO
"ROCKY VII"

Culture Night

Materials: Depends on the culture, refreshments
Effort Quotient: ✋✋
Time: ⬛⬛⬛
Planning: ★★

Cultural activities aren't as popular as they once were, so a good activities planner looks for ways to keep culture alive. Plan a poetry reading (or combine it with an on-site poetry-writing contest), a group sing-along, a dance lesson, a play reading, or some other sort of cultural activity. If you make culture fun, people will attend your cultural events.

Couples Night

Materials: Dinner, refreshments, costumes, guest speaker or discussion leader
Effort Quotient: ♛♛
Time: ▨▨▨
Planning: ★★

The idea is to have each couple come dressed as their favorite couple. For example, you may have Batman and Catwoman, Frankenstein and his bride, George and Martha Washington—or you can go in another direction and find other famous pairs, such as bits and bytes, green eggs and ham, or a dish and a spoon. Plan a simple but nice meal and end the activity with a discussion on improving marriage relations. Depending on timing, you could end the activity with a dance.

Sneaky Secret
As you can see, there is nothing scientific about some of the ideas we have come up with. The key is to find others in your congregation that enjoy some of the same things you like to do, then get together and do them. Most of the time it takes only an idea, creative or not, and others will willingly join you. You know, "build it and they will come." Come up with an idea or something you like doing, such as dinner, a movie, a play, reading, poetry, sports, and so on. Do a little planning, and we guarantee, "They will come!"

It's a Guy Thing

Face it. If you're a man, you may have been born with a genetic inability to plan a good party. Kent is proud to admit that he can be a captain of industry, run a multi-million-dollar company, or wield awesome political power, but he can't plan a worthwhile activity by himself to save his life.

However, men need to get together with other men and form friendships with them, just as women do. This section will give a few ideas of how this can be accomplished with a small amount of effort. After all, if it takes any effort whatsoever, a party by men, for men, will probably never come to fruition.

Tube Ball

Materials: TV, snacks (chili is mandatory), beverages, dessert
Effort Quotient: ✺
Time: ☒☒☒
Planning: ★

This kind of activity is especially good if someone in your ward has cable or a satellite dish and can pick up more channels than just the big three. Select the game you want to watch several weeks in advance and make sure to give it plenty of publicity before the day of the event. The cost of admission is some sort of snack or finger food.

The host's responsibility is to make the mandatory chili. Make sure you have plenty of napkins around and don't make too much of a mess, or you won't have the privilege of returning to that home the next time there's a great game on satellite.

At halftime, go out and throw a football around or shoot a few hoops. However, make sure you get back into the TV room in plenty of time to watch the second half of the game.

A variation of this idea is to have a mini-tailgate party at the host's home and have everyone bring the appropriate barbecue food so they can pig out before the game. This takes a little more time, but it really adds to the feeling of almost being at the game.

Game watching is also a good time to do some manly socializing and provides a pretty nonthreatening environment for nonmembers. Make sure to clean up afterwards, though. And if you really want to ingratiate yourself to the host's family, spring for some movie tickets that will take the host's wife and children off the premises while the men are taking over the family dwelling.

Sports Night—Live and In Person

Materials: Game, tickets, transportation, money for food
Effort Quotient: ✺
Time: ☒☒☒
Planning: ★★

There are so many different types of athletic events that it shouldn't be too difficult to find something in your area. If there aren't any pro teams in your vicinity, some substitute will have to be made. If tickets aren't available or are too expensive for your group, find a local college team, a high school game, a semi-pro team, or even a bowling league to cheer on. The idea is to get a big group of your quorum cohorts together for some good, old-fashioned fellowshipping. This is especially good if you have to travel a couple of hours to get to the game. Plan to sit together, carpool together, and tailgate party together. If you organize some tailgating, you'll have to do a little planning on the food. But don't go overboard—the object is not to serve a professional spread but to have a good time together.

Make sure you give yourselves plenty of travel time, especially if you aren't familiar with the city where your game is being played. It's not too cool to come into a close-fought game and have to disturb everybody as you try to get to your seat. Plan ahead and give yourselves plenty of time.

Sneaky Secret

You don't have to spend a lot of money on tickets to have a good time at a professional sporting event. Keep your eye on your local newspaper, which may advertise periodic group deals. For instance, during basketball season, the Washington Wizards sell group discount tickets to certain games. The tickets run $12.50 per ticket, which includes a reserved seat in the nosebleed section, a hot dog, and a medium drink. You can't beat that kind of deal! The Baltimore Orioles do a similar kind of thing by offering family discount deals at some games held during the week. These deals can save you a ton on tickets and snacks. If you want an even better deal, attend a semi-pro or a farm team game in your local area. Tickets to these games rarely exceed $10 per ticket. You get wholesome fun for a fair price. Similar deals can be had with many professional teams, with the exclusion of pro football, in most cities. You may also have success in locating discount tickets by writing or logging onto any professional team's customer service office or Web site.

Feats of Strength

Materials: Sports equipment, field, gym, and a lot of Ben-Gay®
Effort Quotient: ✋✋✋
Time: ⌛⌛⌛
Planning: ★★

For a good workout and an enjoyable activity, nothing beats meeting with your priesthood quorum for an evening of sports, sweat, and homemade root beer. Name your favorite activity, from volleyball to Ping-Pong, and organize a group to share it with you. Remember, sports get-togethers are excellent activities in which to include nonmembers and

investigators—provided the atmosphere is friendly. If your ward participates in cutthroat competition, nonmembers and investigators should not
be part of the equation. (In fact, if your ward is cutthroat where sports
are concerned, perhaps you should forget about participating in sports
and find another male bonding experience.)

One of Kent's favorite activities is the traditional Thanksgiving
morning football game between the Aaronic Priesthood and the
Melchizedek Priesthood quorums in our ward. This annual event gets the
men out of the house while the women cook Thanksgiving dinner, and its
success depends on the level of planning and the amount of hot chocolate
and chili available. If you plan on emulating the tradition, please note
that the wives should not be responsible for providing the chili and the
hot chocolate. They're already working on Thanksgiving dinner, and
that's more than enough to occupy their morning.

Men's Ice Cream Excursion

Materials: Transportation to a local ice cream parlor and money to
  pay for individual treats
Effort Quotient: ♆
Time: ✕✕✕
Planning: ★

Men are so excited about ice cream that many of them will even get
together with other men in order to eat it. All it takes is a car and a local
ice cream parlor—in addition to whatever cash is involved in paying for
ice cream treats. The end of a bishopric meeting or elders quorum presidency meeting is an ideal time to go out for ice cream, because the men
are already on hand to make the trip.

Socializing over ice cream gives men the opportunity to solve the
world's problems and get to know one another in the process. And it
never hurts to buy some extra ice cream to take home to the wife and
kids so they can share the fun of ice cream if not the manly camaraderie.

Men's Game Night

Materials: A board game such as Risk®, or a war game; snack foods,
  beverages, dessert
Effort Quotient: ♆

Time: ▨▨▨▨
Planning: ★

This type of activity is perfect for men because it doesn't require a whole lot of planning and it allows their animal instincts to slither forth. This is an activity for a small group, but participants often become so enthusiastic that they make men's game night a regular event.

Playing a manly game like Risk® is competitive, but it also requires luck. Since there is some strategizing that's involved, there should be plenty of time for socializing and solving the real world's problems. Have everyone bring his favorite finger foods. Set a time limit to play, because these games tend to go on forever. At the end of the time limit, the person who is ahead is declared the winner. There's always time for a rematch next month.

Hands-on Tutorial

Materials: Whatever is required for the project at hand
Effort Quotient: ↡
Time: ▨▨▨▨ (It may take several sessions to complete a project.)
Planning: ★★★

If there are men in the ward who have particular skills, you may be able to coerce them into teaching you to do what they do. Clark is adept at making stained glass, and about once a year he'll teach a free stained-glass class to ward members who have expressed interest in learning the skill. The secret of teaching a class is to give the participants hands-on experience. If you show people how to do something, it isn't nearly as effective as walking them through their own projects.

The best way to teach a skill is to assemble a kit of materials that participants can use to make their own project. You can charge a minimal amount for these supplies, or the teacher can give them away for free if he has them on hand. Make sure the project is big enough to whet the interest of the participants, but small enough that they can finish a project during the course of the class. The idea is not to teach people how to become master craftsmen, but to give them enough exposure to the skill so they'll know whether they're interested in pursuing the hobby in a more extensive manner.

General Conference Ice Cream Feast

Materials: Ice cream or ice cream bars, toppings, bowls, napkins, and spoons
Effort Quotient: ✴
Time: ⧖ before (or after) the priesthood session of general conference
Planning: ★

This is sort of like a mini-tailgate party before the priesthood session of general conference. All priesthood holders who are attending the priesthood session in the building should be invited to gather about forty-five minutes before the session for ice cream and visiting. This is an excellent time to mingle, which is something that men don't do terribly often. It is also a good incentive to get young priesthood holders out to this important session.

Move-Ins/Move-Outs

Materials: Strong backs
Effort Quotient: ✴✴✴
Time: ⧖⧖⧖
Planning: ★

Add a little enjoyment to this often backbreaking endeavor by meeting afterward for donuts and milk, or going out for burgers to replenish your strength. Helping a family move is an excellent way to get to know the new family, but the socialization afterwards gives an opportunity for existing quorum members to get to know each other better. Besides—adding food to the equation is one way to inspire quorum members to give this important service.

Ladies' Night Out

Women are natural socializers who love to get together for no reason other than to visit with one another. This social tendency is demonstrated every Sunday, as desperate men make every attempt to pry their wives out of the ward meetinghouse after church meetings have ended. But once women sit down to organize a formal activity, you'll find that most of those activities require far more planning than any party that is put together by men. Needless to say, the effort that is put into an activity for women is reflected in the success of those social occasions.

Progressive Dinner

Materials: Theme, menu, homes, food
Effort Quotient: ♈♈♈
Timing: ▧▧▧
Planning: ★★

If you have never had the opportunity to experience a progressive dinner, you have been missing out on a great activity. As the name implies, these dinners are progressive in nature—with different courses of the meal being served at different locations. Progressive dinners require some planning, especially in regard to the theme, menu, route to be taken, and the transportation. If you have a large group, you may have to double up houses for the same courses of meals. It's always nice to end up at the church for dessert and socializing.

Although progressive dinners don't have to have themes, a dinner can be enhanced by the use of a theme that ties all the homes together. One option is to have a dinner with an international flavor, with each house representing a different country. Or the theme can take a scriptural turn, with each hostess taking a scripture and planning around it. Other possible themes could revolve around seasons, holidays, books, colors, or historical characters. The sky is the limit; use your imagination and see what you can invent.

A variation of the house-to-house progressive dinner is one that is held progressively through rooms at the meetinghouse. Each area (cultural hall, Young Women room, Primary room, Relief Society room, and priesthood areas) can represent a different house. Pick a theme and divide up the women to work with each course of the dinner, making sure to decorate each room differently, just as different hostesses would do if you were meeting in their homes. This eliminates the need to drive long distances if you are in a ward where members are spaced far apart, but preserves the flavor of a traditional progressive dinner.

Women's Overnight Retreat

Materials Needed: Everyone brings her own bedding, plus a treat to share

Effort Quotient: ♨♨
Time: ▨▨▨
Planning: ★★★

Men may not be able to comprehend why grown women would want to attend a slumber party, but overnight retreats are extremely popular in some wards. The ideal way to plan such a retreat is to begin the party shortly after supper at the home of one of the women. Be sure to choose a home that is large enough to accommodate a group, and where children are not present. If the hostess has children of her own, perhaps they can be farmed out to other homes for the event.

Games can be organized during the evening for the benefit of women who want to attend but who cannot stay all night. Other possible activities include making cookies, quilting, watching a movie, studying scriptures, or participating in craft projects. In fact, you may want to organize several different activities in different locations throughout the house in order to accommodate those with different interests. The following morning, women can meet at the ward for a breakfast and a seminar, with attendance open to women who were unable to attend the overnight festivities.

Night on the Town

Materials: None
Effort Quotient: ♨♨
Time: ▨▨▨
Planning: ★

This activity can take on many different aspects. Some women's groups like to meet once a month (or more often) and go to different restaurants, movies, plays, playgrounds, museums, or even shopping malls. This is a great activity for women who like to do similar things but at different places or locations. This is a great way to socialize or just be around people you are comfortable with. If you're sponsoring a night on the town as a ward activity, don't forget to open your activity to all women in your ward. You won't get everybody, but you'd be surprised who may come out periodically to join you.

Lunch Bunch

Materials: None
Effort Quotient: ♉
Time: ▨▨▨
Planning: ★

If you live in a ward where women have trouble getting to know one another, a monthly lunch bunch could be a lifesaver. Set aside one day a month for the women in the ward to go to lunch. If children are part of the picture, the best place to host this event is in the meetinghouse because the nursery toys are accessible. (Be sure to put the toys away after using them!)

The object is for everyone to bring one item to share with the group for a potluck lunch. You may choose to have children bring sack lunches, or to allow the children to share their mothers' food. Be sure to read the food guidelines in chapter 9 before allowing children to participate in the buffet table.

Lunch bunch women tend to bring lots of salads and finger foods, but fewer main course meals. If your lunch bunch is sponsored by the Relief Society, you may want to secretly assign the members of the Relief Society presidency to each provide a main course at the monthly lunch bunch. That way nobody will go home hungry. The food doesn't have to be fancy—a pizza or a bucket of chicken is sufficient.

Big Sister Activity

Materials: None
Effort Quotient: ♉♉♉
Time: ▨▨▨▨
Planning: ★★

This activity takes on two forms. First, issue an invitation to the Laurels to attend one of your home, family, and personal enrichment meetings. Plan some type of activity that would intrigue teenage girls. This could be an Oriental cooking class, a craft class, or a class that offers makeup or grooming tips. The purpose of the activity is to show the Laurels how much enjoyment they will get out of Relief Society.

The second part of this activity is to assign one of your Relief Society members to be a "big sister" to each of the Laurels. Good choices to serve as big sisters are single women or other women who are young enough or charismatic enough to relate well to teenagers. The "big sisters" are to take an active, but not intrusive, role in the lives of their "little sisters." The idea is to help the Laurels make a smooth transition into Relief Society by helping dispel the rumor that Relief Society is a program for stodgy old people.

Winter Picnic

Materials: Blankets, sunglasses, suntan lotion, umbrellas, picnic baskets, picnic supplies
Effort Quotient: ♦♦♦
Time: ▨▨▨
Planning: ★★

Bring summer to your ward even in the dead of winter by having a summer picnic in your cultural hall, even if you have two feet of snow on the ground outside. Plan your menu, but at a minimum make sure it includes fried chicken, potato salad, baked beans, and soda pop. Optional items could include corn on the cob, ice cream, and watermelon. To add to the authenticity of the affair, make sure you set up your beach umbrellas, wear your sunglasses, and smear on the suntan lotion. Your husband is really going to wonder what you've been up to all day. Wink and smile. This is another activity where your creativity can make a big difference in the success of the event.

Cookie Exchange/Ice Cream Social

Materials: Plates of cookies, ice cream, and toppings
Effort Quotient: ♦♦♦

Time: ☒☒☒
Planning: ★★

The object here is for each participant to bring a plate of cookies and a recipe that will be exchanged for another plate of cookies and recipe. If that isn't caloric enough, add to the food fest by ending the evening with ice cream. The cookie exchange gives women the opportunity to try out all those cookie recipes that they have been saving for years. Make sure to have a couple of extra plates of cookies on hand for those who arrive without cookies of their own. You may also want to encourage sisters to bring something other than chocolate chip cookies—that way, you'll be certain to get a variety of cookies.

Secret Lives

Materials: An item belonging to each participant, pencil and paper
Effort Quotient: ♥
Time: ☒☒☒
Planning: ★★

The object of this activity is to guess who is associated with which treasured object. Each participant is asked to bring in an item that illustrates some facet of her life. Objects can include sheet music, a ballet slipper, a prize they may have won in a contest, a favorite food, a treasured book, a piece of art the woman created but that nobody in the ward has seen, or a picture that is unrecognizable as the adult woman. Encourage the women to think of things that others may not know about them.

When all items have been collected, each should be numbered. Each participant will be given a piece of paper and a pencil so she can guess which display goes with what person. Participants may even want to write why they guessed a particular item belonged to a particular person. After everyone has guessed, go around the room and connect the items to the women who brought them. As the items are identified, give each participant an opportunity to tell why she picked the item she did. You may want to give a small prize to the woman who connected the highest number of objects to the correct women.

International Night

Materials: Varies
Effort Quotient: ✋
Time: ⌛⌛⌛
Planning: ★★

If your ward includes women who were born in or who have lived in different countries, give them the opportunity to talk about and show things from those countries. The discussions can include music, culture, food, history, arts and crafts, and language. This activity gives women the opportunity to experience another culture, if only for a few minutes. If you live in an area where you don't have a lot of cultural diversity, a variation would be to have women bring a typical dish from the country of their ancestors. Compare and contrast the foods from different countries.

Salon Night

Materials: Varies
Effort Quotient: ✋
Time: ⌛⌛⌛
Planning: ★★

The purpose of this activity is to focus on you. Provide classes or services that are available at salons, such as manicures or makeovers, haircuts or styling. Don't forget the stress-relieving exercises! End the evening with healthy refreshments such as raw vegetable platters and fruit slushes, or maybe a little frozen yogurt.

Get to Know Your Local Area

Materials: Varies
Effort Quotient: ✋✋
Time: ⌛⌛⌛
Planning: ★★

Plan a picnic at a local park. Have someone familiar with your local area come in and talk about things that families can do in your local area or state. You could also have someone come from one of your local health spas and talk about walking or running for exercise. You might even include a class on summer cooking. Plan a walk around the park, perhaps accompanied by somebody who can tell you what flowers and trees have been planted there or how to spot local birds and other wildlife.

Home, Family, and Personal Enrichment Meetings

There's a myth in the Church that homemaking meeting had its origins in the Victorian era, when society looked for devices that would make women busy in a superfluous way. If they were taught how to play the piano and to cross-stitch, they would have something to display when their indulgent husbands trotted them out to greet visitors. If women didn't have some sort of distraction to keep them busy, they were liable to get into all sorts of mischief. Thus homemaking meeting was born.

A lot of women believed this myth, at least to the extent of deciding that homemaking meeting was designed for people who didn't have anything better to do. Because their lives were busy (and *all* modern women are busy) they considered themselves exempt from homemaking meeting as it was originally designed. And if they didn't *do* crafts (if they didn't have the interest, or if their homes were already full of crafts, or if the crafts they were accustomed to seeing in homemaking meetings were too ugly or useless for any sentient human being to want to make), it was just another excuse for them to stay home.

The very name "homemaking meeting" was an archaic term that reminded people of life in the 1950s. But the 1950s are ancient history. By the late 1990s, many women had no passion for staying home and baking cookies. Many others had the inclination, but their circumstances made it impossible for them to do so. For these women, the idea of homemaking meeting made them feel angry or guilty. Angry and guilty women avoided homemaking meeting, too.

All this changed in the closing years of the twentieth century, as the name "homemaking meeting" was scuttled in favor of the more modern "home, family, and personal enrichment meeting." Women were soberly counseled not to shorten the title, but everyone immediately abandoned the unwieldy new name in favor of "enrichment meeting," so that's how it will be referred to here.

Unfortunately, changing the name from "homemaking meeting" to "enrichment meeting" didn't entirely solve the problem. In fact, as new enrichment programs moved away from crafts into more politically correct areas, women who had been loyal to homemaking meeting for decades because it was meeting their needs suddenly found themselves staying home on enrichment night. But the idea behind enrichment meetings is still a sound one. Women look for opportunities to learn, to be inspired, and to spend time with other women. Enrichment meetings provide an ideal forum to offer those opportunities.

No matter what you call the monthly meeting for adult women in the Church, the first thing to do to get women to that meeting is to plan programs that will entice them to attend. Look at the Questions from the Clueless at the end of this chapter for some ideas that will help you plan worthwhile enrichment meetings.

After the program has been enhanced with exciting classes and projects, the next thing for someone who plans enrichment meetings to do is solicit the help of your bishop and female ward leaders. When the bishop and ward auxiliary leaders fully support enrichment meeting, others will be inclined to follow. Supporting enrichment meeting takes a real time commitment. Mere words won't do it. If the bishop fully supports your enrichment meetings, he'll be in the building when enrichment meetings are being held—or he will send his wife to enrichment meeting while he stays at home with the children. If the bishop makes a personal appearance, he may sample the food in the cooking classes, or teach an occasional class of his own. He may also lend a hand by using his woodworking tools to make craft supplies for the women. If your bishop thinks enrichment meeting is important, his attitude will carry over to the women of your ward. And if your Primary presidency and Young Women presidency support enrichment meeting, the teaching staffs of those organizations will follow the example of their leaders. Perhaps these leaders can be convinced of the importance of enrichment meeting over lunch in a local restaurant—paid for, of course, by the enrichment leader.

Once women arrive at enrichment meeting, they need a variety of experiences. One of the good things that has come from the enrichment night format is that enrichment leaders are now counseled to have a theme for every meeting. The easiest way to do this is to have all women meet together in a single theme-based session. But the easiest way to do something isn't necessarily the best way to bring women out to enrichment meeting. Some women will not attend enrichment meeting unless crafts are part of the menu. Others have no need for crafts, but instead need a spiritual boost. A third group will be attracted by practical classes in homemaking arts or other educational fields.

There is a way to meet all these needs and still have your enrichment night follow a prearranged theme. When planning your enrichment meetings for the coming year, choose your themes and then decide on classes that will fit that theme. Experiment to see what works in your ward. Three basic selections include a lesson with a spiritually enriching nature, a hands-on class in the home arts, and the standard craft class. If you have one class in each of those three areas, you'll be a lot more likely to have something in your enrichment meeting that will appeal to everyone. In fact, your goal should be to hear complaints from women that they don't know which class to choose because they all sound equally good.

There's no way to predict what classes are going to pique the interest of the women in your ward. Here are a few suggestions that may work in your area:

- Stress-management
- Inexpensive vacations
- Games to play in the car on long road trips
- Planning children's parties
- Wrapping presents
- How to mark scriptures
- Haircutting at home
- Auto mechanics for women
- Computer basics
- Photography basics
- Painting and wallpapering techniques
- Basic cooking
- Ethnic cooking
- Making school lunches
- Soup-making
- Food additives and children's behavior
- Stained glass

- Drawing
- Ceramics
- Planning family reunions
- Gardening basics
- Filling our homes with uplifting music
- Personal finance
- Physical fitness

Ideas to Enrich Your Enrichment Night

Materials: Varies
Effort Quotient: ⍓
Time: ⧖
Planning: ★★

➡ You might want to spice up your enrichment nights with one of the following ideas:

- Include a "give or take" table at each of your activities, whereby women can bring in useable things they no longer need or want and can take away things that other women no longer need or want. Any items not taken at the end of a given enrichment night can be donated to a local charity.

- Include a "nifty idea table" at each of your activities. The idea is to have a table for just that: nifty ideas, timesavers, bonus buys at local stores, places to pick fruit, ideas on stain removal, inexpensive Christmas ideas, and so on.

- You might also want to have a recipe table set up at your next enrichment night for women to share their favorite recipes or to pass on recipes that they haven't necessarily tried but that look good. Having a few samples is always a good idea.

- Use an early-bird special to entice women to arrive on time to their enrichment meetings. This can be in the form of a terrific piece of information or a mini-lesson that begins exactly on time and that is available only to people who are there when the special treat is presented. A lot of thought should go into these five-minute demonstrations. You can teach people how to make edible

Christmas trees using ice cream cones (a project that's good for mothers with young children) or show them quick and easy ways to make gifts for the neighbors or the people they visit teach. Make sure to have an extra snack for these women who come right on time—a nice box of candy to pass around, or homemade cookies. The early-bird special is successful as long as the rules are enforced. The moment you start waiting even five minutes to give that early-bird special or bend the rules to give late-comers some of the leftover treats, you've lost your incentive for people to come on time.

Dinner with Something Extra

Materials: Dinner, decorations, presentations by a half dozen women
Effort Quotient: ♥
Time: 🔺🔺🔺
Planning: ★★★

Everyone knows they should do their visiting teaching, but nobody wants to have to feel guilty about it. Here's a way to inspire women to go visiting teaching, but without burdening them with guilt.

Plan a light meal such as a soup-and-salad dinner. You don't have to spend a lot of money, but make the dinner a nice one so that women would be glad they attended even if that were the extent of the evening. As the participants eat dessert, have various women give five-minute presentations related to different aspects of visiting teaching. Some of these may include the following:

- How visiting teaching can change people's lives
- How to reach women who don't want contact with the Church
- How to work well with your companion
- How to make friends of the women you visit teach
- How to teach the lesson to people who have been giving the lesson all month
- How to find ways to serve the women on your visiting teaching route

End the evening with a short class on making small gifts that can be given to people on your visiting teaching route. This will give the women souvenirs of the evening, as well as ideas that will help them be more effective visiting teachers.

Service/Talent Auction

Materials: Varies
Effort Quotient: ♥♥♥
Time: ⌛⌛⌛
Planning: ★★

This is an alternative to the service exchange that is fully described in chapter 6. The difference here is that the evening is livened up with an actual auction. Often we don't realize the talents the women amidst us possess. One function of the auction is to make the women aware of those talents.

The premise is that each woman brings something that she has made (or a coupon for a service she can perform) to an auction. Once there, the auctioneer holds up the various items for bid.

Items that are auctioned can be paid for with play money or with points earned during a pre-auction quiz (use your creativity to invent other fun ways to earn points). If you use play money, fill a bunch of envelopes with varying amounts of Monopoly® money. Women will draw envelopes from a hat, and that's the money they'll begin with. As the evening progresses, however, a woman may be left with "change" after making her purchase. Women with leftover cash may spice up the evening by giving their leftover money to others, raising the stakes at the end.

Having a successful auction depends on finding a dynamic auctioneer. You need to choose someone who will be entertaining but who will also make each woman feel her offering is important and valuable. Bidding starts at one dollar and goes up from there. You may want to consider having the enrichment board bid on items that aren't getting many bids. And remember, no one can bid again once she has successfully won an auction—even if an item comes up later that is more attractive than the one she originally purchased.

➲ Ideas of what you could suggest the women bring for auction include but aren't limited to:

- Loaves of bread
- A dessert

- A whole meal
- Home-canned items or other delicacies
- A coupon for baby-sitting
- An offer to weed a garden
- A family night for another family
- An offer to go grocery shopping for someone else
- An offer to wash someone's windows
- A craft or the offer to complete a craft for another
- An offer to take pictures of the winner's family
- A floral arrangement
- A handcrafted wooden item
- An offer to drive and attend the temple with someone
- An offer to tole paint a project for someone who is painting-impaired
- An offer to sew an item for someone else
- An offer to cross-stitch a work of art for the winner
- A sewing lesson
- A lesson in the fine art of home canning
- A music lesson
- A dance lesson
- An offer to help someone make a scrapbook
- A lesson in the fine art of floral arranging

This activity has been such a success in some wards that they've made it an annual tradition. Besides being an evening of fun and friendship, it can network the sisters together as they become more aware of each other's interests—and it may show the enrichment leader which women should be drafted to teach a mini-class in the future.

Summertime Car Wash

Materials: Water, soap, drying cloths, portable vacuum cleaner
Effort Quotient: ✹✹✹
Time: ⌛⌛⌛
Planning: ★

For a cool summertime activity, have the women work together to wash everyone's car. The women have the fun of interacting with each other and everyone goes home with a clean car.

Women's Health Fair

Materials: Local nurse or doctor (preferably female), light dinner, refreshments
Effort Quotient: ✲✲✲
Time: ⬡⬡⬡
Planning: ★★

Invite a registered nurse or a local female doctor to come to your meeting and speak about women's health care. You may want to invite your Laurels to share the evening because there is vital information that applies to young women, too. The visiting health care practitioner should be able to bring pamphlets and videos that cover a variety of women's health care issues, as well as artificial breasts to help women learn how to do breast self-examinations.

Super Saturday Craft Day

Materials: Varies depending on craft ideas chosen, luncheon
Effort Quotient: ✲✲✲
Time: ⬡⬡⬡⬡
Planning: ★★★

The super Saturday craft day provides an opportunity for women in a ward or group of wards to get together and make attractive and yet inexpensive gifts and decorations for the holidays. This type of activity can be the highlight of the year, taking place just before the holiday season gets into full bloom. If your super Saturday activity takes place in the springtime, it can become a spring bazaar.

Those who are planning the activity should meet at the end of summer to select eight to twelve worthwhile and appealing items that can be made quickly and inexpensively. Examples include holiday wreaths, food items, ornaments, Christmas cards, clothing, nativity scenes, advent calendars, and other items that can be found regularly in Christmas project magazines. Be sure to choose items that are inexpensive, foolproof, and can be completed within the time allotted for the activity. Create one prototype of each item and calculate the estimated cost and the time to make the item. Display the sample projects along with sign-up sheets (include the cost and time estimate on each sheet) outside the Relief Society room for several Sundays. Encourage women to sign-up for as many projects as they have the time and energy to make. Payment should be made at the time of sign-up in order to give teachers the opportunity to purchase all the materials before the event.

When the project day arrives (usually a Saturday early in December), the women gather together in the cultural hall (and other rooms as needed) and spend most of the day (or as much time as they would like to spend) visiting the various project stations and making the projects they signed up to make. Consider including one area where women can gather and work on projects which they've brought from home. (And encourage women who haven't signed up for a craft to pop in during the day to chat with those who are working—and maybe even lend a hand.) Serve a luncheon in the middle of the day to break up the work and to give women time to visit with each other.

To make the activity more successful and reduce the amount of work involved, several wards may wish to

Sneaky Secret

Don't feel overwhelmed if you can't think of any good craft ideas, because there are literally thousands of resources available. They come in the form of hundreds of books in your local library, ideas taken from your local newspaper, other church groups in your area, family members living outside your local area, friends, neighbors, many Internet sites, various clubs in your local area, and local craft and hobby stores in your area. Start with a couple of phone calls to family, friends, and neighbors. If you're unsuccessful, expand your search.

As you're planning your craft day, don't limit the pool of available talent for teaching your classes. If you don't have crafty women in your Relief Society, there are many people in your own community who have excellent craft skills and would love to teach them to others.

do this together and share the costs and responsibilities. For example, one ward may be responsible for craft classes, one for the luncheon, and one for decorations and cleanup. Also consider inviting the young women so that moms and daughters can enjoy working on projects together. Make sure to invite nonmember friends and neighbors too, because craft-oriented activities have a great deal of appeal to women outside the Church. (You could take pictures of each craft and send the ward mission leaders to these women with a visual aid in hand.)

Questions from the Clueless

? *I can't get people to attend my home, family, and personal enrichment meetings, even though it's a commandment for them to do so. Do you have any suggestions?*

If you're ever going to succeed, the first thing you'll have to do is to learn that women are not commanded to attend enrichment meetings. The only meeting that women in the Church are commanded to attend is sacrament meeting. As much as we may want women to attend enrichment meeting, or even Relief Society, attendance at those meetings is strictly optional.

That being the case, it's your responsibility as enrichment leader or home, family, and personal enrichment counselor to make enrichment meeting such a terrific event that women can't imagine staying home.

This is not an easy task. When the homemaking program was revitalized in the late 1990s, many Relief Society presidents decided that the exclusive function of the new enrichment night should be to inspire women on a spiritual level. They determined that because spiritual classes are good for women, Relief Society members don't need anything else. In fact, the trend in many wards has been to abandon the practice of having women divide into groups after opening exercises, instead giving them a one-size-fits-all session where all the women gather together to be spiritually fed.

The problem with the one-size-fits-all motif is that one size *never* fits all. This is as true for enrichment night as it is for clothing. Even if ninety percent of the women in your ward are mothers with young children who need a spiritual boost once a month, the other ten percent either don't have children or don't need to leave their homes that extra night every month in order to get a spiritual boost. And who's to say that the ninety percent of the young mothers in your ward who *need* a spiritual boost will actually come to enrichment meeting to get that spiritual infusion? As enrichment leader, you're battling against exhaustion and inertia. You may be giving women exactly what they need, but if you don't give them what they *want,* you may be looking at an empty room on enrichment night.

If you've found that enrichment night attendance is lower than the attendance at your old homemaking meetings, the first thing to do is to examine the format. Talk to Relief Society members who used to attend homemaking meetings but who fell by the wayside after the transition to enrichment night. If your one-size-fits-all motif is squeezing out a segment of your Relief Society members, it is easy enough to fix the problem.

Modern trends aside, a wise enrichment leader will never abandon crafts as part of an enrichment meeting. There is a reason for this, and it has nothing to do with the wreath or other knickknack that is produced by the women who sit around the craft table. The secret to appreciating crafts is knowing what crafts really are. Crafts aren't grapevine wreaths. Crafts aren't plastic bottle Santa Clauses. Crafts are the glue that holds enrichment meetings—and, ultimately, even the ward—together.

Think about it. Enrichment leaders don't offer those craft classes so people can learn how to make stained glass sun-catchers. Yes, the crafts have to be something the women want, or they won't go. But the real reason we have craft classes is so the women will have an excuse to get together and have something to do with their hands while they talk.

Craft classes, as well as cooking classes and other classes where women interact with one another, are successful because women have a subconscious need to bond with one another. You can't bond with other people while you're sitting in a room staring at the teacher, no matter how "good for you" the knowledge in that class may be. No, you bond with them while you're doing something together.

Painting a wooden family home evening assignment pegboard doesn't occupy a woman's mental faculties. While her hands are busy, she visits with the people next to her. She gets to know them. She observes their strengths and hears them tell about their weaknesses. She listens as they drop hints about their wants and their needs. She discovers the things she has in common with them. In short, she forms friendships.

The friendships made in enrichment meetings tie the whole ward together. Find a family who doesn't feel at home in the ward, and more often than not you'll see a woman who doesn't go to enrichment meetings.

The friendship factor should be exploited shamelessly when promoting your ward's enrichment meetings. When you make announcements or send out flyers, stress the friendship aspect even more than the classes that are going to be held. This attitude is contagious; if you're diligent about it, you'll soon be hearing Relief Society members telling a new person in the ward to "be sure to come out to enrichment meetings. That's where you'll meet everyone and make friends."

On a more pragmatic level, women also make contacts in enrichment meeting. They spend time with women they may never choose as friends and see those women in action. When the time comes for a new Primary president to find her counselors or a Young Women leader to find just the right Beehive advisor, inspiration often comes because she worked with the perfect woman for the job in an enrichment class. Mothers find women to exchange baby-sitting chores with or share children's play-groups in enrichment meeting, and there's no better place for a new member of the ward to present herself to rest the of the congregation.

This is not to say an enrichment leader can never have an evening where women don't divide into small groups. Some programs, such as the white elephant service exchange described in chapter 6 or the service/talent auction detailed above, are so enjoyable and worthwhile that they really do appeal to just about everyone. But most of the time, the tried and true formula of offering a variety of classes is the program that works. If you give women what they want, they will come.

Once you've gotten a woman out to enrichment meeting, you have to get her out again next month. She'll come willingly if her previous experience with enrichment meeting was a good one. If she has learned a new skill in an educational seminar, she'll return to take advantage of other worthwhile classes. If she has taken home a craft or home arts project that pleases her family and herself, she'll return to make new crafts that appeal to her. If she has been spiritually fed, she'll return when her spiritual batteries need recharging.

But the one thing that will bring her back even if she doesn't need the classes is the knowledge that *she* is needed—that the enrichment meeting won't be a success unless she is there. Maybe she has been drafted to teach a class. Maybe she is on the food committee, or has signed up to bring an item for dinner. Perhaps she feels needed because people tell her they miss her when she isn't there. No matter what the case, she'll return to enrichment meeting to feel that spirit of friendship and the sense of belonging.

Because so many women consider themselves exempt from enrichment night, the biggest challenge an enrichment leader may face is to convince women that enrichment meeting is necessary. She won't even have to lie to do this, because enrichment meeting is necessary. It gives women ties to the ward. After sacrament meeting itself, enrichment meeting may be the most important meeting held in the Church. If an enrichment leader can give the women in her ward the vision of enrichment meeting, everything else about the calling will fall magically into place. If she can't infuse women with the vision of enrichment meeting, she might as well cancel the whole thing.

? *How do I advertise my enrichment meetings?*

Before women ever attend their first enrichment meeting, they have to be convinced enrichment meetings are worthwhile. One way to do this is to make an enrichment packet for each woman to take home with her. Packets can be mailed or hand-carried to women who do not attend church, so every woman in the ward has a personal invitation to enrichment meeting.

If you're handing out these packets at the beginning of the year, you could include twelve stickers for women to place on the correct week and day of each month of her calendar. That way she can't help but notice when enrichment meeting is coming up, and she'll be less likely to forget to attend.

The focus of the enrichment packet is a personalized letter inviting the woman to enrichment meeting by name and telling her how important it is for her to attend. One thing you may want to point out is that in many areas women may move into a ward without any friends or family living nearby. Enrichment meeting is the perfect opportunity for women to form the bonds that take the place of family in far-flung settings.

Two other items are essential components of an enrichment packet. The first is a schedule of all enrichment dates and classes throughout the year, so that women can keep this ready reference on hand to know what is going to be presented on which date. This schedule can take the form of a brochure or a laminated card. The other item is a refrigerator magnet that proclaims the joys of enrichment meeting and is a constant reminder that enrichment meeting is less than four weeks away. This magnet doesn't carry the message, "Come to enrichment meeting and learn to make potholders." Instead, it reminds women to come to enrichment meeting and make friends.

In addition to carrying a message of their own, the refrigerator magnets serve a second purpose. Once or twice a month, as needed, your enrichment committee may want to produce a "Refrigerator News," which is a flyer printed on a half sheet of brightly colored paper. The flyers can be stuck on ward refrigerators for as long as they're needed, reminding women of upcoming enrichment events.

The final weapon in an enrichment arsenal doesn't go inside the packet, but it is just as important as the enrichment schedule itself. This is a telephone call to remind women that enrichment meeting is near and that their presence is sorely needed. Telephone calls are especially important to keep Primary and Young Women workers abreast of enrichment activities. The regular telephone calls remind women who can't attend Relief Society on Sundays that they are a valuable part of the Relief Society group, and that their absence at enrichment night would be missed.

? *What do I do when a teacher doesn't show up for an enrichment class?*

Sooner or later, you're going to find yourself with a teacherless class in your enrichment meeting. Do not panic. If the enrichment leader and the home, family, and enrichment counselor are prepared, the evening can proceed without a hitch.

Once a person has been drafted to teach a class, there should always be a backup plan. You may not be able to have the scripture-marking class that was advertised, but if you know of a woman in the ward who has made a lifelong study of the Atonement, you can ask her to be a backup teacher for your spiritual classes. Once you've used her services, find another backup teacher. Home arts classes may be more tricky, but backups can be found for them too. There is always someone who can teach a class on container gardening if the regular teacher falls through—especially if the regular teacher prepared her lesson materials and made her handouts before she got the flu.

Craft classes are the hardest ones to improvise. Because of this, the enrichment leader or her assistant should always know how to make the craft that is scheduled for the upcoming meeting. That person should follow up on the craft throughout the month preceding the enrichment meeting, to make sure supplies have been purchased and the teacher hasn't run into any obstacles. If there has been a regular progress report from the teacher of a craft class, she'll be less likely to bail out if she's in a bad mood on the night of the event. But if she *does* bail, at least the supplies will have been purchased and the substitute teacher will be able to step in and teach the class.

Because last-minute improvising is so often necessary, the enrichment leader and the home, family, and personal enrichment counselor should never have any assignments during an enrichment meeting. They should always be available to step in at a moment's notice and take over for any Relief Society member who is unable to fulfill her assignment. If they aren't needed to substitute as teachers or work on the refreshments, both women will have the opportunity to act as cheerleaders throughout the night, drifting from class to class and participating as needed, or seeking out women who appear to need a friend while everyone else is busy having fun.

? *I'm just not sold on the idea of craft classes. What about doing service projects instead?*

Substituting service projects for craft classes would be an excellent option, if only it worked. It doesn't matter what service project you pick . . . quilts for AIDS babies, kits for women in Bosnia, gifts for women in shelters for battered women. After a hard day battling the kids or going to work or battling the kids *and* work, and then putting dinner on the table, most women figure they've *done* their quota of service for the day. Most service projects—no matter how noble—don't get people out to enrichment meetings.

Service projects aren't completely off-limits at enrichment meetings. An enrichment leader can schedule a service project as part of the evening's program and everyone will gladly pitch in, but in most wards, women won't go to enrichment meeting specifically to do service projects. After all, she can reason that staying home with her children and spending time with them is a valid service project, too.

It's not that women in the Church aren't good-hearted, but the incentive to stay home after a long day is a big one. Every woman needs to know that materials have been purchased or work was done for *her,* or that the cooking class won't succeed unless she produces the bunch of spinach she was assigned to bring. Otherwise, when enrichment night comes and she's too tired to move, the odds are she's just going to put up her feet and stay home.

Don't give up on the idea without a little experimentation, though. All wards are different. Maybe your ward will be one of the blessed few that wholeheartedly embrace service projects as enrichment night activities. You never know unless you try.

? *I'm sold on the idea of crafts, but I don't know how to pick them.*

There's an art to picking crafts that will be made by women in church settings. Each craft that is chosen must satisfy four factors, or the craft will not be a success. These are the four essential characteristics of a successful craft project:

The craft cannot be expensive. Period. In fact, unless there are other classes for women to choose, the craft class shouldn't cost anything. Women should never be made to feel as though they can't attend enrichment night because they can't afford to pay for a craft project, or even a food item. Five dollars is a good maximum amount to charge for a craft class in most American wards, although the ceiling may be raised for some crafts at a craft day where there are many alternatives to choose from.

The craft cannot look cheap. Forget about making lovely doodads out of bleach bottles. As long as it is possible to spend three dollars on fabric and make scarves that sell for twenty-five dollars in the stores, you don't have to settle for garbage. Don't present any craft that you wouldn't buy in a store if you had the money to do so, or that you wouldn't be glad to receive as a gift.

The craft should be absolutely foolproof. Self-esteem is so hard to come by that the last thing you want is to have women be demoralized by failure in a craft class. There are plenty of foolproof classes you can choose. Don't settle for a craft that can be successfully made by some women, but that will be destroyed by others.

The craft should be finished before enrichment night ends. Choose crafts that take less than an hour for a skilled person to make, and then determine to help an unskilled woman finish her craft even if it takes twice as long as you anticipate. *Women do not finish craft projects once they have left the building.* If a woman goes home with an unfinished project, it will end up in the back of her closet. Her self-esteem will suffer, and she may not return to try again next month.

One more thing to consider is to teach skills rather than projects. A ceramics workshop may take six months. A series of drawing classes may take a year. Quilting may be an ongoing project once it gets started in your ward. Look beyond the scope of one enrichment meeting and see if you can teach skills that will provide years of satisfaction. You're not just filling class slots when you pick enrichment classes—you can also change lives.

CHAPTER 4
Focus on the Youth

It takes both ideas and creativity to (1) keep the youth interested as you try to teach them gospel principles and (2) stay within a very limited budget. In this chapter we hope to give you a variety of enjoyable activity ideas that can be adapted to your youth, your building, your geographical area, and your ward's customs. We also hope to make it easy for you to incorporate the teaching of gospel principles into the activities you plan.

Some of the most effective activities in this section rely on a surprise at the end to make them work. This may seem to be at odds with the rule that youth are supposed to plan and carry out their own activities. If you sponsor an activity that relies on the element of surprise, you may want to involve youth in other aspects of the planning, such as publicity or refreshments. See if you can find ways for your youth to be event planners without having the event ruined for them. In any case, having a surprise event that is primarily planned by adults should be the exception rather than the rule.

When you're planning youth activities, look back at chapter 1 to determine the purpose each activity should serve. Some activities may serve to inspire; others may serve to develop talents. Occasionally an entire activity may be planned with the purpose of enticing one wayward young man or young woman to attend. If you always plan your event with your purpose in mind, the parties you plan will be far more successful.

Many of the activities presented here will be just for fun, but having fun with friends in a church environment has a place in our youth programs, too. Activities that don't teach a principle but provide fun are the best occasions to invite nonmembers or members who rarely come to church. These activities can also serve the purpose of unifying your group. Remember—youth want to have fun. If they don't have fun in a church setting, they'll seek their fun someplace else.

Some of the following ideas were adapted from different LDS Web sites and are included for those who haven't yet discovered the vast resources that are available on the Web. Whether these ideas are old or new, we hope they will help spark your creativity. As far as ward activities are concerned, the secret of success is to take an idea and adapt it to your individual situation.

It goes without saying that whenever you plan an activity for youth—or for any other church group, for that matter—the appropriateness of any situation must be considered. Don't let your youth run pell-mell through the chapel as part of a treasure hunt or other game. Don't end an activity in the chapel unless you've instructed your youth ahead of time to dress appropriately. Don't cook in the conveniently-provided meetinghouse ovens if it is against your ward policy to do so. Don't plan an activity that costs money, if money is an issue for some of your families. Joseph Smith knew the wisdom of teaching correct principles and letting people govern themselves, and we're going to assume that you have the common sense to plan activities that are reverent when they should be, and that otherwise follow Church guidelines. By the same token, you should guide youth who are planning their own activities to remember these basic rules of comportment.

Remember to check out some of the warm-up activities in chapter 8, because there is a section that focuses just on youth activities. Warming up your group before the main activity may be even more important with the youth than it is with the adults.

An Emphasis on the Spiritual

Young men and women are fun-loving creatures, so it's great to find enjoyable activities that also have a spiritual message. Here are a few ideas to adapt and use the next time you're planning a party with a spiritual twist.

Skit-in-a-Bag

Materials: Miscellaneous items placed in grocery bags, one for each group
Effort Quotient: ✋✋
Time: ⌛⌛⌛
Planning: ★★

This one is an old favorite, and with good reason. It inspires youth to use their creativity, and it gets them working together. Choose funny, unusual items you find around your house and place between five and seven items in each bag. Divide the youth into groups of four to five and have one person from each group pick a bag without looking in it. The groups then spend the next fifteen to twenty minutes creating a skit, using every item in the bag. The way that Skit-in-a-Bag becomes spiritual in nature is that leaders can choose the topics of the skits. If you're trying to teach a concept to the youth, assign that concept and let them decide how to present it. These concepts can include character traits such as courage or responsibility, but they can also include scriptural stories or themes. Another twist to this activity might be to have youth come up with commercials that would sell something in Book of Mormon lands, or give them a word from the Topical Guide that they have to make a commercial for. Or you can use fairy tales, such as Cinderella, and have youth rewrite the endings, giving them a spiritual twist. For instance, Cinderella finally married the Prince in the temple. Or Rumplestiltskin was converted to the Church and became the greatest missionary ever. Let them use their imaginations and you will be amazed at what they invent.

Straw Towers

Materials: Unbendable drinking straws (50 to 100 per group), 1 to 2 rolls of tape per group
Effort Quotient: ✋
Time: ⌛
Planning: ★★

Break into groups of five or six individuals, have each group take the straws and tape, and claim a space to work. Give them ten to fifteen minutes to build the tallest self-supporting structure that they can. At the end of this time, have the groups carry the structures to the front of the room and place them in a row on a table. Have a leader speak about what makes a good life or about the importance of values in creating a solid life foundation. As the leader speaks, everyone's focus will be more on watching the structures as they topple one by one. Most all of them should eventually topple, collapse, or get blown over by movement or a slight breeze in the room. The speaker or group leader should acknowledge each tower as it drops. After all the towers topple that are going to fall, lead a discussion about what makes the good ones stay up while others have fallen. Make sure to focus on the foundations of the structures, tying that to the foundation of our lives.

River Crossing

Materials: Paper or fabric cut into 18x18-inch "rocks," 3 per team (you may want to laminate the "rocks" or use sturdy material so they don't fall apart during the activity)
Effort Quotient: 🐝🐝
Time: ⏳
Planning: ★

This game is best played in your cultural hall or parking lot. First, mark the boundaries of your "river" so the shores are approximately thirty to forty feet apart. The object is for each team to cross the river, using only their rocks and not touching the alligator-infested water, in the quickest time possible. You'll need to move the rocks as you go. The youth will quickly discern that only two people can cross at a time, with one returning with the rocks to fetch the next person. This activity is an excellent one to use to teach your youth the importance of working together and looking out for one another as they travel the perilous waves of life.

The Maze of Life

Materials: A maze that is constructed with available materials or is located in your locale; clues to help youth navigate the maze
Effort Quotient: 🐝🐝

Time: ▨▨▨
Planning: ★★★

This is an activity that can be lots of work for the adults, but the youth really enjoy it. Several of our friends have done this activity in their own wards, with positive feedback from the kids. The idea is to create a maze that the youth must explore. As with any maze, youth will come to points where the path leads in two or more directions, and they must choose which path to take. If they make the wrong choice, they will reach a dead end, or may even circle back to the same spot. Youth do not make these decisions randomly, but are given hints and advice whenever they reach a point that calls for the decision. Even though the activity is fun, it does show the results of the choices we make in life—making the right choices results in a joyful life, while wrong choices cause unhappiness and confusion.

One way to build the maze is to use blankets, cardboard boxes, and lots of tape to hold the thing together. Rather than make the pathways large enough to walk through, you can save time and materials by making the paths tunnel-sized and having the youth crawl through them.

There is a public park in our stake that creates a corn field maze each summer. The employees plant a large field of corn, let it grow tall, and then carve a maze into it and charge about five dollars a head to let people explore it. There are decision points throughout the maze, and a selection of clue sheets to help you decide when you come to each point. Depending on the clue sheet you select, the clues will relate to such things as Boy Scout knowledge, Girl Scout knowledge, popular children's books, or books of the Bible. The folks that staff the maze will also help groups create their own clue sheets so that the clues given will be something applicable to your group. You may want to check in your own area to see if something similar is available. That will shoot some of your budget, but will also save you a lot of work.

If the cardboard maze is too much effort, and there are no commercial mazes in your area, there are still other options. You could use different colors of tape placed on the floor of the building to mark the different paths. This does, however, lend itself to cheating because there are no walls to stop youth from jumping to a different place if they have been trapped by a wrong decision. But you can minimize this problem if you plan the maze correctly. Another option would be to design a modified treasure hunt (see chapter 9), where each location has two clues that correspond to the choice that is made. Making the correct choice will take youth to the next clue, while making a bad choice will just lead to a clue that says, "You made the wrong choice—go back to the last clue location and try again." There should be a number of ways to adapt this same idea using different implementations that will be less work.

Take special care to design clues that are fun and not too obvious. You don't want to have clues such as, "Should you go to the mall with your friends on Monday night, or go to family home evening," because everyone will pick the answer that they're supposed to pick rather than the answer they'd necessarily choose. You may want to use the clues to test their knowledge of the scriptures, or of the various values that the youth are supposed to be learning in their classes.

Scripture Detective

Materials: Sets of scriptures, colored 3x5-inch cards, pencils, paper
Effort Quotient: ♈♈
Time: ▨▨▨
Planning: ★★

This is a scavenger hunt that takes place throughout your building and church property and is good for any number of youth teams, as long as you have planned for the number of teams in advance. The object is to have each team go to different locations on or near the meetinghouse property by using colored clue cards as a guide. (If your meetinghouse is in use by other wards, you may want to transfer your location to a park or shopping area.)

To prepare, map the layout of your ward meetinghouse and list or mark stations where you will place clues. After you are satisfied, place each of your routes on paper. Each team should start and end at the same place, but should have different routes to reach the final destination. Name each team according to the color they are seeking. For example, the blue team will look only for its own colored cards at any given location. When you have decided where to place the clues throughout the building and have mapped out the different routes, then use your scriptures to create anywhere from five to ten clues, depending on the length of time you have for the activity. Tape the clues in inconspicuous places.

To start, each team is given a colored card that provides a clue (see, not everyone is clueless!) of where the team is to go next. Once they figure out the clue, they use the directions to find their next

> **Sneaky Secret**
> Use a computerized scripture base to do a word search for some of the more obscure words in the scriptures, such as "under" or "behind." This saves time that would otherwise be spent searching randomly through scripture pages.

clue card, and so on until they arrive at the final destination. The clues will be something that team members have to find from using the scriptures. This can be done by looking up references for separate words, for example: 1 Nephi 11:24, twelfth word (look); Matthew 5:15, tenth word (under); Psalm 21:9, eighth word (oven); Revelation 3:8, thirteenth word (door). Another option is to use a verse or verses to imply an area of the building so the teams will have to reason it out, such as using 3 Nephi 7:24–25 to represent the baptismal font. *Note: Any team that disturbs clue cards of other teams will be disqualified, so make sure to leave other teams' cards alone!*

This is a great activity that gives your youth another opportunity to familiarize themselves with the scriptures, to think, and to work together.

YW Values Hunt

Materials: One envelope per girl, and twenty-one more for the questions and clues; sheets of typing or construction paper in each of the seven value colors

Effort Quotient: 🖐🖐

Time: ⌛

Planning: ★★★

 Preparation:

- Choose six value choices for each of the seven Young Women values, using the Personal Progress book or your Young Women organization experience. "Be selective about the television

programs you watch" could be a *Choice and Accountability* value choice. "Work to stop criticizing, complaining, or speaking unkindly to or about another" could be a *Divine Nature* value choice. Place your choices in pairs so that two different values are paired together, such as *Faith* ("Bear your testimony") and *Good Works* ("Baby-sit for free"). You should now have twenty-one pairs of value choices. Assign each pair of value choices an envelope, and write the two choices on the front of it, along with the question, "which would you choose?"

- Decide where in your building you would like to place the twenty-one envelopes, and create clues to indicate each location. You can use clues such as those in the Scripture Detective activity, or you can direct the girls by using simple descriptions such as "Bishop's home away from home" to lead them to the bishop's office. The clues should indicate where the next clue can be found, leading teams of girls from one location to another and ending at the same place they started. Write a different clue on the back of each of the twenty-one envelopes.

- Cut the colored paper into 1x2-inch squares. The colors you use in each envelope should reflect the color represented by the two value choices listed on the front of the envelope (white for *Faith,* purple for *Integrity).* For each of the twenty-one envelopes, you will need one square of each color for each girl. For example, if you have fifteen girls, one envelope might have fifteen yellow squares and fifteen purple squares. There is no specific order necessary for the clues or the questions. Have the clues taped in place before the girls arrive. Make sure to inform other youth leaders who are holding activities in the building about what you are doing so they can instruct their youth to leave the envelopes alone.

- To begin the hunt, divide the girls into small groups. Each group should have a set of scriptures. Give each girl an empty envelope. Start each group in a different place to avoid everyone being in the same place at the same time. Remember, the clues should lead from one to another and back to where they started.

Girls will travel in their groups, going from envelope to envelope as they answer the clues. Every time the girls find a new envelope, they should do three things:

- They should read the different value choices on the front of the envelope as a group.

- Each girl should decide for herself which colored square from inside the envelope would correspond to the value choice she would choose. She should take a piece of paper in that color from the clue envelope and put it in her own envelope.

- The group should read the clue on the back of the envelope that will lead them to the next envelope, leave the envelope where they found it, and move on to the next question. It's important that they follow the clues in order. If they happen to spot an envelope while going from one clue to another they should leave it alone until the clues lead them to it.

When a group reaches its starting point again, the group is finished as long as all the girls have twenty-one squares of paper. If they don't have all twenty-one, then you may need to help them figure out where they missed one.

Once the groups have all finished, gather everyone together. Help them to understand that there were no right or wrong choices. Then have them sort their paper squares into colors. If they have more squares of one color, that may indicate a personal strength. For the colors they have few of, encourage them to set Personal Progress goals to help develop those values.

Here are a few ideas for value choices, along with the corresponding color for each value. Make sure to tailor your value choices to the needs of the girls in your group:

- *Faith* (white)—bear your testimony; learn about the sacrament and then listen to the sacrament prayers during sacrament meeting; earn money and donate it to your ward mission fund.

- *Divine Nature* (blue)—make a concentrated effort to strengthen your relationship with a friend or family member; ask a married couple to describe the blessings an eternal marriage brings; learn about and apply a divine quality such as charity, patience, or humility to your life.

- *Individual Worth* (red)—evaluate your activities at the end of each day and list in your journal one good thing you did; develop a friendship with someone who may be feeling lonely or discouraged; prepare for your patriarchal blessing.

- *Knowledge* (green)—read *The New Era;* learn a new recipe; work on developing a talent you have.
- *Choice and Accountability* (orange)—make and wear a modest article of clothing; apologize to someone you have hurt; plan and participate in activities that help you keep the Sabbath day holy.
- *Good Works* (yellow)—baby-sit for free for someone who is attending the temple; tutor a child who needs help with schoolwork; perform a small act of service for a different family member each day for a week.
- *Integrity* (purple)—commit to not listen to or repeat unclean or unkind stories; think about how to "Stand for Truth and Righteousness" (the Young Women motto) throughout each day; always tell the truth.

The New Era *Chair Grab*

Materials: A copy of *The New Era,* paper, pencils
Effort Quotient: ✋✋✋
Time: ⌛⌛⌛
Planning: ★★

The object of this activity is to have the youth become familiar with the great stuff contained in the Church magazine written especially for them, *The New Era.* (Depending on the needs of your youth, this game can also be played with the *For the Strength of Youth* pamphlet, the Personal Progress handbook, or a Scouting handbook.)

Tell the youth well in advance of the activity which issue of *The New Era* will be used for this game. Make sure everyone has access to that issue. Then have your youth come prepared to answer questions about that month's issue of *The New Era.*

Before the activity, you will need to read through *The New Era* and write down about forty questions from the articles. You will then need to create a set of answers *for each team* to all forty questions. Each answer needs to be on a separate slip of paper, so if you've got five teams, you're going to have two hundred slips of paper with answers written on them. Each team will have the same set of answers.

Place five chairs on one side of the room, each labeled with a number one through five. Divide the group into five teams. Group the teams on the opposite side of the room from the chairs. Give each team a set of answers to the questions and have them divide the questions evenly among themselves. When play begins, a leader reads a question and the person from each team who is holding the correct answer runs across the room and sits in the highest numbered chair he can. For instance, the first person who reaches the chairs will sit in the chair labeled with the number five. If he has the correct answer, his team gets five points. If the answer is not correct, the team loses five points. The second person will sit in the chair labeled number four, and will get four points for a correct answer (or lose four points for an incorrect answer), and so on down to chair number one. The team having the highest score at the end of the game is declared the winner. Be sure to award a valuable prize!

Patriarchal Dinner

Materials: Elegant table settings and linens provided by each age group, dinner
Effort Quotient: ↡
Time: ▨▨▨
Planning: ★★★

Depending on the size of your group, assign each class to decorate a table for the meal using linens and dishes from home. Round tables add a touch of class if they are available. Invite the stake patriarch and his wife to have dinner with you. Have the youth dress for dinner. Enlist the help of several ward members to prepare the meal and serve it. During dessert have the patriarch and his wife introduce themselves and speak about patriarchal blessings. This activity can help break the ice between the youth and your patriarch. If he doesn't live in your ward, the youth may not really know him.

World's Fair

Materials: Varies
Effort Quotient: ↡↡↡
Time: ▨▨▨▨
Planning: ★★★

The key to this event is that the youth should have no idea exactly what this activity is about. The less they suspect what is happening, the more effective the activity becomes. Prepare them to come by telling them that it will be a youth fair or a game night that the leaders are planning for them, but that they should not wear very casual attire. This activity is to be done in phases. Phase one will be a game night with a carnival-like atmosphere in the cultural hall. Phase two will take place in the chapel. Enlist the help of several volunteers, some to be in the cultural hall (which will represent the world), and some to be in the chapel (which will represent crossing through the veil). All the volunteers who are in the chapel, including the bishopric, should be dressed in white. Don't let the youth see the chapel volunteers until they're taken to the chapel later in the evening!

Phase One: Each youth is given a certain number of tickets (between fifty and one hundred) upon arriving at the fair. Activities are taking place in the cultural hall that allow the youth to spend their tickets. Carnival games such as shooting hoops, tossing a ring around the neck of a bottle, or playing darts, might be appropriate. Dessert booths where youth can purchase junk food for tickets should also be available. You may want to use your scriptures to determine different ways that we can be tempted into losing sight of our eternal goals and pick activities to represent those. Use your imagination!

The adult volunteers should quietly try to win the tickets away from the youth by betting them that they can't accomplish a certain thing, such as making a basket or a series of baskets. The volunteers should use other subtle tricks to entice the youth to squander their tickets. Don't forget to collect those tickets! Remember—nothing at the fair is free.

You can also set up booths in which the youth use tickets to perform a good deed and are then rewarded with additional tickets. These booths could host activities such as tying quilts for kids at the local children's hospital, writing letters to missionaries serving from your ward, or assembling care packages for the widows in the ward.

Let the youth spend some time taking in the sights and activities and spending their tickets until eventually a designated person who has been in the room the entire time requests that the youth, one at a time, go with him. This should be done so discreetly that the youth who are involved in the games and service booths won't even notice what is going on. He takes them to the chapel, where phase two begins.

Phase Two: From the time the chapel is opened, reverent music should be playing. The bishopric should be seated on the stand, dressed in white. The escort who takes a young person to the chapel should escort the young person to the bishop. The bishop will ask how many tickets the young man or woman has left and will quietly take the remaining tickets without giving praise or condemnation, and ask the young person to take a seat in the chapel. This continues until all the youth are in the chapel.

When everyone is in the chapel and their tickets have been turned in to the bishop, have someone speak to the youth about the subtle ways that we are tempted to squander our lives and our talents and how being aware of these can help us to recognize when Satan is influencing us to lose sight of our eternal goals. Equate the number of tickets lost with the time we waste on matters that do not prepare us for eternity. Tickets earned and saved can be compared to the good and charitable things we do on earth.

GIGO (Garbage In, Garbage Out)

Materials: Scriptures, paper, pencils
Effort Quotient: ♦
Time: ⧖
Planning: ★★

Begin by playing, singing, or saying a variety of television and radio jingles and slogans. Have the youth write down what the product is for each one. Use everything from baby food to beer. Then, read the beginning words of several well-known scriptures and have the youth write down the correct endings for each. Most likely they will know many of the commercials and few of the scriptures. Discuss with them the powerful influence of music and the media, and teach them that we need to be selective about what we allow into our minds.

Scripture Chase Basketball

Materials: Basketballs and hoop, set of scriptures for each youth
Effort Quotient: ♦♦♦
Time: ⧖⧖⧖
Planning: ★★

Divide the youth into two teams. Have a leader call out a scripture reference or clue. While one team looks for the scripture, the other team takes turns shooting the basketball. When the whole team has found the scripture, the basketball shooters count how many baskets they made during the time the other team was searching. Then the teams switch places. Do this for several rounds. The highest score wins. If the youth aren't too familiar with the scriptures, then make the scripture clues easy enough that they can use the Topical Guide to find the scripture. If the youth are *really* unfamiliar with the scriptures, they can try to find books in the scriptures as well. How fast can your group find Moses, or Habakkuk, or 2 Peter?

Faithful Reminders

Materials: Large sheets of poster board, pens, pencils, markers, bags, a basket
Effort Quotient: ✋
Time: ⧗
Planning: ★★

Gather a variety of objects from around your house, such as a small statue, flower arrangement, coat hanger, seashell, and place them in a bag or bags. Set up large tables in the cultural hall, enough to fit six youth around each. Number each table. Put a sheet of poster board and drawing supplies on each table. When the youth arrive, have them choose a number from a basket. This will be their table assignment. This mixes up the youth so there are a variety of ages at each table. When the activity starts, have someone from each table go to the bag and pick out the first two items he touches, taking those items back to the rest of the group. The groups then design an inspirational poster that incorporates one or both of the items. If you make it a contest or have a place to display the posters when they are finished, the youth will take more pride in their efforts.

Missionary Night

Materials: Varies
Effort Quotient: ✋✋
Time: Depends on the type of activity your looking for
Planning: ★★★

The possibilities are endless for a missionary activity. Missionary activities can last all evening or all week, depending on your youth and the circumstances in your ward. There aren't any rules here. Choose the options that will provide the best missionary experience in your ward. After all, some youth respond to spiritual activities, while others benefit more from something that is lighthearted. Know your youth before you plan a missionary activity in order for your activity to do the most good.

Here are some options you may consider for your youth missionary experience. Choose the ones that sound good to you, or use these ideas as a springboard to plan something entirely different:

- Have the bishop issue mission calls before the activity, interviewing each young man and young woman individually.

- Have the youth follow mission rules for the week of the event. (Keeping missionary hours and staying away from television and music is a real eye-opener for some youth.)

- Have youth learn the first discussion.

- Have a missionary fair with different booths that emphasize different aspects of missionary preparation. Don't forget those all-important social skills, such as getting along with a companion and combating loneliness and homesickness.

- Have the youth go on splits with the missionaries and help teach the discussions.

- If the missionaries in your area are allowed to tract, have the youth go tracting with the missionaries. This is a great event to close out a youth mission week, with the youth tracting with missionaries on a Saturday morning and then sharing their testimonies in sacrament meeting the following day.

- Prepare and serve dinner to your current ward missionaries. Ask them to come prepared to tell you stories from their own mission experience.

- Prepare and send packages and letters of support to missionaries serving from your ward.

- Poll missionaries and former missionaries, both male and female, about what things they wish they had known before leaving for their missions. Then have a skills night revolving around some or all of the items.

- Have a Missionary Olympics, with such events as shirt-ironing, simple clothing repair, simple bicycle repair, suitcase-packing, door approaches, and memorization of missionary scriptures.

- One effective missionary activity takes some extra preparation. Send a blank tape to each of the missionaries who are serving from your ward (without letting the parents know), asking them to tell the youth on tape how their mothers and fathers played a role in preparing them to serve. Make it clear to the missionary what you are doing, and stress that the tape needs to be returned as soon as possible. Send a self-addressed envelope with the correct amount of postage on it to make it easy for the missionaries to return their tapes to you. Also, don't forget to allow extra time for missionaries in foreign countries.

  Then invite the parents to come to a missionary activity night to share how they prepared their missionary sons and daughters to serve. After each set of parents speak, play the tape that was sent by the missionary son or daughter. Give the tapes to the parents after the event as a souvenir of the occasion.

Firesides

Firesides provide young men and women a chance to spend time together in a spiritual setting. Generally these are held on a Sunday night, which helps set the reverent tone of the activity. Because there has been an increased emphasis on eliminating extraneous Sunday meetings, nobody should hold a fireside just to hold a fireside. There should always be a worthwhile activity that will justify the time leaders and youth spend away from home.

Although firesides should be uplifting to the youth, not all firesides need to have a church-related theme. Youth are at a sensitive period in their lives, and they need guidance in all areas that are important to them. Here are some possible topics for firesides, followed by plans for two firesides that are spiritual in nature:

- **Moral Standards and Dating Panel.** Ask several men and women from your stake presidency, bishopric, young adult leadership, or others to participate on a panel to answer youth's questions about the standards we try to teach them, why they are vitally important to live by, and why the world has such different standards from ours. Be sure to choose panelists who relate well to youth, and whose ideas they respect. You may want to have youth submit their questions in writing ahead of time, or even provide a box where questions can be anonymously deposited during the fireside. This will give young people an opportunity to ask the questions that really matter, without being embarrassed because of the questions they pose.

- **Book of Mormon/Bible Stories.** Do you have a great story-teller in your ward? Take any scripture story and retell it in a modern setting, with fictional names and places. See if the youth can figure out which story it is.

- **Bible Parables.** Pick three or four Bible parables and talk to the youth about how they apply to us today.

- **Patriarchal Blessings.** Invite the stake patriarch to talk to the youth about how to receive their blessings and why these blessings are important.

- **How Well Do You Know Your Parents?** Prior to the evening of the fireside, give one of each youth's parents a survey of basic questions about themselves. At the fireside have the youth and parents sit across the room from each other. Have a designated person read a question and answer from one of the surveys. All youth who think it was one of their parents who wrote the answer should raise their hands, and the corresponding parents should stand. When the parents are asked who wrote the response, all parents should sit except for the one who wrote that particular answer. At the end of the evening let each youth take home the survey from their parents, so they can read the answers together.

For the Strength of Youth *Fireside*

Materials: Three small signs labeled "Agree," "Disagree," and "Undecided"
Effort Quotient: ♦
Time: ⌛
Planning: ★★

Before the fireside, prepare approximately fifteen statements that come from the *For the Strength of Youth* pamphlet. Hang the prepared signs in different areas of the same room. As you read each statement, have all the youth move to the sign that indicates their answer. After all youth are in place underneath a sign, ask someone from each group why they answered the way they did. Make sure to correct any of their statements or opinions that are against church doctrine, but be careful of their feelings and views. If you can provide a quote from one of the prophets or general authorities about each statement you have prepared, the quotes could be used to correct any misunderstandings that the youth have about what is expected of them. As the saying goes, "When the prophet speaks, the debate is over." If you find that any of the youth are hanging out under the "Undecided" sign, temporarily take it down so they have to choose another answer. This fireside has at least two clear benefits. First, your youth get to move around, thus avoiding boredom. The greater benefit, though, is that youth get to express their opinions rather than just being lectured. This fireside can be adapted to any subject where your youth would benefit from an interactive discussion. Be sure when you prepare your statements that you have a variety of correct answers. The greater the variety of true and false statements, and the more obscure your statements are, the more thought-provoking the fireside will be.

The Savior Walk

Materials: Various volunteers in period costume, construction-paper footprint cutouts
Effort Quotient: ♥♥
Time: ▨▨▨
Planning: ★★★

This fireside takes a lot of preparation to be effective. Choose several people from the scriptures who knew the Savior in his mortal life. These might include Mary, his mother; John the Baptist; Peter; Mary, the sister of Martha; Mary Magdalene; a leper who was healed; the woman who touched the hem of his robe to be healed; the blind man who received his sight; or any others that you feel inspired to include. Find volunteers to play the part of each character, and ask each to fast, pray, and study his character. Based on the knowledge received through this study, each volunteer should prepare a short first-person narration about that person's experience with the Savior. Meanwhile, have the youth help cut out many construction-paper footprints. The night of the fireside, place the characters in separate rooms in your church building. The footprint cutouts should be placed on the floors like a pathway, connecting the rooms and ending where they began so you have a circular pathway through the church. The youth are then divided into small groups. Each group will begin in a different room, and will follow the pathway through the building and back to where they started. Send a leader with each group. When the groups are finished, have them all move into a final room that has been designated as the Garden of Gethsemane. In this room, have someone portray the Savior kneeling by a tree, with persons representing Peter, James, and John "sleeping" in a corner. Have reverent music playing, and use a narrator to speak about the Savior and the Atonement. If you have time, end with a testimony meeting. Make sure the youth come dressed in Sunday best in order to remind them of the reverence of the occasion. It would be a good idea to have all participants join in a fast the day of the fireside. Also, a fireside of this magnitude may require a dress rehearsal the day before.

Indoor Fun

It may be weather that keeps you indoors, or merely the nighttime schedule of your activity. In either case, most youth activities take place within the confines of a ward meetinghouse or other building. Here are suggestions for activities that take place within four walls.

Hijacked!

Materials: Varies, depending on your resources
Effort Quotient: ✸
Time: ▧▧▧
Planning: ★★★

This activity gives the youth a taste of different cultures. Use the resources in your ward, stake, or community to pick four or five countries that will be featured during the activity. If you have access to a real pilot or Air Force personnel, it would add to the authenticity of the activity to ask him to dress in uniform and be the pilot. You will also need to ask one or two other people to be airport security. The class who is hosting the activity acts as the flight attendants. The evening should begin in a room that is designated as the airport, and decorated with travel posters and travel-related paraphernalia. As the youth arrive in the airport, have a flight attendant check them in by giving each a passport, boarding pass, and seat assignment. Have them wait in this room until the flight attendants call them to board the airplane. Then take them to a room that has been decorated like the interior of a plane that can seat all the youth who attend, with chairs lined up in two sections and an aisle down the middle. Number the seats so each ticket holder can find his assigned seat. As everyone takes his assigned seat and waits for takeoff, have the flight attendants give a humorous orientation of in-flight safety. When the pilot arrives, it's time to take off! As the flight begins, one of your visitors should hijack the plane to his country. This can be done by bringing a food native to that country, telling stories, bringing items of interest, teaching a children's game (such as having a piñata to represent Mexico), or doing something else that will teach the culture of that country in an interesting way. When a visitor has completed his presentation, have airport security arrest him and take him away so someone else can hijack the plane. At the end, the plane arrives safely at its destination.

Task Relay

Materials: Two containers (basket, hat, bowl, etc.) to hold slips of paper
Effort Quotient: ♛♛♛
Time: ⧗
Planning: ★

Prepare two sets of slips of paper listing different activities and place them in the two containers. Set the containers at the front of the room. Divide your group into two teams and have them line up at the back of the room. At the signal, have the first person on each team run up to the container, take out a slip of paper, and do the activity listed. Everyone on the team will need to complete one activity from the container. The first team finished wins. Tasks might include quoting a favorite scripture, naming three national monuments, lining up the team and having them hop around the room on one foot, singing "Jesus Wants Me for a Sunbeam," having the whole team laugh aloud for thirty seconds, having the whole team *not* laugh aloud for thirty seconds, or doing any similar task you can invent. Make sure the tasks are designed to be fun and not *make* fun. Youth are easily embarrassed; don't ask them to do anything that might cause distress to the person who draws a particular task.

Stocking Ball

Materials: Several pairs of knee-length queen-sized stockings, same amount of athletic socks
Effort Quotient: ✋✋✋
Time: ⌛
Planning: ★

Create stocking balls by rolling up one athletic sock and stuffing it into the toe of one of the queen-sized stockings. You'll need several backup stocking balls because stocking balls can get sweaty or ruined in the heat of competition. Split into two teams, with each team sitting on opposite sides of a blanket. Ask for a volunteer from each team and have the volunteers face each other on their knees in the center of the blanket. They'll need to stay on their knees at all times, and cannot use hands except to put their stocking balls on before the match begins. Give the volunteers a stocking ball and have them put it on their heads and over their ears like a stocking cap. It needs to be on as securely as possible without covering the participant's eyes. Give the contestants a little time to get used to the device. Before they begin play, they should each be able to swing the ball around their heads like a propeller in both directions. When both contestants are able to do this, have the combat begin. Each person will try to pull the stocking ball off the head of his opponent by swinging his own stocking ball around in circles until it is entangled with his opponent's. The first person to pull his opponent's stocking ball off the opponent's head without losing his own is the winner. This works best if the opponents swing their stocking balls in opposite directions. The youth will either love this or hate it because it tends to make the combatants look silly. But if everyone takes a turn, everyone will have the opportunity to look as silly as everyone else.

Play-Doh® Pictionary

Materials: Play-Doh®, wet towels to clean up the mess (Trust us, you'll *need* those wet towels.)
Effort Quotient: ✋

Time: ⌛⌛
Planning: ★

The title is self-explanatory. When this game is used for a youth activity, pick a theme and create your own list of words that go along with the theme. If you're playing with a larger group, divide your group into teams and have them sit around tables. The youth leader has a master list and sits up front. A member of each team goes to the youth leader for the first word, goes back to the table and uses the clay to get his team to guess the word. When a team thinks they know the word, they send another person to the youth leader with their answer. If they get it right, the youth leader gives the next word to the person who brought the answer. Each team works independently this way until they have completed the list, with the first team finishing the relay being the team that wins. If you have a smaller group, the teams can play in competition, with both teams trying to be first to guess the word that is being illustrated in Play-Doh®. Remember . . . no spelling, no numbers, and no letters.

Human Sports Night

This is an all-human, all-the-time event that features several human activities. After an evening playing Human Geometry, Human Bowling, and Human Dartboard, finish off with a refreshing dessert of Human Whistling Crackers and Human Lemonade.

▶ Human Geometry

Materials: None
Effort Quotient: ♈♈♈
Time: ⌛⌛⌛
Planning: ★

Divide the group into multiple teams. Have each team congregate into a group in front of the leader. So as not to confuse anyone, this is known as the starting position. The leader then calls out a shape. Each team then rushes to form the shape, using their bodies on the floor. As soon as the shape is completed, the team is to notify the leader. After each round, each team is to go back to the starting position. Start out with relatively simple shapes and then get progressively more challenging. For example, start off with a triangle or a square and then move to numbers or letters. Finally, move to complex shapes like a human, a cat, the state of Virginia, or the planet Saturn. The teams will learn very quickly the importance of selecting a leader and using teamwork. This activity can also be used by itself as a warm-up activity, as it can be adapted to any size group including an entire ward.

▶ Human Bowling

Materials: Huge rubber ball, plastic wrap or tape
Effort Quotient: ♥♥
Time: ⧗⧗
Planning: ★

Kids, this is your chance to take a shot (literally!) at your leaders. Use plastic wrap or tape to immobilize five to ten leaders or youth, so that they can't move their arms or legs. They should only be able to stand up straight like a bowling pin. Try not to cut off circulation, and only immobilize your "bowling pins." Set your "bowling pins" in the shape of a triangle as in a bowling alley. Roll the large ball at the "bowling pins" with enough impact to knock some of the "pins" over and into each other. A certain number of people will fall down, depending on how good the throw is. Each person scores by how many pins fall down, but the most fun is watching the "pins" hobble, wobble, and finally fall down when the huge "bowling ball" hits them.

▶ Human Dartboard

Materials: Aerosol whipped cream and round Cheetos®; towels
Effort Quotient: ♥
Time: ⧗
Planning: ★

Divide the group into boy/girl pairs. Have the boys spread a thick layer of whipped cream on their faces. Have the leaders stand the boys side-by-side in a row. Each girl should stand a few feet in front of her partner. Give the girls a handful of Cheetos® and, at the leader's signal, have the girls throw the Cheetos® at the faces of their partners. The pair with the most Cheetos® stuck to the boy's face at the end of the time limit wins.

▶ Human Whistling Crackers

Materials: Crackers, a long table, a vacuum cleaner to sweep up
  cracker crumbs
Effort Quotient: ✸
Time: ⧖
Planning: ★

This is a simple relay that is good for a lot of laughs. Divide the group
into teams, and place a pile of crackers on the table for each team. Have
the teams stand behind a starting line. At the starting whistle, the first
person on each team runs to the table, eats a cracker from his team's
cracker pile, faces the rest of the team, and whistles. Only after a successful whistle has escaped the cracker-eater's mouth is the cracker-eater
allowed to run back and tag the next member of the team. Note: Some
people just aren't good whistlers, and nobody can whistle really well with
a mouthful of cracker. Anything that remotely sounds like a whistle
counts in a cracker race.

▶ Human Lemonade

Materials: Three-ounce paper cups, lemons cut in wedges, sugar,
  water, a long table
Effort Quotient: ✸✸
Time: ⧖
Planning: ★

Divide the youth into two teams and put a team at each end of the
table. Place paper cups at each end of the table in rows of three cups
across, creating as many rows of cups as you have youth on that team.
Place a lemon wedge in the first cup of each row. In the second cup, place
a teaspoon of sugar. Fill the third cup halfway with water. Have each
team stand behind a starting line near its end of the table, with each
team facing the table. At the starting signal, the first person on each
team runs to his end of the table, picks up the first cup, and bites into
the lemon; picks up the second cup and pours the sugar into his mouth;
and picks up the third cup and pours the water into his mouth. Mix the
lemonade by jumping up and down three times. Then the player runs
back to tag the next person in line. The winning team gets a valuable
prize—perhaps a pitcher of *real* lemonade.

Basket/Box Picnic

Materials: Basketball, numbered slips of paper placed in a hat, pre-
   assigned food items
Effort Quotient: ⍏
Time: ⌛⌛⌛
Planning: ★

Assign the young men to each bring a dessert and a drink for two.
Assign the young women to bring a meal (lunch or dinner) for two in a
decorated box. There aren't any rules here. The young women can make
their boxes look like gift baskets where everything is displayed so the
young men can see the contents, or they can hide the contents from view.
They can make their own food or even use fast foods. Let them use their
own creativity. Place the boxes in a line on the stage and number them.
Place the same numbers in a hat. Line up the young men and let the first
one in line throw the basketball from the free throw line. If he misses the
basket, he goes to the end of the line. (The last boy does *not* have to keep
shooting until he makes a basket!) As each boy makes a basket, he gets
to choose a number from the hat. He will then take the box with the corresponding number and eat with the young woman who brought the box.
Have several blankets available, and as they get their box lunch they can
take a blanket and spread it out on the cultural hall floor to eat on. The
object is that hopefully unlikely pairs (such as a Deacon and a Laurel)
will be able to get to know one another.

Chair Balloon Hockey

Materials: Non-carpeted surface (hard gym floor), chairs, balloons
Effort Quotient: ⍏⍏⍏
Time: ⌛⌛
Planning: ★

Have everyone blow up one balloon before the game starts. Divide
the group into two teams and have each team select a goalie. Have the
goalies stationed at each end of the "field," where they can move around
behind a predetermined line. The rest of the players move around the
room on chairs, hitting the balloon with one hand toward their team's
goalie, and holding the chair with the other. The players may not get out
of their chairs while the game is in progress. The goalie's role is to get

the balloon, sit on it, and pop it before the other team can count loudly to three. A point is scored each time the goalie sits on and pops a balloon.

Airplane Dog Fight

Materials: Lots of scrap paper
Effort Quotient: ✺✺
Time: ⧗
Planning: ★

While the youth spend several minutes making lots of paper airplanes, divide the room in half with portable chalkboards. Put half the youth and half the airplanes on each side of the dividers. At the starting whistle, have the youth throw the airplanes over the divider as fast as they can for three minutes. When the time is up, count the airplanes on each side of the divider. The team with the least number of planes on its side wins. There are only two rules to this game: Only one plane can be thrown at a time, and participants must stop exactly when the leader says to stop. Play a tournament by repeating several times. For variety, use a bag of socks or wad newspaper into balls (you might need to put a small amount of tape on these to hold them together).

Bad Bowling

Materials: Bowling alley, shoes, bowling ball
Effort Quotient: ✺✺✺
Time: ⧗⧗⧗
Planning: ★

This game is for all of us who whine about our bowling skills. At a local bowling alley, break your group into a few teams. The object of the game is to get the worst score possible. Sounds easy, doesn't it. But there's a catch—gutter balls count as strikes. It's amazing how good your youth get when the pressure is off.

Sound Effects Skits

Materials: Recorded sound effects
Effort Quotient: ✺✺✺

Time: ⌛
Planning: ★

Divide the youth into small groups. Give each group a scenario to act out, and let them know that they have to integrate sound effects into their skits. The sound effects should have nothing to do with the skit. For instance, if the skit is about a birthday party at the zoo, you may want to have them use sound effects such as the sound of an automobile horn or bacon sizzling. The object is to come up with the most humorous skit.

Indoor Mini Golf

Materials: Paper plates, tape, golf putters, golf balls
Effort quotient: ⅋⅋⅋
Time: ⌛
Planning: ★★

Here is an activity for groups that have carpeted cultural halls. This activity is as much fun to make as it is to play. Cut holes in paper plates, turn upside down, and tape them to the floor in various locations. Use your creativity in creating obstacles. You can ask to borrow putters from your local mini-golf center. Use the same rules as you would at the mini-golf center, scoring points by how many hits it takes to get the ball into each hole. Remember—the lowest score wins. You can add variety by either playing with teams or as singles. Make sure to firmly remind your youth about safety and respect for church property. Before they begin, have a demonstration on how to hit the ball *gently*. Have a leader posted at each hole to monitor safety.

Black Light Volleyball for Youth

Materials: Volleyball net, volleyball, 4 to 6 tube black lights, reflective sport tape, white shirts on all participants
Effort Quotient: ⅋⅋⅋
Time: ⌛
Planning: ★★

Tape the black lights up in the cultural hall on the walls, consistently spaced. Two work really well taped to the bottoms of the basketball backboards on each end of the cultural hall. Wrap the reflective tape across the top of the volleyball net and around the ball. Neither needs to be covered totally. Use a yellow highlighter on the reflective tape to help it show up better if necessary. Have everyone wear a white shirt, then play volleyball! This was mentioned earlier as a ward activity, but the youth love it too.

Surprise Dinner

Materials: Planned meal, menus, pencils, tables, chairs
Effort Quotient: ✺
Time: ⌛⌛⌛
Planning: ★★

This is a meal that the adults serve to the youth. You will need to plan for kitchen help, and for a waiter for each table. Plan a normal meal of several courses, but write the menu in code. Put only tablecloths (butcher block paper or similar), crayons or colored pencils (or something else to write with), and the menus on the tables. Have the youth sit at the tables and fill out their menus. Pre-determine how many items you want to offer per course (three to six is sufficient). Make sure to include silverware, napkins, drinks, and even toothpicks among the menu selections (all listed by their code names, of course). The menus should instruct guests to:

- read through the numbered menu selections for each course

- choose one number for each blank on the menu

- use each number only once

- sit back and savor the meal

A sample menu will follow. After the youth indicate what they want to order, their marked menus will be collected. The dinner will then be served, one course at a time. All of one course will be cleared away before the next course is served. Youth cannot save anything from one course to the next. The fun of this meal is that the menu items are disguised, and the guests have to make educated guesses about which items should go together. If they think through what they're reading, and if you haven't made the clues excessively difficult, they will be able to enjoy a fairly normal meal. Have your waiters and youth dress for the theme.

For our sample menu we have chosen a beach theme. The dinner will

SAMPLE MENU

Instructions:

1. Read through the menu selections.
2. Choose one number for each blank below. Be sure to fill in each blank for each course.
3. Use each number only once.
4. Sit back and dine in style.

After all orders are completed, they will be collected. You will be served a course, and then all of that course will be cleared away before the next course is served.

1. Swordfish	8. Sand and Sea
2. Suntan Lotion	9. King Trident
3. Beach Towel	10. Jellyfish
4. Schooner	11. Sea Foam
5. Sun Goddess	12. Starfish Family
6. Seagull	13. Sand Castle
7. Sand Pail	14. Pelican

APPETIZER: _____ _____ _____ _____

MAIN COURSE: _____ _____ _____ _____ _____

DESSERT: _____ _____ _____ _____ _____

Key

1. Swordfish (knife)	8. Sand and Sea (spaghetti with sauce)
2. Suntan Lotion (hot fudge sauce)	9. King Trident (fork)
3. Beach Towel (napkin)	10. Jellyfish (Jell-O® square)
4. Schooner (garlic bread)	11. Sea Foam (whipped cream)
5. Sun Goddess (brownie)	12. Starfish Family (6 carrot and celery sticks)
6. Seagull (ice cream)	13. Sand Castle (straw)
7. Sand Pail (glass of water)	14. Pelican (spoon)

consist of a three-course meal. The first course will be a Jell-O® square salad with whipped cream. This will be followed by a main course of spaghetti with sauce, garlic bread, and carrot and celery sticks. Dessert will be a brownie with vanilla ice cream and hot fudge sauce. We will add water to the menu for the drink.

Of course, you aren't limited to the beach theme shown on the menu. Here are a few other theme ideas, along with some meal suggestions:

- A **Sports** theme first course (appetizer) could include "Pom-poms" (salad); "Whistle" (salad dressing); "Goalpost" (fork).

- A **Scripture** theme second course (main course) could include "Matthew 8:31–32" (ham), "Ether 2:16" (potato boat = stuffed potatoes); "Zechariah 5:1" (roll). If you choose this theme, make sure the youth bring their scriptures.

- A **Circus** theme third course (dessert) could include Big Top (ice cream); Cannon (spoon); Clowns (colored sprinkles).

Money Management Fair

Materials: Magazines, newspaper clippings, Monopoly® money or equivalent, other various supplies
Effort Quotient: ♥♥
Time: ▨▨▨
Planning: ★★★★

Young men and young women will be divided into pairs of "married couples." Create two different monthly financial scenarios for each youth couple that you expect to attend. The couples will receive one scenario (month) at the beginning of the activity, and the second scenario about halfway through the activity. If they started their first month unemployed and not doing well financially, their second month may have them finding a terrific job with stocks offered worth $100,000. When developing the scenarios, try to consider many lifestyles and income levels (student to CEO), employed in a steady job or unemployed, and so on. Here is a sample monthly scenario:

- You have just lost your job and have not yet found another.
- You have $2,800 in savings.
- Your apartment rent is $680 a month.

- Your car payment is $340 a month.
- Your utilities cost $60 a month.
- Cable television is $45 a month.
- Groceries cost $300 a month.

Before the activity, each youth age group should prepare one or more booths that will represent various financial expenses or resources. Booths to consider having are a bank, mortgage or real estate office, bishop's office, employment office, auto dealership, utilities (include cable television here), supermarket, mall, entertainment, and so on depending on the different scenarios you develop. Stock the booths with inventory by cutting many different kinds of items out of magazines. For example, you can create an inventory of cars for the auto dealership, from clunker to luxury. You can illustrate different types of housing for the real estate "office," too. A supermarket may show peanut butter and jelly sandwiches or steaks and shrimp that youth can purchase with their fake money.

As young women arrive for the activity, they should put their names on a piece of paper in a paper bag. Pass the bag around and have the young men pick their "wives" out of the bag. When everyone is paired off, hand out the scenarios, and an appropriate amount of fake money, possibly a credit card, and an ATM card. The couples will then go from booth to booth to buy or make payments on their car, home, utilities, entertainment, food, and church contributions. If they buy a large item like a car or house they will need to go to the bank to get approval and a loan.

As youth move from booth to booth, the leaders manning each booth will write what they did on the scenario cards and make appropriate financial adjustments, creating a record on the scenario cards so the leaders will know if the couple has enough resources to complete their transactions. Make sure to include enticing entertainment like basketball or Nintendo® that the youth have to pay for, as well as refreshment stands that sell tempting real snacks for play money. Halfway through the activity, give each couple the second half of their financial scenario. If the couple has a lot of money, they can choose to buy nice things with it or put some or all of it in savings to save for later. Some of them may want to give their excess to less fortunate couples. This activity takes a good deal of forethought, but it is very fun and worth every effort. Have a discussion after to find out what everyone learned and to emphasize good money management skills.

Outdoor Fun

For warm summer nights or those spring and autumn nights when the weather is cool and yet still pleasant, take your group outside and entertain them with some of the activities found here.

Video/Photo Scavenger Hunt

Materials: Video cameras or Polaroid® cameras for each team
Effort Quotient: ✹✹✹
Time: ⏳⏳⏳
Planning: ★★

Here's an old favorite. You will need to line up a few adult volunteers to drive the youth around the night of the activity. Divide the youth into teams of four to six, or enough to fill one car. Give the teams a video camera or Polaroid® camera. They will have a certain amount of time allotted to get a certain number of tasks recorded or photographed. Make up a creative list of feats and assign point values for each task, giving more points for more difficult shots. Make sure to use some ideas that would be unique to your area (Shannon gave points for having youth stand in the Potomac River). Whether you have chosen to use video cameras or Polaroid® cameras, plan for the youth to be back to the building in plenty of time to either watch the videos or vote for the best pictures. Make sure the youth understand that they can be as creative as they want in their pictures. For instance, "someone on your team riding a horse" might refer to riding a hobbyhorse, or even the mechanical horse at Kmart. Some ideas for your scavenger hunt might include:

- Team members shaking hands with missionaries

- The entire team giving the bishop "bunny ears"

- Team members in front of Brother and Sister _____'s house, wearing their bathrobes

- A team member helping to carry a stranger's groceries

- A team member standing by the greeter at Wal-Mart and greeting the customers

- A member of your team singing "I Wish I Were an Oscar Meyer Wiener" while standing in the hot dog section of a grocery store
- Team members admiring Brother and Sister _______'s kitchen garbage can
- Team members in front of a fish tank

Watermelon Football

Materials: Medium-sized watermelons, towels for cleanup
Effort Quotient: ✋✋✋
Time: ⌛
Planning: ★

Here's a fun game for those who live where watermelons are plentiful. Divide into teams and play tackle football.

Tennis Baseball

Materials: Tennis racket and tennis ball
Effort Quotient: ✋✋✋
Time: ⌛
Planning: ★

This is played the same way as baseball, except that you use a tennis racket and ball. When you play with tennis balls, no baseball gloves are needed. If you have too many youth, divide into three teams and have two teams in the field at all times. After all, you'll need a lot of outfielders playing far back in the field. A tennis ball can really sail!

Slide Battle

Materials: Large plastic tarp, hose, bar of soap
Effort Quotient: ✋✋✋

Time: ⌛⌛
Planning: ★

Split your group into teams and have each team stand at opposite ends of the tarp. Keep a low stream of water flowing onto the tarp during the activity. Have the team members number off. The leader then calls out a number and the two people with that number get on their hands and knees on the wet tarp and try to get the soap back to their own side. This will probably work best with teams of girls against girls and boys against boys to avoid any accidental hand slips. Also, remind the girls to avoid white shirts. It wouldn't hurt to have a few extra dark shirts on hand for those who forget.

Flourball

Materials: Pantyhose (half your group will need one leg of the hose at a time), flour, clothes that can get dirty
Effort Quotient: ♥♥♥
Time: ⌛⌛
Planning: ★

This is a unique variation of paintball. Divide your youth into two teams, equipping each member of only one team with a stocking leg filled with a small amount of flour about the size of a fist. The two teams face off on a playing field, with each team having control of half the field. A base is identified at the end of each side of the field. The object of the game is for the unarmed team to run through the armed team and make it to the base without getting hit. The people who get hit are taken prisoner by the armed team and have to sit on the side of the field. Both sides should have a chance to be the armed team, and the winner is the team who gets the most people to the base without getting hit by the sock or flying flour.

Air Raid

Materials: Buckets filled with water; 7 to 8 large soft sponges cut into 3 pieces each, or about 20 rags; 5 to 6 large obstacles such as tables
Effort Quotient: ♥♥♥

Time: ⧗
Planning: ★★

Mark start and finish lines approximately fifty feet apart, with obstacles placed randomly on the field between the start and finish lines. Assign two people to be the "bombers" and give them each a bucket full of water with ten small sponge pieces or rags. Place one "bomber" about halfway between start and finish, and the other about ten feet past the finish line. The object of the game is to get from start to finish, going from obstacle to obstacle, without getting hit by a wet sponge. The job of the "bombers" is to try to hit the runners. (The bomber who is assigned to the halfway point is only allowed to try to hit the runner until the runner has passed him.) If you choose, you may assign point values to each obstacle. Otherwise, everyone is wet and happy.

Bigger or Better

Materials: A small, silly item such as a rubber toad for each group; enough vans, pickups, and adult drivers for your teams.
Effort Quotient: ♉♉
Time: ⧗
Planning: ★

Split the youth into groups, with each group traveling in a van and a pickup truck following behind each van. The groups then go to people's homes and ask if they will trade them something bigger or better for the object the group began with. You'll need the pickups because the objects the youth collect may get large. Give assorted prizes for the teams that end up with the biggest, most valuable, most useful, or ugliest items. The treasures you collect can be donated to charity at the end of the night.

Orange Golf

Materials: Three pairs of old pantyhose, four large oranges
Effort Quotient: ♉♉♉
Time: ⧗
Planning: ★

Divide your youth into two teams and have them get into lines. Use the socks to make makeshift belts by wrapping an entire pair of pantyhose around the waist of the first team member in each line and tying it tightly. Cut the legs off the third pair of pantyhose, put an orange in each leg and tie one leg to the back of the belts so that the first team member in each team has an orange-filled "tail" that hangs almost to the ground. Mark a line or place an object such as a chair to be the turn-around point. The first person on each team then uses his orange "tail" to bat another orange down to the turnaround point and back to the starting line. When he returns to the starting line, he slips off the belt and tail and gives it to the second person in the relay. Continue until everyone on the team has had a turn. The first team to finish wins. Because this tends to be a shorter activity, combine it with one or more of the other shorter athletic events in this section.

Water Softball

Materials: Bats, sponge balls, Slip n' Slide®
Effort Quotient: ♛♛♛
Time: ⧗
Planning: ★

Set up the baseball field by placing some inexpensive sponge balls in a bucket of water and placing it at the pitcher's mound. Place the Slip n' Slide® between third base and home plate. Divide the youth into teams. Have each team choose a pitcher and then enjoy a fun game of water softball. Youth won't need baseball gloves for this game! If players don't use the Slip n' Slide® when running to home plate, it is counted as an automatic out.

Parent/Youth Activities

If there's any time in a person's life that he needs to be reminded how great his parents are, it's during the teenage years. Parent/youth activities can perform a vital service by getting teenagers and their parents to spend time together and to learn to appreciate one another. Here are a few activities that are designed for parents and teens.

The only caution in planning a parent/youth activity is to be mindful that not all of your youth may have parents who are available or willing to participate. Once they reach their teenage years, a beloved leader can privately discuss the situation with these youth and ask if there might be an acceptable substitute for Mom or Dad who could fill in for the activity.

Pudding Bull's-Eye

Materials: Ice cream cones, pudding, towels
Effort Quotient: ✋
Time: ⌛
Planning: ★

Have parents lie on their backs with an ice cream cone in their mouths, open side up. The youth stand on a chair above their parent with a bowl of pudding (tapioca is a good choice) and a spoon. Each youth tries to fill his ice cream cone with the pudding before anyone else. The youth better be nice, because they get to take a turn with the cone in their mouths next!

Dining Out Relay

Materials: Various food items, two large paper bags
Effort Quotient: ✋✋✋
Time: ⌛
Planning: ★★

Place identical food items in two large paper bags. Place the bags on chairs on the opposite side of the room. Divide into two teams and have one person at a time race to the bag, pull something out without looking, eat it completely (have him open his mouth to prove it), then run back to his team. Each person on the team takes a turn. The first team done is the winner. Some ideas might include a few pieces of peanut brittle, a large dill pickle, hard-boiled egg, fruit snacks or a fruit roll-up, a juice box, a banana, a can of Vienna sausages, a bottle of baby food, bubble gum to be chewed and one bubble blown, and a few crackers. Don't forget to put garbage cans by each chair.

Glamour Pix

Materials: Various, depending on the classes chosen; camera
Effort Quotient: ✋

Time: ☒☒☒
Planning: ★★★

This activity is for mothers and daughters. Have three or four classes on hair, makeup, manicures, and modest clothing, or other age-appropriate classes. After some "professional" instruction from the class teachers, let the moms work on the daughters, and the daughters fix up their mothers. At the end, take pictures of mother and daughter together as a keepsake of the evening.

My Mom Is a Queen/My Dad Is a King

Materials: Potluck food
Effort Quotient: ♀
Time: ☒☒☒
Planning: ★★★

Ask each parent/youth to bring a favorite family dish or a dish from their heritage for a potluck meal. A few weeks before the activity, ask the youth to find out different things about the parent who will be honored, such as basic vital statistics of where he was born and grew up, how many brothers and sisters he had, his favorite school subjects, favorite foods, favorite sweets, favorite color, and so forth. Then have the youth learn more specific things, such as the parent's favorite childhood memory, an embarrassing moment, what he wanted to be when he grew up, what he is most proud of, what he'd like to change about himself, and so on. Ask each youth to tell a story about the parent's life using this information. Provide beautiful paper for the final copy of each story. This is a big project, but could be used to fulfill goals in many different programs that we have for our youth. During the evening have the youth read their stories for the group. Roll up each paper like a scroll after it has been read, and tie it with a ribbon. Each author should present this to his parent as a souvenir of the evening.

Dance Mixers and Ideas

Although dances are traditionally organized on a stake level, each ward takes a turn at being in charge of them. Here are some ideas to get people mingling with one another, guaranteeing that your dance will become the "event of the month."

Dance Themes

Materials: Music and decorations to match theme, dance instructor, light refreshments
Effort Quotient: ♛♛♛
Time: ⌛
Planning: ★★★

- Barn Dance
- Parking Lot Dance or "A Night Under the Stars"
- Theme Dance—60s, Western, Disco, Disney
- Line Dancing
- Latin Dance
- Square Dance
- Ballroom Dance

Whose Shoe?

Materials: None
Effort Quotient: ♛
Time: ⌛
Planning: ★

Have the boys move to the edges of the room, then have the girls take off one shoe and throw it into a pile in the center of the room. Let the boys then pick a shoe from the pile, find the girl to whom it belongs, and dance with her.

Dance Cards

Materials: Prepared dance "cards"
Effort Quotient: ♛♛
Time: Varies
Planning: ★

Prepare the dance cards by designing them on a computer with spaces for about ten signatures and instructions that each cardholder needs to get a certain number of signatures to earn refreshments. Signatures are given only by dancing with the person whose signature is being sought. The completed card can be turned in to receive the refreshments. A variation is to have youth collect as many signatures (and therefore dances) as possible to earn different components of the refreshments. For example, if you choose to have ice cream sundaes, each ingredient or topping can be earned with a certain number of signatures.

Door Prize

Materials: Paper, scissors, marker, and door prize
Effort Quotient: ♥
Time: ⧗
Planning: ★

Hand out the numbered tickets to those who arrive in the first half hour. Those with tickets can participate in a drawing for a door prize at the end of the dance.

Ugly Box

Materials: Some of the ugliest and most outdated but modest clothing items you can find, a large box
Effort Quotient: The ability to show up appropriately dressed or swallow your pride and make use of the ugly box
Time: ⧗
Planning: ★

Do you ever have a problem with your youth showing up to dances or other activities in inappropriate clothing? Keep the Ugly Box on hand and let them choose something more modest if they forget to dress appropriately. A few things make this really successful. One is to make sure through many humorous announcements disguised as threats that your youth know what the box is and what it is for. Be firm when they show up dressed inappropriately that they must put something else on, either from the box or something of their own, and *don't back down!* Most of all, use a *lot* of humor, because humor will get your point across in a way that bullying won't. Once you have the respect of the youth and they know that you won't cave in, they will usually cooperate with no further incidents.

Ding and Ditch Ideas

Materials: Varies
Effort Quotient: ♥♥♥
Time: ⏳
Planning: ★★

- **Heart Attacks:** Have your group cut out many cardstock or construction-paper hearts and write nice things on them for the person or people they are going to Heart Attack. The youth then sneak over to the person's house and either tape them to the front door or tape them to plastic forks and leave them stuck in the ground all over the front yard. You can leave a plate of goodies, ring the bell, and run as well. As noted in chapter 7, this is an excellent idea for an activity near Valentine's Day.

- **Teepees:** Do the same thing as above except cut out Indian teepee shapes. Write "You Have Been T-Ped" on them. It's funnier than using toilet paper and is less wasteful—to say nothing of being easier to clean up afterwards.

- **Chalking:** Have your group use sidewalk chalk and write sweet notes to the person on his driveway or front step late in the evening when they won't get caught. Chalking the bishop or a youth leader is a creative way for the youth to let him know how much they care. Chalking an inactive youth can help break the ice. The chalk wears off in anywhere from a few days to a week.

- **Others:** How about doing something for the season? The Twelve Days of Christmas for a family in the ward (one of something the first day, two of something the second day, and so on)? Or a plant in painted clay pots for the spring? Or fruit-filled cornucopia for fall? These are sure to please the recipients. After all, people are always glad to learn that somebody cares about them.

Questions from the Clueless

? *How can I design activities that will appeal to all the youth?*

There's no way you can make everyone happy all the time. The only way to do it is to make everyone happy some of the time. A variety of activities should be presented, so that everyone's needs are met.

As you're helping youth plan their activities, make sure to remind them to choose a purpose for each activity before deciding what activity to hold. Knowing an activity's purpose will give youth the framework to plan an event that will meet the needs of more of the group's members. In addition, when events are planned ahead of time, youth won't be left with the default option of playing basketball instead of engaging in any meaningful activity.

? *How can I use activities to reach those who are not more involved?*

Adults who work successfully with youth understand that they must know each young person individually. Each member of a quorum or class has individual talents and strengths. They each have personality quirks and challenges. Once an activity has been determined by your planning committee, make sure to utilize the talents and needs of people who will be attending. A class clown may make an excellent emcee, and a shy person may have computer skills that will result in excellent publicity or decorations. If you play to everyone's needs and strengths, you'll be more likely to involve them in your activities. Remember—young people are different, and they want to be recognized for who they are. If you can make each member of your group feel valued and needed, you'll have a better level of involvement for all your activities.

One final piece of advice is to assign youth to teams randomly. Make it so that every member of every group has to be involved to accomplish the desired result. If you rely on a few stars to do the majority of the work and receive the majority of the glory, you'll be feeding the needs of the few instead of reaching the entire flock of sheep.

CHAPTER 5
Suffer the Little Children

It is quite an undertaking to find activities for Primary-age children. There are so many programs for children, and so many varied abilities in this group. What the three-year-old will enjoy, the eleven-year-old will look at with disdain. It may not even be possible to find a single activity that will appeal to the youngest children in a Primary as well as the oldest.

The activities included here are not organized according to age group. They are broadly categorized by activity type, giving you the opportunity to select a general category, read through the activities in that group, find an appealing activity that fills your goals, and adapt that activity to interest your age group. But don't stop there. These activities are only skeletons; use your creative genius to flesh them out and make them your own.

Spiritual in Nature

Most of the activities we plan in the Church should have spiritual underpinnings, because we, as Church members, have our basis in spiritual things. Thus you will see spiritual roots in just about any party you organize—if you look for those connections.

Here are some activities that are based directly on spiritual pursuits. Adapt them or enhance them for your group, or combine several small activities into one mega-party.

Thirteen Flavors

Materials: Thirteen ingredients for banana splits, such as bowls, spoons, napkins, ice cream, bananas, different toppings, nuts, whipped cream, cherries, even small brownies or cake; Articles of Faith charts from the ward library, or scriptures
Effort Quotient: ♥
Time: ⧗
Planning: ★

After having the children memorize the thirteen Articles of Faith, have a party where they earn ingredients for banana splits. For each Article of Faith they can recite from memory, they earn one ingredient. Use the charts or scriptures for quick review.

As I Have Loved You

Materials: Varies depending on theme. For sample activity you will need several wicker baskets; clean, empty baby food jars; candlewick, enough for each child to have a two-inch length; salt (you will need approximately ⅓ cup per child); food coloring; spoons; mixing bowls; paraffin; empty soup cans or other large aluminum cans; masking tape; pens; paper; crayons; glitter; ribbon; stickers; several cassette tapes; cassette recorder
Effort Quotient: ♥♥♥
Time: ⧗⧗⧗
Planning: ★★★

For your quarterly Primary activity, create baskets or boxes of treats to give to several individuals in the ward who would appreciate a kind gesture and a bit of Primary cheer. The bishop can help you select individuals who would most benefit from the gift.

The first step in this activity is to pick a theme. This activity works especially well around Valentine's Day, which is the theme we have chosen to use as our example here. Purchase baskets and other materials listed above. You may also want to purchase some sort of basket filler and a ribbon to dress up the baskets just a bit.

⮕ When the children arrive, talk briefly about why we serve others. Explain that when we help others, we show our love for them. Tell them that you have picked three or four people in the ward who would benefit from knowing how much they are loved. Divide the children into three groups and have them rotate through each group, meeting in the Primary room when each activity is complete.

▶ Layered "Sand" Candles

Make a few candles beforehand to have on display (it is best to put these candles in the baskets that you will give away and let the children take home their own candles).

Before the activity begins, pour salt into several different bowls. Add food coloring into the salt, one color per bowl. Stir until color is even. Place several spoons near each bowl and line up the bowls along a table. Cut the candlewick into 2-inch lengths and dip into melted wax to strengthen.

Give each child a baby food jar and a piece of masking tape. Have them write their names on the tape and then place the tape on the jars. Give the children instructions to spoon the colored salt into their jars, making each layer of color about ½-inch deep. Children will need to leave an inch of empty space at the top of each jar. Remind the children to be careful not to shake the contents of jar or they will mix the colors together!

In the meantime, have a teacher melt the wax carefully in a can placed in the top of a double boiler at very low heat (make sure both top and bottom of the double boiler have water in them).

Have the children bring their baby food jars to the teacher, who will then pour melted wax into the jars, over the top of the salt, filling them almost to the top. After the wax has set just a bit, have the child insert the wick, leaving about 1 inch of the wick sticking out at the top for lighting the candle. The child will need to hold the wick in place for a minute or two.

Leave the candles on a countertop to set. The candles will firm up while the children participate in the rest of the activities. Children can peel off their names once the activity is over and they have picked up their own creations.

▶ The Gift of Music

Teach the children several songs about love (use the index to the *Children's Songbook* for ideas). Have them spend 15 or 20 minutes practicing the songs and perhaps learning how to say, "I love you" in several different languages.

▶ Greeting Cards

Have the children make simple notes and cards on colored paper with glitter, markers, stickers, crayons, and other art supplies. Each child should make a note for each basket recipient. Remind the children to sign their names and even tell a little bit about themselves if they'd like. When the notes are complete, punch a hole in the top of each paper and tie them together with a ribbon. This makes for a sweet booklet to place in each basket.

At the end of the activity, the children should meet back together in the Primary room. Show them the finished booklets and the candles that will go in the baskets. Then have them record on tape the songs that they learned in the music activity. You can also record them saying, "I love you" in the languages that they learned. Tell the children that you will make a copy of the tape to put in each basket.

Send the children out the door with a Valentine's cookie and their candles as souvenirs.

Arrange with the Achievement Days leader to have the eight- to eleven-year-old girls make cookies at their next activity to place in the baskets. Allow this smaller group to hand-deliver the baskets. Invite several of the girls to report on their experiences during opening exercises the next Sunday.

Scripture Scramble

Materials: Paper, pen, scriptures
Effort Quotient: ♛
Time: ⧗
Planning: ★★

This activity is for children who are old enough to read. Write out the words to a verse of scripture or one of the Articles of Faith on paper. Cut the verse into phrases and give each team an identical set. The strips are dumped on the floor or a table. At your signal, have the children assemble the scripture. The first team to assemble the words in the correct order and write the reference or Article of Faith number on the chalkboard is the winner.

Where in the Scriptures?

Materials: Scriptures
Effort Quotient: ✷
Time: ⧗
Planning: ★

This activity is for children who are old enough to read. Choose four to six different things for the children to search for in their scriptures. In the Book of Mormon, children could find the verse where Nephi built the boat, or where King Benjamin gave his address, or where Alma the Younger was converted. If you do this activity often, you can progress to more obscure references as the children master the easier ones. Switch books occasionally and use the Old Testament, New Testament, Doctrine and Covenants, or Pearl of Great Price. Don't forget to involve the Bible Dictionary, Concordance, or the maps once in awhile. This activity, when used often, will give the children a lot of confidence in knowing and using their scriptures.

Scripture-Reading Chain

Materials: Colored typing or construction paper, cut into strips;
markers; stapler
Effort Quotient: ✷
Time: Ongoing
Planning: Ongoing

After deciding on your scripture reading project and the reading assignments given to the children, cut several sheets of different colors of typing paper into strips. Gather these, a set of colored markers, and a stapler into one container to be kept together for the duration of your project. Each week, or once a month if you choose, set time aside in Primary to have the children show you that they finished the assignment. (You may want to get a parent's signature as proof, because younger children have active imaginations.) Then let them write their name on a paper strip and attach it to the chain. Shannon found that since hers was a monthly assignment, it helped to have the children also put the month of the assignment they were "passing off" because sometimes later they couldn't remember if it had been done. Keep this chain in a safe place. It will get very large. At the end of the year, present the chain to the bishop and the ward as a visual token of what has been accomplished.

To estimate the magnitude of how large the chain will get, times the number of children who are participating with the number of months you plan to do it. You can adjust the size by making thinner or shorter strips.

Scripture-Reading Chain Variation

Materials: 8½x11-inch typing paper, white and colored; dark marker; staplers or glue sticks
Effort Quotient: ✸
Time: Ongoing
Planning: ★★

Use this activity to reinforce any concept you are currently teaching the children and to reinforce the monthly Primary theme. This can be done for as short or as long a time as you would like. Just remember that the length of time is going to coincide with the length of the chain.

Divide four pieces of white typing paper into eight equal sections each by folding the eleven-inch side in half like a half-fold card to make two sections; then folding each half into half, making four sections; and once again folding each of the four sections in half, making eight equal sections. Flatten the papers back out to their original shape. With the black marker write one scripture reference or reading assignment on each of the sections. You will be able to fit eight references/reading assignments on each piece of paper. (You may also want to draw a line along each paper fold to give you a cutting line later.) These are your patterns. Now copy each pattern onto as many colored sheets of paper as you have children. Each child will have four colored

> **Sneaky Secret**
> For a holiday variation on the scripture chain, you can have the children create Advent chains, so they will have a scripture or reading about the Savior and his birth each day of December up to Christmas Eve day.

copies (or thirty-two strips of paper). You may choose to leave strips blank if you plan to have a shorter chain.

Allow the children to cut their strips apart (or have them pre-cut to save time); then glue or staple them together into a chain. They can take them home, mount the chain on a wall, and tear off one link each day for a month to read, alone or with their family, a scripture or reading about the subject you are teaching them.

Nephite Nate the Storyteller

Materials: Paper plates or card stock, flashlight
Effort Quotient: ✷
Time: ⧗
Planning: ★

Make a face from the card stock or paper plates by cutting out eyes, nose, and mouth to resemble a Nephite. Have the storyteller stand at the back of the darkened room, hold a flashlight behind the face so that the shadows are projected onto the wall in the front of the room. You will notice that the face comes to life as the flashlight moves. Have "Nate" tell the children stories from the scriptures. To add a little more interest, make more faces and have them interact to tell a story.

Eight Is Great (Baptism Preview)

Materials: Varies, see each activity
Effort Quotient: ✷
Time: ⧗⧗⧗
Planning: ★★

This is a program that can be done on a Saturday morning or on an evening a month or so before the first child of the CTR–8 class celebrates his eighth birthday. Invite the entire class and their parents. Plan for about an hour. Here are things to consider adding to your program:

- Introductions to or explanations of the Gospel in Action award, the Cub Scouts, and the Achievement Days program. You can have the Cub leader and Achievement Days leader show some of the projects they have done.

- Short talks on why baptism is important, how to prepare for baptism, and the importance of the Holy Ghost. Since the children have been and will be hearing about the importance of baptism, and the gift of the Holy Ghost in Primary throughout the year, keep these remarks brief.

- Preparation for parents (letting them know what needs to be done from scheduling the building to what to bring to the baptism).

- A talk from the bishop, telling children what to expect in the interview he will have with them.

- A session where children can ask questions of the bishop.

- A tour of the baptismal font (if it is in the building at which you are meeting).

- A matching or guessing game relating to baptism information.

- A talk from a recently baptized child, telling about the experience. (Don't forget to allow for questions afterwards!)

- A demonstration on how the baptism will be done without repeating the baptism prayer.

- A Fourth Article of Faith activity where the children rotate from station to station. They would start with Faith, move to Repentance, then Baptism by Immersion, and finally Laying on of Hands for the Gift of the Holy Ghost. Have speakers at each station, or a simple activity relating to each topic.

Make sure that the speakers speak to the children at their level, unless they are specifically speaking to the parents. Some wards have found that they prefer to provide a meal or refreshments, such as breakfast on a Saturday morning or refreshments during the evening.

Conference Bingo!

Materials: Paper; pencil; copied pictures of the First Presidency and Twelve Apostles; other appropriate photographs that are specific to general conference; current chart of the First Presidency and Twelve Apostles; glue stick; contact paper (optional); markers

Effort Quotient: ♛

Time: ⏳
Planning: ★★

This game will help prepare children for general conference. Prepare a 5x5-inch bingo grid, five rows down and five rows across. Copy pictures of the current First Presidency and Quorum of the Twelve so they are sized to fit in the squares. Use a current chart of the general authorities (available in the most recent conference issue of the *Ensign*) for reference. Because each card has twenty-five squares to fill, you'll need to supplement the card with other illustrations such as the Salt Lake Temple, the Conference Center, the First Presidency, a hymnbook, the Quorum of the Twelve, the Assembly Hall, the Tabernacle organ, the angel Moroni, and the general Primary president. Cut out the pictures and glue them randomly onto the squares, making each card different. In the center square, write FREE. Make as many cards as you need for your group.

If you would like to protect the cards, cover each with contact paper or have them laminated. These can be used for other activities, too.

Write a description of each picture (name of the person pictured, or the illustration) on slips of paper and place them in a container. On the day of the activity, familiarize the children with the names and faces of the apostles and prophet, as well as the other illustrations. Try to get the children to associate names with faces, then hand each a playing board and a handful of markers (anything from a handful of beans to small candies). Pick slips of paper from the container till someone gets "Conference," which is five in a row in any direction. It's okay to leave the chart where the children can see it. It will help them to learn better.

Junior Missionary

Materials: Varies
Effort Quotient: 🖐🖐
Time: ⏳⏳⏳
Planning: ★★★

The primary purpose of missionary work is to preach the gospel, but any missionary who enters the field without preparation in a number of areas will be unprepared for the rigors of missionary work. This activity is an enjoyable way to emphasize the various aspects of serving as a missionary. If it's done right, it will stress to children at a young age that

there is much to do in preparation for missionary service.

➡   Assign children to be companions, if you'd like, or just let them go through the stations alone. Either way, designing missionary name tags on your computer (using blank address labels), or simply hand-lettering them will be a big hit. Make sure to call them "Elders" and "Sisters" throughout the activity.

▶ Spiritual Preparedness

Have the older children assemble a scripture that has been cut up into pieces. Give them part of the reference, such as _____ 1:14, and let them see if they can determine that it is Mosiah 1:14. Give the younger children a picture of missionaries, scriptures, or a person in the scriptures that has been cut up and can be reassembled as a jigsaw puzzle. If the puzzle picture represents a person in the scriptures, have the child identify the character. Also, you may want to have the children name one book from the scriptures, such as Matthew or Mosiah. Older children can have a contest to see who can name the most books.

▶ Domestic Skills

For younger children, draw a picture of a sock on cardstock, making the outline large enough to fill the page. Then make as many copies as you have children. Punch holes around the edges and let them "mend" the sock with yarn. Have the older children try sewing buttons onto a piece of fabric.

▶ Nutrition and Health

Gather the following materials: long, skinny balloons (at least ten); clothespins; marking pen; several 20x1-inch poster board strips; glue; large box or piece of Styrofoam to use as a target (if playing indoors).

Glue the poster board strips into rings. Blow up ten balloons and tie shut. Using the marker, draw or write the names of ten foods on the balloons or on a sign next to the balloons. (About half of these foods should be healthy; the others shouldn't.) Place a clothespin on the knotted end of the balloons. Anchor each of these in the ground if outside, or in the cardboard box or Styrofoam if indoors. Place them in the shape of a triangle like bowling pins, with one in the front, two placed behind it, and so forth. Give each player a chance to toss five or six rings to see if they can "choose" the healthy food choices.

▶ Physical and Mental Stamina

Missionaries must be able to walk or ride to each of their appointments. Organize a treasure hunt where children are allowed to run from one area to another to pick up colored strips of paper that will award them a prize. This activity works better outdoors, but it can be adapted to an indoor activity. It can also be adapted for children who are young enough that they do not have reading skills. One way to do this is to station adults at each of the spots the children need to visit (the red car in the parking lot, the Dumpster, the satellite dish, or other locations). Start off by telling the children to go to the back corner of the parking lot. When the children get there, the volunteer at that station will give them a purple strip of paper. That volunteer will tell them to go to the flagpole. The volunteer at the flagpole will exchange purple strips of paper for yellow ones. Sites must be visited in order, because the volunteer will issue her color only in exchange for the color of the previous site. When children reach the finish line with the proper color strip of paper in hand, they will be awarded a fabulous prize. This activity can be modified by making two routes with a different color sequence for both, so that all the children aren't running in the same direction.

▶ Social Interaction

Have a three-legged race with each missionary and a "companion," or do some other cooperative endeavor to show that missionaries succeed when they find ways to work well together.

Cultural

We live in an age when being cultured could be described as preferring television dramas to situation comedies. But we don't have to bow to popular culture. Fine art and music entertainment are still available for people who seek them out.

When planning a cultural activity for Primary children, you don't have to strap them to a chair and force them to listen to Beethoven's ninth symphony. By starting small, you'll be able to give children bits of exposure to culture that may carry over into their adult lives. Here are a few activities that can be loosely described as cultural. When your group is ready to move to something more sophisticated, there are countless other ways you'll be able to expose them to art.

A Day at the Louvre

Materials: Art media of your choice for children—crayons, colored pencils, paint, paper, Play-Doh®, clay, glue, salt, seeds and beans (optional)
Effort Quotient: ✋✋
Time: ⌛⌛⌛
Planning: ★★

Before the activity, pick several themes for your art exhibit. You may choose to focus on the Primary theme for the year or to include artwork that centers on stories from the Book of Mormon or other works of scriptures. Family, nature, and friends are also good subjects to pick from. After picking your themes, designate several different areas in the building where you will display the artwork. Plan to place all the Book of Mormon artwork in one hall, and the nature exhibits in the next hall, and so forth.

THE BALANCE...
THE COLOR...
THE USE OF
MACARONI NOODLES...
IT'S A MASTERPIECE!

Prepare stickers (computer mailing labels work well) with the different subject titles written on them. As the children arrive for the activity, give each a sticker. When ready, divide them into groups according to their stickers. All those with Book of Mormon stickers will be one group, and so forth. Have the groups gather around tables that have been stocked with art supplies.

Give them a certain amount of time to create their masterpieces. Younger children will draw quickly, and will probably want to do more than one piece of art. That is okay. You might even let them draw one picture from each category, if you have enough time and supplies and interest to allow for that. Make sure to emphasize that children need to do their best work, because it is a masterpiece.

As each child finishes his masterpiece, have him sign it—just as real artists do. Have a leader help the child hang the artwork in the appropriate "gallery." Be sure to hang the pictures at the children's eye levels, rather than the leaders'! If you are using standard sheets of paper, leaders can prepare frames out of brown and black construction paper to set off each piece of fine art. After a certain time limit, have the groups go on guided tours of the "museum." Leaders will be the guides. Make sure they point out use of color, picture details, and ask questions of the children about what they are seeing. If your building situation and your bishop allow it, the pictures could be left up for the ward to enjoy for a week or so.

Here are some variations that will enhance the experience of your young artists:

- **Salt Pictures.** After the picture is drawn you can texture it with glue and salt. Let the child apply white glue to selected parts of the picture and then sprinkle salt on top of the glue. Let the picture sit for ten to fifteen minutes, then dump off the excess salt.

- **Vegetable Patch Pictures.** You can also texture pictures with dried foods such as beans, peas, rice, macaroni, popcorn, and spaghetti. Dried spices such as parsley flakes, sesame seeds, pepper, and paprika may also be used to good effect. You won't need to buy new spices; most kitchen cabinets are full of spices that are old and dusty and need to be replaced. Nevertheless, even old spices have some potency to them. Make sure the children don't touch their eyes when working with the spices.

Music Festival

Materials: Varies, each instrument will have materials listed
Effort Quotient: ♦♦
Time: ⧗⧗⧗
Planning: ★★★

➲   Here are some ideas for constructing homemade musical instruments. Once the children have their instruments, let them sing and perform all the familiar songs they know really well and love.

▶ Kazoo

Gather the following materials: cardboard toilet paper rolls, wax paper cut into 3½-inch circles (one for each kazoo), construction paper cut into 4½x6-inch rectangles (one rectangle for each kazoo), rubber bands, white glue, hole punch.

Glue the construction paper around the toilet paper tube. Using the hole punch, make a hole about one inch from the end of the tube. Wrap a wax paper circle over the end of the tube with the hole. Keep the hole uncovered. Glue in place. Wrap a rubber band tightly around the end of the tube, and over the wax paper. To use the kazoo, put mouth near open end and hum, or sing "dah dah dah" into it.

▶ Rhythm Shakers

Make shakers from plastic Easter eggs with a tablespoon of uncooked rice, lentils, or popcorn placed inside. Or use any empty plastic bottle. Small water bottles also make good shakers, if you have access to them. Place some colorful buttons inside and tie a cute ribbon around the lid.

▶ Jingle Bell Bracelets

Gather the following materials: elastic thread; small jingle bells, five to six per bracelet; needle and thread.

Make one bracelet per child. Use a child's wrist as a guide to how large to cut each piece of elastic thread. String five to six bells on each thread; tie the ends of the thread together. Place a touch of glue on the knot to keep the ends from coming apart. Space each bell the same distance from each other and use the needle and thread to sew the bells into place on the elastic.

▶ Castanets

Using two short lengths of elastic string and four buttons per set, string each elastic through two buttons so that each button can be placed on a finger or a thumb. Put one on each pointer finger and each thumb and click away!

City of Nephi

Materials: Empty cardboard boxes, approximately the size of cereal boxes; brown wrapping paper; pencils; markers; white glue; glue sticks; poster paint; brushes; scissors; cardboard; pictures from the ward library

Effort Quotient: ♉♉♉

Time: ⧖

Planning: ★★★★

To make this a real learning activity, the leader may have to do some scripture study first. Look through the Book of Mormon, gleaning all the details you can about city life. As the children build the city, have them look up some of the references you have discovered and try to incorporate those details into their city. Use a large piece of brown wrapping paper as your base. Decide where you want the streets, rivers, lakes, or other formations to be and pencil them in. Arrange and adjust the boxes as the buildings until you're happy with the layout. Don't forget that you can stack smaller boxes on top of bigger ones in creating the buildings. Have pictures of Nephite cities from the ward library so the children can get ideas about what they might have looked like. If any of the boxes are too tall for the city, use the scissors to trim them down. With the pencil, mark where the buildings are going to go, then remove them from the base. Paint the "streets" of the city. Paint any bodies of water. Paint the boxes to look like buildings. Don't forget a temple. When the paint is dry, glue the box buildings to the brown-paper base. Use the cardboard to create any other details, such as trees. You can also use cotton balls to make shrubs and green felt for grass, or any other items from around your home that would help make the city more realistic. Another idea is to give the children an assignment to bring an item from home that may be used to build their city. Don't give them a specific assignment, just let them find something for themselves, but it must be something small that would have been thrown away or left unused. For another activity, you might make play clay (in the craft section of this chapter) for the children to form and paint Lamanites and Nephites, pots, baskets, or animals to bring the City of Nephi to life.

Parking Lot "Beautification"

Materials: Sidewalk chalk
Effort Quotient: ♥♥♥
Time: ⧗⧗
Planning: ★

Get permission from your bishop first! Then gather the children, give them a bucket or two of sidewalk chalk, and let them "decorate" the church parking lot. It would tie the whole activity together if you asked your ward bulletin editor to announce the week before that people should be on the lookout for beautiful art in the parking lot next Sunday. Perhaps the bulletin editor will also print a nice thought or thank-you from the Primary to the ward on the Sunday after the chalking, so your ward will understand the love that went into the artwork. The chalk will wear off in a week or so.

Primary in the News

Materials: Varies
Effort Quotient: Varies
Time: Varies
Planning: Extensive

Depending on the needs of your group, you can get just about any results you're seeking out of a Primary media project. If you want to generate bonds of friendship in the ward, use the Primary reporter to interview ward members from a child's perspective. If you want to excite the children about the scriptures, the Primary television station may be just the vehicle for you. The possibilities are endless! First, assess your group, Primary, or ward needs. Does your ward need more interaction among members? Is your ward transient, therefore making it difficult for everyone to get to know one another? Second, assess the interest of your group, and their ability to stick to a project. Do you want this to be a one-time project or an ongoing project? Our ward is fairly transient. We seem to get a whole new ward each summer. And each year the process of "bonding" our ward family starts over. We use our ward bulletin as one way to help with ward bonding, and we try to include the children and youth through mentioning special achievements and including their artwork. An especially successful part of our ward bulletin has been the spotlighting of different ward members, families, or couples. The same ideas can be used for Primary alone or can be incorporated into the entire ward family. Here are a few ideas to get you started.

▶ Primary Reporter

Assign an individual or group to interview someone in the Primary or ward. Have them decide on the questions to be asked beforehand. Help them to come up with a few creative questions as well as what we call basic information questions. A creative question might be, "What is your most embarrassing moment?" A basic information question would be, "Where were you born?" Ask the ward bulletin editor if, when written up neatly, the interview can be placed in the bulletin. Or ask your bishop for space to place it on your ward bulletin board. If it is done on a regular basis, this provides an effective way for your ward members to get to know one another. It also teaches the "reporter" how news gathering is done in the real world.

▶ Primary Television Station

This is a project the children will enjoy because it is something new and it gives them a chance to be taught by adults other than those they see each week. Design a television out of a large box (this can be a refrigerator box that people can actually step into, or a large box that can be set on a table). And designate a time (once a month or so) to have a live television interview. This gives the children something to look forward to. Use ward members who are not involved with Primary to come in dressed as someone from the scriptures to tell his or her story through an interview. Putting the scriptures on "television" gives children the opportunity to learn about scriptural figures from a child's perspective. What would it have been like to have been swallowed by a big fish as Jonah was? How did Moses feel when he saw the burning bush? Were Shadrach, Meshach, and Abed-nego nervous when they were thrown into the furnace? What was it like to be Elijah and witness the things he did? What would it have been like to be a leper, then to be healed completely by Jesus? Would you remember to return and thank him? Make sure that your chosen people know very well the stories that they are to be interviewed about. Let them come up with their own costume, and you have an exciting activity to share with the children. All you will need to provide is the interviewer! Once you have a television in

WE COME TO YOU
LIVE FROM THE STAKE CENTER...

Primary, you may begin asking children to "appear" every now and then to perform a song or tell a story.

▶ Primary Radio

If you want to get Primary children to perform in front of their peers, you may want to design a radio show rather than a television station. Children will usually be less shy about singing or telling a story if they know they can't be seen. If you're making a Primary radio, design a huge radio that looks just like the old-fashioned ones. A large appliance box can be customized by cutting a hole for the "speaker" and covering it with a piece of fabric. (Make sure to keep the back of the box open so the child who is tucked inside it will have some light!) Now tune in for some lively radio programs. Set a specific time each month when the radio will be used because anticipation is part of the pleasure.

▶ Time Machine

This can be done two ways. Decorate either a large refrigerator box or use paper cut to the size of the Primary room door to make a time machine. Once a month or every other month have a character from the scriptures visit Primary by falling out of the time machine or falling through the door. Make sure they are dressed in the costume of their character and have them visit with the children for a few minutes about who they are. Use ward members that the children don't get to see very often. Consider using time travelers from the young men and young women once in awhile, too.

▶ Primary Newspaper

Some Primary groups have discovered that making a newspaper page about each child for his birthday makes the children feel special. Information about the world and/or Church on the day they were born, information about their lives obtained from parents, and a picture or two of them can be included.

Japanese "Tea" Party

Materials: Store-bought Japanese noodles; rice cakes; honey; apple juice to represent the tea; colored paper; felt-tip pens; stapler or tape; pink tissue paper; pipe cleaners
Effort Quotient: ⍦
Time: ⊠⊠⊠
Planning: ★★

If you don't have the privilege of having someone from Japan in your ward to help make this really authentic, then you can do a few things to make your party feel like the real thing. Adapt this idea for any country or culture, but be sure to include food samples, a craft or two, and a custom.

▶ The Food

Plan to serve Japanese-style noodle soup (buy at the grocery store and follow the directions on the package); sweet rice cakes (spread the rice cakes with a thin layer of honey, put them on a cookie sheet and broil for 1 minute just before serving); and hot apple juice. Be careful not to make the juice too hot, though. It's better to sacrifice the authenticity than it is to risk burning little fingers or tongues.

▶ Japanese Fans.

Make Japanese fans by providing everyone with colored paper. Have them draw pictures of cherry blossoms, butterflies, and other beautiful designs, then fold into a fan and tape or staple the bottom. It would be helpful to provide books with Japanese art so the children have something to look at while they create their own.

▶ Cherry Blossom Decorations

Find a small branch for each child and strip off the leaves. For each blossom, cut an 8-inch square of pink tissue paper. Gently crumple the paper. Grab the square in the middle and give your wrist a quick, hard flick to create an instant blossom. Twist one end of the pipe cleaner around the outside of the cherry blossom, and the other end around the branch to form cherry blossoms. Tuck in or trim off any edges. Make three or four blossoms per branch.

▶ Japanese Wish Tree

Set up a small tree (real or silk). Place some paper slips, pencils, and twist-ties on a stand under or beside the tree. Design and place a sign near the tree explaining that it is a "wish tree" and anyone can write out a wish and attach it to the tree. Make sure to mention that for the wishes to come true they should be happy and positive thoughts for themselves and others, and most important should not be selfish. When a wish has been written, the paper is folded over and twisted into the semblance of a flower shape. The twist-tie is then wrapped around the bottom of the flower shape (similar to the cherry blossom decoration) and wrapped around the tree.

Hawaiian Vacation

Materials: Plastic straws, cut into 2-inch segments (most stores carry brightly colored straws that make for more colorful leis); yarn; flowers cut from different shades of colored cardstock (punch a hole through the middle of each flower); hula hoops; Hawaiian music on tape; a variety of tropical fruit for tasting; a real coconut to crack and sample; pineapple-shaped sugar cookies and frosting; knives; paper towels

Effort Quotient: ♨♨♨
Time: ▨▨▨▨
Planning: ★★★

This activity is great for your Primary's quarterly activity day. Do this on a summer's day, so the activities can be performed outside and facilitate cleanup. First, invite each child to join the Primary on a trip to Hawaii—issue plane tickets as the invitations. When the children arrive at the activity, help them assemble paper leis. This is relatively simple if you pre-cut lengths of yarn and straws and flowers, so the children simply have to assemble the leis. To assemble, children pull the yarn through a segment of straw, then through a paper flower, then through another straw until the yarn is covered. They can then get help to tie both ends together and place the leis around their necks.

Explain to the children that visitors to Hawaii are almost always greeted with flowered leis and a friendly "Aloha!" At this point, divide the children into several smaller groups and have them rotate through each activity.

▶ The Hula

Teach the children how to "hula." Most local elementary schools will let groups check out equipment for periods of time. Borrow hula hoops from your local school, put on some Hawaiian music, and let the kids work out their energy. Have a Primary teacher or other leader show the kids how to "hula," then hold a contest—award certificates for the children in each group who can "hula" for the longest period of time or with the most creativity (around their knees or neck, for example).

▶ A Taste of Hawaii

Check out a book on Hawaiian life and culture from the library and read up a bit. Treat the children to samples of fresh pineapple, mango, papaya, and coconut. Demonstrate how a coconut is cracked open, and have a few daring kids taste the bitter milk.

▶ The Sound of Hawaii

The Hawaiian language is relatively easy to speak if you know how to pronounce it. Get someone to do a little research and teach the children a few Hawaiian words and a fun Hawaiian song. Your local library will have lots of helpful books.

To finish up the activity, have the children meet back together again to prepare for the trip back to the mainland. Tell them that many tourists bring home fresh pineapples to share with their families. Have the children frost pineapple-shaped sugar cookies to take home.

Primary Mural

Materials: A large sheet of paper, such as blank newsprint; art media, such as pencils, markers, crayons, paints

Effort Quotient: ☙
Time: ⧖
Planning: ★★

Have the children gather together around the paper and let them choose a place where they can write their names and draw a picture of themselves. For younger children who haven't learned to write, have an older child write their names or guide their hands. Save room around each name and face to have the children draw things about being a member of the Church that are important to them—the Primary theme, the temple, the bishop, their families, or the Savior. Display the mural in your Primary room. If spaces are left blank, they can be filled in before Primary starts, or after it is over. This activity can also be done with the Book of Mormon, other scripture stories, Jesus Christ, or holidays.

Indoor Fun

It's amazing to see what diversity can be found within the walls of our own meetinghouses. Depending on your own creativity, your cultural hall or Primary room can be transformed into a pirate ship, an African jungle, or the celestial kingdom. Anything goes—as long as you respect the building. Always remember that the first function of your meetinghouse is as a house of worship. Stay out of the chapel unless your activity is a spiritual one that requires the chapel, and maintain reverence for the building in all you do. Remember to clean up the building after you use it, too. If you leave the place cleaner than you found it, you'll be able to use the building next time you need a space station for your Primary lunar activity.

Primary Family Dance

Materials: Stereo equipment, CDs, decorations, lamps, refreshments, craft items
Effort Quotient: ☙☙☙
Time: ⧖⧖⧖
Planning: ★★

This activity is such a popular event for the children and their families who have tried it that it may even become an annual tradition in your ward. As the name implies, this is an activity for the entire family, including grandparents and small children who may tag along with Mom and Dad. This is an evening event, but it shouldn't last any longer than two hours. (Two hours is all the time it will take to wear out everyone—including the people who plan the party.) Choose a theme for the dance. Assign a group to decorate, but keep the decorations to a minimum. Lighting can be done with lamps and stage lights so that it's neither too light nor too dark and can help promote a family atmosphere. Assign a group to be in charge of providing simple refreshments. Someone will need to choose good dance music. One option is to focus on songs from Disney movies.

Set up the cultural hall with the following areas, each of which will be explained below in more detail: a dance area, a "family room" area, a craft table, and a refreshment table. The dance area is self-explanatory. For the parents with babies and small children, a "family room" area using the foyer furniture can be set up in a corner of the cultural hall in a square formation so the parents can visit while their babies are able to play in a "fenced in" area. The added benefit to this setup is that the parents who have to tend to babies can also watch their older children dance. Toys from the nursery can be placed in this "family room" area. The craft table is a long table set on one side of the room with paper, simple games, and other things that children enjoy. It is for those who don't want to dance or who would like to take a break from dancing. The refreshment table is also set up in a corner of the cultural hall. This way the entire activity takes place in one large room, so nobody will be tempted to wander off. Fathers and mothers enjoy dancing with their children; the children enjoy dancing with each other; the parents who need to tend to the babies have a comfortable place to visit with one another while the babies play with the toys; some children will find their entertainment at the craft table; and through the entire two hours everyone will be able to visit the refreshment table as they like. Halfway through the activity, turn off the music for a twenty-minute break. This is a good time to have a dance demonstration or other scheduled entertainment.

Indoor Camping

Materials: Tents, either homemade or real; various supplies listed below
Effort Quotient: ♦♦♦

Time: ⌛
Planning: ★★★

What children don't like tents? We don't know of any! Do you want
to take your group on a hike through the wilderness like Lehi? Or have
them pitch their tents and get ready to listen to King Benjamin's
address? How about giving them some pioneer experiences, or even just
an exciting "camping" experience? Tents can help make a memorable full
Primary activity or can be scaled down and personalized for smaller
groups. Here, we give several different ideas, but the sky is the limit.
Smaller dome tents are very popular with the children because of the
windows and zippers and other little goodies that fascinate children. But
you can easily set up makeshift tents using blankets or sheets, and
chairs. Just be warned that the makeshift tents are harder to keep
straight because children can get a little rambunctious and blankets can
move.

One thing that makes indoor camping fun is to isolate the tent
groups from one another by placing the tent doorways facing away from
each other. But it is nice to face them all toward the middle if you choose
to create a flashlight campfire (see below).

If you're feeling ambitious, you can add foil-covered stars to the walls.
Or punch holes in one point of the foil stars, tie a long string through
each, and attach them to the ceiling. Glowing plastic stars are also nice.
These are available at most toy stores or large chain drugstores.

▶ Flashlight Campfire

To make a flashlight campfire you will need six or more brown paper
bags, tape, and two flashlights with fresh batteries. Roll each bag into
the shape of a log, starting at the open edge and rolling tightly. Tape the
edges. Place the flashlights on the floor where your campfire is going to
be and lean the paper logs against each other to form a teepee around
the flashlights. Add pieces of yellow, orange, or red cellophane paper to
add "fire" color. Turn the flashlights on and adjust them so they glow just
like you want them to.

▶ Cheyenne Indian Game

Gather the following materials: four flat sticks (because we don't really live in the wilderness we can just use tongue depressor sticks), colored markers, twelve pebbles.

This game is for two players. To have more than two play at the same time, just make more sets of sticks. The Indians used dirt, leaves, berries, and other materials found in nature to color the sticks; but we will use our trusty colored markers. Color each stick a different color on one side only. You can embellish the stick with Indian designs if you like. Number the sticks one through four. This might be done by adding one nice Indian design to one stick, two Indian designs to the next stick, three designs to the third stick, and four to the fourth. Leave three sticks plain on the back and score three black lines on the back of the fourth stick. The twelve pebbles will be used as counters. To play the game, throw the sticks into the air. When they land, add up the numbers on the sticks, and take that number of pebbles for yourself. If a stick lands plain side up, then you get no points for that stick. If the black lines land face up, you get no points at all for that turn regardless of what the other sticks say. When you have thrown the sticks, whether you get any points or not, your turn is over and it is the next person's turn to toss the sticks. If there are no more pebbles in the center when a player earns them, then he just takes them from the other player. The one who wins is the first to get all twelve pebbles into his hand.

▶ Silly Fishing Tricks

Gather the following materials: balloons, curling ribbon or string, paper and pencil, a large cardboard box or a large church table turned on its side and decorated as "the local fishing hole."

This game has no hooks or worms. But the balloons will be filled with funny, silly things to do. Cut your paper into strips long enough to hold a short message and write different messages on each strip. Insert the message strips into the balloons, blow up balloons, and tie off. Attach a piece of curling ribbon to each balloon. Put the balloons behind a table, with the strings hanging out. The children take turns pulling out balloons by their strings, popping them, and following the instructions on the message strip. Ideas for messages might include:

- Stick out your tongue and say "Ahhhhh!"
- Sing the first line of "I Belong to the Church of Jesus Christ" as loud as you can.
- Make the silliest face you can.

- Throw kisses to everyone as you say, "Thank you! Thank you! Thank you!"
- Jump up and down and shout, "A bug! A bug! A bug!"
- Repeat the first Article of Faith.
- March around in a circle three times like a stripling warrior.
- Pretend you are Nephi, and design your ship by air drawing it.
- Flap your arms like a bird while saying, "Caw! Caw! Caw!"
- Pretend to sneeze ten times in a row.
- Laugh and don't stop until everyone else is laughing, too.

▶ Another Fishing Game

Gather the following materials: plastic straws (cut in half, if desired), colored tissue paper, and a fish bowl. Before the activity, cut out several fish (about three inches long) from colored tissue paper. This is a relay, so divide the children into teams and give each person a straw. The first member of each team needs to inhale through the straw to hold a paper fish in place and transport it from the start line to the fish bowl that has been placed across the room. If a person drops the fish from the straw, he has to start over. The first team to finish wins.

▶ Campin' Pete (or Patty), the Storyteller

Gather the following materials: cardstock or paper plates, a flashlight, and a good storyteller.

This is the same idea as Nephite Nate the Storyteller, which is listed in the "Spiritual in Nature" section of this chapter. Once you have created your face, more commonly known as Campin' Pete (or Patty), tell a funny camping story. Make sure to stay away from scary stories. To add a little more interest, make more faces and have the characters help one another tell a story.

▶ Make a Bird Feeder

Gather the following materials: a pinecone for each child, creamy peanut butter, birdseed, plastic knives, and a bunch of string or ribbon.

If you don't live in an area with pine trees, you can purchase pinecones from a craft store. Tie a string or ribbon loop tightly to one end of the pinecone. Have the children spread creamy peanut butter on a pinecone with a plastic knife. Roll the pinecones in the bird seed. Place each pinecone on separate squares of wax paper, write the child's name on the wax paper, and they will have bird treats to take home and hang in their trees.

▶ Writing in the Book of Mormon

Gather the following materials: sheet(s) of copper or metal plating from a hardware or craft store, large nails, and masking tape. Use metal cutters to cut the sheets of copper into small squares. Place tape over the sides of the copper plates if there are rough edges. Give each child a piece of the metal and a nail. Let them write their names or make designs, like the Book of Mormon prophets may have written on the gold plates.

Picture Scavenger Hunt

Materials: Several pieces of paper, pictures or drawings
Effort Quotient: ✋✋✋
Time: ⌛⌛⌛
Planning: ★★

Everyone loves a well-planned scavenger hunt, but younger children can't read. To solve this little problem, lead them through a hunt using picture clues. Your pictures can be hand drawn or cut out of magazines. You can even take photographs before the event. One consideration is the prize that should be awaiting the children at the end of the hunt. This could consist of anything from a bowl of treats to a small picture of Jesus for each child. As you decide on your prize, think about what you are trying to teach the children. Maybe that will spark a great idea for an end-of-the-hunt reward. Keep in mind that younger children are more interested in the process of an activity than they are in a competition that has winners and losers.

If you are using this activity for older Primary-aged children, then make it more complicated by making your pictures somewhat cryptic. If you are having your hunt in the church building and have chosen to place a clue in the room where one of the CTR classes meets, you may want to give a picture of a CTR ring. If you have a picture of a lectern, the children will have to decide whether the lectern is the one in the Primary room or the one in the Relief Society room. Six to ten clues is a good number for younger children, although older children can handle as many as sixteen clues.

The Search for Captain Moroni

Materials: Small plastic figurine to represent Captain Moroni (a real one can be bought through church bookstores, or you can use a plastic figurine from a child's toy box); construction paper
Effort Quotient: ✋✋✋
Time: ⧗
Planning: ★★

Before the game, hide Captain Moroni in an out-of-the-way place. Draw a map on construction paper (simpler for younger children, more detailed and complex for older children) that indicates where Captain Moroni is hidden. Cut the construction paper map into between eight and twenty different pieces, depending on how difficult you want to make the game. Hide the puzzle pieces. When you gather the children, tell them that Captain Moroni has disappeared and it is their job to find him. Explain that they will have to find the puzzle pieces in order to assemble a map that will guide them to his location. As they find the puzzle pieces they need to bring them to a central location (Nephite headquarters) where they will begin to put the puzzle together. Continue play till all the puzzle pieces are found and Captain Moroni has been located. This is a game of team effort and working together. Older children prefer a decent challenge. Avoid the mistake of trying to make it too simple. They just might outsmart you by figuring it out too quickly.

Outdoor Fun

Outdoor activities are particularly beneficial to children in these modern times, when the lure of television and the computer keeps them indoors and away from the sunlight. Here are some activities that will help Primary children rediscover the joys of being outdoors.

Pioneer Activity Day

Materials: Varied, listed with each activity below
Effort Quotient: ✋✋✋
Time: ⧗⧗⧗
Planning: ★★★

Unless you live in Utah, pioneer celebrations are few and far between. Pioneers were fascinating people, and their lives can teach us a lot. This terrific activity will give Primary children a new appreciation for our pioneer forebears. The event is divided into four or five different activities, and children can take turns sampling each.

▶ Make Butter

You will need several of the smallest baby food jars you can collect and enough whipping cream to fill the jars ¼ to ½ full.

Place a small amount of cream in each jar and have the children shake it vigorously until butter is formed. Provide small sections of johnnycake (or bread) and a plastic knife to let them try their creation.

▶ Eat Johnnycake

Johnnycake was a staple in the pioneer diet because it used only basic ingredients. It was often made with just cornmeal and water. Here is a more appealing recipe that can be made to serve with the homemade butter.

Johnnycake

2 eggs
1 cup water
¾ cup milk
2 tablespoons oil
1 teaspoon salt
2 cups yellow cornmeal
Butter

Mix the eggs, water, milk, oil, and salt together in a bowl. Stir in the cornmeal until smooth. Heat the griddle or frying pan. Put a small amount of oil on the griddle to keep the cakes from sticking. Pour about ¼ cup (less for bite-sized samples) of batter onto the heated griddle. Fry the cake until done on one side, then turn over and cook the other side. Makes twelve cakes.

▶ Wade through an Icy River

You will need a plastic child's wading pool and a *lot* of ice.

Let the children take their shoes and socks off and wade through the water. Explain to them that the pioneers had to endure icy rivers even when the weather was very cold. Tell a true story about the pioneers crossing a river.

▶ Dance the Apple Dance

All you need for this game are apples.

Have the children choose partners and link hands. The partners should try to dance for a whole song with an apple pressed between their foreheads.

▶ Make Candles

You will need sheets of honeycomb beeswax (from a craft store), lengths of candlewick (about two inches longer per candle than the length of the beeswax), paring knife, scissors, and towels.

There are several ways to make candles; but this method is quick and, because you cut the honeycomb wax to the size you want, the candles can be small enough to make them economical. To make candles, lay the towel on a table to provide a soft surface to work on. Adults in the group should use the knife to cut the wax to the desired length. Lay the wick along the edge of the wax sheet (the length of the candle plus two inches) and gently begin rolling it up. As you roll the wax, press firmly and evenly until the whole sheet is rolled up around the wick. Trim the wick so it is about a half-inch above the wax.

▶ Make Oiled Paper Windows

You will need brown paper grocery bags, scissors, cooking oil, and paper towels.

When pioneers built homes, they often didn't have enough money to buy glass windows. Instead of using glass, they used oiled paper in their window frames to let in the light and help keep the wind and bugs out. Try this activity to let the children see how oiled paper can become translucent. Cut the brown paper grocery sack into small enough sections to work with, about 12x12 inches square. Use a paper towel to spread the cooking oil onto both sides of the square paper grocery sacks. Wipe the squares with a clean paper towel to remove the excess oil. You now have paper ready to become a window.

▶ Hand Sewing

The pioneers didn't have sewing machines, so everything they sewed was by hand. Let the children see how nice a seam they can sew with real fabric—that has been cut in the shape of pants, shirts, or dresses— needles, and thread. For the younger children, cut out shapes of clothing from cardstock (the children can decorate them later with markers) with holes punched around the outside. To get them started, either help them tie a big knot in the end of the yarn, or show them how to keep the yarn from going through the hole by taping the tail to the back of the card and close to the first hole to be laced. Make sure to wrap a piece of tape around the "needle" end to keep the yarn from unraveling as they stitch.

Teddy Bear Picnic

Materials: Teddy bear, picnic lunch, various supplies depending on the activity
Effort Quotient: ♥
Time: ⧗
Planning: ★★

➲ Teddy bear picnics can be used to teach a variety of things to young children while they are sharing a fun time with one of their favorite pals—their teddy.

- Have parents help each child dress Teddy up as their favorite scripture person. Have the children come prepared to tell the scripture story using Teddy's help.

- Teach the children about manners and have them teach them to Teddy.

- Have each child let his teddy bear "help" make or prepare an item to give to needy children.

- Have the children dress their teddy bears in the period costume of an ancestor, and be able to tell something about that ancestor.

- Teach the children about safety (from knowing how to dial 911 and then talking to the person on the other end of the line, to fire safety, to dealing with strangers) and have them teach Teddy, or use Teddy to demonstrate what they learned.

- Have the children teach Teddy a song, or who the latter-day prophets are, or about the Word of Wisdom, or how to pray.

As you can see, teddy bears can be used in a variety of ways. Children love to include them in their lives and in situations where they are learning. It also helps the children to feel important, and gives the added benefit of reinforcing whatever you are trying to teach them. Since it is a picnic, don't forget to add a snack or lunch.

Bubble Festival

Materials: Bubble wands or tools, bubble solution
Effort Quotient: ♥♥♥
Time: ⌛
Planning: ★

Here is a terrific mid-summer activity. Children (and adults, too) can't resist bubbles. Provide the children with any and all possible bubble-making tools, from straws to bent hangers to empty milk containers. Don't forget to have them use their own hands as a bubble wand. To round out your bubble activity, add other things for the children to do, such as water activities, or a boat race.

Bubble Recipe

1 cup Joy® or Dawn® dish washing liquid
10 cups water
¼ cup glycerin or white Karo® syrup

Mix together and let settle at least overnight; for best results, let it sit for two to three days. Make several batches for a Bubble Festival.

▶ Bubble Art

You will need tempera or poster paint in three or more colors; white construction paper; bubble solution, bubble wand or drinking straw;

three or more small containers; teaspoon; and a one-cup measurer.

To make sure clothing doesn't get stained, make sure the children are wearing old clothes for this activity. Pour a cup of bubble solution in each of the three containers. Add a teaspoon of paint to each container. Gently stir till mixed. Have the children take turns blowing bubbles while their partner "catches" them on the paper. As the bubbles break, a design of brightly colored splotches will take shape on the paper. Add more paint for darker colors.

▶ Inside a Bubble

Put bubble solution into a child's wading pool. Place a hula-hoop in the solution. Have the child stand inside the hula-hoop and gently lift it up till the child is "trapped" inside a bubble. Use a stool in the center of the pool that children can grab to keep from slipping in the solution, as it will be slippery.

Sneaky Secret
- Bubbles pop mostly because of dryness, such as dry air or contact with a dry surface.
- Best conditions for a "bubble day" are cool and humid days and shady areas.
- If possible, have a "bubble day" in more humid weather such as right after a rainstorm.
- Keep all tools really wet with the solution.
- If you get a lot of small bubbles instead of a big one, you might be blowing too hard or have the tool (wand) too close to your mouth.
- Finish off your bubble with a quick twist of the wrist to seal it.
- Don't slosh your bubble tool in the solution because it creates suds and foam which isn't good for making bubbles.
- To get a bubble to land on your finger or any surface without popping make sure it is wet.

Primary Olympics

Materials: Various
Effort Quotient: ♧♧♧
Time: ▩▩▩
Planning: ★★★

There are many ideas listed in this book for Olympics competitions. These contests provide a wonderful activity for any age group because of the exercise the different events provide. Here are a few ideas that are geared specifically for children.

▶ Marshmallow Juggling

Bring a few bags of regular-sized marshmallows. Almost everyone loves marshmallows, and almost everyone loves to try a hand at juggling. So it seems pretty natural to have marshmallow juggling as an Olympic contest. Kent and Shannon, who have lived in Greece, are sure that if there had been marshmallows in Ancient Greece, the Greeks would have added this event. Start out by giving basic juggling instruction. Have each child take one marshmallow, toss it into the air, and catch it with his other hand. Have the children continue to throw their marshmallows back and forth from hand to hand until they can do it pretty well. Then give the children a second marshmallow and have them try tossing one into the air while shifting the second one to the opposite hand. Catch the tossed marshmallow with the empty hand. If you have trouble visualizing this, think of a circle. One marshmallow is arcing through the air from right to left, while the other marshmallow is being shifted from the left hand to the right. For the younger children, you may want to just stick with one marshmallow. If they can toss one marshmallow up in the air with one hand and catch it with the other, they will be doing very well.

▶ High Jump

Bring a bunch of mittens from home, blow up a number of balloons, and hang them at different lengths along a rope or string. Some balloons should be easy to reach and some should hang high enough so the children have to jump to reach them. Let the children bat at the balloons with mittened hands.

▶ Easy-Kneezie Relay (Biathlon)

This is an exciting relay that is funny to watch. You will need two beach balls and two books. Place a starting line and finish line about fifteen to twenty feet apart. Divide your group into two teams and make a line for each team behind the starting line. The first person on each team starts the race with a beach ball squeezed between his knees and a book balanced on his head. Both players race, as best as they can, to the finish line. When they reach the finish line, they get to carry the ball and book back to the next person on their team. If in the process of the race anyone drops the book or ball, that player must go back to the start line and try again.

▶ Shot Put (Peanut Toss)

You will need six cardboard party hats, or six cones made from card-stock; duct tape; and a bowl of unshelled peanuts. Tape the six party hats to a wall—open side facing out—approximately six inches apart. Mark a throwing line (closer for younger children, farther away for older children). Have the children line up single-file behind the throwing line and take turns trying to toss six peanuts into the hats.

▶ Long Jump (Backward Beanbag Throw)

You will need a five-gallon bucket or a cardboard box, dry beans, and six to ten small, mismatched socks. Fill each sock half full with beans and tie a knot at the open end of the sock to make beanbags. Have the children stand at a challenging distance from the bucket or box and, facing away from it, throw the beanbags over their shoulders and into the target.

▶ Baton Pass (Spoon Race)

You will need a spoon for each child and a small item such as a cotton ball, Ping-Pong ball, olive, grape, or piece of popped corn. Divide the group into two teams and have them stand single-file in two lines. Give each player a spoon. Give the first person in each line the small item, which will be passed to each team member down the line using only their spoons (no moving of the object with hands is allowed). The first person passes the object into the spoon of the next person in line, and so on down the line. When the object is dropped, the team will need to start over. For smaller children, just have them pick the dropped object off the floor and continue passing.

Parent/Child Activities

Many of these activities can be used for any combination of parent/child get-togethers. But a quick glance at this section will show you that some of the activities listed in this section are going to be more appropriate for a specific gender. For instance, a fashion show is probably not going to be an activity that a father and his son would enjoy sharing, nor a mother and her son. Likewise, a nice game of tackle football is not necessarily something that a mother would enjoy sharing with her child.

Here is a word of caution for planning parent/child activities. There are so many split families and single-parent families now that leaders need to be extremely prayerful and sensitive to the youth they are called to serve. Don't assume that a child without a father would love to have the bishop fill in as a father figure. Nor can you assume that a child without parents would *not* like to have the bishop fill in as a father figure. Some youth will feel that they don't want a reminder that one of their parents is not playing an active role in their lives, while others will be grateful that someone cared. We can't say it forcefully enough: Leaders need to be extremely prayerful and sensitive to the youth they are called to serve.

Ice Cream Sculptures

Materials: Various candies (provided by you), half gallons of very hard ice cream (provided by the teams)
Effort Quotient: ✺✺
Time: ⧗
Planning: ★

Ask each parent/child team to bring a half gallon of very hard ice cream and whatever tools they would like to use to sculpt a creation out of the ice cream. (Have a few bricks of ice cream on hand for those children who may not bring their own or cannot afford to.) You provide the candies for decorations and let each team choose what they would like to use to decorate their masterpieces. Give awards for the funniest, most creative, most un-melted, or any other creative category that comes to mind. Pass out bowls and spoons to end the activity.

Family Snoop

Materials: Paper, black marker
Effort Quotient: ⬇
Time: ⧗⧗⧗
Planning: ★★★

This adaptation of "The Newlywed Game" is always a hit with kids and youth. The kids enjoy being with their parents in an informal situation, and this is a fun way for parents and children to get to know one another a little better. Make a list of six to ten questions—that have three or four possible answers—for the parents, such as, "What is your daughter's favorite school subject?" or, "If you told your son about what a brain you were in high school, how would he react?" Then make a list of six to ten questions for the youth to answer, such as, "What TV character reminds you of your father?" or "What does your mother say that drives you crazy?" Once you have the questions and answers, you'll need four parent/child pairs per game. These can be chosen from names drawn from a hat or by some other means of random selection. First seat the children on the stage, sending the parents to a "soundproof booth" so they can't hear the children's answers. Ask the children four questions (one at a time), and have someone write the answers on individual pieces of poster board. Then bring the parents back to guess the children's answers. Give each parent/child team five points for each correct answer. Then send the children to the soundproof booth and ask five questions to the parents. The first four questions will be ten-point questions, and the last question will be a twenty-five-point bonus question. The team scoring the highest gets a fabulous prize, and everyone in the group will enjoy an evening of laughter. This is a great way for children and parents to get to know each other—and for children to get to know other parents in the ward. It's also a game that new ward members can enjoy without knowing anyone else or having any particular talent.

Silly Dates

Materials: See each event
Effort Quotient: ⬇⬇⬇
Time: ⧗⧗⧗
Planning: ★★

➲   Mix and match these events to make your own unique parent/child activity:

- Have the parents take off their shoes and socks and roll up their pant legs a little. Have them stand behind something so that only their feet and ankles are showing. See if the kids can pick out their own parents. You can switch and see if the parents can pick their own children.

- Have an Olympics, with events such as the javelin throw using toothpicks; the shot put with cotton balls; trying to eat a cracker and then whistle; the 100-meter dash; a curler toss using real hair curlers. See chapter 2 (Book of Mormon Olympics) for more ideas.

- Have a parent/child wheelbarrow race using real wheelbarrows. Have the parent wheel a child across the field, and let the child wheel the parent back.

- Are you serving watermelon? How about a watermelon seed spitting contest? Go for distance, height, or hitting a target.

- Ask the parents before the planned evening to tell about one crazy thing that they did when they were younger. Write them down on slips of paper and read them one at a time. Have the kids vote for who they think did what.

- Have parent and child tied to each other for the duration of the activity. Tie wrists together like handcuffs. Parents and children will then need to run, throw, and catch together. If the parent has more than one child at the activity, tie the second child to the parent's other wrist.

- Have a daddy/daughter theme dance, such as a 50s dance. Dress the girls in poodle skirts. Put the dads in white T-shirts with slicked back hair and teach them to jitterbug. A western theme with line dancing would also be fun. Other options include a costume ball, a barn dance, or a parking lot dance under the stars.

Broom Air Hockey

Materials: Brooms, socks
Effort Quotient: ♥♥♥

Time: ⧗
Planning: ★

Line up the kids on one side of a playing area and their parents on the other. Arm each with a broom and a pair of rolled up socks. Have them hit the socks back and forth in a battle similar to air hockey, with each trying to get the socks past his partner. It's not necessary to keep score on this one. This is best played on a non-carpeted floor, but can also be played on carpet if contestants are moved a little closer together.

Water Balloon Volleyball

Materials: Volleyball net, filled water balloons, towels
Effort Quotient: ♥♥♥
Time: ⧗
Planning: ★

This is a favorite summer activity of many groups, and often ends up in a water fight. Set up a volleyball net outside and have many water balloons filled and ready. Divide into equal teams. Each parent/child team needs to hold a towel between them and, when a water balloon is launched over the net, catch the balloon in the towel. They then launch the balloon back over the net using the towel like a slingshot. Continue with one or two balloons rocketing back and forth at a time. When a balloon breaks, simply replace it with another one. Don't forget to bring extra towels and several plastic bags to protect car seats on the drive home.

Mom and Me Fashion Night

Materials: Various
Effort Quotient: ♥♥♥
Time: ⧗⧗⧗
Planning: ★★★

Here is an activity that will tap the creativity of your girls and their moms. Assign each girl and mom an article of clothing to create and model. For example, a "Sunday Dress" might be adorned with items pertaining to ice cream sundaes. These could include ice cream scoops, topping jars, ice cream cones, or whatever your girl and her mom can create. Another option is a "Bathing Suit"—a woman's suit decorated with bathing items such as bath scrubbies and toy boats. The possibilities are endless; and all you need to do is assign the article of clothing to the girl and mom then wait to see what happens the night of your activity. It would be great if they could create matching outfits and model them together; but at least one should plan to model their creation. Don't forget a camera.

Night on the Town with Mom or Dad

Materials: A planned meal, elegant decorations, nice linens, place settings, silverware, centerpieces, music, camera, picture props
Effort Quotient: ✦
Time: ▨▨▨
Planning: ★★★

This makes an especially nice daddy/daughter date, but would be equally nice for mothers and sons. Decorate the cultural hall as a fancy restaurant complete with maitre d' and waiters. Ask for volunteers in your ward to help plan, prepare, and serve dinner. Use the nicest linens, dishes, silverware, and centerpieces that you can find. (Nice, yet simple decorations could include silk ficus trees that have been decorated with white mini Christmas lights. You could also hang lace on the walls with white mini Christmas lights behind.) Ask the parent and child to come dressed in their very best clothes. Don't forget the soft, elegant music. After dinner have someone come in to teach the waltz or other ballroom dances. To end the evening, have a photographer take individual pictures of the parent and child. For the pictures, try to find some fancy props such as a parasol for the ladies and a top hat for the gentlemen. Check your local high school drama department for appropriate props.

Crafts

Crafts serve a multitude of purposes for those who participate in them; and the least important factor is the craft itself. Creating a successful craft project gives an increased sense of self-esteem to the child. Occasionally, a well-picked craft project can launch a lifelong interest in a particular art or skill. And don't forget the opportunity children have to interact with one another as they all work together on their individual projects. A craft activity may be the favorite activity for some children—and if crafts can also serve as presents, they can help children create lasting gifts for parents at Valentine's Day, Mother's Day, Father's Day, or Christmas.

For your help in planning, these activities include a "skill quotient" to tell you what age child can be expected to finish these crafts successfully. An easy project might be acceptable for kindergartners or first-graders; a medium project might be appropriate for second-, third-, and fourth-graders; a difficult project might be reserved for fifth- or sixth-graders. However, you as a leader should know your children well enough to determine which projects will be attainable for your particular group.

⮕ When you're making a craft with children (or adults, for that matter), look for foolproof projects that can be completed within the allotted time. The teacher should know how to make the project, and should indeed have a finished sample on hand to show children what they're working to create. People do not complete craft projects after they have gone home; make an effort to work with the children until a successful project has been finished. And don't forget to buy extra materials in case extra people attend, or replacement parts are needed.

Candy Rose

Materials: Two Hershey's Kisses® for each rose; red cellophane wrap; green floral tape; artificial stem or lollipop stick; artificial rose leaves (optional); ribbon
Skill Quotient: Medium
Time: ⧗
Planning: ★★

These pretty little rosebuds make a great gift for mothers or for teachers, or for anyone else who would appreciate a token of affection. To make them, hold the two Hershey's Kisses® with the flat sides together. Smoothly and tightly wrap the piece of cellophane over the tip of one of the kisses and down over the other kiss. Give the excess cellophane a twist below the tip of the second kiss. Lay the stem on top of the excess cellophane and hold snugly. Start wrapping the floral tape around the stem and cellophane just beneath the kisses, making sure to wrap a little onto the point of the bottom kiss. Add an artificial leaf close to the "bud" while wrapping the tape down the stem. Make sure to overlap the floral tape and pull it tight. When you reach the bottom, tear off the excess tape. Tie a bow onto the stem with the ribbon.

Candy Heart

Materials: Clear vinyl (can get it by the yard at the fabric store); paper hole punch; red yarn; candy
Skill Quotient: Easy
Time: ⌛⌛
Planning: ★★

To prepare, find a heart pattern, or make your own pattern for a five-inch heart. Trace the heart onto the vinyl several times. You will need two vinyl hearts per candy heart. Lay two vinyl hearts on top of each other and punch holes every half inch along the edges, about ¼-inch from the edge. Cut yarn into three-foot lengths and put tape around one end of each length of yarn. (Hint: Before cutting all the yarn, try lacing one heart together to make sure that your heart size and the size of the yarn are compatible.)

To assemble the hearts, give each child a set of vinyl hearts and a section of yarn. Have the children begin lacing the heart together by sticking the taped end of the yarn through the hole at the top of the heart, leaving a tail of about six inches to be used to tie a bow when the lacing is done. Stitching is done by bringing the yarn up and over the edge of the vinyl and then back up through the next hole. The stitches will loop around the edge of the heart. Continue lacing the heart to within two inches of the top. At this point, help the child fill the heart with small candies, being careful to not overfill. Finish lacing the heart until you reach the starting point. Tie both ends of the yarn into a bow, and snip off the ends of the yarn to even up the bow. If the children would like to write a message on the heart, they could use a permanent marker.

Shannon's Favorite Play Clay

Materials: For each child, one cup each flour, water, and salt; 1 tablespoon cream of tartar; food coloring
Skill Quotient: Easy
Time: ⌛
Planning: ★★

Mix all ingredients and cook on low heat until a ball forms. Take out of pan and knead in a few drops of color at a time until the clay is the right shade. Store dough in plastic bags. This clay is ideal for making Noah's ark and animals, or to illustrate Book of Mormon stories in Primary classes.

Tiny Gingerbread Houses

Materials: Half-pint milk cartons; brown grocery bags or brown construction paper; white glue; stapler; colored markers; edible decorations such as sugared cereals, cake decorations, candies, miniature marshmallows
Skill Quotient: Easy
Time: ⌛
Planning: ★★

These gingerbread houses are not edible, but are fun and quick for children to decorate. Thoroughly wash and dry the empty milk cartons. Cut a piece of brown paper sized to wrap around the four sides of the milk carton. Glue in place. Cut a piece of brown paper sized to cover the peak and make a V-shaped roof. Staple or glue this into place. Let the children use the markers to draw on windows and doors if they choose to do so. Then have them glue on the edible decorations to create a "gingerbread house" effect.

Camping Activities

Many children love the concept of camping, and you don't even need to do the actual camping to make them happy. Instead, you can make camp gear as an activity, or do camp-style activities without having to spend the night in the woods. Camping teaches resourcefulness and an appreciation for nature. Even if you have no intentions of having an actual camping experience, you can have a camping party activity right in the ward meetinghouse—or even in the parking lot.

Make Your Own Camp Gear

Materials: Listed below with each item
Effort Quotient: ♉♉
Time: ⌛
Planning: ★★

▶ Puffy Camp Cushion

You will need two 16x16-inch pieces of vinyl for each child (use a shower curtain); newspapers; a hole punch; yarn and yarn needle; and a pair of scissors. Place the two pieces of vinyl together with wrong sides facing each other and right sides facing out. Punch holes about one inch apart and approximately one inch from the edge through both pieces at the same time. Use the yarn and needle to sew three sides and half of the fourth side together with a whipstitch. Tear newspaper into strips and stuff it into the cushion case. Continue stuffing the cushion until the right amount of cushioning for you is achieved. Stitch the rest of the fourth side with the yarn. Tie off the yarn with a tight knot, and sit on your personal camp cushion.

▶ Soap-on-a-Rope

For each child, you will need a bar of soap and 1½ to 2 feet of heavy cord. You will also need one large nail. Before the activity, the adult leader should work a hole in each bar of soap with the nail. The children can thread the cord through the hole and tie a strong knot. When they get to your campsite, children can hang the cord from a tree branch to keep the soap clean and dry between uses.

▶ Cattail Mat

You will need cattail leaves, scissors, and shipping tape. If you are camping near any kind of wet area, you will be able to find cattails growing there. Have an adult use the scissors to cut down a large bundle of cattail leaves close to the ground. Take them to a flat area and lay the leaves one at a time, side-by-side until they are as wide as a placemat or a mat to sit on. Once this is done, insert another leaf crosswise to the ones laying on the ground, weaving it over a leaf, under the next, and continuing this pattern to the end of the leaves lying on the ground. Get another leaf and weave it the same as the first except that you will begin by going under a leaf first, and over the next. As each new leaf is woven into the mat, be sure to push it tight against the previous one so you won't have any loose spots or spaces in the mat. When you have finished all the weaving, trim the edges with the scissors and press half the width of the tape around all four edges on the top of the mat. Fold the other half of the tape over and press it onto the bottom side of the mat. This will hold all the weaving in place.

Under-Water Watcher

Materials: 1 cardboard-type milk carton for each child; plastic wrap; large rubber bands or duct tape; scissors
Effort Quotient: 🖐
Time: ⧗
Planning: ★★

Adults should cut off the top of each milk carton to make a cube that is open on one side. Cut another opening in the bottom of the carton. This will be the window. Children can place plastic wrap over the window and partially up the sides of the carton. Pull it tight. Duct tape or rubber band the plastic wrap into place. To view what's beneath the dark surface of still water, lower the watcher into the water, window first, and look through the clear bottom. When this is placed in the water correctly, you will be looking into the milk carton from where the top was cut off. Use a small flashlight to help illuminate objects under the water.

Rock Collecting with a Soil-Sifting Screen

Materials: An old, sturdy wooden picture frame; mesh window screen (cut a piece that is large enough to fit over the frame); tacks and hammer or staple gun (with grown-up help); old spoon to dig with; empty egg carton; glue; marker; rock and mineral field guide
Effort Quotient: 🖐🖐
Time: ⧗
Planning: ★★

Make the soil-sifting screen by stretching the screen across the picture frame and either tacking or stapling it every inch around the entire frame. *Make sure you pull the screening as tightly as possible before tacking.* When you sift the dirt, make sure the wooden frame part is on the bottom and the tacked side is facing up. This keeps the screen from being torn lose by the weight of the dirt and rocks. Scoop some dirt onto the screen and sift the dirt through the holes by rubbing your hand gently back and forth over the dirt. It will fall through the holes, and the rocks, roots, and sticks will stay on the screen. Look through your siftings to see if you have any rocks or fossils you might want to add to a collection. After children have collected the rocks and other samples they want, they can glue the treasures into the egg carton. Label each one with the date that it was found, where it was found, and what it is. Use the field guide to identify any items that may be unfamiliar.

Flip-a-Coin Hike

Materials: Coin, paper, pencil
Effort Quotient: ✹✹✹
Time: ⧖
Planning: ★

Take the coin, the paper, a pencil, and your Primary class out for a hike. Every five minutes, have a child flip the coin to see if you should go left or right. Help the children use the paper and pencil to make a map of your hike so you can find your way back again. Also, make sure you mark the trail clearly to make the return easy.

Outdoor Golf Course

Materials: Toy golf clubs, curved sticks, or clubs made from rolled-up newspaper and tape; golf balls; nine or more empty soup cans; nine small paper cups; nine foot-long sticks; black marker; spoon or garden trowel for digging; can opener
Effort Quotient: ✹✹✹
Time: ⧖
Planning: ★★

Choose a good place for your golf course. Look for an area that is away from where other people are camping or fishing. Plan out your course, deciding where each of the nine holes will go. Use the spoon or garden trowel to dig holes big enough to hold a can, so that the top of the can is level with the ground or even just below ground level. Pat the soil back around the can. Turn the paper cups upside-down and write a number—from one to nine—on each. Pound the foot-long sticks into the ground next to each hole and hang a numbered cup on each stick to mark the holes. If you have extra cans, use the can opener to cut off the other end of the cans to create tunnels that the ball must pass through between holes. Make sure to pull the cans out of the ground, fill in the holes, and pick up all trash when you're finished golfing.

Camp Crafts

Materials: Listed below with each craft
Effort Quotient: ♆♆♆
Time: ⧖
Planning: ★★★

▶ Twiggies

You will need to gather supplies from nature, such as twigs, moss, pine needles, pinecones, and bark. You will also need small white pebbles or seeds, glue, and a fine-tipped black marker. A Twiggie is an unusual creature because it gives full rein to a child's creativity. Gather together your supplies. Decide how you want your Twiggie to look. Do you want to create a person Twiggie, or an animal Twiggie? How about a replica of your favorite pet, or your pesky little brother or sister? Don't forget about the beautiful deer with the large set of antlers that you saw last year. Break the twigs to fit the shape you want. Glue the pieces together. Glue the white pebbles or seeds in place to form eyes and nose, and use the marker to make them look like eyes. When the Twiggie is finished, brush a coat of thinned glue over it to give it a shiny look. When it is completely dry, use moss for hair and leaves or dried grass for clothing.

▶ Nutty-Buddies

You will need: nuts in shells (various kinds), small wiggly eyes (from a craft store), white glue, ribbons, yarn, and a variety of trims, such as mini pompons. Have the children look for small pieces of wood or bark that can serve as platforms for a Nutty-Buddy or Nutty-Buddy family. Place the nuts, glue, and all other supplies on tables. Have each child first glue one or more nuts on his piece of wood. Children can build a Nutty-Buddy family by gluing more than one nut on the same piece of wood. Let the glue dry before continuing with the decorations. When ready, let the children decorate the nuts to look like faces. This craft can be done with smooth stones as well, but those aren't Nutty-Buddies, they are called Rock Jocks.

▶ **Totem Poles**

You will need: empty thread spools (wooden are best and can be obtained at a craft store), pencils, scissors, paint and brushes or colored markers, paper, and white glue. Give each child four or five spools to decorate with paint or colored markers. Let them use their imagination to cut out beaks, tails, wings, or any other parts they would like from the paper. Glue these in place. When the spools dry, glue them together. Bigger totem poles can be made from large soup cans, #10 cans, or even round oatmeal containers.

Questions from the Clueless

? *As an activity planner, what can I do about discipline problems? We have a child in the Primary who is totally out of control, and who ruins every activity. How do I deal with this?*

This is a very delicate situation. On one hand, some disruptive children may have a medical condition that makes it hard for them to sit still. Other troublemakers may be desperately seeking attention they can't get elsewhere. These children need love and understanding.

However, no child should be allowed to hold the rest of the Primary hostage. Somehow, the disruptive child's behavior should be controlled so the other children can enjoy the activity.

Fortunately for you, this is a problem that is bigger than you are. You should take your concern to the Primary president and have her offer suggestions. If you *are* the Primary president, the matter should be discussed with the bishopric counselor who advises the Primary, or with the bishop himself.

Before you go up the ladder, you may want to determine if seeking help is even necessary. Your first recourse should be fervent prayer, which may give you all the answers you need. If after prayer you still don't know how to deal with the problem, prepare yourself with ideas that can potentially ease the situation. The child may need a parent at each activity, or perhaps an adult or teenager can be called as a companion to him. Maybe a conversation with the child's parents or even the child himself may give illuminating answers. Take your list of possible suggestions to your Primary president and see what she suggests.

In any case, the actual decision belongs to the Primary president, working in conjunction with the bishopric. Together, you should be able to come up with a decision that will be fair and compassionate to everyone involved.

CHAPTER 6
Service:
The Feel-Good Chapter

★ **IN THIS CHAPTER**
 ✔ Giving Service to Ward Members
 ✔ Performing Service in Your Community
 ✔ Planning Missionary Service Projects
 ✔ Questions from the Clueless

No self-respecting book written about activities would consider itself complete if it did not include at least one chapter on service and service-related activities. Here is that chapter, just for you.

We've started where a ward activities book should start, with service activities that are given by ward members, to ward members. From there we've branched out to services that can be given from ward members to benefit the community. The chapter ends with some great activities to spice up your ward's missionary effort.

Some of the projects in this chapter require a whole lot of work; others require an hour or two of free time. But no matter which service activity you choose, you'll help at least two groups of people when your ward or auxiliary group performs a service—the givers and the receivers.

By the time you've skimmed the ideas in this chapter, you should have some general ideas relating to the breadth and expanse of service that can be rendered. As you can plainly see, each idea has at least two or three variations. Although it is easy to think about service during the holiday season, the idea is to keep the spirit of service throughout the entire year. If you do nothing else other than smile more than you did the day before, you are well on your way to making your community a better place in which to live.

One more thing before we move into the meat and potatoes of service activities is to acknowledge that there are many reasons why we get involved and participate in service projects. Some reasons are noble and some are pretty selfish. Don't be discouraged if you find your group participating in service activities for the wrong reasons. Many times the giver learns a lesson along the way and ends up giving service for the right reasons, even if he didn't start out that way. But even if the lesson isn't learned this time around, the act of service can help people despite the giver's motivations. As Congresswoman Connie Morella once said, "It doesn't matter who gets credit, it only matters what gets done."

Service Begins at Home

There's a great need for ward members to serve other ward members. A ward is a miniature city, and every home in that city has a different set of problems and challenges. Even though the Relief Society is dedicated to the task of helping those in need, providing for the needs of all the ward members, all the time, is more than any Relief Society can handle.

These projects represent ways ward members can serve one another. Later on we'll expand to projects that allow ward members to help other members of the community.

Volunteer Bank Staffing

Everyone has talents that others don't have, or abilities that others are unable to perform. You may not think that being able to efficiently and quickly rake leaves is a gift, but it could be a great blessing to someone who can't get out in the yard and do the work.

If there are needs in your ward that are not being fulfilled, consider establishing a volunteer bank to match people with projects. This can work in several ways. It can be organized as a direct exchange, where people take services in exchange for something else. Or it can be organized as an indirect exchange, where Thelma Jones may volunteer to bake cookies for Joe Smurf, who will mow the lawn for Kitty Culpepper, who will do some grocery shopping for Thelma Jones. Or it can be organized on a no-return policy, where volunteers are matched with people who need help, without needing any service in return.

Coordinating a volunteer bank is a big job. The coordinator will have to come up with a list of volunteers, as well as a list of the tasks that each volunteer is willing to perform and a schedule of how often the volunteer will be available. Even harder will be the job of coming up with recipients. Some ward members may need the services but be reluctant to impose on fellow Saints, but other ward members may request more than their share. In any case, kindness and tact—as well as a backbone—are essential qualities for the volunteer bank coordinator.

Staffing a volunteer bank doesn't have to involve the whole ward. This can be a project that is sponsored by the Young Men or Young Women organizations, which then perform services for people who need them. Priesthood quorums or the Relief Society may want to consider a volunteer bank, or it can be sponsored under the auspices of the activities committee.

No matter who sponsors the volunteer bank in your ward, you're going to need sample talents that people can donate or exchange. Here are a few to get you started:

- Shop for someone who is incapacitated
- Mow a lawn
- Organize a yard sale for someone else
- Create a piece of artwork or a craft to give to someone
- Rake the leaves
- Shovel the snow
- Paint, wallpaper, or do other home improvement projects
- Organize a closet
- Baby-sit
- Do laundry
- Run errands
- Take someone to a doctor's appointment
- Prepare and deliver a meal to someone.
- Plant flowers in someone's yard
- Help someone study for a test or organize a term paper
- Take someone shopping for a prom dress
- Sew, knit, or crochet an item for someone else
- Teach a skill (artwork, music, or some other talent)
- Chauffeur someone else's children to seminary
- Clean a kitchen

White Elephant Service Exchange

Materials: Gift-wrapped, white elephant gifts with a service note included—one per person who attends; decorations; light refreshments

Effort Quotient: ✹

Timing: ⌛

Planning: ★★

➡ This activity is appropriate for the Relief Society sisters or the Young Women organization in a ward. The object of a white elephant service exchange is to share talents with other people by offering service to others. Each woman who attends should come with a wrapped package that contains an offer of service. Here are some sample ideas to get you started:

- Cook an Italian meal (or some other specialty) and deliver it to the home of the recipient.

- Bake homemade bread once a month for the recipient.

- Baby-sit a family of children for an evening or a weekend.

- Paint a ward member's bathroom.

- Write a holiday letter for a family in the ward.

- Clean a cluttered closet.

- Spend ten hours doing family history research for the recipient.

- Do a person's visiting teaching for the month. (This one is very popular among women who are soon to be incapacitated by childbirth.)

- Make a braided rug for the recipient.

- Wash the recipient's windows.

- Give a haircut, a tinting, or a permanent to a woman who wants one. (Only offer this service if you're qualified to do so!)

- Do temple work for the recipient's family names.

- Do the recipient's grocery shopping for a week.

- Make a Christmas nativity scene for the recipient, or take young family members Christmas shopping for their parents.

- Make homemade stationery for the recipient.

As you can see, the gifts that are offered at a white elephant service exchange are limited only by the imagination of the donors. Any talent a woman has can be appreciated by somebody else. Indeed, seeing how important her talents are to others is one of the benefits of hosting a white elephant service exchange.

Be sure that everyone who attends the activity donates a gift. Keep some gift wrap on hand in case women arrive without having been prepared, and help them think of possible services to donate if they're having trouble.

Once every participant has a wrapped service to donate, the activity is similar to a white elephant exchange, with the exception that presents are unwrapped as they are received. Everyone sits in a circle, with the attractively wrapped gifts in the center. Select a person to go first, perhaps singling out the woman whose birthday is the closest to the date of the party. That person chooses an item from the center of the floor and unwraps it, telling everyone what treasure she has been given. Then go left around the circle, with each person having a choice of taking any gift from the center or stealing a service that was selected by someone who went before. Whenever a woman's white elephant is stolen, she must take another item from the center of the circle or from somebody else's lap. (A player can't steal back something that was just stolen away, but she can reclaim a cherished treasure if the opportunity presents itself later.) Swapping and stealing goes on until all the presents have been distributed.

Make sure to have some sort of follow-through after the event. Perhaps there can be a time limit on when the services can be claimed. After the services have been claimed, make sure to publicize some of the success stories to inspire women to participate next year.

Tithing Settlement Care Packages

The bishop is an unsung hero all year, but no time is more stressful for him than the annual tithing settlement. At a time when most families are spending their holidays together, the bishop and his financial clerk have the responsibility of meeting with every member of every family in the ward to determine tithing status. Not only that, but the bishop also uses this meeting to check up on families in the ward and visit with each member for only a moment or two, just to make sure there are no hidden problems that he should be aware of.

Because so many families have to be met, the bishop and those who assist him will often go directly to the ward meetinghouse from work, or stay at the meetinghouse all day on a Saturday or Sunday, just to finish their task. They have to do this, but they don't have to be hungry while they're doing it.

If your ward auxiliary is looking for a holiday service activity, you may want to consider taking care packages to the people who are working on tithing settlement. This should consist of food that can be consumed in hurried gulps between appointments. This isn't a good time to make submarine sandwiches. Finger food is more appropriate. Some foods to consider are these:

- Cookies
- Small sandwiches that aren't messy
- Chips, with or without dip
- Single-serving bottles of water or juice
- Candy
- Small pieces of fruit (grapes are excellent, as are many dried fruits)
- Vegetable sticks, with or without dip
- Bite-sized appetizers that taste good cold

If your organization takes on this project, the first thing you'll need to obtain is the bishop's schedule for tithing settlement. The best person to give you this is the ward financial clerk, who will be on hand for every appointment. Be sure to ask him to let you know if additional appointment days are added to the calendar! The financial clerk should also be able to tell you how many people will be helping the bishop during tithing settlement. You can't feed just the bishop without providing food for the clerks and counselors who are on hand to help him.

After you know how many days are involved, the next thing to do is to coordinate your activity with the bishop's wife. She can tell you if the bishop has any food allergies or any favorite (or unfavorite) snack foods. Working with her will also guarantee that she won't make a big meal for her husband before sending him off to tithing settlement. After all, feeding the bishop at tithing settlement is a service to the bishop's wife as well as to the bishop.

After you have talked to the ward financial clerk and the bishop's wife, the next thing to do is to make your assignments. Members of your organization can sign up for different days, or your auxiliary members can work as a group. The bishop and his assistants will obviously not need as much food if they're meeting for two hours one evening as they will if they're meeting from sunup to sundown on a Saturday, and this should be taken into account.

Once you and your organization have committed to supply food at tithing settlement, make sure you follow through. If food is promised, it should be delivered. The bishop and his assistants may not have asked for this service, but they'll look forward to it once they know it's coming. Don't let them starve on your account.

Adopt a Missionary

This is an especially good activity for the youth, and it works equally well to serve either the missionaries assigned to your ward or the elders or sisters from your ward who are serving in other places. Some of the adoption activities might include the following:

- Taking turns writing monthly letters

- Making and decorating special cards (Christmas, birthday, other special days) to send your missionaries

- Taking pictures of your class and sending them with personal notes from your class members, telling the missionaries how much the class members love and appreciate them

- Baking cookies and clipping articles out of the local newspaper to send to your missionaries

No matter how you do it, the idea is to make sure your missionaries know that they are thought of often and that your youth appreciate the importance of missionary work.

Ward Gardens

If someone in the ward has a plot of land to donate to the cause, you're on your way to a ward garden. Ward gardens can be subdivided into family-sized portions, with each portion being planted, weeded, and watered by the family who is assigned to that piece of ground. Or the garden can be planted and maintained by a ward auxiliary, with the fruits of their labors being distributed to widows and shut-ins. Youth are especially good at dealing with gardens, and they're likely to want to take on a project like this if boys and girls can work together.

Shopping for Shut-ins

If your ward doesn't want to take on anything as extensive as a volunteer bank, consider shopping for shut-ins as an auxiliary project. This is an ideal activity for busy priesthood quorums because it is relatively simple and doesn't take a lot of time.

There are numerous ways to organize a shopping for shut-ins project. The activity can be done only once, or it can become an ongoing activity. Shut-ins can be paired up with priesthood members via home teaching assignments, or assignments can be made in other ways.

The most common way to shop for shut-ins is to pick up grocery or pharmacy items for them. However, there may be occasions when other items need to be purchased—items from discount stores, Christmas trees, automotive supplies, or home repair supplies. Be assured that female shut-ins wouldn't ask a priesthood holder to pick up a pair of pantyhose or other female item. Most shopping that is done by men for widows would consist of staples such as bread, milk, and cheese.

The shut-in should give a detailed list to the volunteer before the shopper ever leaves on the shopping expedition. Don't forget to find out what size cans or bottles are needed before you find yourself looking at a shelf of similar items at the supermarket. If brand names are specified, the shut-in may want to tell the shopper which store carries that particular brand. The shut-in should either give the volunteer enough cash to pay for the purchases, or should reimburse the volunteer with a personal check at the time of delivery.

Adult Baby-sitting Co-ops

This is an activity that can be a great boon to the members of your ward who participate. Assemble a group of parents whose child-rearing skills you trust. Offer to trade baby-sitting chores with other members of the co-op.

The most effective way to run the co-op is to do it on a credit system. Credits can be awarded per fifteen-minute increments, awarding one credit per child who is being watched. It goes without saying that there are some children who should be worth a whole lot more credits than other children, but there may not be any way to take that into account without hurting someone's feelings. Additional credits should also be awarded to a sitter who feeds a meal to children, or who acts as a chauffeur.

The participating parents should get together ahead of time and determine what the rules are, as well as how those rules should be enforced. There should also be a coordinator to determine whose turn it is to do the sitting, because parents may not end up watching the children of the parents who tended their own children last time. Be sure to provide a peaceful way to resolve any disagreements that may come up. Baby-sitting co-ops should make parenting easier, but not at the expense of having to call the bishop in as referee.

Adopt a Family for Sacrament Meeting

Every bishopric member or ward clerk who sits on the stand in sacrament meeting represents a father who is not able to help his wife take care of their children during the meeting. Other men are lost to stake callings such as the high council, and still other families don't have fathers at all. If you're looking for an excellent ongoing youth activity, one option is to have young women, and young men who are not needed to pass the sacrament, adopt a family to offer help during sacrament meeting.

If you're considering having youth adopt a family, several things need to be considered:

- The volunteer can't be someone who is needed to ride herd on his own brothers and sisters.

- The volunteer cannot be someone who himself needs a chaperone. For this reason, youth should absolutely not go in pairs to take care of children. If they go in pairs, they're likely to visit with one another instead of performing their duties, making more noise than the children would make without the "help."

- The volunteer should be someone who relates well to children, and who can play with them quietly or perform other tasks that may be directed by the mother.

- No young man or young woman should volunteer if he comes from a family where youth are strictly expected to sit with their parents during sacrament meeting. A small number of parents are adamant about having the family sit together, and their wishes should be honored. Even if mothers need the services a youth can offer, service should not be given at the risk of antagonizing the youth's own parents.

Meals on Wheels

One of the functions of the Relief Society is to provide food to people in need. However, some wards have so many new mothers or such an extensive list of shut-ins that additional help is appreciated. One option for a youth group is to have them volunteer to lend a hand providing meals for

families with special needs. The bishop or the Relief Society president may be able to offer names of families who would benefit from this project.

In the case of elderly shut-ins, a visit may be appreciated even more than the food. When your volunteers deliver a meal, make sure they deliver a little friendship and companionship as well. They needn't stay long—a five-minute visit is usually sufficient. Volunteers should stay long enough to find out if the recipient has other needs and to make the recipient feel loved and appreciated.

When you're considering Meals on Wheels as a service project, don't overlook the older Primary-age children. Meals can also be delivered in wagons, and visits from children may be especially enjoyed by the recipient of the food.

Finally, don't forget to take food to shut-ins after ward dinners. If the ward has served a nice meal and there is food left over, people who have missed the festivities may be considerably cheered by being offered some of the food.

Baby-sitting Squads

This is a great activity for getting the youth of your congregation involved in service activities. But is also extremely helpful for parents who are the recipients of the service.

Having youth do volunteer baby-sitting can be especially helpful for a single parent during the holiday season, allowing the parent to do holiday shopping. But it can also be helpful during ward adult activities, such as temple excursions and dinners. Youth baby-sitting could also be a birthday gift to a single parent or a parent with special needs. Mother's Day is a good opportunity to do volunteer sitting—as long as the sitters don't neglect their own mothers on that hallowed day. Think about offering sitting services during the monthly Relief Society enrichment night, too.

As the youth get more organized, they will enjoy coming up with excuses to volunteer to help out a single parent. For example, this could include watching the kids during a total or partial eclipse of the sun, on Groundhog Day, or at any other time when the parent might appreciate some free time alone.

Flower Patrol

Most ward meetinghouses in the United States are decorated with silk flowers and silk plants. Some of these artificial decorations look almost real, but others bear little resemblance to any flower that appears in nature—especially when the silk imitations are coated with a thick layer of dust.

Unfortunately, budget constraints will probably never allow for real flowers in the chapel during sacrament meeting. But real flowers are appreciated by worshippers, and can greatly enhance the spirit of reverence. If you want to launch a service project that will brighten the lives of others, you may want to consider having your group provide flowers on Sunday throughout the year. These can be grown in home gardens, or the participants can communally farm the same plot of ground by planting and tending bulbs and seeds. During weeks when no flowers are blooming, the ward can always fall back on the silk plants. In fact, looking at those silk plants during the off weeks will make ward members appreciate your contributions all the more.

As a variation to the Sunday flower group, you may want to think of having your group plant flowers in the beds around the meetinghouse. These can be replaced as the season passes so that flowers adorn the grounds from early spring until the last days of autumn.

Twelve Days before Christmas

This is a great service activity that can be done right before (say twelve days before) a holiday, such as Christmas. The object is for your group or quorum to adopt a member of the group who doesn't usually attend church activities, and give some sort of recognition to that person for the twelve days before Christmas. To make this service activity even more fun, do it anonymously.

Decide what you want to do for the twelve days and then divide up the days by the number in your group. You will need to gear your surprises to the age and gender of the recipient. For example, for a teacher-age boy, gifts might include: one box of donuts, two movie tickets, three bags of candy, four cans of soda, five packs of gum, and so on. Sponsoring a Twelve Days before Christmas project can be as much fun for the givers as for the receivers.

A variation on this theme is to be "Christmas Pixies" and do three weeks of Christmas service projects for the three weeks leading up to Christmas. For example, the first week could be dedicated to your community. Activities might include visiting, singing, and helping out at a rest home or local hospital. The second week could be dedicated to your neighborhood. Activities might include baking cookies and delivering them to your local police, firemen, or public works office. The third and final week could be dedicated to your fellow ward members, your family, or your extended family. Activities might include writing and delivering Christmas cards, doing extra chores around the house, or volunteering to wrap presents.

Mixed-up Holiday Service Activity

This activity can be so much fun for the participants that they won't even know they are performing a service. Choose one of the minor holidays, such as Valentine's Day or President's Day, or even New Year's Eve. The object is to celebrate that holiday by doing service activities geared to other holidays in the year. For example, if your group picks Valentine's Day, and has chosen to deliver cookies to shut-ins, sick people, or rest homes, the cookies may be in the shape of Thanksgiving turkeys or Easter eggs, and the delivery may be made in Halloween costumes. Don't forget to sing Christmas carols when you deliver the goods!

After making your deliveries, return to the meetinghouse to have a dance or play a few games, followed by the inevitable refreshments.

Volunteer Yard Work

Have the bishop give you a list of families in your ward that are in need of general yard work. Divide up your group and fit the tasks with the talents of your group members. This type of service activity can be done either overtly or covertly. You'll probably be able to accomplish a lot more if you work with your various families and schedule the things that need to be done. This is especially helpful if the mother or father is ill, traveling, or otherwise unavailable. This type of volunteer work can include watering, snow shoveling, raking leaves, cutting lawns, trimming hedges, painting exterior walls, and many other jobs that may need extra hands to get done. This service project is also not just limited to members; you can include nonmember friends as recipients or volunteers. This can be a great missionary project, or it can soften the hearts of people who would otherwise be hostile to Church members.

Bishop's Chore Corps

Most bishops spend so much time providing service for others that they may neglect their own yard work and home repairs. This is where your group comes in. Working in conjunction with the bishop's wife, compile a list of "honey-do" projects that the bishop just can't get to. One by one, work to knock each project off your list.

This is a great service activity for the youth, and it may be even more fun if your group conspires with the bishop's wife to do the work without ever letting the bishop know how "his" household chores are being done. The end results will be a grateful bishop and nicer surroundings for the bishop's wife. Have a lot of fun with this one.

Meetinghouse Cleaning Crews

In an effort to save tithing dollars and teach Church members personal responsibility, Church officials have asked that members be responsible for doing the regular cleaning of ward meetinghouses. This includes making sure the bathrooms, classrooms, chapel, hallways, sacrament area, and entrance areas are cleaned and vacuumed and that the trash has been taken out, at least once a week.

Depending on the number of people in your family or group, the total time commitment to clean a meetinghouse is usually less than three hours. Make a game out of it by enlisting members of your organization to be responsible for different areas of the building. You could even start out the activity with a breakfast or end it with a light dinner, snack, or dessert. You may want to offer an extra incentive for volunteers by awarding small prizes or certificates at the end of the project, tailored to individuals who did the work.

If you want to go the extra mile, have your group volunteer to help clean another church, not of our faith, in your area. This can be an especially rewarding experience, and can lead to a lot of goodwill and possibly a missionary opportunity or two.

Service Projects for the Neighborhood

Charity may begin at home, but it shouldn't end there. Performing acts of service in the community can have a twofold benefit. In addition to providing a service for our towns and neighborhoods, it also demonstrates that Latter-day Saints are good citizens and neighbors. The eyes of the world are on Church members, and every act of kindness we perform reflects kindly on our religion.

One caution, however, is that if we fail to follow through on our service commitments, we're not just giving ourselves a black eye. People who are unfamiliar with our doctrine can judge the Church only by what they see our members do. Just as performing acts of service gives us a good name in the neighborhood, promising to serve and then failing to do so is worse than never making the commitment. Before you decide to sponsor an act of community service, make sure you have enough people to fulfill your promises. Once you make that promise, it's up to you to make sure the promise is kept—even if it means having your family do the work that was agreed upon by an entire Scout troop.

Used-Goods Collection Drives

This is a great service project that could involve your Young Men and Young Women organizations. If it is organized properly, it doesn't take too much time or effort from any one group or individual.

The idea is to organize a drive to collect new or nearly new things that can then be donated to a local charity, library, shelter, or hospital. Most people have attics, basements, and garages that are packed full of things that could be much better utilized by somebody who can't afford to buy them. This project puts our clutter in the hands of people who would appreciate it more than we do.

The key to a successful collection is to set a start date and an end date. Because this is a good activity to do over a period of several months, it is essential to have a clean, dry place for storing and sorting items that have been collected. Items that are especially needed are new and used books, coats, and other types of clothing. However, it may appeal to your youth more to collect music tapes, as well as music and game CDs.

At the end of your collection effort, have a party to celebrate your achievement. You might ask a speaker to come from the organization that will receive your items, telling your group what the organization does and what kinds of help are needed.

Clean the Town

Occasionally your town may sponsor a citywide cleanup, a park cleanup, a school-yard cleanup, or any number of other community-wide cleanup efforts. This is a great way for Church members to get out and meet some of their neighbors, and to have neighbors rub shoulders with them.

Neighborhood cleanups often take place in the fall and spring. Fall is the time to rake leaves, cut grass, pull up flowers, mulch, and generally prepare areas for winter. Spring cleanup involves planting flowers, mulching, weeding, and generally preparing areas for the summer. Neighborhood cleanups can also take place after natural disasters or after a large community event, such as a fair or other celebration. There is plenty of opportunity for neighborhood participation in multiple cleanup efforts. Most are just a phone call or page in the local paper away.

National/Local Safety Week

Not only is this a great activity or series of activities for your group, it also is a great way to learn and practice good safety techniques. You or your group could volunteer to pass out smoke detectors and smoke alarms at a local fair or you could even go house to house or door to door. Your local fire department may even donate the smoke detectors and fire alarms. If that isn't possible, then you may be able to get a corporate sponsor to buy a large quantity of smoke detectors and fire alarms for donation to needy families. You could begin and end your activity at your local fire station with a picnic and talks on the importance of fire and home safety.

Adopt a Street, Trail, Park, Spot in Neighborhood

If you're willing to make a long-term commitment, this is an excellent activity that will be an ongoing project for a ward, a Scout troop, or just a group of families from the ward. The key here is *commitment,* because once the promise has been made, follow-through is mandatory.

As you have no doubt seen, people who adopt an area by promising to keep it clean are given a goodly amount of free publicity, in the form of a group name appearing on a metal placard to designate your area. This can be excellent advertising for the Church, if and only if the group follows through and keeps the area spotless. If the group promises to keep a specific area clean and then doesn't police the area on a regular basis, motorists will receive a negative impression of the Church every time they drive down that segment of the road or visit that particular neighborhood or section of parkland.

If you believe your group may be interested in adopting a street or park, the first step is to go to your city or county public works department. However, you may want to adopt a trail instead. In this case, contact your local forest service or Bureau of Land Management office for information. If you are interested in adopting a segment of your local neighborhood, there may be a neighborhood association that can help you get started. You will need plenty of tools, including rakes, hoes, clippers, brooms, and of course, plenty of waste containers. Many organizations that own the properties you'll tend will donate equipment to your group. Don't forget to have plenty of safety vests if you're going to be doing any cleanup near busy streets.

If the time comes that the ward wants to focus its efforts in other areas, be sure to go to the government agency and terminate your agreement. Keep the area clean even after the agreement is terminated—as long as your group name is on the sign. Adopting an area is no casual decision. Before you get involved with this sort of project, you and your group should know exactly what is expected of you (even during the summer months when everyone is on vacation, or during the dead of winter, when snow and ice may make outdoor activities dangerous and unpleasant).

This Old House

This project has different names in different areas, but the gist is to help renovate or build a house for a needy family or worthy group. Many organizations get involved in this type of endeavor, sometimes setting aside a day when numerous groups will go to different homes throughout the area and do some sort of renovation. Skilled technicians such as plumbers, roofers, electricians, general contractors, painters, and others are essential to the success of this type of service project, but there is plenty of work for everyone else to do. Unskilled workers can help haul building materials around the site, help paint, sweep, hammer, cut wood, deliver water, serve food to the other workers, make telephone calls, buy materials, clean up the work area, do some general gardening or deep cleaning of the home, and perform numerous other essential activities.

Building a house or doing any major renovations requires more than one day, and often several weekends. Participate as much or as little as your schedule may afford you; whatever service you and your group give will be greatly appreciated.

All ages, from senior Primary children to senior citizens can find something to do, so this activity is good as a whole ward project (especially if you provide some sort of off-site diversion for young children). Be sure to include the young men and young women so they can get the sense of accomplishment that comes from completing well a major task.

Special Olympics

Getting involved in any level of Special Olympics is exceptionally rewarding. Fortunately, Special Olympics is an organization that always has need of volunteers. Your whole ward, your auxiliary, or even individual ward members could volunteer to help at a local, state, national, or international Special Olympics. Some ways that help may be needed include the following:

- Judging events
- Selling tickets
- Officiating and scoring
- Escorting participants
- Housing Olympians
- Delivering food
- Translating for Olympians who speak other languages or need signing

Cheering and encouraging the participants is a prerequisite for any and all Special Olympics volunteer assistance. Contact your Special Olympics chapter and find out when the next competition will be taking place, and ask how you or your group can help out.

Adopt a Cemetery

Large cemeteries have custodians who are paid to take care of the grounds, but small cemeteries may have a desperate need for care. This is a great activity for an entire ward, elders quorum, or youth group. Grounds care is needed in the winter, just as it is in the summer. In the summer and fall, your group can volunteer to trim around the grave-stones, cut grass, trim hedges, collect garbage, rake leaves, and gener-ally clean and make aesthetic improvements to the cemetery grounds. In the winter, ensure that the entrance/exit roads are kept clear of snow and other debris. You can also ensure that snow is removed from the head-stones and grave sites.

One activity that may be greatly appreciated would be to put a flower at each headstone early on the morning of Memorial Day, so relatives vis-iting the graves will know their loved ones have been remembered. And don't forget to map the cemetery, making a record of the location of each headstone, together with the information that is recorded on it. As head-stones age, they begin to crumble, and information that isn't collected today may be lost tomorrow. If there is no place to keep such information, it may be appropriate to have it recorded at the local courthouse or kept in a local library.

Blood Donation

The Red Cross is always in need of whole blood, platelets, and plasma. A healthy person who weighs at least 105 pounds and is at least seventeen years of age can donate whole blood every fifty-six days.

Although people who have never donated blood may be nervous their first time around, they'll find that blood donation is really simple, relatively painless, and so vitally important that it's worth the sacrifice. Not only that, but donors are rewarded with orange juice and cookies to help them regain their strength.

From start to finish, donations usually take less than an hour, includ-ing the paperwork. Call 1-800-Give-Life for a donation center or blood drive near you. You can also call your local Red Cross for other types of volunteer services that are needed in your area. Blood drives are fre-quently organized by young men who are looking for an Eagle Scout proj-ect, but they can just as easily be sponsored by priesthood quorums and Relief Societies or a Laurel in need of a Personal Progress Value Project.

Adopt a Family

This type of service project is best done by a family, a Young Men or Young Women group, or even a Primary class. The object is to secretly adopt a family in your ward boundaries, member or nonmember, and do service projects for them for a certain period of time. The family that you adopt can be a family that needs help or even a family that seemingly has everything, but is in need of some extra friendship.

The challenge is to continue doing little acts of kindness for your chosen family without getting caught. Shovel their snow while they are at the store. Rake their leaves while they are at a movie. Wash the outside walls of their house while they are on vacation. Leave goodies, toys, gifts and the like at their doorstep, ring the bell, and run like crazy. The acts of kindness don't have to be elaborate activities, but simple things that will bring joy and satisfaction to your adopted family and a real sense of fun and accomplishment to your group.

When the time period ends, you may want to send an anonymous note telling the family you've enjoyed being their friend, and telling them you'll never forget the pleasure you had on their behalf.

Sneaky Secret

If you don't know how to hook up with service opportunities in your community, let your fingers do the walking. Most communities, by way of their city or county government, have hot lines or clearing houses for volunteer efforts. These clearing houses for volunteer services try to match volunteers with organizations and agencies according to the needs of the organizations and the interests and skills of the volunteers. For example, where the authors live in Loudoun County, Virginia, there are twelve organizations represented by the Office of Volunteer Services. These range from the Association for Retarded Citizens to the Office of Solid Waste.

If you don't know how to locate a volunteer clearing house, your local library can help you find organizations in need of your services, and you may find further resources by looking in your local telephone book or reading the local newspaper.

Abused Women's Shelter

Abused women's shelters exist in almost all of our communities, and there are always opportunities for donated time and efforts. These efforts range from helping move heavy furniture and doing general house and yard work to helping baby-sit some of the kids while the mothers rest, shop, or do other things. This type of service is great for a priesthood quorum or

Young Men or Young Women group, although you may want to check with the women's shelter and see if visits from men are allowed.

Helping at an abused women's shelter can be done on a one-time basis or as a regular program, depending on the needs of the shelter and the time commitment of the group. Don't just drop in, though. Call ahead and work out a schedule with the head of the shelter.

Many shelters house both women and their children. And the children are often overlooked on Easter, Halloween, Christmas, and other holidays. A ward could easily do a drive for Easter baskets and new toys, coloring books, crayons, and candy to fill the baskets with, then have them delivered to the shelter. This takes a huge burden off the mother who is trying to make a new life, and it gives the child a good memory to hold on to during this rough time.

Adopt a Statue

Taking care of a statue or monument is one way to show respect to the area and give something back to our community. Even if the grounds surrounding the statue are maintained by the city, other things often take precedence over cleaning, raking, washing, or mowing a small public area. Be on the lookout for untended sites, and pitch in as your group is able.

One advantage of finding a site and taking care of it without being asked is that your group won't have to make as formal or long-term a commitment as you would if you adopted a section of roadside. If you pick a statue and take care of it on a regular basis, you may not have the glory of a permanent placard erected next to the statue, but you also won't have to worry about recriminations if your group is less committed during summer vacations.

Beautifying the public areas of your town is good for the city, and it's also good for the people who do the work. As we work to make our surroundings cleaner and more beautiful, we also make our towns and cities more enjoyable places to live.

Local School Volunteers

There are many areas in your local school district where volunteer service can be rendered. You or your small group could volunteer to work in the library one or two mornings or afternoons per week. You could also volunteer to read to children who need extra reading time.

➲   But volunteer work doesn't end in the school library. Here are other areas where your volunteer efforts could be greatly appreciated:

- Do clerical work in a nearby school office.

- Offer free tutoring for students who need extra help.

- Help chaperone field trips.

- Help in a school play or band activity.

- Serve as teacher's aides.

- Do clerical work, such as copying, typing, or sending out E-mail for various teachers.

- Help coach a local sports team, run the concessions stand, or help sell tickets.

- Volunteer to referee sports events or like activities.

Volunteering at a local school depends on the amount of time you or your group are willing to commit and the type of assistance that is needed by the various schools in the area. You don't even have to have children enrolled in a school in order to serve as a volunteer. Regardless of how much—or how little—experience you have with children, your knowledge and talents can be put to good use.

Service Scavenger Hunt

A service scavenger hunt is similar to a regular scavenger hunt, but instead of just begging for useless items, you will be trading service for the things on your list. For example, one of the items on your list may be, "Collect a brochure at your local fire station on fire safety, and clean ten fire truck windows." Another suggestion might be, "Collect your bishop's signature, and wash his car." A third idea might be to "Collect a cup of water from a local stream, lake, or river, and fill two garbage bags with litter." The ideas are endless, and for that matter, the areas for meaningful service are also. The only real preparation for this activity is to make the list of things to be collected and the service that is to be rendered for each item on the list.

Rest Home Visitors

Plant some plants at a rest home or assisted living center. Or do mulching in the springtime, weeding in the summer, raking in the fall, and snow-shoveling in the winter. Most living centers have to pay for these services to be performed. By volunteering to do help with the yard work, your group can be a big help to the organizations involved. You could also brighten the lives of the residents by beautifying their surroundings.

When you're thinking of helping out at these centers, don't forget about volunteering to work inside with the residents. Help patients write letters to loved ones or address Christmas cards or birthday cards to loved ones and friends. Patients also need help getting ready for the day, or being moved around the facility. Volunteering to read to patients or helping patients with their meals is also a great service and is typically well received. Sometimes just volunteering to talk and be friendly goes a long way to bringing a smile to a person who needs it. Take a flower to the women on Mother's Day, or a small box of candy to the men on Father's Day. Find some way to show the residents they haven't been forgotten, and you'll be performing a service that one day you may wish for someone to perform for you.

Public Library Volunteers

Most public libraries have a staff member who handles and coordinates volunteer efforts and requests. Projects can involve shelving books, dusting and wiping bookshelves, helping repair covers or putting on temporary book covers, helping with summer and winter reading programs, helping set up chairs for larger group meetings, doing outside yard work, washing windows, and doing a number of other things. Helping with clerical and general communications is also a big help to the library staff because it allows them time to do more important library work. A simple call to the coordinator, stating your group size

Sneaky Secret

Volunteer efforts don't have to be big or important in order to make a difference. Whether you donate your time to help dust bookshelves at a local library or volunteer to host the Russian Ambassador to the United States, your efforts will be appreciated by someone. Even little acts of kindness go a long way toward relieving the burdens of our fellowmen.

and the amount of time you'll be able to donate, can get you on the road to helping out your community.

Thrift Shop Clothes Sorting

Most areas have thrift shops that cater to the less fortunate citizens in our communities. These thrift shops are strictly run on a volunteer basis, with the clerks, the cashiers, and the stockers all donating their time for free. Most thrift shops are open until later in the evening to accommodate their unique clientele, so volunteering after school or work shouldn't be too difficult. If having your group volunteer at a thrift shop appeals to you, contact your local thrift shop and ask about their policies and procedures on volunteering. You can also call your local county volunteer coordinator for assistance.

Animal Service Projects

Youth groups have a particular affinity for animals, so it should be easy to find animal-related projects for them to do as a group. Check with the local humane society or a pet shelter to see if volunteers are needed, and how you can help out.

If there isn't a place for you at an organized animal shelter, you can offer spontaneous help within the neighborhood. Volunteer to walk the dogs of shut-ins or to take care of animals while their owners are on vacation. You may also find elderly owners who could use help with bathing dogs, as well as caring for cats and other four-legged pets. You may be able to exercise other small animals or help clean their cages or boxes. Cleaning aquariums is nasty work, and your group may be able to volunteer their services in this area too.

Remember that volunteer work is just that. No payment can or should be received for your help. But that doesn't mean your help shouldn't be competent. Don't clean an aquarium or house-sit a pet if you don't know how to do it. Owners think of their pets as members of the family. They may not be able to pay for your services, but they'd rather not use your services at all if your "help" will culminate in a funeral service for little Flipper or Fluffy.

Post Office Elves

Have you ever wondered what happens to those letters that arrive at your local post office addressed to Santa Claus, the Easter Bunny, or the Tooth Fairy? Most of the time they just go into the dead letter drop. However, there are times when the letters have legitimate return addresses and the senders actually expect to receive a reply.

Here's where your assistance comes in. Have your young men or young women go the second mile and try to fulfill the wishes of the small senders. Ask your local Post Office to give these dead letters to your group. Then find someone with a creative mind to write responses where only a letter is needed, and someone with excellent handwriting to provide the penmanship. Others in your group can think up clever and unique ways to fill the wishes and requests. This can be a good character-building activity for your entire group because it shows them how fortunate they are to have so much. At the same time, performing this service may quite possibly fulfill the wishes of someone whose needs would otherwise be unfulfilled.

Missionary Service Projects

Missionary work is so central to our faith that every activity we perform should have a missionary aspect. Even if an activity doesn't have overt missionary implications, you never know when a nonmember is going to be invited to the event by one of the ward members. Equally common is that a member who never darkens the door of the meeting-house may show up to a ward party, even if he was dragged there kicking and screaming by a determined spouse. If your event is exciting enough, and if he is made welcome enough, that wayward member may come back to your next activity of his own volition.

There are numerous activities throughout this chapter that further the missionary efforts in your ward. Any act of service that is performed by our members reflects on our faith as well, which is why we have stressed several times during this chapter that care must be taken that service projects are performed to the best of our ability.

But sometimes you want to plan activities that have overt missionary implications. Several ideas for missionary projects follow on the next few pages. Don't limit yourself to these few projects, however. As you browse through the text of this book, be on the lookout for ways to adapt other activities to missionary service. A financial seminar that you are planning to help the members of your priesthood quorum may benefit the whole community. A craft day sponsored by the women of the ward may have particular appeal for women outside the Church. Whenever you plan an event, be aware of ways to expand your focus. Latter-day Saints don't have to knock on doors in order to do missionary work. Quite often, the best missionary service we can perform is through quiet acts of friendship and fellowship. One way to extend that hand of fellowship is to invite nonmember friends to nonthreatening activities such as the ones in this book.

Welcome Neighbor Packets

This is a great missionary project if you live in an area with a lot of turnover. The idea is to prepare a packet of useful community and neighborhood information, and present that packet to new families who move into the area. This is an excellent way to do a little missionary work without being too pushy.

Items that should be included in this packet are those that would be useful to someone who is new to the area. You can include such things as school locations and schedules, maps, and contact information for schools, governments, and other public facilities such as libraries and swimming pools. You might even want to get creative and include listings and reviews of restaurants in the area. Perhaps you could visit local merchants and get some discount coupons to include in the packets as well. And don't forget to revise the packet as needed to make sure the information it contains is current.

Because another purpose of the packet is to introduce the new family to the ward and the Church, make sure to include some material about those topics as well. You may have a welcome letter from the bishop, plus directions to the meetinghouse and meeting times. Include material about Church programs, such as the family history libraries and family home evening. Don't include so much church information that people are overloaded, though. In this case, a little information goes a long way.

Once the packets are complete, the next step is to come up with a method for identifying new families and delivering the packets to them. If you have a real estate agent in the ward, he can be a great help in identifying recent sales in your area. Existing ward members can also target new families who move into their neighborhoods.

The trickiest part of the Welcome Neighbor Packet project is the mode of delivery. The preferred method of delivery is to have a neighbor give it to the family, as part of welcoming them to the neighborhood. If no ward members live close by, have the packet delivered by stake missionaries or leaders from the ward. One tactic that does *not* work is to give a packet to every family in the ward and challenge everyone to distribute them when the opportunity arises. This sort of challenge guarantees that packets will end up trampled on the floor of the family automobile instead of being delivered to the home of people who would greatly benefit from their contents.

Neighborhood Cleaning Crew

If you want to create a lot of goodwill in the neighborhood around your meetinghouse, an excellent activity is to get a group together to do volunteer cleanup in the immediate neighborhood. This could include going door-to-door volunteering to rake leaves, pick up trash, mow lawns, wash windows, sweep driveways and gutters, walk dogs, and remove trash. Be sure to stress that there will be no charge for this activity, and that it is being performed as a neighborhood service by members of The Church of Jesus Christ of Latter-day Saints.

Another project that may be done in conjunction with the neighborhood cleanup (or shortly afterwards, when local residents may still recognize your faces) is to collect nonperishable goods for a local food bank. This can be done at the same time as the cleanup, or flyers can be passed out during the cleanup with a pickup at a later date.

Once the donations have been collected, everything should be sorted and delivered in boxes to the local food bank or homeless shelter. After everything has been delivered, return to the meetinghouse for pizza and root beer.

Christmas Cookbooks

This is an activity that emphasizes the culinary skills of ward members while also promoting goodwill in the community. The idea is to have ward members compile a book of Christmas recipes and thoughts, and then distribute that book free of charge to nonmembers in the community or to members of the ward who do not usually participate.

When choosing an editor, select someone from the ward who has good typing and desktop publishing skills. This should be done near the end of the summer so that there will be plenty of time to get the project completed before Christmas. Solicit Christmas recipes and stories from all ward members. You want the book to be a useful kitchen resource for the people who receive it, but you also want to use it to teach them a little about the Church and your ward. Perhaps the bishop should write an introduction, plus you should also include items such as meeting times and the phone numbers to reach ward leaders and the missionaries. Also include brief stories, quotes, traditions, and scriptures that emphasize the spiritual nature of Christmas and the fact that we are celebrating the birth of Christ. But make sure the main content of the book is recipes, because that's what will cause the recipients to keep the book on their kitchen shelves and refer to it throughout the year.

Print copies of the book on the ward copier, or using a local copy service if that is cheaper. You can probably get away with using standard letter-sized paper, perhaps folded in half so that it makes a small booklet just smaller than a hymn book. If your budget will allow, use heavier, colored paper for the cover.

There are a number of options for distributing the book. Home teachers, visiting teachers, auxiliary leaders, and priesthood leaders can deliver them to the members of the ward. Stake missionaries could visit the families in the neighborhood and leave a booklet as a gift. Individual members and families can be asked to give them to their neighbors. You may also wish to distribute the book as part of another activity, such as a community Christmas concert. Advertising the book as part of the concert may get people to attend who ordinarily would not. This gives you a double chance to influence them, as they feel the spirit of the program and then have that spirit reinforced by reading excerpts from the book.

Valuable Coupon Books

This concept is similar to the Christmas Cookbook, except that you give neighbors a "Valuable Coupon Book" instead. As they redeem the coupons throughout the coming year, this will bring them into contact with ward members and bring them to the ward building a number of times.

You can have a lot of fun and involve many ward groups in the design of the coupons. The youth may wish to offer a car wash in the summer, and then include a coupon so neighbors can bring their cars over for a free wash. You can also include coupons for ward events such as summer parties, Christmas parties, and talent shows. Also provide coupons that provide admission to educational activities such as financial planning and budgeting seminars, health fairs, and family history classes. Although most of these are offered without cost to any member of the public, having a date on a coupon will serve as a reminder throughout the year.

The biggest challenge to pulling off the activity is being able to plan things a year in advance so that the dates of the events can be listed on the coupons. For some events (family history instruction), you do not need to print a specific date on the coupon, but just list a number and have the coupon holders call for their free appointment. Another challenge is to devise a series of events that will really interest people, and will get them out to socialize with ward members on a regular basis.

Sponsor a Crèche Display

This is an activity that serves two functions. Its overt purpose is to get people into the Christmas spirit as they view manger scenes in your ward setting. But the second purpose is a missionary effort. So many people who are not familiar with the Church do not know of our deep commitment to Christ. Having an annual crèche display will remind them that Jesus Christ is at the center of our religion. What better missionary opportunity could there be during the Christmas season?

Organizing a crèche display is easy. Many people in your ward are likely to collect manger scenes, so it should be easy to get people to donate theirs to put on display in the cultural hall during the Christmas season. Because many of our members have been on foreign missions, you'll probably be able to find manger scenes from many of the world's nations. This is good, because you'll want a whole lot of them to make the display worthwhile, attractive, and interesting.

Find an attractive way to display the manger scenes, and make sure the local newspaper advertises the dates and times that the crèches will be on display. Also arrange for ward members to be on hand to keep children from touching or even walking off with the small pieces. Crowd control is important if you're expecting a lot of viewers.

As people exit the display, you may want to serve hot apple cider in disposable cups. It wouldn't hurt to have a table where people can pick up free copies of the New Testament or the Book of Mormon, as well as other Church pamphlets, so that people who are inspired to do so can pick up literature that will teach them more about our religion.

Questions from the Clueless

? *What happens if my service or volunteer work is not gratefully received by the intended recipient?*

Most of us, needy or not, don't receive acts of kindness very well. We perform acts of service much more easily than we receive those acts of charity. This same reasoning also applies to people you'll be serving as you and your group embark on service projects. Some recipients may be so grateful they'll embarrass you with their effusiveness; others will accept the service but act almost annoyed or resentful to do so.

Just as there are recipients who are delighted to receive service but do not know how to say thank you, there are also people who are so uncomfortable at being the recipients of charity that they would rather not have the service performed for them at all. If you try to perform an act of service for someone who resists your efforts, you and your group will almost have to be psychic to figure out the motivations of that particular person. If you determine that the person does want help but doesn't know how to accept it graciously, you may want to come up with some way to involve the person so he or she isn't just receiving charity, but is also working alongside your group. For example, you may enlist the disabled father of a family to direct you as you work on his property. Or you may ask an elderly lady to keep you supplied with cool water or to tell you about her life as you work in her garden. Try to come up with some way to make the reluctant recipient feel useful and needed, and your recipient may be as happy for your company as he is with your service.

Eventually you'll have a bad experience. You may work all day to help someone, only to have the person criticize your work at day's end. Or the ingratitude may be even worse. Clark and Kent have horrible memories of spending an entire summer working with the rest of the ward to remodel a woman's home, only to have the woman move her boyfriend into the house and cut off all contact with the Church the moment the work was finished.

When bad experiences happen, try to push all that aside and consider who is the actual recipient of the service. The scriptures have told us that when we perform acts of kindness to others, it is the same as performing those acts for the Savior. The Savior is not an ungrateful recipient.

Continue to render service whenever and wherever you see it is needed. If you are giving service or performing an act of kindness and find yourself unhappy with the amount of gratitude that is being shown on your behalf, ask yourself why you performed the good deed in the first place. If you are performing your acts of kindness in order to gain any sort of reward, a change of heart may be in order.

? *Do acts of kindness or service projects need to be spontaneous to be worthwhile?*

Acts of kindness or acts of service can be spontaneous. You may suddenly get the idea to make cookies for someone, or see a neighbor's walk that needs shoveling just as you're standing there holding a snow shovel. These spontaneous acts of kindness brighten the lives of others and can even change their lives. However, there is something to be said about organizing a large service project—doing the planning and organization that is involved in bringing a small or big project to execution. Often the planning involves many acts of kindness and service. Remember: it doesn't matter who gets credit; it matters what gets done.

? *What happens if my youth group is not interested in participating in a service project that might not be very exciting or stimulating to them?*

Just as you have to keep your group interested in doing service projects, you also have to instill in them the reasoning behind doing acts of service. The idea is not to look at what the givers are or aren't getting out of the project, but rather focus on the outcome for the people being served. If the recipients are somehow benefited, the project is a success and should be repeated in the future.

However, it doesn't hurt to look for projects that appeal to the specific group that will be performing the service. For example, a group of young people may be able to relate to clothing drives if the recipients will be other teenagers who don't have decent clothing to wear. Or they may be interested in working on a service project if boys and girls are working together, giving them a bit of social interaction as they do the service work. It doesn't hurt to ask the members of your group ahead of time to see what sort of project appeals to them. You'll get more participation out of them if they work on the project from beginning to end, rather than being given a project when they show up to a weeknight meeting and have a service project thrown in their laps.

? *Does a service project have to be ongoing to be successful?*

There are so many opportunities to do acts of kindness that we should always have our eyes open for service opportunities. Sometimes these activities can be ongoing projects, but they are just as likely to be one-time shots that address a need for a few hours or a day. Remember, there are enough things that need to be done and enough people to serve, that every effort helps.

CHAPTER 7
'Tis the Season

★ **IN THIS CHAPTER**
- ✔ Great Christmas Party Ideas
- ✔ Ideas for Holidays Throughout the Year
- ✔ Seasonal Suggestions
- ✔ An Activity for Every Day of the Year
- ✔ Questions from the Clueless

Those who are newly assigned the task of planning activities will soon learn that much of their work is dictated by the calendar because many of the activities they will be planning relate to a specific holiday, season, or occasion.

The biggest events in most wards are those associated with Christmas. The ward Christmas party may well be the most elaborate activity that is held in your ward during the year, and will typically consume the lion's share of the activity budget. Because of the importance of this holiday in the lives of most Church members, it is also the most critical in terms of having a successful activity. We will try to give you some ideas in this chapter that will start you down the right path toward planning a successful Christmas activity.

But Christmas comes only once a year, and most of us expect to be entertained the other eleven months as well. Fortunately, the calendar is filled with many other holidays and seasons that will provide plenty of opportunities for ward members to have some fun. This chapter will also provide some ideas that should get you started on planning a successful activity during any month of the year. In fact, towards the end of the chapter we will provide an activity idea for every single day on the calendar.

This chapter will not provide a lot of details about planning the activity or getting the needed supplies. Unless you have skipped all of the previous chapters, you should already be an expert in the process of planning and coordinating your activities. The function of this chapter is to give you a lot of little ideas that you can germinate into multiple activities that will entertain any size group.

We have also tried to include many ideas here that work well for small groups, or that can be scaled for any sized group from a single family to an entire ward. These should prove valuable for youth leaders, and also for activities planners in those smaller branches of the Church that struggle for ideas that can apply to their limited number of Saints.

With that introduction, let's decorate the tree, hang up the lights, dust off the carols, and get ready for Christmas!

Christmas Activities

No matter where you live, it is most likely there will be some kind of ward activity to celebrate Christmas. Although you may be forgiven for ignoring any other event during the year, most wards have strong traditions relating to Christmas, and you will almost certainly be expected to provide some kind of celebration for the Saints over which you have stewardship. Clark and Kathy once lived in a ward where the Christmas programs were so elaborate that they rivaled the parties that must have been held in Russia's royal court—right before the revolution. Christmas parties are a huge deal in most ward settings, so it's essential that you go all out to plan this event even if you don't have a czar's pocketbook to pay for it.

Although there are multiple challenges to planning the ward Christmas party, the biggest is how to anticipate and accommodate the large crowd. The Christmas party is the one event that most members in all stages of activity, as well as many of their friends and neighbors, plan to attend. There are no easy answers on how to handle the large crowd; however, thorough planning, especially for the unexpected, is probably the best guard against getting surprised. As you meet with your committee, make sure to place special emphasis on ideas that will help you deal with a larger number of people than you expected.

But before you lose much sleep over the anticipation of producing a Christmas event, consider that it is one of the easier events of the year to plan. The theme of the event is already decided (celebrating the birth of Christ), as are the decorations, the content of the program, and often the foods that are served. That does not mean you don't have some latitude in terms of what can be done (we recall a southwestern Christmas party where Tex-Mex food was served), but at least many of the decisions will be made for you unless you decide to be somewhat nontraditional.

Preliminary planning for the Christmas party should usually begin just after school starts in the fall and gets into full swing just after your Halloween activity. Although the bishop may call major committee members to help you, he is just as likely to ask you for your suggestions or leave you to choose your own committee. If this happens, it is essential to pick good, reliable members to help you out. Be careful not to pick the same people all the time. The trick is to find creative people with good follow-through when staffing the major committee positions. Try to spread the workload around and get as many people as possible involved. You'll never know the talents of those around you if you don't widen your sphere of helpers.

Although the program will set the tone of your party, most of your time will be spent on the food. Generous amounts of tasty food can cover up a multitude of other shortcomings, and those shortcomings will inevitably come. The major challenge with the food will be getting everyone fed quickly and efficiently. The best solution is to have at least two food serving locations—more, if your cultural hall can handle it. You'll need to decide whether to serve a dinner, just desserts, or heavy appetizers followed by desserts, and whether meals should be served buffet style or in another manner.

The next major aspect of your ward party is the entertainment. Here the key is simplicity. As much as you may want to have a Hollywood production, ward members will already be under a lot of stress due to the many projects they undertake during the Christmas season. Your potential cast members will simply be too tired from working, shopping, and attending office parties to want to devote weeks of their lives to working on a program for the Christmas party. They would much rather enjoy a pleasant meal and some simple entertainment and then go home for some quiet time with their families.

There are numerous ways that enjoyable entertainment can be had without a lot of time being expended. If you want a spiritual tone to your party, the congregation can sing Christmas carols and then listen to a message from the bishop. Or talented ward members can each sing or play one Christmas hymn, followed by a congregational sing-along. A live nativity scene reenacted by Primary members is a good accompaniment to the reading of the Christmas story. There are many options you can choose for a simple, yet spiritual, Christmas program.

Not all wards choose a spiritual program. Kent and Shannon once planned a Christmas party where each ward auxiliary and priesthood group was asked to perform a skit. They were given the assignment about a month in advance so they could do some planning in their groups. The stipulation was that each skit could last no longer than five minutes, and each skit had to follow a basic theme. Some of the themes were Christmas on Noah's Ark, Christmas on the Starship Enterprise, Christmas in a silent movie, and Christmas at the home of Santa's chief elf. Although most groups didn't do much preparation until the last minute, the results were nonetheless hilarious. You could even end the skits on a more contemplative note by having Christmas on a Christmas tree lot, or Christmas at the inn in Bethlehem.

No matter what tone you are trying to achieve, remember to keep the Christmas party elegant but simple—elegant simplicity is how you might want to think of it—and everyone will enjoy the evening.

If you are in a new ward, or one that has no expectations for the format of a Christmas event, you should be able to use one or more of the events in this section. Even if you are in a tradition-bound ward, perhaps some of the ideas in this section can be partially implemented to improve your celebration. Remember, however, that Christmas is supposed to be a peaceful season. If you find that people are only reluctantly agreeing to help you stage an elaborate Christmas party, consider scaling back and giving the participants the opportunity to enjoy the event.

A Christmas Spectacular

Most ward Christmas party planners place such a heavy emphasis on the food that any program is an afterthought. In fact, there may be no program at all. For variety, you might want to experiment with a format that reverses this. Have the Christmas program in the chapel, and place most of the emphasis on musical numbers, including congregational singing. If you want some non-musical content, have a member read a Christmas story, or conclude with the bishop giving a short message.

It is important that you gauge your ward as you plan the event. Young children in some wards are able to enjoy a formal program, but in other wards they are not. If reverence is a problem in your ward to the point that a formal program will be drowned out by fidgeting and screaming youngsters, you may want to provide a separate activity for them. Have the children involved with drawing, making crafts, and watching videos while the adults are enjoying the program in the chapel.

When the program has concluded, meet back together in the cultural hall. Serve light refreshments (or even more serious food if your time and budget allow) and then let the participants visit until they are ready to head home.

Christmas Plays

If there are those in your ward with a theatrical bent, Christmas is the ideal time to let them get up on stage and strut their stuff. The most popular vehicle is, of course, the Christmas story, with various ward members assigned to play the parts of Mary, Joseph, the baby Jesus, the innkeeper, the shepherds, and even the various animals in the stable. To eliminate the sound problems that always seem to occur in such productions, you may want to consider using a narrator to provide the story and dialogue. There are also other plays that could be used, such as Dickens's *A Christmas Carol.* If you are going with a more humorous approach, you might act out the song "The Twelve Days of Christmas," with ward members wearing silly props and playing the various parts. For example, one person could dress entirely in green (pear tree) and could wear a hat with a partridge painted on it. The person for the fifth day could be spinning five hula hoops painted gold (golden rings).

Christmas Talent Show

Many wards seem to have a talent show at least once a year, and the holidays may be an ideal time to let ward members share their talents. All of the performers should use material appropriate to the Christmas season. One precaution is to have a talent coordinator review all the acts to make sure their content is tasteful and appropriate. It might be difficult for a performer such as a comedian or a magician to find material suitable to the solemnity of the season (although anything is possible).

Christmas Eve in Bethlehem

This is certainly not your traditional Christmas party, but several friends have reported good results when their wards have tried this approach. Everyone should be instructed to dress in clothes like those worn in the days of Christ—bathrobes, towels, blankets, and scarves may be used as wardrobe enhancements. Each family should also bring enough blankets to seat the entire family. Decorate the room with booths, each serving a different kind of food. Use authentic foods such as fruits, flatbread, crackers, honey, olives, cheese, nuts, juices, and almond cakes. Have those attending go around to the different booths to obtain the items for their meal. Optionally, you can give each attendee a bag of candy coins and have them "barter" for their food at the booths. While eating, families or groups should gather together and sit on their blankets on the floor. To increase reverence and enhance the mood, avoid the overhead lights and use small electrical lamps scattered in and around the various booths. As families are eating, you may want to have a couple who will represent Mary and Joseph ask families if there is any room to share their blankets. (Make sure everyone says no to this request!) After everyone has eaten, lower the lights and open the curtains to reveal a live nativity scene on the stage. Have a narrator read the portions of the Christmas story related to Christ's birth. End with having the audience sing a few Christmas carols, particularly those related to the birth of the Savior. This makes for a memorable and unique ward Christmas party.

Christmas in Many Lands

One common idea for adding some variety to the standard Christmas party is to focus on differing Christmas traditions in cultures around the world. You could focus on one culture (such as the Tex-Mex party mentioned earlier), or represent many cultures at the same activity. Once you decide to do this, you can follow the same cultural theme in the decorations, the food served, and the program presented. If you have a potluck dinner, ask every family to bring a favorite ethnic dish (when our ward did this, we were surprised at the variety of foods that appeared). You might also ask selected members to decorate one table in the style of a particular culture. If your ward has a number of former missionaries who served in foreign lands, this should be an easy and enjoyable assignment.

Christmas in the Lodge

Although most Christmas activities are probably held in the ward meetinghouse, consider an alternate location if you can find one that would be suitable and the price is reasonable. One friend in Montana reports that her former ward used to rent a winter lodge for its Christmas activity. The Primary children come early in the afternoon to put up a Christmas tree and decorate it. That evening, members get together for sledding, visiting, and a buffet dinner. The ward provides soup, drinks, and dessert, and the members are asked to bring a salad or other side dish. The building is large enough that members can dance or gather together to sing carols, and the setting makes for a memorable occasion.

Progressive Christmas Party

This is another idea for a Christmas activity that expands its scope beyond the four walls of the cultural hall. The evening starts with a short Christmas program in the chapel. Members are then encouraged to travel around to other rooms in the building. Christmas carols are sung in the Relief Society room, and people can drop in or out as they please. The Primary room features a live nativity scene presented by the children—always a favorite. Another room houses a Christmas service project, where ward members assemble toiletry kits for a homeless shelter. Christmas cookies can be decorated in the kitchen. After about an hour of traveling, all members go back to the cultural hall for light refreshments. With some imagination, you could probably think of enough different activities to fill most of the rooms of the meetinghouse.

Ward Christmas Tree

During December, many wards have a Christmas tree that is decorated and placed in the foyer near the chapel. If your ward does this, consider putting up the tree without decorations, and asking each ward family to provide an ornament. (Make sure the family is on the hook that attaches the ornament to the tree.) Encourage families to create homemade ornaments, or to provide an ornament that has particular meaning to their family. Another idea is to unify the ward by bringing out the personalities of ward members through their ornaments. One way to do this would be to include ornaments that relate to the specific countries or areas where family members served on missions or in government work. Primary children and teenagers can make ornaments in their classes that can then be hung on the tree. You may even sponsor a contest, where each ornament is numbered and contestants guess which person or family belongs to which ornament. Make sure each contributor gets his ornament back before the tree is put away at the end of the season.

Holiday Piñata

This is a service activity that works well for Primary or youth classes. Inflate a large balloon and then cover it with papier-mâché. Decorate the balloon with a snow scene, or the face of Santa, or a snowman's face. When the papier-mâché is dry, make a hole in the top of the piñata, and then carefully make another hole in the balloon to let the air out. Fill the inside with small toys and candy. Attach a heavy string to the top of the piñata, and patch up the hole that was used to insert the treasures. Once the piñatas are completed, the next question is to determine who will receive them. They could be given to a large family in the ward, or to a charitable organization in the community. They could also be used as part of the program during the ward Christmas party. For the recipients of the gift, the idea is to hit the piñata with a stick until it breaks open and the contents spill out. This can be made more difficult by having the stick-bearers wear blindfolds, and by attaching the piñata to the end of a stick so that it can be moved around.

A Visit from Santa's Elves

This is a good youth activity that provides added benefits related to missionary work and the fellowshipping of ward members. Have the youth of the ward dress up as elves and visit families within the ward or neighborhood that have young children. If you plan to visit a large number of homes, it would be good to break into smaller sized groups of two to four elves each. It is a good idea to coordinate the visits with the parents first, to make sure the family will be home and to get an idea of the kinds of activities that would be appropriate for the children. Once the elves have arrived, they can engage the children in such activities as reading the Christmas story, helping them say their prayers, or helping them write a letter to Santa. If the parents approve, the elves can also bring Christmas treats such as milk and cookies.

The Bare Manger

This idea works well for a Primary class, or as part of a family home evening lesson. Early in December, prepare and display a manger scene. Have the Christ child lying in a bare manger that contains no straw. Provide a small bag of straw near the scene, and tell the children that they must help provide the straw for the Savior's bed. Instruct them that every time they perform a good deed, they may place one piece of straw in the manger. Encourage and remind them of this task throughout the entire month. This is a simple exercise, but one that seems to be quite effective in getting young minds focused on acts of service. If the group is small enough, consider providing a manger and bag of straw for each child.

Shared Christmas Traditions

This idea works well for smaller groups of adults and older youth. Instruct each person to come prepared to share a Christmas tradition from his or her family. Examples would include poems, stories, crafts (such as homemade ornaments and decorations), and edible treats. Those who bring poems and stories should bring enough copies for the entire group. Likewise, those bringing goodies and crafts should have enough to share with everyone. You may also consider making the crafts and the edibles as part of the event. If the large size of the group makes it impractical for everyone to participate, ask selected members to contribute (and then rotate the assignment each year so that everyone gets a chance to be involved).

Advent Jar

This is a project that gets you in the Christmas spirit not only when you make it, but also every time you use it. One of the nice things about Christmas is sharing the many stories, poems, and scriptures that put us in the mood for the season. Collect twenty-five of these and print each one on a small sheet of colored paper (red, green, or white). Roll each piece of paper into a scroll and secure it with a colored ribbon (silver or gold). Place each scroll into a fancy jar or basket. Make enough advent jars for each member of the group, and the members can participate in the construction of the project. When completed, each jar should be taken home and used as a daily reminder of the season. Every day in December, perhaps prior to family prayers, have a family member select and open a scroll and read the contents. You may want to save the Christmas story for the final day, and print it on a unique color of paper (gold) so that it will not be selected until Christmas Eve.

Sneaky Secret

Always look for opportunities to involve multiple groups in your activities. Join with other wards for some of your yearly parties. Have service and project activities where adults and youth work together. You can even involve the youth and the Primary for many types of activities. Not only will these combined groups result in an activity that is more successful, but they will work towards your ultimate goal of building ward unity.

Christmas Project Day

Refer to the activity "Super Saturday Craft Day" in chapter 3 for a full description of this activity. It provides an excellent opportunity for multiple wards and multiple groups to come together for a day of fun and productivity. The crafts produced make excellent Christmas gifts, and will not wreak havoc with your budget.

The Sounds of Christmas

This is a good icebreaker to get people warmed up for the real program during a Christmas party, and it works well with larger groups. Divide the audience into smaller groups, assign each group a number or a color, and make each group responsible for producing a sound effect. For example, one group may have the number two or the color purple, and may be responsible for making a thudding sound by stomping their feet on the floor. Then have a narrator read a story (in the interest of good taste, it should probably involve Santa Claus or some other secular theme). At appropriate times during the story, another helper should hold up large cards with the number or color that indicates the sound effect that is needed. When they see their number or color, each person should perform his assigned sound, producing a story with very amateurish (but somewhat amusing) sound effects.

Secret Santa

Refer to the activity "Secret Admirer" described in chapter 9. This works well as a Christmas activity for smaller groups and classes, and can also be adapted as a family activity for families with several children. As part of morning family prayer and scripture study, have each family member select a piece of paper containing the name of someone else in the family (have them draw again if they select their own name). During that day, each person should try to provide some act of kindness or service for the person he selected. The next morning, each family member should try and guess the identity of his Secret Santa, and the process should be repeated again each day throughout the holiday season.

Sleeping under the Tree

This is an activity that works well for families, and for small groups of same-sex youth. Have a sleepover where everyone brings a sleeping bag and sleeps on the floor under the Christmas tree. Gather in a leader's home, and make sure there are enough adults present to chaperone the youth that attend. Prior to lights out, serve light refreshments and sing Christmas songs. Then have everyone pitch their bags on the floor around the tree, and turn out the lights except for the decorations on the tree. Prior to going to sleep, allow the participants to share Christmas stories and thoughts, and sing more songs if that is appropriate.

Christmas Service Projects

There are many opportunities to provide acts of service during the Christmas season, and it is not unusual for classes and groups of ward members to participate in these community events. One thing that will make the service even more meaningful is to assign the group members the responsibility for locating the opportunities and finding out the particulars for participating. After some preliminary investigation, the group should meet together to hear the ideas for service, and to select the ones that will work best for the group. For smaller groups, it may be possible for each member to select a service project and have all of them performed. Adult leaders should also approve each activity, and hold veto power over suggestions that may be inappropriate or impractical. Group members planning the event should also plan some kind of treat afterwards.

Activities for Other Holidays

Although the Christmas activity will probably be your major holiday assignment of the year, there are other days that lend themselves to celebration as well. Here are some ideas for enjoyable activities that are associated with some of these other holidays.

New Year's Eve

▶ New Year's Tree

If your ward or group has decorated a Christmas tree, have an activity on New Year's Eve to transform it into a New Year's tree. Remove the Christmas decorations and replace them with decorations such as paper hats, confetti, horns, and streamers. Optionally, ask each person to anonymously write down their goals for the next year, roll up the list into a scroll, and attach it to the tree. When the tree is taken down, set the scrolls aside and save them for later in the year, perhaps for use during a summer party. Then open each scroll and reveal the goals for that year. Because they are submitted anonymously, no one will be embarrassed over goals that have been forgotten.

▶ New Year's Reflections and Resolutions

For a smaller class or group, ask each member to reflect upon their blessings and accomplishments for the past year, share their goals and resolutions for the new year, and express appreciation to other class members for their friendship and acts of kindness over the past year. End the activity with light refreshments such as popcorn and hot cider. This makes for a memorable activity if you have a group that is mature enough to approach the activity seriously.

▶ New Year's Decorating

Although the decorations are usually expected to be in place before the activity, New Year's decorations are so simple that you might want the attendees to decorate the room as part of the activity. Adults can hang colored paper streamers, the youth can inflate and place balloons, and even the Primary kids can draw pictures to be hung up around the room. Or, consider dividing into teams and having each team decorate a portion of the room with the materials provided. Set a time limit, and award silly prizes for the teams doing the best and worst jobs of decorating. Once the decorations are in place, have music for those who wish to dance, appetizers for those who wish to eat, and simple games for the younger children. If the activity lasts into the New Year, sing hymns just before midnight, then toast in the New Year with sparkling cider, and finally conclude with having the bishop offer a prayer for the ward as the first prayer of the New Year.

Valentine's Day

▶ Valentine Heart Attack

Identify members of the ward or the class who could use a little attention. For each person, prepare a plate of goodies (cookies, candy, nuts) and about twenty hearts cut out of construction paper. Have members of the class write something complimentary or uplifting on each heart. When you arrive at the house of each recipient, carefully tape all of the hearts to the front door, leave the plate of goodies in front of the door, then knock on the door and run.

▶ Valentine Dinner's on Me

This is a great service project the young women can perform for the young men (or vice versa), or that the youth can perform for the adults of the ward. Host and sponsor a Valentine dinner for another group in the ward. Your group should take care of all of the arrangements, including publicity, menu planning, cooking, serving, decorations, program (optional), and cleanup. At the end of the meal, present each attendee with a small box of candy, a flower, or similar memento. As an alternative to Valentine's Day, have the dinner close to Saint Patrick's Day and serve only green foods.

Saint Patrick's Day

▶ Saint Patrick's Day Green Party

The obvious idea for a Saint Patrick's Day party is to emphasize the color green. Request that everyone wear a green costume, and give prizes for the best ones. Continue that theme with the food, and make sure that all the food served is green (green punch, green frosting on the cookies and cakes, maybe even green mashed potatoes). If members are requested to bring food, give prizes for the green dishes that look *and* taste good.

▶ Saint Patrick's Day Shamrock Cookies

As a class activity, make and decorate shamrock cookies. You can find shamrock-shaped cookie cutters in most kitchen stores. Remember to add green food coloring to the frosting.

▶ Saint Patrick's Day Irish Dancing

If you have anyone experienced in Irish dancing, have them put on a performance and then teach the audience members some of the more basic routines.

▶ Saint Patrick's Day Green Service Project

Make gift baskets for members of the ward or the community. Make sure the contents of the baskets are green, or have some other Irish connection. Have class members deliver the completed baskets, and have them wish the recipients a happy Saint Patrick's Day.

▶ Saint Patrick's Day Green Scavenger Hunt

Divide into teams and equip each team with a video camera. Give each team a list of items they need to film, and a time limit for when they must be back to the meeting place (30 to 60 minutes). Specify whether or not cars may be used (if so, require that an adult be the driver). At the conclusion of the time limit, watch each video, determine the winner (based on creativity and the number of items filmed), and have refreshments. Examples of items you could have on the list would be: a green house, a green automobile, a man wearing green clothes, a woman wearing green clothes, a billboard with green lettering, a can of green beans, a whole watermelon, and a package of frozen broccoli.

Easter

▶ **Easter Gift Baskets**

Although Easter baskets usually relate to the more secular side of the holiday, they can also be used as a service project to reach those members of a class or group who are not active in class activities. Identify those members who would benefit from such a gift. On a day prior to Easter, have class members gather to assemble the baskets. Include the traditional candy, but also small items such as toiletries or small toys. You may also wish to include plastic eggs that contain scriptures or comments related to the recipient. For example, have each class member write down one attribute they really like about the recipient, and include those as well. Decorate all the baskets nicely, and then assign class members to deliver them on or before Easter Sunday.

▶ **Easter Story Eggs**

You can make one of these as a teaching aid for a class, or make one for each class member so they can take it home and relate the Easter story to their entire family. Obtain an egg carton (or an Easter basket) and twelve plastic Easter eggs that can be opened. Number the eggs from one to twelve with a permanent marker. Provide a printed sheet of twelve scriptures that tell the Easter story, starting with the Garden of Gethsemane and ending with the resurrection of the Savior. Have the scriptures numbered one through twelve. Class members should cut up the sheet so they have the twelve different scriptures, and should fold and place each scripture in the proper egg. For smaller children, you may want to include small objects in each egg that relate to the scripture. For example, if you include the scripture about Pilate washing his hands, include a small piece of soap. To tell the Easter story, simply distribute the eggs to the audience, and have them open the eggs and read the enclosed scripture in the proper sequence. You can select any twelve scriptures that are meaningful, but here is one example:

1. "Then cometh Jesus with them unto a place called Gethsemane, and saith unto the disciples, Sit ye here, while I go and pray yonder. . . . And he went a little further, and fell on his face, and prayed saying, O my Father, if it be possible, let this cup pass

from me; nevertheless, not as I will, but as thou wilt" (Matthew 26:36, 39).

2. "What think ye? They answered and said, He is guilty and worthy of death. Then did they spit in his face, and buffeted him; and others smote him with the palms of their hands" (JST Matthew 26:66–67).

3. "When the morning was come, all the chief priests and elders of the people took counsel against Jesus to put him to death: And when they had bound him, they led him away, and delivered him to Pontius Pilate the governor" (Matthew 27:1–2).

4. "Then Judas, which had betrayed him, when he saw that he was condemned, repented himself, and brought again the thirty pieces of silver to the chief priests and elders" (Matthew 27:3).

5. "And they stripped him, and put on him a scarlet robe. And when they had platted a crown of thorns, they put it upon his head, and a reed in his right hand: and they bowed the knee before him, and mocked him, saying, Hail, King of the Jews! And they spit upon him and took the reed, and smote him on the head" (Matthew 27:28–30).

6. "And after that they had mocked him, they took the robe off from him, and put his own raiment on him, and led him away to crucify him. And as they came out, they found a man of Cyrene, Simon by name: him they compelled to bear his cross" (Matthew 27:31–32).

7. "And they crucified him, and parted his garments, casting lots: that it might be fulfilled which was spoken by the prophet, They parted my garments among them, and upon my vesture did they cast lots. And sitting down they watched him there" (Matthew 27:35–36).

8. "And straightway one of them ran, and took a spunge, and filled it with vinegar, and put it on a reed, and gave him to drink" (Matthew 27:48).

9. "[Joseph of Arimathaea] went to Pilate, and begged the body of Jesus. Then Pilate commanded the body to be delivered. And when Joseph had taken the body, he wrapped it in a clean linen

cloth, and laid it in his own new tomb, which he had hewn out in the rock: and he rolled a great stone to the door of the sepulchre, and departed" (Matthew 27:58–60).

10. "And, behold, there was a great earthquake: for the angel of the Lord descended from heaven, and came and rolled back the stone from the door, and sat upon it" (Matthew 28:2).

11. "His countenance was like lightning, and his raiment white as snow" (Matthew 28:3).

12. "He is not here: for he is risen, as he said. Come, see the place where the Lord lay" (Matthew 28:6).

▶ Easter Scripture Chase

Although this is probably not appropriate for Easter Sunday itself, it makes for a good weeknight activity during the week before or after Easter. Bring an Easter basket filled with large candy eggs (chocolate, marshmallow, peanut butter). On each egg, tape a scripture and its corresponding reference. For example, you could list: "If any of you lack wisdom, let him ask of God, that giveth to all men liberally, and upbraideth not; and it shall be given him" (James 1:5). Remove the eggs, one by one, from the basket, and read either the scripture or the reference. If you read a scripture, then the first student to provide the corresponding reference wins the egg. Similarly, if you provide the reference, then the first person to read or quote the corresponding scripture will win it. In fairness to the class, you may want to limit the number of eggs that any one person may win. If someone reaches the limit, have him be the one who selects and awards the eggs.

Mother's Day

▶ Mother's Day Bunch of Kisses

Most Moms (and Dads) enjoy getting chocolate kisses—not only because they taste good, but because of the symbolism inherent in the kisses. There are a number of ways chocolate kisses can be prepared for presentation. One idea is to give each child or youth a small paper bag, and have him decorate it for his mother. Somewhere on the sack, the child should make sure to include words to the effect: "Many kisses to the best mom in the world." When the decoration process is complete, put a handful of chocolate kisses in each sack, seal it, then give it back to the young artist for presentation to his mother.

▶ Mother's Day Fancy Pots

This activity works well for Primary classes or young women. Visit a nursery or garden supply store, and buy a small clay pot for each class member. During class time, have each member of the group decorate her pot with fabric, lace, buttons, and ribbon. As an option to fabric, the pots could be painted. When the decoration is complete, either put a plant in each pot, or line the pot with foil and place a candle inside. Optionally, prepare a poem and attach it to the outside.

▶ Mother's Day Memory Jar

Purchase a fancy wide-mouth jar for each class member, or use wide-mouthed canning jars that can be decorated. Provide small slips of paper, and have each class member write a pleasant memory of his mother on each slip of paper. Once each child has recorded a suitable number of memories (at least a dozen, and as many as one a day for a year), have them fold up the slips of paper and place them into the jars. These can be any types of memories, such as the events of a pleasant vacation, something particularly funny that Mom said, or a teaching moment still remembered. Even the most stoic of mothers will have a hard time not shedding a tear or two when she reads the contents of the jar.

▶ Mother's Day Vacation Treat

It is quite common for family members to give Mom the day off on Mother's Day, serving her breakfast in bed and taking over other family chores she normally does. But how about giving her the day off from her Church responsibilities as well? The young women (and young men in some cases) could be asked to substitute for those women with other callings, so that they could attend Relief Society and just relax for one week. For that matter, the young women could also take over for the Relief Society instructor and give her a break as well. This not only gives the women a rest, but it gives them a chance to see their daughters and sons assume leadership roles for a day.

Father's Day

▶ **Father's Day Popcorn Greetings**

This is a great idea for a Primary class. Purchase a box of microwave popcorn for each child, or put regular popping corn into a glass jar. Prepare labels for each jar or box. The labels should be blank, except for the words "For the Greatest POP in the World!" near the top. Now allow each child to decorate the label with crayons or colored pencils. Then affix the labels to the boxes or jars, and the gift is ready to give to the dads.

▶ **Father's Day Chocolate Treats**

This is another idea that works well for children or youth who wish to prepare a small gift for their fathers. Purchase a chocolate bar for each child or youth involved. Make sure to get a traditional chocolate bar that is wrapped in foil and then covered with a paper wrapper. Carefully remove all of the paper wrappers from the bars, measure the size of the wrapper, and then design your own replacement wrappers. Use a name such as the "Super Dad Bar," perhaps with a slogan of "The Favorite Treat of Great Dads Everywhere." On the back, you can include an ingredients section (chocolate, love, sugar, understanding, patience, wisdom), and perhaps a section showing how each bar provides your daily nutritional requirements (provides 45% of your daily kindness). Include a blank "Serving Suggestions" area where each child or youth can write a personal message. Once the labels are complete, paste them on the bars, which will now be ready to be presented to the proud fathers.

▶ **Father's Day Book of Love**

This activity works well when you are dealing with a rather large class, and you have the necessary preparation time before Father's Day (it would also work well for Mother's Day). Ask each class member a question such as, "Why do you love your father?" or "What does your father do for you that you really appreciate?" Have them write down their answers, or record the responses of younger children. Compile all the comments into a booklet that will be given to the fathers. You may want to credit each comment to the contributor, or it may be more fun to let the parents decide which comments came from their own loving offspring.

▶ Father's Day Coupon Book

We have all received those little books of coupons in the mail that are good for free gifts, or discounts on things we already buy. How about making a coupon book for Dad, containing coupons for things we can do for him? Decorate ordinary letter-sized envelopes with the words "Valuable Coupons," and add other artwork of your choosing. Prepare ten to twelve "coupons" for each envelope. These should measure approximately 3½x8½ inches, and should be made from thicker paper stock. Have each class member write on each coupon the free gift or the service he is willing to provide. Examples might be "Good for one (1) lawn mowing without cost," or "Good for one (1) evening of free baby-sitting," or "Good for one (1) ice cream sundae of your choice at your favorite ice cream parlor." These should obviously be services that the class member doesn't already provide, or these coupons will really not be all that valuable! To make the coupons more humorous, add some "fine print," such as expiration dates and conditions for use.

Halloween

▶ Halloween Carols

Singing carols at Halloween is an interesting way for youth leaders to surprise their young charges, or for any group in the ward to spread some cheer to both members and nonmembers in the neighborhood or at a local rest home. It is best if this is done a couple of days before or after Halloween. Those involved should dress up in costumes and prepare small bags of candy for those who will be visited. (If you choose to visit a rest home, avoid candies that would be difficult for people with false teeth to chew.) You also need to come up with some "Halloween Carols," by customizing the lyrics to familiar songs. If many people are involved (such as an entire ward), you can break into smaller groups of five to ten people each so that more people can be visited. As you visit the front porch of each house, simply burst into Halloween song. If the occupants of the house come out to visit, present them with a bag of candy. If you are visiting nonmembers as a missionary project, consider also giving them some missionary materials, such as an invitation to visit the ward, a listing of meeting times, and a map for finding the chapel. Another idea is to have a party back at the meetinghouse after the caroling, and to invite those you visit to attend for donuts and hot cider.

▶ Halloween Trick-or-Trunk

This is becoming a popular idea for parents with young children, or for people concerned with the dangers of sending their children trick-or-treating. Hold a traditional Halloween or autumn party at the meetinghouse. Invite children to come in costume, and you may even hold a parade of the costumes if that is appropriate. Towards the end of the party, invite everyone to adjourn to the parking lot, where the children in costume will visit each of the parked cars. Adults should open their car trunks, and should distribute goodies to the children as they come to visit each car. Some people even decorate the inside of their trunks with Halloween decorations. After a set period of time, meet back inside the meetinghouse for dessert and a closing prayer. This is also an effective missionary activity, because many nonmember neighbors are interested in finding a safer way to take their children trick-or-treating.

▶ Halloween Pumpkin Carving Contest

If you are holding a Halloween or autumn party, invite people to carve pumpkins ahead of time and bring them to the party. To generate more interest, announce that prizes will be awarded in several categories, such as "largest pumpkin," "most creative," and "most scary." As the pumpkins arrive, put them on display for all to see. Later during the program, you can announce the winners and give out small prizes. Not only does this type of event generate interest in the activity but it also helps complement the decorations and provides part of the program. Similar contests can also be held in areas such as apple bobbing or pie baking.

Thanksgiving

▶ Thanksgiving Candles of Gratitude

This is a good activity for a smaller group, such as a class of ten to forty people (or even as a family home evening activity). This is something that has to be done at night or in a dark room. Provide each person with a candle, and seat them around the room in some kind of circular or square pattern. Have the instructor light the candle and name one thing for which he is thankful. Have him then light the candle of the person next to him. Following this pattern, go around the room and have each person do likewise, naming a blessing as the candle is lit. As each blessing is mentioned, the room gets lighter, reminding us of the light that comes into our lives because of the gospel and the Lord's blessings. When all the candles have been lighted, sing a hymn of thanks.

▶ Thanksgiving Time Capsule

This idea works well for the entire ward, or for a smaller group—but you must be patient, because it takes more than a year to come to fruition. Before Thanksgiving, ask each family (or class member) to provide a short written paragraph or two listing the things for which they are thankful. Make sure the name of the family or the individual is also written on the paper. Keep all of the papers in a "time capsule" (a jar or envelope), and put it in a place where it will not be lost over the next year. One year later, during a Thanksgiving celebration, open the jar and read all the papers, including the names of the authors. If you want to maintain this as an ongoing tradition, create a new time capsule each year before reading the contents of the previous year's capsule. This activity is especially effective if you live in a ward with a lot of turnover, because reading the blessings will remind you of families and individuals who no longer reside with you. The idea of a time capsule could also be used for a Christmas or New Year's party (the New Year's capsule could contain members' resolutions for the next year).

▶ Thanksgiving Leftover Feast

This is a good informal activity that can be held the Friday or Saturday after Thanksgiving. The only rule is that each family should bring enough leftover food to feed their entire family. Just put all of the leftovers on a serving table, and have a potluck dinner. With a little bit of luck, you will have a wide assortment of Thanksgiving food. The ward may want to supplement the food by providing drinks, breads, or desserts. Have some kind of games after the meal or just let everyone relax and enjoy the conversation.

Seasonal Ideas

Not all activity ideas need to be related to a specific holiday. Some are also associated with a specific season or time of year. Below you will find some suggestions for these types of activities.

Back-to-School Party

You don't have to be going back to school to enjoy a back-to-school or end-of-summer ward party. If you're serving a potluck dinner, eat first and get things cleaned up quickly so you can move into a couple of games. To add a little more to the festive atmosphere, have everyone dress in their loudest summer shirts or souvenir T-shirts from their vacations. Regardless of the reason for getting together (back to school or end or summer), plan for some kind of gag gift to give all the kids going back to school. The gag gift could be a pencil engraved with something—"I love school!"—a brochure from one of your local amusement parks, or any other idea you can come up with to rub into the kids the fact that summer's over and it will soon be time to hit the books again. This is a good way to close out the summer and get everyone back together from summer vacations.

Meteor Shower Activity

This is a sure winner for those budding astronomers in the ward, plus a lot of fun for those with just an average interest in the nighttime sky. There are a couple of times during the year when a large amount of meteor activity can be seen—as many as forty meteors per hour in optimum conditions. The two primary meteor showers of the year are the Perseids (August 11–13) and the Geminids (December 13–15). For best viewing, select an area that is very dark and away from the lights of nearby cities. This means that urban ward members may need to travel some distance to remote parks or campgrounds. Try to select an area that allows fires to be built. In the early part of the evening, build a fire and have members gather around it. Provide food that can be cooked in the fire, such as hot dogs, marshmallows, and foil dinners. If the weather is cold, provide hot chocolate or hot cider as well. After everyone has been fed, let the fire die out, so that members may begin to observe the showers. Check with local weather sources to determine the optimum viewing times in your area. Because such an event can easily be thwarted by clouds or bad weather, plan an alternate activity if the weather does not cooperate.

An Idea for Every Day of the Year

When you are first called to a position that requires you to plan activities, you often perceive the calendar as being your enemy. It seems to be a thankless master that dictates the time and theme of many of your activities. But as you become more experienced in planning and executing activities, you come to view the calendar as a valuable friend. Not only does it force you to plan regular activities, but it often dictates the nature of the foods that will be served, the decorations that will be used, and the program that will be presented. As we noted previously in the Christmas section, Christmas activities are easy to plan, because the theme, decorations, program, and menu are already set if you choose to be traditional.

Often the most difficult part of planning an activity is to come up with the theme. Once the theme is established, it is easy to come up with ideas that relate that theme to the other aspects of the activity—such as the decorations, the menu, the program, and even the publicity that will be used to promote it. Thus, the calendar can be your friend by helping you in choosing that all-important theme.

On the following pages you will find twelve monthly calendars that give you party ideas for all 366 days of the year. These include holidays and historical dates significant to United States residents (readers in other countries are certainly free to include their own important dates), as well as important events in Church history, and other dates that are just plain silly (Opposites Day) but have been officially declared as such and have the potential to inspire great activities.

January

01 New Year's Day. Hold an informal party to get rid of that extra holiday food, and launch a ward goal program.

02 In Haiti, this is known as Hero's Day, or Ancestry Day. It is a good day for honoring one's ancestors.

03 Sir Edmund Hillary reached the South Pole in 1958. Have an activity featuring large bowls of ice cream. Celebrate penguins.

04 Utah Statehood Day. Utah became the forty-fifth state on this day in 1896.

05 The longest Monopoly® game on record ended after 264 hours. This is a good excuse to have a game party.

06 Today is both Bean Day and Apple Tree Day. How about a chili cook-off with apple pie for dessert (yes, we know that real men don't put beans in their chili).

07 The comic strip *Tarzan* began on this day in 1929. How about a jungle party?

08 Rock 'n' Roll Day. Sounds like a good day for a '50s or '60s party.

09 National Static Electricity Day. This brings to mind several interesting activities.

10 Peculiar People Day. The possibilities here are endless.

11 International Thank-You Day. Plan an activity to say "Thank You" to someone.

12 Carrots are a great winter vegetable. Have a celebration of carrots, complete with weird costumes, crazy games, and a menu featuring you-know-what.

13 National Peach Melba Day. Just another excuse to serve some fattening desserts.

14 Take a Missionary to Lunch Day. Serve dinner to honor your stake and full-time missionaries.

15 Tchaikovsky's *Sleeping Beauty* premiered in 1890. How about a program of music, dance, and other cultural entertainment?

16 The radio program *Love a Mystery* debuted in 1939. A good day for a mystery party.

17 The first International Exhibition of Surrealism opened in Paris in 1938. This would be a good day for any activity related to the arts, or just a surrealistic party.

18 Today is both Winnie the Pooh Day and Jazz Day. Lots of possibilities with either (or both) themes.

19 National Popcorn Day. Another good excuse for making tasty treats. Perhaps a carmel popcorn sculpture contest?

20 Inauguration Day. Every four years the newly elected United States president is sworn into office on this date. It's a good day to "inaugurate" new ward programs, or have a bogus election party and elect ward members to outlandish positions.

21 National Hugging Day. Many possibilities here.

22 In 1878 Texan John Martin saw a UFO fly over his farm. How about a UFO costume party?

23 National Pie Day. Can you say "Pie Baking Contest"?

24 The first Boy Scout troop was organized in England in 1908. A good day to honor Scouts, or have a Scouting-related activity.

25 This is both Dinner Party Day and Opposite Day. If you can't come up with something here, you haven't been paying attention.

26 On this day the first electric dental drill was built. Throw a "try not to think about it" party.

27 National Chocolate Cake Day. Enough said.

28 National Kazoo Day. A kazoo party would be great fun. Remember prizes for the best performances . . . and for the worst.

29 This is both National Puzzle Day and National Corn Chip Day. Sounds like the food and program are already planned.

30 The *Lone Ranger* program debuted on radio in 1933. Perform a service project and then watch old television shows.

31 Zane Grey's birthday. Have a cowboy and cowgirl party.

February

01 National Freedom Day commemorates the abolition of slavery, which occurred when President Lincoln signed the Thirteenth Amendment to the Constitution in 1865.

02 The first lie detector test was given on this date in 1935. Play a game where players tell tall tales and the audience must locate the fibbers. "To Tell the Truth" is a good option.

03 Felix Mendelssohn's birthday. An evening of classical music would be nice.

04 On this day in 1831, Edward Partridge was called and ordained first bishop of the restored Church. How about an activity to honor your bishop?

05 National Chocolate Fondue Day. Have a fondue party, assuming you can find anyone who admits to owning a fondue pot.

06 Norman Rockwell's first colored *Saturday Evening Post* magazine cover appeared in 1926. How about having a nostalgia party?

07 National Fettuccine Alfredo Day. Parties with Italian food are always popular.

08 Jules Verne's birthday. Hold an "Under the Sea" party.

09 The Beatles first appeared on Ed Sullivan on this day in 1964. Host an Ed Sullivan-type program for the ward. Be sure to find a host who can make it a "rilly big shew."

10   The first singing telegram was delivered on this day in 1933. It also is World Marriage Day. Have sweethearts compose and sing telegrams to each other, and give prizes for the best ones.

11   *The French Chef,* starring Julia Child, premiered on television in 1963. A good day to hold a cooking class, or serve a French dinner to ward members.

12   Abraham Lincoln's birthday. You can have a debate, or even a party with a log cabin theme.

13   Exorbitant Price Day. A good day for a seminar on smart shopping and creating and using budgets.

14   Saint Valentine's Day. If you can't think of an idea for today, you're beyond help.

15   Disney's *Cinderella* premiered in movie theaters on this day in 1950. That's as good a theme as any for a fancy-dress ball.

16   Feast of Sticky Buns. Another excuse to not feel guilty about making some decadent desserts.

17   Random Acts of Kindness Day. Plan a service activity and do something nice for those who least expect it.

18   On this date in 1979, the one thousandth stake of the Church was organized in Nauvoo, Illinois. How about serving a steak dinner?

19   Today is the birthday of Nicolaus Copernicus, the Polish astronomer who originated the Copernican theory (sun is the center of our universe). Have a stargazing party.

20   Today is the birthday of nature photographer Ansel Adams. Have an activity where ward members bring and show their favorite photographs. Award prizes for the best ones in each category.

21   Former President Richard Nixon visited China on this day in 1972. Have an activity celebrating Chinese culture and cuisine.

22   The birthday of George Washington, the first president of the United States. Have a party with an honesty theme, and don't forget to serve cherry pie for dessert.

23   National Banana Bread Day. The women can bake the bread, and the men can taste and judge the results (or vice versa).

24   National Tortilla Chip Day. Chips and dips are a great snack when playing board games. Have a salsa contest—either salsa as in salsa, or salsa dancing.

25   International Clam Chowder Festival. Celebrate bivalves with a hot winter soup competition. Supplement your chowder with a bread-baking contest.

26   Today marks the birthday of both Levi Strauss (the creator of blue jeans) and Buffalo Bill Cody (American frontiersman and showman). It must certainly be time for another western party.

27 On this day in 1833, the revelation known as the Word of Wisdom (D&C 89) was received by Joseph Smith. How about an activity featuring all healthy foods?

28 The first Vaudeville theater opened on this day in 1883. It must be time for another ward talent show.

29 Leap Year Day. This day only occurs approximately once every four years. A good excuse to have a party.

March

01 Today marks the birthday of both Fredric Chopin and Glenn Miller. A good day for classical or jazz music.

02 Elmer Fudd first appeared in a Warner Brothers cartoon in 1940. Pop the popcorn, and let's watch cartoons.

03 I Want You to Be Happy Day. A good day for a service activity.

04 *People* magazine was first published on this day in 1974. Hold a costume party where people dress as their favorite celebrity.

05 National Cheese Doodle Day. How about a build-your-own-sandwich extravaganza, accompanied by a vast array of snack foods?

06 National Chocolate Cheesecake Day. That certainly sounds better than snack foods.

07 The Gibraltar Mission was formed on this day in 1853. Have a Spanish fiesta to celebrate.

08 Soap opera writers went on strike on this day in 1988. Write your own soap opera (*As the Ward Turns, All My Primary Children*),

and have ward members play the parts.

09 National Crabmeat Day. A good seafood dinner would really hit the spot.

10 The first film was shot in Hollywood on this day in 1910. Have a contest for the best home movies.

11 Mary Shelley's novel *Frankenstein* was published on this day in 1818. Let's have a scary costume party. In fact, Halloween in March isn't a bad idea.

12 Alfred Hitchcock Day. How about a trivia contest relating to his movies?

13 Halley's Comet passed near the Earth and was noticed for the first time on this date in 1758. This brings to mind a clean-the-ward service activity (starring Comet® cleanser). Be sure to serve refreshments afterwards and award silly prizes to the participants.

14 Albert Einstein's birthday. Hold a science fair or borrow some old science filmstrips from a local school.

15 The first blood bank opened on this day in 1937. Arrange for ward members to donate blood as a service project.

16 National Artichoke Hearts Day. And who will win the prize for the most creative dish using one of these tasty treats?

17 On this day in 1842, the Relief Society was organized in Nauvoo, Illinois. Have a Relief Society birthday party and invite the husbands—or have the men host a dinner for the Relief Society members.

18 Roger Bannister became the first man to run a mile in under four minutes in 1950. How about an indoor Olympics activity, featuring strenuous activities such as a beanbag toss?

19 Elvis Presley bought Graceland on this day in 1957. It must be about time for an Elvis look-alike party, featuring prizes for the best costumes.

20 The first detective story (Edgar Allen Poe's *Murders in the Rue Morgue)* was published on this date in 1841. Time for a mystery party (or just watch an old mystery movie).

21 National Teenagers Day. Have the adults throw a party for the kids. Treat them for one day as they would like to be treated all year long.

22 National Goof-Off Day. Have contests featuring yo-yos, paper airplanes, jigsaw puzzles, and other worthless but enjoyable activities.

23 National Chip and Dip Day. You provide the chips, members provide the dips. Prizes for the best ones. What could be easier?

24 Harry Houdini's birthday. How about a magic show?

25 Jimmy Stewart's birthday. Because many of his movies are family-oriented, this would be a good day for a film festival. Watch *Mr. Krueger's Christmas.*

26 On this day in 1830, the first copies of the Book of Mormon were made available at the Grandin Bookstore. Have an activity centered on the scriptures, with scripture chases and puzzles, and a scripture-marking class. End with a meeting where participants tell which is their favorite scripture—and why.

27 On this day in 1836, the Kirtland Temple was dedicated. Celebrate with a temple excursion.

28 Something on a Stick Day. Have everyone bring a food served on a stick. Prizes for the most tasty and creative.

29 The first Comic Relief benefit concert was held on this day in 1986. Have a stand-up comedy competition.

30 National Badminton Day. Shall it be men versus women, or adults versus the teens?

31 The musical *Oklahoma!* premiered on Broadway on this day in 1940. Have ward members create and star in their own musical, or have an Oklahoma party.

April

01 April Fools' Day. Have a dinner party with blue punch, and serve all the food courses backwards (dessert first, appetizers last).

02 On this day in an undetermined year the first human cannonball stunt was performed. How about a talent show featuring unusual talents?

03 National Find-a-Rainbow Day. Although you might not find one in the sky, consider a party with rainbow decorations.

04 The television program *Star Trek* was canceled on this day (a day of mourning for all fans). How about a *Star Trek* party, complete with costumes? For a real laugh, feature a showing of the hilarious documentary, *Trekkies*.

05 New York City's Central Park was first proposed on this date in 1851. If the weather is nice, have an activity at a local park or campground.

06 The Church of Jesus Christ of Latter-day Saints was officially organized on this day in 1830. There is also scriptural evidence (D&C 20:1) that this is the birthday of Jesus Christ. This is certainly reason for any dignified birthday celebration.

07 No Housework Day. Have a party where the men do all the work (now that's a real challenge!).

08 Hank Aaron hits home run number 715 on this day in 1974. If it's too cold for a baseball game, have a baseball party.

09 The first Academy Awards were held on this day in 1927. How about an Academy Awards theme party?

10 Bananas were first offered for sale in England on this day in 1633. Banana splits and banana bread for everyone!

11 Barbershop Quartet Day. If that doesn't appeal to you, how about teaching a class on home haircutting and grooming?

12 The Salk Polio Vaccine was announced on this day in 1955. Organize a health fair and invite the community.

13 Thomas Jefferson's birthday. Because he was an amateur inventor as well as the third American president, have a crazy inventions contest. If you're looking for dessert to serve afterwards, this is also National Peach Cobbler Day.

14 Ripley's "Believe It or Not" column was first published on this date. Reveal unusual facts about ward members, and have the audience guess which ones are true versus fabricated.

15 Federal Tax Return Deadline. Celebrate with a party where each guest is served bread, water, and a pound of flesh.

16 National Eggs Benedict Day.

Come dressed like an egg, serve eggs to eat, and have an egg toss for entertainment. Present "You're a Good Egg" awards to ward members.

17 National Cheeseball Day. Ward provides the crackers, members provide the cheeseballs. Prizes for the best ones. Also provide cheesy decorations and entertainment.

18 The first crossword puzzle book was published on this date. Have a puzzle party or a mystery night.

19 Summer vacations are just around the corner. Have a vacation seminar, giving hints on how to vacation with children and what destinations to visit close to home.

20 National Pineapple Upside-down Cake Day. Prizes for the best recipes.

21 Webster's Dictionary was first published on this date in 1828. Hold a party featuring Scrabble® and other word games.

22 The first Earth Day was observed on this day in 1970. Perform a service project that improves something in the community.

23 William Shakespeare's birthday. If the Bard holds no appeal, it is also Picnic Day.

24 The soda fountain was patented on this day in 1833. Chocolate sodas and ice cream sundaes for everyone!

25 The first Jane Fonda workout video was released on this day in 1982. Hold a fitness activity, followed by healthy treats.

26 Today is Richter Scale Day, Static Cling Day, and Hug an Australian Day. How many more ideas do you want?

27 Today is Write an Old Friend Today Day and also National Prime Rib Day. Have everyone write letters of appreciation to other ward members. Reward them with a big slab of you-know-what.

28 The first animated electric sign was built on this day. Hold a trivia party where you quiz people about advertising slogans.

29 The Ford Motor Company made its 50 millionth car on this day in 1959. Hold a community seminar to teach basic auto repair and maintenance.

30 The dial weighing machine was patented on this day in 1772. Hold a "don't worry about the calories" party (or a nutrition seminar if you have no sense of irony).

May

01 On this day in 1846, the Nauvoo Temple was publicly dedicated by Orson Hyde. Consider taking Primary children to tour the temple grounds, having them first receive a "temple recommend" from the bishop. If there is no temple near you, come up with a temple-related activity.

02 The first American Booksellers Convention was held on this day in 1912. Have everyone come dressed as a favorite literary character. Prizes for the best costumes and for those who identify the most characters.

03 Tweety Bird and Sylvester first appeared together in a Warner Brothers cartoon in 1947. Show cartoons and other funny movies, or have a seminar on pet care. Serve popcorn.

04 Invisible ink was invented. How about an activity related to spies or quirky inventions?

05 The stock market crash of 1893 occurred on this day. Time for another seminar on financial planning or investing?

06 Orson Welles' birthday. Play his controversial "War of the Worlds" radio broadcast that caused such panic.

07 Bucks County (Pennsylvania) Kite Day. Make and fly homemade kites.

08 No Socks Day. Wear any kind of clothes you want to this party, but no socks allowed!

09 National Teacher Day. Hold an activity to honor outstanding teachers in your community or outstanding teachers in your ward.

10 Human Kindness Day. Hold a service activity and spread joy to others in the ward or community.

11 The first regularly televised TV show was broadcast on this day in 1928. Play TV trivia games or invite a local news personality to speak about the media and its history.

12 The first wedding in the United States was performed on this day, centuries ago. Have a seminar on building better marriages.

13 The term "Bogey" was first used in a golf game on this day. Design a miniature golf course in the cultural hall and play a round of golf, or have a Bogart film festival.

14 Help Clean up Your Street Day. Hold an activity to clean the meetinghouse grounds and the interior of the building. Reward your group with nonmessy treats.

15 On this day in 1829, John the Baptist conferred the Aaronic Priesthood on Joseph Smith and Oliver Cowdery. Celebrate the restoration of the Aaronic Priesthood.

16 Wear Purple for Peace Day. Have a party where everyone wears purple. Pray for world peace and for the missionary efforts throughout the world.

17 Pack Rat Day. Bring all those things you never use and have an exchange party—or box them up for charity.

18 International Museum Day. Take your group to visit a museum.

19 The first Frog Jumping Contest was held in Calaveras County, California, on this day in 1918. Frogs may be too exotic for ward members, but how about some human jumping events such as relay races?

20 The first speeding ticket was issued on this day. Sponsor a seminar on safe driving.

21 The television game show *Let's Make a Deal* debuted. Have an activity featuring versions of favorite TV game shows, and choose contestants from the audience. Don't forget to award those fabulous prizes!

22 On this day rattlesnake meat was first sold in cans. Have a dinner party featuring exotic foods and recipes. It need not feature anything as exotic as rattlesnake.

23 The first cross-country automobile trip from New York to San Francisco began today. If the weather is nice, a road rally would be fun.

24 The Brooklyn Bridge opened on this day in 1883. Show slides from favorite vacation trips and have the audience try to guess the locations.

25 The first national spelling bee was held on this day. How about a

contest between the young men and the young women?

26 John Wayne's birthday. Throw a cowboy party.

27 The first International Master chess tournament was held on this day in 1851. Hold your own chess tournament.

28 National Hamburger Day. Have the ward provide the meat and buns, let the members bring the fixings. Award prizes for the most exotic creations. Hot fudge hamburger, anyone?

29 The movie *Vertigo* premiered. Have a phobia party, sitting thirteen people at each table and offering plenty of ladders to walk under.

30 The first ice cream freezer was patented on this day. This would be a good time for a party featuring homemade ice cream.

31 Superman debuted on this day in 1938 in Action Comic number 1. Have a costume party where people dress as their favorite action hero or comic character.

June

01 Brigham Young was born on this day in 1801. Celebrate his birth with a start-of-summer party.

02 Festival of Utter Confusion. Use your imagination to come up with some great ideas.

03 The movie *Star Wars* premiered on this day in 1977. Have a party with an outer space motif. Thanks to the proliferation of video cameras, you could even make and show your own 1950s-style science fiction movie.

04 The grocery cart was introduced on this day in 1937. Sponsor a seminar on being a smart shopper.

05 On this day the first Smile Girl contest was held. Take close-up pictures of ward members smiling and have a contest where people identify the person from the smile.

06 The first drive-in movie opened in 1933 in Camden, New Jersey. Set up the cultural hall with a movie screen in front and clusters of chairs to represent the cars. Have members walk to the snack bar to get treats.

07 The *New York Times* first reported that alligators were living in the sewer under the city. Have a tabloid party and award prizes for the best tall tales.

08 On this day in 1978, the First Presidency issued a letter announcing the revelation granting the priesthood to worthy men of all races. Celebrate in an appropriate manner.

09 Senior Citizens Day is celebrated on this day in Oklahoma. Hold an event to honor your older members and celebrate their lives.

10 Construction at America's first public zoo, founded by Benjamin Franklin in Philadelphia, was completed this month. How about a trip to the nearest zoo? If that isn't feasible, have an Africa party and go on safari in your neighborhood.

11 The kitchen stove was patented on this day. Give it a rest by having an activity where none of the refreshments need to be cooked before serving.

12 On this day the first documentary film was finished. Make a ward documentary starring ward members.

13 Kitchen Klutzes of America Day. Sponsor a cooking class with recipes so easy that anyone can make a successful meal.

14 Flag Day. This day celebrates the anniversary of adopting the flag in 1777. Have a flag party. Design your own family flags, or a ward flag.

15 A Friend in Need Is a Friend Indeed Day. Sponsor a service project.

16 Wish Fulfillment Day. Try and make a wish come true for someone in the ward or the community.

17 Eat All of Your Vegetables Day. What an exciting menu idea for a ward activity! Pumpkin ice cream is an option.

18 International Picnic Day. Plan a picnic in a local park, at a member's home, or on the meetinghouse grounds.

19 The first issue of *Cycling Journal* was published today. Meet at the ward and then bicycle a short distance to a park or member's house. Have treats and then ride back.

20 National Vanilla Milkshake Day. A good excuse to have a '50s party complete with '50s food. Or have an ice cream-making contest with prizes awarded for the most unusual flavors.

21 Aimless Wandering Day. Sponsor a seminar on setting and reaching goals.

22 The pin-making machine was patented on this day. Organize a bowling activity and give prizes for the lowest scores.

23 A Volkswagen Beetle reached the 1,400,000-mile mark on this day in 1992. If you've already had your seminar on auto maintenance, have a "bug" party and center the theme on the things that bug us.

24 A ninety-three-pound salmon was caught on this day. Celebrate with a fish fry or a salmon bake.

25 Legislation to mandate an eight-hour workday was passed in 1868.

Sponsor a job fair to help people improve their job skills.

26 A thirty-foot diameter pancake was made on this day in 1988. Celebrate with a pancake breakfast (or supper).

27 The Prophet Joseph Smith was murdered by a mob on this day in 1844. Plan an activity to celebrate his life and accomplishments.

28 On this day in 1820 the tomato was first proven to not be poisonous. Throw a pizza party to celebrate.

29 Flower and Camera Day. Show flower pictures taken by ward photographers, or go on a nature photography walk and take pictures of flowers.

30 Circus Comes to Town Day. Sponsor a ward circus or carnival.

July

01 American Stamp Day. Sponsor an activity where members bring and display the various items they collect, such as stamps, coins, dolls, refrigerator magnets, or whatever. Have a craft class and teach people the art of rubber stamping.

02 National Literacy Day. Sponsor events to promote literacy in your ward and community.

03 Idaho became the forty-third state on this day in 1890. Any activity on this day should certainly feature a potato bar (and yes, we realize that Idaho is known for other things as well).

04 Independence Day. On this day in 1776, patriots from the original thirteen colonies signed the Declaration of Independence from England. Have a pancake breakfast or an evening program.

05 Workaholics Day. Sponsor a relaxing activity where you just sit around and eat and visit.

06 National Fried Chicken Day. Prizes for the most tasty. Need we say more?

07 Macaroni Day. Have an "all pasta" dinner or a Yankee Doodle party. (If you can't make the connection, sing the song.)

08 On this day in 1838, the revelation on tithing was received (D&C 119). This would be a good day for a seminar on financial goals and management.

09 The donut cutter was patented on this day. Some homemade donuts and cold milk would taste awfully good.

10 The program *Your Hit Parade* debuted on this day in 1950. Yet another excuse to break out those old singles (even if they probably are all on CDs these days).

11 *The Newlywed Game* debuted on television in 1966. Playing this on a ward level can uncover some eyebrow-raising secrets.

12 Video Games Day. The kids will love this as an activity idea, but will the parents be able to stand it?

13 This was the date of the New York City power blackout that occurred in 1977. Celebrate by playing black light volleyball.

14 Comedy Celebration Day. Are there any budding comedians in the ward?

15 On this day in 1929, the Mormon Tabernacle Choir began its weekly network radio broadcasts. Celebrate with an evening of highbrow music, or have a "Messiah" sing-along in July.

16 The movie *Gentlemen Prefer Blondes* premiered. Are your ward members ladies and gentlemen? Have a Gentlemen and Gentle Ladies night. The possibilities are endless. On one hand you can teach manners and perhaps even ballroom dancing. On the other hand, you can remember those original gentle men and gentle ladies and celebrate the Knights of the Round Table.

17 Disneyland opened on this day in 1955. Celebrate by creating your own "theme park" in the cultural hall.

18 Hog Calling Contest Day. Time for another festival of little-known talents?

19 This is Flitch Day, when bacon is given to any married couple who can prove they have lived in harmony and fidelity for the past year. This could make for an interesting program.

20 Man first walked on the moon in 1969. Hold an event to set and share your own ambitious goals. Be sure to have a Moonwalk for the kids.

21 National Junk Food Day. Finally—an activity where people can bring the foods they really eat!

22 Preparedness Day. Plan activities related to personal and family preparedness.

23 Music was banned in Iran on this day in 1979. You know what to do.

24 Pioneer Day (a Utah state holiday) commemorates the arrival of pioneers in the Salt Lake Valley in 1847. Whether you live in Utah or not, throw a party to honor pioneers in your own ward. Remember, everyone is a pioneer of some sort. This is the time for a little personal recognition.

25 Act Like a Caveman Day. That brings to mind several activity ideas, a few of which are moderately tasteful.

26 Benjamin Franklin was appointed the Postmaster General on this day in 1775. Why not create and mail care packages to the missionaries from your ward or to friends who have moved away?

27 Confucius's birthday. Sponsor a party spotlighting Chinese food and culture. Make fortune cookies on the premises and award prizes for the most creative sayings.

28 An indoor record was set on this day in 1987, when a paper airplane flew 196 feet, 2 inches. Have members create and fly their own paper airplanes and give prizes in several categories. Serve airplane meals for dinner (just kidding about that part!).

29 National Lasagna Day. Award prizes for the best, but nobody tops Kathy's recipe.

30 Arnold Schwarzenegger's birthday. Have a humorous body-building competition.

31 Jimmy Hoffa was last seen on this day in 1975. This would be a good evening for a mystery party or a treasure hunt.

August

01 This is Herman Melville's birthday, and also the date that Shredded Wheat® cereal was patented. Hold a costume party using *Moby Dick* as the theme. Serve breakfast food for refreshments.

02 The first skating rink opened on this day. Sponsor an activity where your group goes ice or roller-skating.

03 Columbus set sail on his first voyage in 1492. Sponsor a treasure hunt.

04 National Chocolate Chip Day. Award prizes for the best homemade recipes featuring these little nuggets of temptation.

05 The television program *American Bandstand* debuted on this day. Give a beauty seminar featuring age-defying secrets, or teach young girls to make poodle skirts.

06 Friendship Day. Sponsor an activity, such as a progressive dinner, that helps someone find a new friend in the ward.

07 The first photograph of Earth from space was taken on this day in 1959. Sponsor a seminar on taking better photographs. Invite the entire neighborhood.

08 A sixty-five-pound trout was caught on this day. Go fishing if you have a nearby pond or stream. If you don't, serve a seafood dinner and tell fish stories.

09 National Polka Festival Day. Sponsor a dance. You don't really have to do the polka unless you are adventurous.

10 The movie *Gidget Goes Hawaiian* premiered on this day in 1961. How about a luau?

11 The animated cartoon process was patented on this day. Come dressed as your favorite characters and watch cartoons.

12 Today marks the height of the Perseids meteor shower. If the sky is clear, have a meteor shower party. If it's Friday night, have a family campout under the stars.

13 International Left-handers Day. Hold a party honoring south paws. Have the right-handed people serve dinner.

14 The U.S. Social Security System was created on this day in 1935. Sponsor a seminar that teaches about retirement and investing.

15 On this day in 1839, the doctrine of baptism for the dead was publicly announced by Joseph Smith. This would be a good day for a youth baptism trip.

16 Watermelon Festival. A good day for a cookout, followed by lots of ice-cold watermelon for dessert.

17 National Thrift Shop Day. Organize a drive to collect unwanted household goods, box them up, and deliver them to your favorite thrift shop.

18 Bad Poetry Day. Who will win the prize for writing the worst poetry?

19 Festival of Random Access Memory. Sponsor a seminar to teach members more about their home computers. Or teach a class on building a better memory. Mnemonics, anyone?

20 The Voyager 2 satellite was launched on this day in 1977. Hold a movie night featuring films on space exploration.

21 Hawaii became the fiftieth state on this day in 1959. Celebrate by wearing loud floral clothes. Give prizes for the best and worst. Eat pineapple ice cream sundaes as a treat.

22 Science fiction writer Ray Bradbury's birthday. Celebrate space travel or circuses—two of Bradbury's chief fascinations.

23 Permanent Press Day. Dig out some of those tacky polyester clothes from the '70s and have a costume party.

24 The Parcel Post System was authorized by the U.S. Congress on this day in 1913. Sponsor an activity to create and mail care packages to ward members away at college or in the military.

25 On this day in 1878, Aurelia Spencer Rogers founded the Primary organization in Farmington, Utah. Have a Primary birthday party.

26 Women's Equality Day commemorates the passing of the Nineteenth Amendment in 1920, which gave women the right to

vote. Honor the women in your
ward or group.

27 Today was the first day someone
was jailed for speeding in an automobile. Celebrate by having a road
rally and obeying the speed limit.

28 National Cherry Turnover Day.
Ask members to bring any dish
containing cherries (cooked,
frozen, or fresh). Award prizes for
the most tasty and creative.

29 Chop suey was invented on this

day at the Waldorf Hotel in New
York City. Teach a class in oriental cooking. Let attendees consume
the results.

30 National Toasted Marshmallow
Day. Schedule a ward campout.
Cook hot dogs and marshmallows
over the fire.

31 Wisconsin State Cow-Chip Throw.
If cow chips are in short supply,
find a more tasteful alternative.

September

01 The wreck of the ocean liner
Titanic was found on this day in
1985. Host a cruise party with
theme costumes and dancing, and
lots of fancy food (as fancy as your
budget will allow).

02 Autumn's hay fever season is in
full swing. Celebrate allergies with
humor and games, or give an
allergy seminar and teach useful
information.

03 *The Muppet Show* debuted on this
day. Make puppets and put on a
puppet show.

04 The first self-service restaurant
opened on this day. Take a group
to a restaurant or have a party in
the ward where everyone serves
himself (what else is new?).

05 National Cheese Pizza Day. Have
a contest where teams compete to
make the best pizza. Prizes for the
best ones, and everyone gets to eat
the results.

06 Read a Book Day. Start a program

to encourage members to read the
Book of Mormon.

07 Grandfathers' Day. Honor grandfathers in the ward, or have an
activity to encourage children to
write to their grandfathers.

08 National Neighborhood Day.
Promote an activity to clean up or
improve the neighborhoods within
the ward boundaries.

09 Colonel Sanders's birthday (the
inventor of Kentucky Fried
Chicken®). Hold a chicken dinner
in his honor.

10 National Wiener Schnitzel Day.
Have an activity spotlighting
German food and culture.

11 Pretty Boy Floyd robbed his first
grocery store on this day in 1925.
Hold a seminar on self-defense and
crime prevention.

12 The television program *Lassie*
debuted on this day in 1954. Have
a dog show, where dog lovers can

exhibit their prized pets. Have the dog-haters award hilarious prizes.

13 The birthday of Judith "Miss Manners" Martin. Hold a formal dinner for the adults, and have the youth learn proper etiquette by setting the tables and serving the meal.

14 The first board game, *A Journey Through Europe,* was offered for sale on this day in 1759. Celebrate by holding a game party or a European cultural night.

15 National Sand Sculpture Tournament. Have ward members display their artistic talents, such as artwork, sculptures, photographs, and stained glass.

16 Mexico Independence Day. Celebrate Mexican culture in terms of decorations, food, and entertainment.

17 The 33⅓ RPM "long-play" record was introduced on this day in 1931. If you can still find records and a turntable, show the kids how Mom and Dad used to dance.

18 The television program *Get Smart* debuted on this day in 1965. This is a great opportunity to present a seminar on home improvements, or learn a craft or two.

19 Bissell® patented the carpet sweeper on this day in 1876. If you haven't thoroughly cleaned the meetinghouse since Comet® day, it's time for another deep cleaning.

20 Italian National Feast. Sponsor a potluck dinner featuring Italian food.

21 Miniature Golf Day. Construct a course in your cultural hall and let members play. Award prizes for the lowest—and highest— scores.

22 On this day in 1827, Joseph Smith obtained the gold plates from the angel Moroni at the Hill Cumorah. How about giving a journal-writing seminar, so ward members can learn how to write their own "gold plates"?

23 Checkers Day. Does anyone remember how to play checkers anymore? Hold a ward elimination tournament, or make a life-size checkerboard and have players leapfrog over one another.

24 National Bluebird of Happiness Day. Sponsor a service project to bring happiness into someone's life.

25 The first blood transfusion using human blood was performed on this day in 1818. Organize a service project where ward members can donate blood.

26 The C.I.A. (Central Intelligence Agency) was established on this day. Celebrate with a party where everyone comes in disguise and brings some kind of mystery food.

27 The first blues song was published on this day in 1912. Sponsor an activity where members write and perform their own sad songs. Make impossible rules such as having to use the word "refrigerator" in the song, or writing a verse about a dog and a truck. Award prizes for the saddest and most miserable songs.

28 Ask a Stupid Question Day. A good excuse to hold a trivia game party.

29 The telephone answering machine is tested on this day in 1950.

Sponsor a contest where ward members write possible messages for answering machines. Award prizes for the most clever.

30 The television program *The Flintstones* debuted on this day in 1960. Have an outdoor cookout and teach survival skills.

October

01 Julie Andrews's birthday. Have a "My Favorite Things" party.

02 The television program *This Old House* debuted on this day in 1979. Sponsor a seminar about home repair projects.

03 Cartiér discovered Montreal on this day in 1642. Hold an activity to celebrate our friends in Canada.

04 National Taco Day. What better excuse to make and serve all kinds of Mexican food?

05 The PBS (Public Broadcasting System) television network debuted on this day in 1967. Hold an educational or cultural activity.

06 Chowderfest. Who can make the best corn chowder? Or chicken, or mussel? Award prizes for the most tasty and creative. Crown a King and Queen Chowderhead to preside over the festivities.

07 Edgar Allen Poe died on this day in 1849. Read one of his stories or view a movie adaptation suitable for your audience.

08 The first airline movie was shown on this day. Create an "airplane" and show a movie during the

"flight." Have flight attendants serve snacks.

09 Season of Glass. Have someone teach a class on basic stained glass making. Clark will teach it if you pay his expenses.

10 This is National Angel Food Cake Day, and also the day potato chips were first made. Serve either or both of them at your activity of choice.

11 National Bookkeeper's Day. Sponsor a seminar on budgeting and family finances. Then serve refreshments.

12 Global Scream Day. Sponsor a session on stress reduction.

13 Pumpkin Festival. Hold a pumpkin party that features pumpkin carving, pumpkin pies, and pumpkin costumes.

14 National Chocolate Covered Insect Day. Well, if you're going to be that way, then chocolate covered raisins and nuts would be an acceptable alternative.

15 National Grouch Day. Plan a service activity to cheer up the grouches in your ward or neighborhood.

16 Dictionary Day. Have a Scrabble® tournament to improve your vocabulary. Be sure to use all those Scrabble® dictionaries!

17 Big Yellow Hat Day. Have people wear outrageous costumes and award prizes for the best ones.

18 Lincoln began growing his beard on this day in 1860, in response to a letter from an eleven-year-old girl. Sponsor a seminar or class on personal improvement of any type, or get together and write letters to missionaries or public servants.

19 *West Side Story* premiered. Show a musical, or (if you're ambitious) have your group present one.

20 Ellery Queen's birthday. This would be a good day for a mystery party or a Clue® marathon.

21 National Shut-In Day. Dress in costumes and take cookies to people in a rest home or to the homes of ward members.

22 William Miller predicted the world would end on this day in 1844. It did not. Throw a not-quite-the-millennium party.

23 Canning Day. Sponsor a seminar teaching about food preservation and storage. Serve some preserved foods to show they are edible. (The trick is to find foods that actually taste good.)

24 United Nations Day. Celebrate the different nations of the world. Provide an activity with diverse costumes, foods, decorations, and talents.

25 National Greasy Foods Day. Do we really want to celebrate this? Hold an activity that features and serves healthy foods.

26 French Food Festival. We've given other cultures their day. How about the French? And no, French fries are not an acceptable menu item. Snails, however, are.

27 National Potato Day. A potato bar is always good for a simple, inexpensive and yet tasty treat. Let the ward provide the potatoes and the members the toppings.

28 Wild Foods Day. Sponsor an activity where you prepare and serve foods not of the standard meat-and-potatoes variety.

29 National Disgusting Little Pumpkin-Shaped Candies Day. If your ward doesn't "do" Halloween, have an autumn harvest party.

30 Time clock patented. How about a seminar related to getting a better job or keeping your current one?

31 Halloween. Do you really need help with this one?

November

01 All Saints' Day. This is the opposite of Halloween—it is the day when the ghosts return to their graves after their Halloween outing. Turn all those carved pumpkins into pumpkin pies, and celebrate.

02 The first newspaper crossword puzzle was published on this day. Have a party featuring word games.

03 Sandwich Day. Attempt to make a giant hoagie sandwich that will feed your entire group. Have everyone help make the sandwich and then enjoy the spoils.

04 King Tutankhamen's tomb was discovered on this day in 1922. Have a King Tut party, and be sure to serve Egyptian food.

05 Roy Rogers' birthday. Have an indoor rodeo and serve cowboy food around the fake campfire.

06 National Nachos Day. Time for another challenge. Who can make the best plate of nachos?

07 Lewis and Clark reached the Pacific Ocean on this day in 1805. Sponsor a treasure hunt and let everyone search for hidden treasure.

08 X rays were discovered on this day in 1895. Sponsor a health seminar or a class that teaches first aid.

09 The first stealth aircraft was introduced on this day in 1988. Have your ward or group do a good deed in secret for a person or group in the neighborhood.

10 The television program *Sesame Street* debuted on this day in 1969. Show some *Sesame Street* videos to distract the kids while the adults party elsewhere, or have a cookie bakeoff in honor of Cookie Monster.

11 Veteran's Day or Armistice Day. Observes the ending of World War I, and honors all those who served in wars. Honor those in your community who have rendered public service in various ways.

12 The first automated teller machine (ATM) began operation on this day in New York City's Chemical Bank in 1969. Sponsor a service auction where bidders use play money to "buy" acts of service donated by group members.

13 The movie *Fantasia* premiered in 1940. Show it, or any other good family film.

14 Claude Monet's birthday. Teach a seminar on drawing or appreciating fine art.

15 National Clean out Your Refrigerator Day. Have everyone bring an item actually found in their refrigerator. Give prizes for the strangest and oldest items.

16 The first relay race was held on this day. Divide into teams and hold an indoor competition featuring relay races requiring both physical and mental skills.

17   Homemade Bread Day. Have everyone bring a loaf of their favorite recipe. Award prizes for the best, and let the audience eat the entries (after judging).

18   The first teddy bear was made on this day. Organize a drive to collect Christmas toys for children who need them. Repair, wrap, and make them ready for giving.

19   Ford halted production of the Edsel automobile on this day in 1959. Sponsor an exhibit of antiques or one-of-a-kind objects loaned by ward members. This is a great opportunity for a white elephant exchange.

20   The first national crocheting contest was held on this day. Sponsor an exhibit of various crafts created by the members of your ward or group. Avoid hurt feelings by prohibiting buying and selling.

21   Nostalgia for the Future Day. Sponsor an event where group members provide items for a time capsule that will be opened a year from now.

22   National Roast Turkey Day. Sponsor a pre- (or post-) Thanksgiving dinner for those who will be away from their families during the holidays.

23   Great Tinker Toy Extravaganza. Bring toys or games that can be enjoyed down on the carpet. Forget your inhibitions and act like a kid.

24   Use Even If Seal Is Broken Day. Organize a fair where members can give away used (but still serviceable) items they no longer need.

25   The first public performance by a sword swallower occurred on this day. Must be time for another talent show featuring dubious talents.

26   The television program *The Price Is Right* debuted on this day in 1956. Sponsor your own version of a television game show. Offer valuable (but inexpensive) prizes to the winners. Or give a seminar on smart shopping.

27   The movie *Casablanca* premiered. Show a romantic movie while the kids are distracted in another room.

28   The first legal maternity leave is granted in France in 1909. Sponsor an activity where the audience tries to identify group members by their baby pictures.

29   Square Dance Day. If you provide chili and corn bread, even those who don't like to dance should come for the food.

30   Judge a Book by Its Cover Day. Sponsor a favorite old book day that will introduce people to new authors they would enjoy.

December

01 Today begins the advent calendar, counting down the days until Christmas. Sponsor an advent calendar-making fair, where families can make advent calendars to celebrate every day of this festive month.

02 Sugarplum Festival. Produce a Christmas play, or a Christmas talent show. It's never too early to get people into the spirit of the Christmas season.

03 The first successful heart transplant was performed on this day in 1967. Deliver paper hearts and heart-shaped cookies to someone who needs a lift.

04 The first person to die in a bowling ball accident expired on this day in 1982. Sponsor a bowling tournament—but be careful.

05 Tchaikovsky's *Nutcracker* premiered on this day. Sponsor an evening of classical music or ballet. Or get into the Christmas spirit with a "Messiah" sing-along.

06 National Gazpacho Day. Have a potluck dinner featuring everyone's favorite homemade soup (it need not be served cold).

07 The National Fire Safety Council was founded on this day in 1979. Sponsor a seminar on home safety and fire prevention.

08 The Marx Brothers' *Coconuts* premiered on Broadway in 1925.

Have a Marx Brothers film festival and serve coconut cake for dessert.

09 On this day in 1849, the first LDS Sunday School was organized by Richard Ballantyne. Have a birthday party.

10 Nobel Prize Day. Have your own prize program, honoring the accomplishments of your ward or group. These can be serious or silly awards.

11 Laughing gas is first used in pulling a tooth on this day in 1844. Produce a talent show featuring comedy.

12 Poinsettia Day. Take flowers and Christmas treats to those in need of a Christmas visit.

13 National Cocoa Day. What would taste better after a chilly evening singing Christmas carols than mugs of hot cocoa and marshmallows?

14 Today marks the height of the Geminids meteor shower. Put on your warm coats and grab the hot cider.

15 The Bill of Rights (the first ten amendments to the United States Constitution) was adopted on this day. Celebrate the right to worship freely.

16 National Chocolate Covered Anything Day. Who will win the prize for the most unusual chocolate covered food item?

17 Dickens's *A Christmas Carol* was first published. Have your ward present it, with the bishopric playing the parts of the ghosts.

18 On this day in 1833, Joseph Smith, Senior, was ordained the first Church Patriarch. Consider an activity that stresses the importance of patriarchal blessings.

19 Pennsylvania Gingerbread House Invitational. Bake and decorate gingerbread houses, and deliver them to someone who needs some Christmas cheer.

20 Trivial Pursuit® invented. Sponsor a Christmas trivia party.

21 Forefathers' Day. Commemorates the landing of the Pilgrims in 1620 on Plymouth Rock. Have a Pilgrims party.

22 National Date-Nut Bread Day. A good excuse to indulge in any type of Christmas bread or goodies.

23 The first Prophet of the last dispensation, Joseph Smith, was born on this day in 1805. This is certainly cause for celebration.

24 Christmas Eve. Assuming you're prepared for the holiday, visit some friends or go singing Christmas carols.

25 This is probably the greatest day for celebration of the whole year, as most Christians celebrate the birth and life of Jesus Christ.

26 Day after Christmas. Sponsor a white elephant gift party to dispose of those gifts that didn't quite warm the cockles of your heart.

27 National Fruitcake Day. Bake fruitcakes and other goodies. Visit people whom Santa may have missed.

28 Birth of the cinema on this day. Show *It's a Wonderful Life* or some other sentimental Christmas movie.

29 The Philadelphia Pepper Pot dish was invented by George Washington in 1777. Sponsor a meal using recipes all created before 1900.

30 Miracle Day. Organize a service project that will bring a miracle into someone's life.

31 New Year's Eve. Celebrate the accomplishments of the past year, and the promises of the next one.

Questions from the Clueless

? *Is it proper to include Santa Claus as part of a Christmas activity?*

In some wards it would be considered blasphemy to have Santa Claus attend a Christmas activity—in other wards it would be considered blasphemy to *not* have him present. This is something that is highly dependent upon the traditions of the ward, and there will probably be strong opinions on each side of the issue. To change the tradition may require you to have the patience of Job and the wisdom of Solomon.

If your ward is trying to get away from having Santa Claus at ward Christmas parties, you might consider having the bishopric dress as the Three Wise Men and pass out small bags of treats. This seems to work well, and the children enjoy it.

If you like the idea of including Santa as part of the celebration, try to do it in a way that will not distract from the true reason for the holiday—the birth of our Savior, Jesus Christ. Perhaps Santa can arrive at the end of the evening, after all the food has been served and the program has been presented.

No matter when Santa arrives, it may also be reasonable to have him in a separate room from the cultural hall, or wherever the main festivities are occurring. This will be less distracting for everyone involved, and will truly provide at least a physical separation between the spiritual and cultural traditions of Christmas.

CHAPTER 8

Icebreakers and Lifesavers

★ **IN THIS CHAPTER**
✔ Ideas for Keeping Your Activity Moving Along
✔ Lifesavers That Really Save Activities
✔ Warming up the Adults
✔ Warming up the Youth
✔ Warming up the Little Ones

One problem you will always have to deal with when planning an activity is the tendency for certain families to arrive ten, thirty, or even sixty minutes late. This is a fact of life, as parents try to manage large families and still handle their other responsibilities.

Rather than get frustrated over these well-meaning but disorganized folks, one approach is to design your activity so that you can entertain those who arrive early, while holding off the main activity until everyone arrives. That is the purpose of icebreaker activities. They get the crowd warmed up and in a jovial mood, so that when the tardy members finally arrive, everyone will be set to jump right into the main activity. Even if you live in that rare ward where everyone is punctual (if there is such a place), Icebreakers are still a good prelude to the main activity because they give members a chance to have some fun and associate with one another. This is especially important for new members or nonmembers, who may not feel at home when they first arrive on the scene and who may need an excuse to mingle with other participants.

It is quite common during an activity that you will have a lull in the program. For example, the cleaning crew might be clearing off the tables while the program crew is getting ready to present the entertainment. Rather than have your crowd wander off or leave because of boredom, you need to sponsor a short activity that keeps people moving and wakes them up before the next phase of the activity. We refer to these kinds of activities as Lifesavers.

This chapter is simply a collection of short little activities that may be used to give people a laugh and keep them entertained before or between portions of your primary activity. Most of these are suitable as either Icebreakers or Lifesavers, and the few that are not will be readily apparent when you read the descriptions. The activities are listed according to age group.

Warm-Up Activities for Old Fogies

These Icebreakers and Lifesavers are designed for adults, and for general ward activities where adults are present. Most of them are equally successful in both large and small group activities. Human beings are inherently a little bit shy, especially when we get away from our comfort zones. These activities do just that—they force us into that scary realm of human interaction, but they do it without too much trauma. This section includes a variety of entertaining activities, including some tame ones and some that get right in your face, in a good sort of way. If some of the ideas seem lame to you, use others. It's the concept of warm-up activities that we want to convey—the ones you use will depend on the needs of your ward members. Most of these activities involve little or no planning and preparation and can be introduced without much forethought.

Now and Then

Materials: Computer or projector, old photos of people who are attending, pencil and paper
Effort Quotient: ✹
Timing: ⧗
Preparation: ★★

This is an excellent warm-up activity for an auxiliary get-together, but it requires some preparation. A couple of weeks before the activity, have each participant bring a picture of himself as a child. Have someone put the pictures together in a common format (slides, prints, or digital prints on a computer). The object of the game is to identify as many childhood pictures as you can. As the first picture is shown, everyone writes down his guess of whose picture it is. (Assign each picture a number beforehand and announce that number each time the corresponding picture is shown.) This process continues until all the pictures have been shown and everyone has a name for every number. Run through the pictures a couple of times to allow everyone adequate time to guess. The person with the highest score should win a magnificent prize.

Confession

Materials: Paper and pencil for everyone
Effort Quotient: ✦
Time: ⧖
Preparation: ★

Set up tables and chairs in the cultural hall. Divide the group up by using some preconceived method (birth month, numbering people as they enter the cultural hall, or whatever way you want). Seat no more than ten to twelve per table, but make sure each table seats an even number of players. Pair up. The first person in each pair takes three to four minutes to learn as much as possible about his partner and writes these items down on paper. Then the second person quizzes the first one, repeating the process. Finally each person takes one minute to repeat for everyone at the table (from memory—do not use paper) as many facts as he can about his partner. Valuable prizes such as stickers or pieces of candy can be awarded to the person at each table who remembers the most about his partner.

Did You Know?

Materials: Paper and pencil for everyone
Effort Quotient: ✦
Time: ⧖
Preparation: ★

Set up tables and chairs in the cultural hall. Divide the group by some preconceived method and seat no more than ten to twelve persons per table. Each person in the group writes down something he or she doesn't think the rest of the group will know about him or her. The pieces of paper are folded, numbered, and placed in a cup or hat. The slips of paper are then pulled out of the container and read one by one. Each member of the group compiles a list of people they feel best matches the number of each clue. After the last slip is read, the person with the most correct matches wins and is justly and handsomely rewarded with a stick of gum, piece of candy, sticker, or some other treasure. This can also be used with "most embarrassing moment," "my silliest habit," or some similar bit of personal trivia.

All the News That Fits

Materials: Plenty of newspapers or magazines (depending on the size of your group)
Effort Quotient: ✋
Time: ⏳
Preparation: ★

Give everyone a section of newspaper or several pages of magazine. Everybody is to spend three to five minutes looking for words, phrases, and pictures that describe them or something about them. Each person can pick as many things that describe him as he wants; however, everyone will have to take turns telling the group why he picked out the things he did. This is a very enlightening activity.

Stick 'Em Up!

Materials: None
Effort Quotient: ✋✋
Time: ⏳
Preparation: ★

Have your group stand in a circle. The person who's *it* walks around inside the circle, chooses a member of the circle at random, points his finger at the person, and says, "Stick 'em up!" The victim must raise both hands straight up in the air and say his name and the names of the persons to his immediate right and left. The person to the victim's left must raise his right arm straight up, and the person to the right must raise his left arm straight up. If anybody makes a mistake, either by raising the wrong arms or saying the wrong names, that person becomes *it*. Repeat the game until everyone is too tired to raise their arms anymore.

Let's Get Introduced

Materials: Something that makes music
Effort Quotient: 🖐🖐
Time: ⌛
Preparation: ★

Arrange people in two circles (facing each other), women on the inside, men on the outside. There should be an equal number of males and females As the music starts, the women move clockwise and the men move counterclockwise. As the music stops, introduce yourself to the person facing you. Tell each other one thing you like and one thing you don't like. Continue the process until the first person falls from exhaustion.

Mental Block

Materials: One soft rubber ball or aluminum foil ball
Effort Quotient: 🖐🖐
Time: ⌛
Preparation: ★

Have everyone sit in a circle. If there is a chance that names may be unfamiliar to some players, go around the circle and have everyone say his name. Then the first person starts by saying his name and picks a category (fruit, cars, insects, books, cities, countries, current ward Primary teachers, and so on). That person throws the ball to someone else. This person must say the name of the person who threw the ball and something that relates to the chosen category. That person then throws the ball to someone else. The game is repeated until someone makes a mistake or can't immediately think of an answer that fits the category. If someone makes a mistake, everyone in the circle points a finger at the offending person and says, "Mental block. Stop the clock!" Once the game is started again, a new category is chosen. Continue the game until everyone knows each other's name.

Who or What Am I?

Materials: Tape or safety pins and various advertisements cut out
of newspapers or magazines
Effort Quotient: 🖐🖐

Time: ⧗
Preparation: ★★

Attach an advertisement to the back of each person. Everybody mingles and asks questions about their respective advertisements. Responses can only be "yes" or "no." The first person who guesses who or what he is wins an appropriate prize, or at least a round of applause.

John Hancock

Materials: Paper bags and marking pens
Effort Quotient: ♆♆
Time: ⧗
Preparation: ★

Each player receives a paper bag and a marking pen. The bag is placed over the person's writing hand. Everyone mingles and tries to get as many signatures on their bags as possible within a specific time period. The clincher is people can only sign their signatures with their opposite hand. The person with the most signatures (that can be identified) in the time limit wins. Some great prize (sticker, piece of candy, a million dollars) can be awarded.

Oink or Hee Haw Game

Materials: None
Effort Quotient: ♆
Time: ⧗
Preparation: ★

This is actually a popular children's game, but can be played by adults with hilarious results. Have the group form a circle, either sitting on the floor or in chairs. One person starts by snorting at the person to his right. The person receiving the snort turns to his right and passes the snort

along. This process continues around the circle. Neither the person snorting nor the person receiving the snort can laugh. Anyone who laughs in the process of snorting is out. (Laughing is quite permissible unless it's your turn to snort.) If someone is snorted at and can't make a snorting sound, an equally obnoxious "hee haw" can be substituted. This new sound is then passed on down the line. This is a sure fire way to lighten up any group.

Pass the TP, Please

Materials: A roll of toilet paper per group
Effort Quotient: ♥
Time: ⧗
Preparation: ★

Divide group into smaller groups (eight to twelve per group). Have each group sit in a circle or around a table. A roll of toilet paper is then passed around the group. Each person takes as many sheets off the roll as he wants. The minimum is one sheet. Once everyone has taken his share of toilet paper, return the roll to the leader. The clincher is that for every sheet of toilet paper, each person must tell one thing about himself. Start with the leader and go around the circle. Skittles,® M&Ms®, or dried beans can be substituted for toilet paper if you're dealing with a group that might be easily embarrassed.

Bean There, Done That

Materials: Dried red beans (or some other object that can be thrown without rolling)
Effort Quotient: ♥
Time: ⧗
Preparation: ★

Sit or stand in a circle. Pass out an equal number of beans to everyone in the circle. (A medium-sized group may start with five beans per person, depending on how long you want to play the game.) The person who is designated to start the game says the following: "My name is (say name) and I've (done so-and-so)." For example, "My name is Kent and I've lived in Athens." That person throws a bean on the floor in the middle of the circle, and only those in the group who have also done the thing in question can throw a bean in the middle as well. Repeat the process until the first person runs out of beans. This experienced person should win a valuable prize.

Love Me/Love Me Not

Materials: None
Effort Quotient: ✹✹
Time: ⧗
Preparation: ★

Arrange the group into a circle. The group can be seated, standing, or sitting on the floor. *It* goes up to someone and says, "Hey, (say person's first name), do you love me?" The person can respond yes or no. If the person responds with a yes, he must add the phrase, "But I don't love people (name a characteristic of people in the group—people who wear glasses, have on white socks, have black hair, are taller than 5'2," and so on)." The people with the characteristic mentioned must switch places. *It* tries to get one of the vacant spots. Whoever is left without a place is the new *it*. If the person who is asked the question responds, "No," everyone switches places and *it* has an easier job of finding a seat.

Nephite/Lamanite

Materials: None
Effort Quotient: ✹✹✹
Time: ⧗
Preparation: ★

Arrange the group into a circle. Everyone is to introduce themselves to the people on both sides of them. If *it* walks up to someone and says "Nephite," the person must say the name of the person on his right. If the *it* person says "Lamanite," the person is to say the name of the person on his left. If someone messes up, he becomes *it*. Repeat until it's time to move on to some other activity.

Top Dog

Materials: Chairs, 3x5-inch cards, marking pen, tape
Effort Quotient: ✹✹

Time: ⌛
Preparation: ★

Arrange chairs in a circle. Give each person a 3x5-inch card and have him put his first name on it. Tape the card to the back part of the chair so the card is showing when the person gets up. One person is designated as the "top dog," or the number one chair. The "top dog" starts the game by saying, "Hi, my name's _____. Where's _____?" That person is to say "Hi, my name's _____. Where's _____." Repeat the process until somebody makes a mistake. If someone makes a mistake, he moves to the seat at the left of the "top dog" and everyone else moves up a chair. Here's the trick. For those who have moved up, your name becomes the name on the card that is taped to your new chair. This sounds confusing, but it's not. It's plenty of fun, as long as you can get the game rolling by having someone make a mistake early on in the game. (You may have to plant someone in the audience to make that first mistake, but once people have changed chairs, mistakes will be frequent.) Note: The top dog never moves, so this is a great position for someone who isn't mobile.

Investigative Reporter

Materials: Quiz sheet and pencil for all players; tape and 3x5-inch cards for the organizer
Effort Quotient: ♆♆
Time: ⌛
Preparation: ★★

This activity takes a little time to prepare, but it's well worth the effort. As everyone enters the cultural hall, write a number on a 3x5-inch card and tape it to that person's back. Give each person a quiz sheet with instructions to find out certain information about eight to ten other members. For example, write down the shoe size of number 27; learn number 12's favorite flavor of ice cream; determine what color number 3's socks are. All quizzes will have to be slightly different. The first person to complete his or her paper wins some appropriate prize. This activity is a lot of fun and really forces people to mingle.

Rutabaga, Rutabaga, Rutabaga, YUCK!

Materials: None
Effort Quotient: ♦♦♦
Time: ⌛
Preparation: ★

Sneaky Secret
If you are in charge of an activity, large or small, come prepared with at least two Lifesavers. You may never have to use them, but if they are needed, you will thank yourself later. If they aren't needed, then you can store them for the next activity and no one will be the wiser.

Have everyone form a large circle with some space between each person. Each person is to come up with one simple motion (snap your fingers, tap your feet, thump your chest, clap your hands, and so on) that can be repeated as the group says, "Rutabaga, Rutabaga, Rutabaga, Yuck!" Each person need only concentrate on the person to his or her right. At the completion of each, "yuck," each person is to take on the action of the person to his right. Continue doing this until someone messes up. That person leaves the circle, and can help point out other unfortunates who mess up and should be eliminated. Continue the game until it is time for the main activity.

Dynamic Duos

Materials: Pencil or pen and sheet of paper for everyone
Effort Quotient: ♦
Time: ⌛
Preparation: ★

Divide the group into smaller groups (eight to twelve per group), or play the game as one large group. The group is given two minutes to list as many pairs of words (can include opposites, and so on) as they can think of. For example: hot/cold, dark/light, bacon/eggs, India/Pakistan, peanut butter/jelly. After the two minutes are up, the group is told to quit writing. One person starts and begins reading his list of dynamic duos. As the duos are read, everyone who has a duplicate on his own list should scratch off the duplicate. One at a time, have everyone read his list aloud until all the duplicates have been eliminated. The person with the most remaining duos is the winner and should receive an appropriate and valuable prize.

Pat on the Back

Materials: Pencil or pen and sheet of paper for everyone; tape; tissues
Effort Quotient: ♥♥♥
Time: ⧖
Preparation: ★

This is a warm-up activity that seems to appeal to women more than men. Tape a blank sheet of paper to the back of each participant. Have the group mingle, stopping to write one good thing about each person on her sheet of paper. Because the paper is on the person's back, nobody ever knows who wrote what comment. After the time limit is up and everyone's papers are full, sit down and have each person read aloud her own paper. Get out the tissues and wait for the sniffles to start as people realize how many good things others have said about them. This activity is such an ego-boost that women often take home those sheets of paper and keep them forever.

Barnyard

Materials: None
Effort Quotient: ♥♥♥
Time: ⧖
Preparation: ★

Arrange the group in a circle. Count off by fours until everyone has a number. All the ones become chickens. All the twos become goats. All the threes become cows. And all the fours become horses. Call out one and four. All the chickens and all the horses must change places within the circle. Call out three. All the cows must change places. Continue calling out numbers until the group gets bored, then call "barnyard," at which point everyone must change places. The game is now over.

Losing Your Marbles

Materials: Marbles, music
Effort Quotient: ♥
Time: ⧖
Preparation: ★

Arrange the group into a circle. Give a marble to each person. Select five different people and give them several marbles rather than just one. When the music starts, players pass their marbles to the right, one at a time, as fast as possible. When the music stops, the person(s) with the most marbles is out. Continue the game with the same number of marbles, but fewer people. By the way, anyone who drops or throws a marble is also out. This is a simple but interesting activity.

Warming Up the Younger Set

Warm-up activities may be even more invaluable for youth activities than they are in ward activities for adults. The primary purpose of these activities is to break down the unseen barriers that human beings tend to put up when faced with new situations, and youth are especially vulnerable to feelings of insecurity in the face of new situations and new groups.

Icebreakers and Lifesavers for youth serve as distractions that perform a threefold function. They get youth speaking to one another. They initiate physical contact, in a good sense of the word. And they provide a mental distraction so the youth don't have time to be self-conscious. Don't ever underestimate the power of a good warm-up activity to get your youth activity off to a successful start.

Human Knot

Materials: None
Effort Quotient: ♈♈♈
Time: ⧗
Preparation: ★

Form a tight circle. Have everyone reach into the circle and grab someone's hands. If done right, the group should be pretty well entangled. Now the object is to get untangled without anyone letting go of hands. This can be quite entertaining and will certainly knock down any barriers. Can also be played by having someone be the "doctor" and become responsible for untangling the mass of humanity.

Name That Hobby

Materials: None
Effort Quotient: ☙
Time: ⧖
Preparation: ★

Gather the youth into a circle. Have the first person say her name and hobby: "My name is Shannon, and my hobby is playing the piano." The next person repeats that information and adds his own: "Her name is Shannon and her hobby is playing the piano. My name is Kent and my hobby is running." Continue around the circle, each person adding his or her own information to the list. The last person who can recite everyone's name and hobby wins.

Chinese Dragon

Materials: Two bandannas
Effort Quotient: ☙☙☙
Time: ⧖
Preparation: ★

Divide the youth into two teams. Have each team get into a line, with each youth putting his hands on the waist of the person in front of him to form a chain. You now have two chains of youth. Stick the bandannas in the back pockets of the end person in each chain. The goal will be for the front person in the line to try to get the bandanna out of the pocket of the back person in the other line, while the back person tries to avoid losing the bandanna.

Bat the Bunny Tails

Materials: Bag of cotton balls, gloves, table, blindfolds
Effort Quotient: ☙☙
Time: ⧖
Preparation: ★

Pick two volunteers who aren't afraid of looking silly. Have them put on gloves and stand at each end of a long table. Spread the bag of cotton balls on the table and blindfold the players. While instructing them to sweep all the cotton balls off their own side of the table, have someone quietly take the cotton balls off the table. Yell "Go!" and watch the volunteers wildly sweep at an empty table. Have your group cheer and encourage them. Let them bat away for a few minutes before taking off their blindfolds and showing them what they've been doing.

All in Stitches

Materials: One spoon, and a long length of yarn for each team, towels
Effort Quotient: ✹✹
Time: ⧗
Preparation: ★★

Cut one piece of yarn per team into twenty- to forty-foot pieces that average about four feet per person (five to ten youth per team). Tie a spoon onto one end of each piece of yarn. Put the spoons/yarn in the freezer no less than one hour before the start of the game. For added torture (the youth love this!), dip the spoons in water to get ice buildup, or even better, find a small bowl (margarine container size) and freeze the spoon in it with water to create a small block of ice. Hand the first person on each team the spoon and have them thread it through their clothing from their shirt collar down through their pant leg and out. The next person threads the spoon from the bottom of a pant leg up through the shirt and out the collar. Continue this until the entire team is threaded together. Make sure your youth understand that the spoon should not go in undergarments, only inside shirt and pants. See which team can complete the task first. It's fun to watch them squirm.

Dr. Scholl's® Game of Shoes

Materials: None
Effort Quotient: ✹
Time: ⧗
Preparation: ★

This is best for larger groups. Have everyone take off a shoe and throw it into a pile in the center of the room and then move back to the wall of the room. When the leader says "Go," everyone grabs a shoe from the pile. The youth then need to find the shoe owner and learn his name, as well as four things about him that others may not know. When everyone has interviewed his shoe owner, have everyone form a circle and one at a time introduce the person they talked to, telling the group the four things they found out about the person, and then returning the shoe.

Pink Spots

Materials: Pink lipstick and facial tissues
Effort Quotient: ♆
Time: ⧗
Preparation: ★

This is a good game for learning names in a group. Have your youth sit in a circle. The leader begins by standing up and saying, "My name is _____, and I have no pink spots. How many pink spots does (someone else in the group) have?" The person named stands up and repeats exactly what the leader said, except for the obvious difference of using his own name in the first sentence and naming someone else in the group in the second sentence. Any mistakes or hesitation earns the speaker a pink spot of lipstick on the face, and he'll need to try again before sitting down. Now that person has one pink spot and will have to say, "My name is _____, and I have one pink spot. How many pink spots does _____ have?"

Sister Sassy

Materials: None
Effort Quotient: ♆
Time: ⧗
Preparation: ★

Have your youth sit in a circle. The object of this little game is to talk like you have no teeth; youth cannot show any teeth throughout the duration of the game. Pull both your lips in and over your teeth. The game is started by someone asking if anyone has seen Sister Sassy, as she is missing. Continue play around the circle, one at a time. Allow as much discussion and conversation as the youth can creatively come up with about where Sister Sassy is. Anyone who shows his or her teeth will need to leave the circle. Play till one person is left.

Mummy Run

Materials: 1 flat bedsheet for each team (preferably white)
Effort Quotient: ✋✋
Time: ⧖
Preparation: ★

Divide into teams, then split up the teams so that half of each team is on the opposite side of the room or playing area from the other half. The first person on each team wraps himself in the sheet by lying down on it and rolling. The arms need to be inside the sheet, and the wrapping job should be a snug fit. After the person is wrapped, he should stand up (with the help of the rest of the team members on his side of the room, if needed). Then, still wrapped like a mummy, he should run to the other half of the team group across the room, and unroll. The first person on that side wraps up and runs back across the room. Continue the relay until everyone has wrapped and run. The first team finished is the winner.

Gorilla, Man, Rifle

Materials: Lots of warm bodies
Effort Quotient: ✋✋
Time: ⧖
Preparation: ★

This game is played the same way as "Rock, Paper, Scissors," except that you use your entire body to play. Everyone pairs up and stands back to back with his partner. If your group has an odd number of individuals in it, just have those who don't get to play the first time join with a partner after the first round. When a leader says, "Go," everyone turns around to face his partner and make the gesture of his choice. Gorilla roars out loud while beating his chest with his hands. Man stands proudly in place with arms folded and his head held high. Rifle shoots a pretend rifle while saying, "Bang! Bang!" Gorilla beats Man because he is bigger and stronger. Man beats Rifle because he invented it. Rifle beats Gorilla. The winners of each round find another partner who won, and the losers are out. Continue to play till there is one person left.

Back Art

Materials: Paper and pencils
Effort Quotient: ✥
Time: ⧗
Preparation: ★

Divide the youth into several groups. Have each group sit or stand on the floor, single file and facing forward, train-style. Have a simple object drawn on a piece of paper and show it to the last person in each line. They are to draw this object with their fingers on the back of the person in front of them. That person draws the same object on the back of the person in front of him, and so does each person up the line. The first person in the line will draw the object on paper. The first team finished whose beginning and ending pictures resemble each other the most wins.

Eggs-Act Directions

Materials: Hard-boiled eggs, blindfolds, garbage cans
Effort Quotient: ✥
Time: ⧗
Preparation: ★★

Form groups of five and assign each team a number. Each team picks a person who doesn't mind eating a hard-boiled egg. Place all the eggs, which have been labeled with the corresponding team numbers, on a plate at one end of the room. Each team blindfolds its chosen person and then tries to direct him to the egg with the appropriate team number written on it. The trick to this is that the team members can't use the words *left, right, up, down, east, west, forward,* or *back(ward).* They will need to come up with different descriptive words to get the team "egg-eater" to the correct egg. The first team whose egg-eater has totally consumed the correct egg wins.

Jaredite Battle

Materials: Balloons, each team needs its own color
Effort Quotient: ✥✥✥
Time: ⧗
Preparation: ★

Divide the group into two teams, one led by Coriantumr and one led by Shiz. Each team must defend its treasure (a pile of balloons) while attempting to steal or destroy the other team's treasure. Play for a pre-determined amount of time, five to ten minutes is good. When the game is over, each team's unpopped balloons are worth 100 points each. Stolen, unpopped balloons are worth 200 points each.

Bucket and Shoes

Materials: A five-gallon bucket, a few towels
Effort Quotient: ♥♥♥
Time: ⧗
Preparation: ★

This activity has the potential to get the participants quite wet. Make sure you schedule it for a warm summer night, and make sure everyone wears old clothes and brings extra clothes to change into after the activity. Three or four youth lie on their backs in a circle with their legs straight up in the air and their feet making a "table" in the center. A full bucket of water is placed on the "table," and the challenge is for the youth to remove their shoes one by one. You can make it easier or harder by increasing or decreasing the amount of people or water. Be mindful of any girls in white shirts, and make sure the bucket is never in a position where it could fall on someone's head and cause an injury.

The Nose Bone's Connected to the Ankle Bone

Materials: Music that can be stopped quickly (CD/tape player or piano)
Effort Quotient: ♥♥♥
Time: ⧗
Preparation: ★

Have everyone find a partner. The group should make two circles, one inside the other, with one person from each partnership in a different circle. This game is similar to musical chairs. When the music is playing, the youth should be walking in their separate circles. (The circles move in opposite directions.) When the music stops, the leader calls out two body parts. The partners need to find each other, connect the body parts, and hold their position until it's time to circle up again. For example, when the leader calls out *foot* and *head,* the partners quickly find each other, connect one partner's foot to the other's head and hold it till the leader has them get back in their circles. Try a couple of practice rounds first to let the players get used to the game. When the game starts, eliminate the slowest one to three couples (depending on the size of the group). You can use any number of body parts—rump, foot, calf, scalp, back, nose. Be creative but tasteful. When you're down to the last few couples try something like nose to nose, or nose to ear. The youth enjoy this one.

Rounding Up the Primary Posse

Here are some warm-up activities that are appropriate for Primary children. Although children of this age seldom need to be warmed up for any activity, perhaps these activities will burn off extra energy so that the children will pay attention during the real activity.

David and Goliath

Materials: A beanbag for each child
Effort Quotient: ✸✸✸
Time: ⧖
Preparation: ★

Mark off a game area. The start line will also be the finish line. Place two separate piles of beanbags about fifteen to twenty feet away from the start/finish line. The beanbag piles should be several feet apart from one another. Select one child to be Goliath. Divide the remaining children into two teams and line them up single file at the start/finish line. Each child will take turns being David trying to get stones for his slingshot. The first player in each line runs to pick up a "stone" from the beanbag piles, then runs back across the start/finish line and goes to the end of his team's line, still holding his beanbag. The only obstacle stopping David from getting his stones is Goliath! Goliath waits anywhere between the start/finish line and the "stones" and tries to tag David as they (the Davids) run back and forth across the playing field. If Goliath tags a David, then that David has to start over. Two players will be running at all times, one from each team. The first team with all players standing in line and holding a "stone" wins the game. If time allows, trade off playing Goliath. Remember that winning/losing is not always a necessary thing for children's games. To make this a no-win game, simply have the two teams continue running until everyone has a "stone." The children will remember most how much fun it was to try to stay away from Goliath, rather than who won anyway.

Blob Tag

Materials: None
Effort Quotient: ♥♥♥
Time: ⧗
Preparation: ★

The only rule in this game is that everyone must stay within the playing area that you have marked off. Start with one person to be *it*. When *it* tags another person, they join hands and become a Blob. They then run together to try to tag someone else. When the third person has been tagged, he/she joins hands with the second person, and the three become the Blob. The three then run to tag another person. When the Blob catches its fourth player, the Blob has the ability to split into two Blobs. The game continues until all the players have been tagged and have become part of a Blob. If the children enjoy it, then let them play again if time allows. It's a great energy tamer.

Backward Relays

Materials: Two 12-inch rubber balls for the Backward Ball Relay
Effort Quotient: ♥♥♥
Time: ⧗
Preparation: ★

As has been mentioned several times in this book, young children enjoy the process of the activity more than competition, so to make these relays no-win, simply have one team and let each child just enjoy the activity.

- **Backward Relay Race.** Mark a start/finish line and a turn-around point, such as a tree or chair (this should be about fifteen to twenty feet from the start/finish line). Divide the children into two teams. Have each person take a turn running backwards as fast as they can to the turn-around point and back to the finish line. The first team finished wins.

- **Crawling Backward Relay.** Mark a start and finish line about ten feet apart. Divide the children into two teams. Have each team stand single file, facing all one direction, and about arm's length apart from one another with legs spread. Make sure there is plenty of space behind the teams. At the signal, the first person in each line should get down on their hands and knees and crawl backwards through the legs of his team. When they reach the end, have them stand up and become part of the line. The first team to have all the players finish the crawl is the winner.
- **Backward Ball Relay.** Divide the children into two teams. Have each team stand single file, facing all one direction, and about arm's length apart from one another. Make sure there is plenty of space in front of the teams. Then have them all sit on the floor exactly where they are standing. Give a ball to the first person in each line and have him pass it back over his head to the player behind him. When the last player in the line gets the ball, he/she will run to the front of the line, sit down, and continue passing the ball. The first team to have the leader return to the front of the line is the winner.

Static

Materials: Balloons, tissue paper, scissors
Effort Quotient: ✋✋✋
Time: ⌛
Preparation: ★

Here is a no-win game that can be used for a variety of different holidays, activities, and even Primary singing time. From the tissue paper, cut out many of whatever shape you've decided on. If it's near Valentine's Day, you might want to use red hearts. For Christmastime, green Christmas trees. For an indoor camping activity, you could use various colored fish for an interesting fishing game; for singing time use black or white notes. Spread your shapes onto the floor. Have the balloons blown up before the activity. Have the children rub a balloon on their hair and then use them to pick up the tissue paper shapes.

Races and Relays

Materials: Varies
Effort Quotient: ♉♉♉
Time: ⧖
Preparation: ★

- **Lame Dog Race.** Everyone races at the same time in this one. Each child lines up at the starting line on his hands and feet (not knees), faces looking down. At the signal, each one raises a foot off the ground. The players crawl forward on both hands and one foot. The entire race needs to be run with one foot off the ground. If a child touches the raised foot to the ground, he/she must immediately resume the "lame dog" position and turn completely around twice before continuing.

- **Swing Your Trunks.** You will need four bowls and approximately forty unshelled peanuts. Divide the children into two relay teams. Have the teams line up facing each other. Place a bowl of about twenty nuts next to the first person in each line, and place an empty bowl next to the last person in each line. Tell the children that they are elephants, and that they'll be using their trunks to pass peanuts from one team member to the next. Have all the children bend over and clasp their hands together with arms outstretched to mimic an elephant. The first "elephant" picks up a nut in his/her clasped hands, and swings his/her "trunk" to pass the nut to the next "elephant" in line. Continue passing from elephant to elephant till the last person drops the nut into the empty bowl. The first team to pass all of the nuts to the end of the line, wins.

- **Feather Relay.** You will need lots of fluffy feathers for this activity. This is a challenging game. Divide the group into two teams, then divide each team into two groups. Place the groups from each team facing each other, single file, and about ten to fifteen steps away from each other. There should be several feet separating the two teams to allow for feathers that are accidentally blown off-course. At the signal, have the first person on each team keep the feather in the air by blowing it across the ten to fifteen steps to the team member opposite them, who then has to blow it back across to the next team member in line. If a feather falls to the ground, have the "blower" pick it up and continue from where they are. The first team to finish wins.

- **Team Elephant Walk.** Mark a start/finish line, and a turn-around point (like a tree or a chair) about fifteen to twenty feet from the starting line. Divide the children into two teams and have them line up single file behind the start/finish line. Have the first child in each line extend one arm out in front of him to make a "trunk" and the other arm back between his legs as a "tail." The second child holds the first child's tail with his "trunk" and extends his arm back through his legs for the third person to hold. Continue arranging the line until each person is attached to the line "trunk" to "tail." At the signal, the race begins, and the elephant lines then walk together, without breaking the lines, to the turn-around point and back to the finish line. First team to cross the finish line wins.

CHAPTER 9
Tying Up Loose Ends

At this point you should have a pretty good idea of how to plan and execute a good activity—along with lots of ideas for activities you can use or adapt for the members of your ward.

Now that you know these basics, this last chapter will focus on a few areas that will make your activities more successful. These ideas should apply to all activities, whether you are inviting the entire ward or just a handful of Primary children. The goal of this chapter is to help you present an activity that fills the need of your ward members and falls well within your allotted budget.

Another focus of this chapter will be the main communication vehicles within your ward—the ward newsletter and the Sunday bulletin. These publications have a place in a book about ward activities for two reasons. First, you will often find that the same people who are planning the activities are also involved in the production of the newsletter and the bulletin. But even if this isn't the case in your ward, there should be a close link between ward activities and these printed resources. Upcoming activities should be promoted in the newsletter and bulletin, but advertising is only half the story. The newsletter or the bulletin should also be used after the fact to thank the people who helped make your activity a success and to report on the event itself. Even those who typically avoid ward activities might be tempted to attend the next one when they find out how much fun they have been missing. If you have just been called to be the editor of your newsletter or bulletin, this chapter will give you some ideas to make your job easier, so that you can produce a product that is both enjoyable and useful to your readers.

Certainly no one would put a funeral on a list of favorite ward activities. Yet births and deaths are all part of the Lord's plan, and every ward will have its share of both. Funerals provide an opportunity for the members of a ward to perform charitable service directed towards others—in this case, the family of the deceased. One of the ways this is done is with a family dinner that is traditionally served after the funeral. Just as with any other ward activity, proper planning and execution is necessary for these dinners to meet the needs of those who attend. This is certainly one event that you want to come off perfectly, and we will give you some hints to ensure that.

The chapter will conclude with a few ideas for activities that will be effective in increasing the unity within your ward. Most of these can be done in an informal way, because they are much less structured than many of the activities listed in previous chapters.

Staying within the Budget

Those of us who grew up in the Church remember how it was in the old days. Each ward used to establish its own annual budget, and would then solicit ward members for additional contributions to fund it. In some wards, families would be asked to pay a fixed amount each year; in other wards, they would be asked just to pay a certain percentage of their yearly income. Wards in more affluent areas would often have generous budgets, and might spend thousands of dollars on annual events such as summer parties or Christmas programs. The negative aspect to this method of budgeting was that it put an additional strain on parents who were already struggling to feed and clothe their children, in addition to paying tithing, fast offerings, and other contributions.

As the Church evolved and began adopting a more international focus, the tried and true method of soliciting money for a ward budget was abandoned in favor of a new program. Wards no longer solicit funds for ward budgets, but instead receive budget funds from Church headquarters. These budget payments are based on the attendance at sacrament meeting, putting all wards on equal footing as far as receiving money to fund their ward budgets. The budget payments, which come from tithing funds, are sent directly to the stake, which then passes on most of the budget funds to the individual wards.

Most members welcomed this change, because it removed a huge financial obligation from them and provided a more equal distribution of funds to each ward, without regard to the income level of the members. But the budget revision was a drastic change to ward activities committee chairmen, many of whom saw their activity budgets reduced quite dramatically in one year. The typical response to these new smaller budgets was to plan activities that relied more on the members to furnish the food and supplies. Formal dinners that were entirely funded by the ward budget were soon phased out. Instead, activities committee chairmen began relying on potluck dinners, where each family was asked to bring a salad or a dessert, with the ward providing the drinks and the main course.

Dealing with budget constraints is the double-edged sword you wield as you plan activities. On one side, you have the responsibility of presenting an enjoyable activity with a relatively small budget. But on the other hand, you don't want to impose on those who attend by asking them to bring expensive items, or items that will take a lot of time to prepare.

Because financing a royal ball with a pauper's purse is a constant challenge for all activity planners, here are some ideas that may help you pull a rabbit out of your hat and astound the people who attend your next event.

Food on the Cheap

Just about every activity will feature some kind of food, even if it consists only of punch and cookies at the end of the program. Unless refreshments are just an afterthought to another activity, you will often find the food items taking the lion's share of your activity budget. Therefore, it is critical that you find ways to provide good food for modest prices. Here are a few ideas:

▶ Try Your (Pot)luck

The most common way to put on a cheap meal is to ask guests to bring a potluck salad, entrée, or dessert. This takes a little trial and error, and until you perfect the program for your ward you may end up with a whole lot of desserts and salads, and precious few entrées. You may want to assign people to bring a particular item according to the first letters of their last names, while remembering that you'll need a lot more entrées than you will desserts. (A single sheet cake goes a long way!) One potential problem with potluck dinners is dealing with those who are not willing to carry their fair share of the burden. If this is an issue in your ward, you may want to specify that each dish that is brought should serve x-number of people.

▶ Maintain Portion Control

You can also reduce your food budget if you can keep those attending from eating like starved castaways. It seems to be a sad fact of life that those at the end of the line in ward dinners are always the bottom feeders. They fill up their plates with olives and pickles, or with the scrapings of a dozen different casserole dishes. It's not that the people in the front of the line are selfish—sometimes they just don't think, and other times they're deceived into believing there's an endless supply of food. One way to avoid this is to keep some of the food back in the kitchen until the end, rather than putting everything on the buffet table at the beginning of the meal. Having less food out on the table will make the buffet seem less sumptuous, so that those at the front of the line will be less inclined to load their plates. Another advantage of leaving some food in the kitchen is that it will give you some fresh food to serve to those who are coming later.

A second idea is to put controlled portions of food on serving plates, rather than have each person serve himself. We have all been to dinners where pie, cake, or ice cream was served in pre-sized pieces on individual plates. There's no reason why this can't be done for the rest of the meal. One note: if you're serving plates this way, vary the portion size slightly, so that those who want smaller portions don't have to take a large serving that will end up in the garbage.

Finally, if you are serving a meal with a limited number of items, ask servers to stand by the table and serve the food to those coming through the line. Not only is this more sanitary, but it also helps control the amount of food that is taken. Even with servers you should not be too rigid, but should honor requests (within reason) for larger portions or substitutions.

▶ Avoid Wasting Food

You can also stretch your food budget further if you reduce the amount of wasted food. Children are typically the prime culprits here. Unsupervised children tend to put more food on their plates than they can ever eat. Equally serious, many younger children who are allowed to fix their own plates like to touch every food item they see, often picking things up and even tasting them before they decide to put them back on the table for others to consume.

This is not just an aesthetic problem. Having people touch food presents a serious health hazard. Primary-aged children should either have their plates served by their parents, or there should be some other plan to keep them from contaminating the dinner.

Unfortunately, having parents escort their own children through the buffet line may not fix the problem in your ward. An authority figure who has a great amount of tact should be stationed at the table to gently remind children *and their parents* that civilized behavior is expected. A beloved Primary president is a good choice to serve in this authority role.

Another idea is to have a separate serving area designed just for children (perhaps with the tabletops at a lower level so the children can see the food better), and filled with basic foods that have more appeal to children. We have all seen children fill their plates with exotic foods, only to leave most of it untouched when they discover that its odd flavor is not what they expected. Having a child-oriented table can greatly eliminate that problem.

If you have separate serving tables for younger guests, make sure that this is announced and understood by the parents before serving begins. Either the parents should escort their children through the line, or a kindly authority figure should be standing at the head of the table during the serving process. It is just as important that children not be allowed to touch the food on the children's table as it is that they not be allowed to touch the adults' food. Remember—this is a health issue. It is your responsibility as the planner of an activity to make sure nobody goes home with food poisoning.

▶ Sign on the Dotted Line

Sign-up sheets can be very effective for recruiting food items for ward parties. Your budget may cover the main course, but unless people sign up to bring salads, appetizers, and desserts, all you'll be eating is ham. As with potluck dinners, using sign-up sheets takes a little experimentation. In some wards, people want to use their agency and bring whatever they choose. In other wards, people want to be given a specific assignment, including a recipe for them to follow. If you don't know the character of your ward, pass out a sign-up sheet where recipes are included for some items and not for others. If you find people signing up to bring food where recipes are included, but leaving the "free-agency" areas blank, you'll know your ward appreciates a little more structure. One unexpected bonus of providing recipes is that people will often agree to bring something just to get a copy of the recipe. This assumes you provide *good* recipes, however, and not your Aunt Hanna's recipe for creamed eggplant and rattlesnake casserole.

Whether or not you include recipes, be prepared for surprises. Kathy once asked a woman to bring a specific casserole to serve twelve, only to get a frozen commercial meatloaf instead. Then, when she passed out recipes for a no-fail cobbler, people diligently followed the instructions and cooked the cobbler for fifty minutes without regard for the quirks of their own ovens, bringing raw and burned cobbler to the ward dinner. Learn to expect anything and be grateful for everything you get. When you're dealing with volunteers, you have to roll with the punches.

▶ Belly Up to the Bar

A well-stocked bar can be the salvation of any large gathering when participants each bring an ingredient that people can add to a make-it-yourself meal. Not only is a "bar" meal easy for all the participants to prepare, but it's also easy to assemble. A taco bar can feature seasoned meat, taco shells, sour cream, cheese, chopped onions, salsa, sliced black olives, and queso sauce. A baked potato bar can offer butter, sour cream, chives, chili, yogurt, cheese, cheese sauce, bacon bits, or any one of a number of other treats. A sandwich bar may have sliced bread, sliced meat, condiments, lettuce, tomato, cheese, tuna or chicken salad. A pasta bar could have assorted sauces and cheeses to top any one of several pastas. And don't forget the ever-popular salad bar and ice cream sundae bar. Just remember to have someone police the area on a regular basis to clean up spills and replenish depleted ingredients. Be especially careful if children are present, if only to make sure they don't touch food and leave it on the bar for others to consume.

▶ Don't Forget the Value of a Good Contest

You can have a lot of excitement along with your meal if you turn it into a competition. Some wards can get quite competitive over a chili cook-off or an ice cream contest or a cake-baking contest, feeding the ward at the same time. Make sure to award fabulous prizes (or not-so-fabulous prizes) to excite the group, and publicize the event well in advance.

People's feelings can get hurt over contests, so take precautions. Don't let anyone know who prepared each item until the food has been tasted by the judges, and by all means have the contest judged by someone whose family is not participating in the competition. If handled correctly, contests can be a huge source of fun as well as food. If they're handled clumsily, you could end up with a lot of hurt feelings.

▶ Shop at Warehouse Clubs

Our ward building is only a couple of miles from one of those huge warehouse shopping clubs where large quantities of food and household supplies are sold for near-wholesale prices. At just about any ward activity, at least half of the food and party supplies originate from there. In fact, warehouse clubs are such a boon to wards and stakes that people without access to them are under a handicap as they plan their own activities. If you don't have a membership in the nearby warehouse club, perhaps another ward member or a member of your committee will take pity on you and take you shopping. One disadvantage of these stores is that they usually do not have the same assortment of goods as a typical grocery store. If you see something you like, you'd better grab it—because there is a chance it will no longer be on the shelves when you go back to get it on the day of the activity.

If you're not fortunate enough to be close to a shopping club, you will have to make do with buying your food and supplies at regular stores. In most areas, you will find quite significant differences in the prices that different stores charge for the same item—and yet this price difference will not be consistent from item to item. For example, you might find that one store asks higher prices for meat, but offers lower prices for fresh fruit. Familiarize yourself with the stores in your area so that you will know the particular strengths and weaknesses of each store—not only in terms of price but also in terms of the variety of foods they commonly stock. If you are new to the area, throw yourself at the mercies of some of the "old timers" in the ward who will be willing to share their experiences with the local merchants. Although it is usually not cost-effective to visit multiple stores when shopping for a family, it might be worth visiting a second store if you can save fifty cents on an item and you are buying two hundred of them.

▶ Buy in Bulk

Everyone knows that you can usually save money by buying in large quantities. You may find that you can buy one hundred paper plates for $1.25, or five hundred for $2.50. So even though your total cost is higher with the larger quantity, your cost per plate drops in half. Obviously, bulk purchases are probably not practical for food items except perhaps for condiments. However, non-perishables such as paper products and plastic utensils are ideally suited for bulk purchase. Buying in bulk will take

a little more planning and budgeting on your part, but if done properly, it will save money over the long haul. But buying in bulk is only the first half of the process. Bulk buyers should also find a secure place for storing the excess goods until the next activity. You will get no benefit from a great price if someone else "borrows" your supplies, or if you cannot remember where you stored them.

▶ Ask for a Discount

Clark and Kathy once attended a ward dinner where a delicious meal was served, and the organizer then bragged that he hadn't paid a penny for the food. He had approached local businesses and asked the owners to donate food as a charitable contribution that could be used as a tax deduction. Although most people probably don't have the nerve to push for a totally free meal, many companies will at least give you a small discount if you tell them the food will be used for an activity sponsored by a church. Sometimes you can also get permission to shop at wholesale establishments that don't normally sell directly to the public. If you find companies that give discounts and special considerations, show your appreciation by taking your business there in the future—not only for ward-related activities, but for personal purchases as well (although you should be honest and not ask for discounts on personal purchases). And be sure to acknowledge the businesses that have helped you out when you're thanking people in the ward newspaper or bulletin. A little free advertising may encourage business owners to help you out in the future.

Sneaky Secret

Avoid supplies that are tied to a particular theme or holiday, because the leftover supplies will have limited usefulness. Those extra five hundred Christmas plates will not do you much good at the annual ward summer party, although they could be used next Christmas if you don't mind storing them for another year . . . and if they fit the decorating scheme of next year's Christmas party chairman. Although regular old white or red plates will not be quite as nice for Christmas, you will be able to use the leftover ones for any number of future activities. When buying large quantities in bulk, always buy a product that will be appropriate for any number of uses.

▶ Be a Smart Shopper

The same techniques you use to save money on your family grocery bill should be applied to purchases for church activities. This would include using coupons, watching for sales, and (as already noted) buying in bulk and comparison shopping for the best prices. Most stores carry so-called "house brand" products that are generally as good as the more famous brands, but are cheaper in price. These types of moneysaving techniques work best if your activity is planned well in advance, as that will give you time to watch for sales and look for the best prices. With smaller events that are often planned just a few days in advance, you may have to just take your chances and pay the going price.

Sneaky Secret

As we were writing this section, there was a story in the news about a church dinner where many of the attendees became violently ill and had to be hospitalized. One woman died. Although we would all like to save money on the food for a ward activity, our bigger priority should always be the safety of those who will attend. No amount of money saved is worth a person's life or health. If there is ever the slightest question about the safety of the food being purchased, spend a little more money and go for the food that is 100 percent safe.

▶ Sell Excess Food

For large activities where the ward is paying for a lot of the food, it may be appropriate to sell the unused food back to the members who attend. The funds from these purchases may then be given to the activity chairman and deducted from the amount he or she will be reimbursed by the ward for the activity. Any food brought by individual members should, of course be offered to the people who brought it. But food bought with the activity budget can be sold back if done properly.

This is probably something you don't want to deal with if you bought your food with a tax exemption number, but if you paid tax on the food you purchased, there shouldn't be any problem.

There are four considerations in selling excess food.

First, you should not sell any package that has been opened and partially consumed. Give it to someone who helped on the committee or to a ward member who could use the food. Second, make sure the food has been stored properly so that the buyer will not be buying the unexpected gift of food poisoning. Third, sell the food for no more than you paid for it, and you should probably discount it beyond that. Finally, put no pressure on the people present to buy the food. If it is obvious that no one wants the food enough to pay for it, just give it away.

▶ Return Unused Items

For non-food items or certain non-perishable food items, it might be possible to return those items to the store where you bought them for a full refund. Whenever you buy supplies or food, make sure you understand the company's policy in regards to returns. Make sure you retain any receipts or other items that may be required for a return. Be a good example, and don't pressure the store to bend the rules for you. Know what the store's policies are, and follow them.

▶ Serve Lighter Meals

Many people today are eating foods that are much different than what they were eating ten years ago. Heavy "meat and potatoes" meals have generally been replaced by lighter fare such as salads, sandwiches, and soups. This can generally work to your advantage when planning a menu, because lighter menu items are often cheaper to purchase than the more traditional main courses. These types of lighter menus are also easier to feature as part of a potluck dinner—even the worst cook in the ward can bring a salad ingredient or an item to be used in an ice cream bar.

For the spring and summer months, consider serving salads (both lettuce and pasta) and sandwiches. As the air starts to get cooler in the autumn, you might want to serve tacos or baked potatoes. During the frosty months of winter, a serving of soup or chili will take off the chill. Most women will tell you that serving ice cream is appropriate for the sticky summer months. (Most men will tell you that any day—summer or winter—is appropriate for ice cream.)

▶ Serve Only Appetizers or Desserts

One recent trend is to hold activities where members are expected to eat at home before or after an activity. In that case, refreshments consist of a table of appetizers or desserts. If you hold the activity early, serve appetizers and send people home for their full meal. Or start the activity late, after the members have eaten at home, and then just provide desserts. No matter what you plan, however, if you hold your activity at a traditional mealtime, people are going to eat enough appetizers to take the place of the meal.

There is one caution about doing this—make sure your audience understands what you are expecting of them. You don't want to deal with a group of ravenous ward members who descend upon your lone plate of cheese and crackers.

Decorating on a Dime

With the exception of buying the food, decorating for your activity will probably be your biggest expense. Anyone who has ever been involved with decorating can tell you that you can burn through a lot of money quickly if you are not careful. Many of the moneysaving tips in the previous section apply equally well to decorations, but here are a few additional hints that apply only to the decorations:

▶ Involve the Members

Having members involved with the decorating not only saves you time, but it can save you money as well. Kent and Shannon attended an international dinner where foods from various countries were served. The decorations at the individual tables followed the same theme, with each table being decorated to represent a different country. Because a typical ward has many members who have served missions in foreign lands, decorating for this dinner simply involved asking various women in the ward to decorate a table representing the land where she or her spouse served as a missionary. Not only did this result in low-cost (or no-cost) decorations, it also produced a result that was memorable and interesting. Having individual tables for eating lends itself well to this type of decorating, but the same concept can really be adapted to any kind of seating arrangement.

Sneaky Secret

Whenever members provide personal items to be used as decorations, you must take the utmost care to make sure the items are preserved and returned to the members in their original condition. One way you can do this is by making sure the items are out of reach of small children—that is why the idea of table centerpieces works so well. As you plan your decorations, put some thought into keeping the decorations out of the hands of small explorers. During the event, part of your job may be to wander around and make sure someone's precious family heirlooms are not being destroyed by junior terrorists.

Another way to involve ward members is to choose members with specific talents to help you. Kathy once chaired a ward dinner with an *Alice in Wonderland* theme. She solicited the help of an artist in the ward who painted life-sized scenes from the book. Although the only materials purchased were white butcher paper and tempera paints, the paintings were so professionally done that they were suitable for framing. The artwork was such an enhancement to the ward dinner that more people concentrated on the decorations than on the food.

Although asking individual members to decorate is fine for some events, sometimes you may choose to involve people on a group level. Contact the leaders in the youth programs and solicit their help. This will serve the dual function of solving your decorating problems and giving youth the opportunity to perform a service project that could use their creativity and talents. (Just make sure that they don't use their organization's budget to pay for the decorations.) Or ask the Primary president if each Primary class would help provide the decorations for a different table. Not only will this produce interesting decorations, but it will also give the parents the added treat of trying to determine which decorations were made by their own offspring. At the end of the evening, allow the parents to keep their children's creations as a keepsake. Think of it! The children will provide you with free decorations, and their parents will help you clean up.

▶ Sponsor Creative Contests

Contests can also help you in the decorating department. Each autumn our ward has a harvest party, and one of the featured events is a pumpkin-carving contest. Each participating family buys and carves a pumpkin, bringing it to the party on the night of the event. As the pumpkins arrive, they are placed throughout the room and used as decorations. Later, as part of the program, the pumpkins are judged and various prizes are awarded. Not only are the members helping with the decorating, but they are providing part of the program, and also participating in an enjoyable family activity.

▶ Use Basic Materials

Party supply stores have all kinds of fancy materials, but they usually have fancy price tags as well. Most decorations will be cheaper if you buy the raw materials and make them yourself, but there is an obvious trade-off here in terms of how much your time is worth. Buy materials from a warehouse discount store or a school supply store, and then paint and cut out the decorations yourself. If this becomes too much work, involve other people in the ward, either as individuals or in groups.

Don't forget about objects that you normally throw out with the trash. Old newspapers, magazines, cardboard boxes, and empty plastic soda pop bottles can all be put to good use. Combine them with some spray paint, glue, wrapping paper, and ribbons, and you will be surprised at the wonders you can produce.

One of the best illustrations of professional decorations on a shoestring was done for another ward dinner that Clark and Kathy attended.

This one was done with a nostalgia theme, and two artists in the ward were drafted to do the decorations. They bought a number of matting boards in a subdued color and made collages of old items that were glued to each board. Ancient records, tickets, invitations, sheet music, photographs, knick-knacks, campaign buttons, and other treasures were collected from the artists' attics and were artistically arranged in numerous themes on the various boards. The result was so professional that Kathy took home two of the collages, vainly hoping to think of some way to frame them and preserve them forever.

▶ Find Discount Party Stores

In our area we are starting to see stores that sell party supplies at substantial discounts. They carry the same merchandise found in regular party-supply stores, but usually at discounts of 50 percent or more. If you live in an urban area, you may want to check your phone book to see if such stores exist in your area.

▶ Borrow Items from Businesses

Businesses such as nurseries will often let you borrow plants for a day, either at no charge, or for a modest fee. This is good publicity for the business, and it also helps you with your decorating. Determine if there are ward members who own or work at such businesses, because the owners will be more likely to honor your request if you have a contact on the inside. It goes without saying that you should take good care of the borrowed items, and return them promptly. If anything is damaged or broken, it will be your responsibility to pay for its replacement or repair.

▶ Use Rental Stores

Don't forget those stores that rent expensive party equipment on a daily basis. This may be an inexpensive alternative to purchasing something that would be used only once or twice. This could be an option if you are looking to acquire some types of sporting goods or cooking equipment. Clark and Kathy were once members of a ward that always rented a "Moon Bounce" for the ward summer party. It is an inflatable chamber where children take off their shoes and have a great time bouncing and playing. It is unlikely that any ward member would own such an item, or that the bishop would consent to paying for it out of the ward budget. In this situation, renting it for one day a year was the perfect solution.

▶ Sell the Decorations

When you sell excess food to ward members, this is usually because you misjudged the amount of food required, or because the attendance was less than you had hoped. Decorations can be different, however, in that you can sometimes *plan* to sell the decorations at the conclusion of the activity. This works well during the holiday months, when you can create theme-oriented centerpieces and then sell them to the members. If you are decorating for a Christmas party, for example, consider placing a nice Poinsettia in the center of each table, and then selling the plants at the end of the evening. Because there is usually a seasonal demand for such items, you will usually not have a lot of problems in getting rid of them. Remember and follow the same cautions we gave you when selling food—sell only items purchased from the activity budget, sell them for a fair price, and do not put pressure upon members to buy anything.

▶ Emphasize Simple Decorations

Remember that decorating for a ward activity is not as important as decorating for your high school homecoming dance. No one is going to have a miserable time and lose his testimony because you did not transform the basketball court into an undersea paradise. As important as decorations can be, remember that most ward members are coming primarily to support the ward and mingle with each other.

Don't forget the mood that can be set for an event through such simple things as lighting and background music. Play some church hymns or classical music over the speaker system, and set the lights in a way to make the area look warm and inviting. These simple touches can sometimes have as much effect as hundreds of dollars spent on expensive decorations.

> **Sneaky Secret**
> Here's a rule to remember when planning any activity. If you find yourself doubting that people can have fun without spending money, remember how much fun you used to have playing in an empty cardboard box. The money isn't what's important—the memories are important. Make a memory, and nobody will remember how much money you had (or didn't have) to spend.

Programs for Pennies

The program or entertainment for the activity is another area where you might blow your budget if you are not careful. Many of the cost-saving ideas presented previously can be adapted to help you save money on the program as well. Here is a recap of the more important ideas, plus a few additional ones that apply specifically to entertainment programs.

As with all other aspects of your activity, keep the ward members involved as much as possible. Not only does this produce a better activity, but it also reduces the time and money you will personally have to spend in pulling the activity together. Members who are involved in musical numbers or drama productions can be asked to furnish their own costumes. This does not have to be anything fancy. For a western dance, ask everyone on the program to wear jeans, a white shirt, and a colorful bandanna. This will give the appearance of a costume, yet will use items that just about everyone should have in their wardrobe. With a little bit of imagination, you should be able to transform many household items into suitable costumes. If all else fails, there are costume rental stores that will rent you a costume for the evening.

For road shows and other dramatic presentations, use props and scenery that convey the idea without presenting all of the detail. For example, if a scene takes place in a doctor's office, you could have people sitting in chairs reading magazines, with someone dressed as a nurse calling out names, and an eye chart hung on the back wall. Everyone will immediately know the setting of the scene, even though the props don't convey every detail. One of our friends wrote an elaborate ward play that included just a few props plus some brightly colored cardboard boxes that were arranged differently in each scene. Even with this minimal scenery, the audience had no problem understanding the story and the locations of the various acts.

For some activities, you may want to award small prizes as part of the program. These may be related to contests for the best food item, the best decorations, or the best performance on the program. Local businesses will often donate prizes in exchange for a little free publicity. If that fails, give humorous prizes (such as a bottle of antacid tablets for the best chili), or prizes that can be created inexpensively at home (such as certificates that can be printed using home computers). Even better, give prizes related to service. Have a young man in the ward agree to mow a lawn or shovel snow, or have a young woman agree to watch children while the parents are away. These types of prizes cost nothing but a little of your time (to convince people to donate their services), yet they benefit the members of the ward in so many ways.

Getting the Word Out

Anyone who has ever planned an activity can tell you that the worst possible outcome is to plan the perfect event and then have no one attend. To be sure, there are some people who would not attend an activity even if you passed out gold coins and precious gems in the parking lot. But most of the time poor attendance can be blamed on the sad fact that most ward members have an attention span equivalent to that of your average fruit fly—probably because they are constantly being bombarded with about ten thousand other things during a typical week. The only way to counteract that bombardment is to make sure your own message gets through as often as possible.

The best starting point is to use the publicity tools already available in your ward—the ward newsletter and the Sunday bulletin. The advantage of using the newsletter is that you may have virtually unlimited space because most editors are desperate to find anything to fill the space. The disadvantage of using the newsletter is that the newsletter publication is

Sneaky Secret

One way to guarantee poor attendance is to schedule an activity the week after a Sunday in which no meetings were held in the building (such as the week after a stake conference or general conference). Without a reminder the Sunday before, you can be sure most people will have long forgotten about the activity that was announced more than a week ago. Never plan an activity unless you have a calendar nearby that will show you potential conflicts—not just church conflicts but also community and school conflicts. If you learn of the conflict after the activity is already scheduled, you will have to use an alternative system such as a telephone tree to make sure everyone is reminded.

often not very timely. Newsletter editors are notorious for holding an issue until there is enough material to fill it; so it isn't uncommon to receive a newsletter that contains announcements about events that have already happened. The Sunday bulletin is more reliable because it appears each Sunday, but the amount of space available to you will probably be limited. In an ideal situation, you can build enthusiasm for the party with your newsletter, and then just use the bulletin as a reminder

as the date gets closer. Consider providing a separate half-page flyer that will be included with the bulletin on the Sunday before the event. That will give you plenty of room to promote the event, plus it will give the members something to take home to serve as a visual reminder.

Another good publicity vehicle is to have announcements made in church meetings. Many bishops believe that oral announcements distract from the purpose of sacrament meeting by taking time away from the program, compromising the spirit of the meeting in order to do nothing more than repeat the announcements already written in the bulletin. Thus sacrament meetings are not the best platforms to use for announcing your activity. But the format of other Sunday meetings is usually more open to the making of announcements. In some wards, time is even set aside for announcements from the various quorums and ward leaders. Take advantage of this to remind ward members of your activity in a way that they'll remember it until the day of the event.

For most activities, the ward newsletter and Sunday bulletin, together with supplementary announcements in church meetings, should be sufficient to publicize your event. But for some activities, especially those that are missionary—or service-related, you may want to make an extra effort to increase your attendance, or to invite those who don't usually attend. Here are a few ideas that should help.

Kathy once had a job where she wrote fundraising letters used to solicit money for worthy organizations through the mail. (You may have even thrown some of her great prose in the trash.) One common technique used by these letters is the inclusion of an "involvement device." This may be a shiny new penny, or a bumper sticker, or some return address labels, or a bookmark. The idea is to keep the name of the organization in front of you, and to make you feel as though you are part of it.

As a planner of ward activities, you can use a similar technique for publicizing some of your events. Recently we had a ward party, and we were told several weeks before the party that tickets would be required for admission. There was no charge for the tickets, and they could be picked up easily from a number of ward leaders. Using the tickets not only gave the planners an estimate of how many would attend, but it also provided a visual reminder of the activity. Our tickets sat on our bedroom dressing table, and we saw them in the morning and at night. It was a great visual reminder that we had an activity to attend that weekend. Other involvement devices that we have seen used effectively include bookmarks and refrigerator magnets.

If you make promotional flyers for your event, the big question you must ask is "How will the flyers be distributed?" Putting them inside the bulletin is the easiest solution, but then you run the risk of people losing the flyers in the jumble of papers they receive each Sunday. Another drawback of passing out flyers only at church means you will miss ward members who don't come to church on a regular basis, who are out of town, or who are away from the ward on another church assignment. One solution is to ask the home teachers and visiting teachers to deliver the flyers, but that doesn't work very well. Even the home and visiting teachers who faithfully visit their families each month will often forget to take the flyers, or will visit their families after the event has taken place.

If you live in one of those Utah-sized wards, where the entire ward covers a few square blocks, you could probably deliver the flyers by hand in a couple of hours. This may not be a realistic option in wards outside the

Sneaky Secret

Don't forget those people who work in other organizations that might not hear your Sunday announcement. If you are planning a Relief Society activity, don't just announce it in the Sunday Relief Society meeting. Consider the women who are out of the room fulfilling assignments with the Primary or Young Women organizations, or who have stake callings that take them away from your ward frequently, or who may have work conflicts on Sunday but could attend an activity on a weeknight. The best way to include the people who may otherwise be forgotten is to review your membership rolls and identify the people who are missing your announcements. Then come up with an alternate way to make sure they are informed of the activity and are invited to it. Remember—the more personal an invitation, the more likely you are to get a positive response. You may even find greater attendance from those who get personal attention than from the people who hear your announcements in their regular church meetings.

Wasatch Front. The most reliable way to get them delivered is to send them through the mail. Unfortunately, the expense of sending flyers through the mail is so prohibitive that it isn't a practical solution. You may want to try a compromise approach, distributing flyers at church and also mailing them to ward members who may miss them the first time around.

Another way to get the word out is with a telephone tree. This is a lot of work, but is a particularly effective way to contact people in a short period of time. Simply divide up the members of the ward and assign different people to call specific families. When you contact the family, you pass along the news, and then ask the family to pass the news along to the next family down the line. This takes a lot of coordination, but if done properly, you can often contact everyone in the ward within an hour or two. Using a telephone tree isn't the best way to publicize an activity, but it works well if your plans suddenly change at the last minute.

An updated version of the telephone tree is to use an E-mail distribution list to get the word out. Many church members seem to have E-mail these days (at least in some areas), so compiling a list of E-mail addresses could be a great benefit to you as a planner of ward activities. You can send individual reminders or a generalized announcement that goes to a whole list of people. Assuming your recipients read their E-mail regularly, the word will get out almost as quickly as with a telephone tree, but with a lot less work. In most wards, using a combination of an E-mail list and telephone contact should reach all the members in a short period of time.

All of our suggestions thus far have assumed that you are publicizing an activity that is designed primarily for Church members. But what if you are planning a community event such as a health fair or a family history seminar? In that case, your first attempt should be to contact the news media that serve your area. Local newspapers will often run articles about upcoming religious events at no charge to you. Local television outlets may also be interested if you are planning a large event that would be of interest to their viewers. You can also print promotional flyers and ask local merchants to display them in their windows. You could post them yourself on telephone poles and other public places, but make sure you don't break any laws in the process. (Make friends among your neighbors by removing the announcements after the event.)

Unfortunately, the most effective way to promote community events is the same way that is most effective in promoting events within the ward: contacting citizens individually and issuing personal invitations—

a practice that takes a whole lot of energy and time. A few years ago our stake built and dedicated a new stake center, and a number of musical and dramatic programs were presented for the community as part of the open house festivities. For several weeks prior to the open house, stake missionaries teamed up with the full-time missionaries to visit every home in the area, tell them about the open house events, and leave them some promotional literature. This was a lot of work, but it was effective. Numerous members of the community attended, and a large percentage of them were nonmembers from the surrounding neighborhood.

Publishing a Ward Newsletter

It seems to have been Kathy's curse to be called as the ward newsletter editor in just about every ward she has ever attended. Shortly after moving into any ward, the bishopric will arrive for the traditional "welcome to the ward and we'd like to get to know you" visit. As part of the conversation, it eventually comes out that Kathy has a background in journalism and has edited the ward newsletters in most of her previous wards. At about that point, the bishop gets a little gleam in his eye, and you know what is coming. The old ward newsletter that has been dead for years is about to be resurrected, under the guiding hand of a brand new and yet experienced editor.

Sadly, ward newsletters do not seem to be as common as they once were. In some wards, the newsletter is a casualty of the new budget system. After all, if the bishop has a choice between giving the ward a newsletter or paying the heating bill, the heating bill gets the money. Another reason ward newsletters may be dying is that publishing a ward newsletter is no easy feat. It's not just the editor who has to work to put out a newsletter; ward leaders, who already have enough to do, don't even want to think about taking even more time to feed information to the newsletter editor.

If ward newsletters are on the verge of becoming extinct, it's a pity. Despite the work and the costs involved, newsletters serve a valuable function in the ward by helping promote the same ward unity that should be the goal of every activity you produce. Also, the newsletter provides the perfect vehicle not only for promoting future activities but also for serving as a record of past activities and as a vehicle for recognizing the efforts of those who were responsible for the success of those activities. Even if the best your ward can do is a monthly one-page "Common

Bond" newspaper published by the Relief Society, newsletters are excellent tools for keeping ward members in touch with each other's lives.

Perhaps you have just been called as the editor of your ward newsletter. Or, perhaps the ward has not had a newsletter in a while, and you would like to revive it. In either case, here are some possible topics that could be used each month to produce a newsletter that will be enjoyable and informative.

▶ Bishopric Message

By tradition, every ward newsletter seems to include a monthly bishopric message, and bishopric members usually take turns writing the messages. Although the editor should not tamper with the content of the message, it is perfectly acceptable to correct spelling errors, poor sentence structure, and other such items that would make the bishopric look foolish or make the article less readable. If you are working with brethren who would have a difficult time writing a coherent grocery list, your gentle corrections and suggestions will be greatly appreciated.

▶ Calendar Items

An important function of the newsletter is to remind the ward members of future ward and auxiliary activities. This can be done with the use of an actual calendar that has the upcoming month's events marked on the proper days. If you don't have the software to produce such a calendar, a chronological list of future dates and associated activities is just as effective. A calendar is a vital component of the newsletter, so make sure it is done well. And don't forget that producing a calendar of any sort creates an obligation for the editor to publish that newsletter on time. There is nothing worse than getting a newsletter at the end of the month that contains a calendar of all the exciting activities you missed. If you do include a calendar in your newsletter, make sure the readers have it in their hot little hands at the beginning of the month on the calendar, not six weeks after the fact.

▶ Organization News

It is also common in many newsletters to have sections where each ward organization can publicize upcoming events and past accomplishments. These should include news from each priesthood quorum and auxiliary organization, but don't forget the smaller groups such as the ward choir. If you plan to include a monthly contribution from each group, be prepared to make a lot of phone calls and to suffer a lot of aggravation. There are some people who would rather endure a root canal each month than to have to write a monthly column. Make sure your ward leaders know your deadline for articles, regularly encourage them to contribute, and then just run your newsletter with whatever you have at the deadline. This may result in smaller newsletters some months, but it is better than delaying the newsletter or getting an ulcer in an effort to get articles submitted.

▶ Event Reporting

As important as it is to use the newsletter to publicize upcoming activities, it is equally important to use it as a vehicle for reporting on the success of past activities. As part of this event reporting, you can acknowledge those who helped produce the activity. Although this should not take the place of personal thank-you notes or expressions of appreciation, it does serve to publicly acknowledge their contributions on behalf of the rest of the ward. Another thing you may want to consider is to mention unscheduled highlights of the activity. You may want to mention Marsha's great lounge lizard performance or Bishop King's sushi costume. These personal insights, presented in a gentle way, will make people who missed the event wish they'd been on hand to share the fun. Finally, you may consider including information that ward members may want to reproduce at home. If an outstanding recipe was served or a terrific ward trivia game was played, you may want to reproduce the information (assuming it is not copyrighted) as another reminder of the event.

▶ Member Biographies

If you have a ward with a lot of turnover, it becomes a struggle for ward members to become acquainted with new members who move in. You can assist in this process by running regular biographies featuring different ward members. Kent and Shannon do this in our ward, and it has proven to be a real hit. They try to report not only the major events in people's lives, but also interesting little-known bits of trivia that really make us laugh and want to know the people better. Here is an example of a biography that recently appeared (with the names changed to protect the innocent):

Did you know that Tom and Mary Smith first met at their singles' ward during a water-skiing trip? That Tom was born in Provo, Utah, grew up in Logan, but then graduated from high school in Salt Lake City? That Mary was born in Maryland, spent most of her growing-up years in Salt Lake City, and then left home at age 18 to study at the National Art School in Canada? That Tom is the oldest in a family with three brothers and two half-brothers? That Mary is the second child in her family, with one older brother, a younger brother and sister; and eight stepbrothers and sisters? That Tom graduated from the University of Utah in communications and is a media analyst for Acme Anvil Corporation? That Mary painted professionally, majored in political science at the University of Utah with a minor in French, and has a law degree from Seacoast University? That Tom's pet peeve is being late for movies, ball games, and church? That he is eternally late for everything else, including most of his dates with Mary? That Mary had some pretty odd pets while growing up, including a boa constrictor, a tarantula, mice, geese, and chickens? That Tom's most embarrassing moment happened at a furniture store while vigorously chatting with a sales lady and Mary happened to notice (burst out laughing was more like it) his fly was not only opened, but a generous portion of his underwear was showing through? That Mary's most embarrassing moment came when she was 16 and walked by a group of construction workers who hooted, whistled, and hollered as she passed? That while she was initially sort of flattered, she became instantly mortified to find out that her skirt had blown up and gotten tucked into her waistband, and that was what mostly attracted their attention? That Tom and his brothers once tied their petite mom up during a football game so they could watch it undisturbed? That they were so afraid of her that they didn't untie her until partway through the fourth quarter? That Mary's hobbies are working out, reading, playing with her daughters, and puttering around on her computer? That Tom enjoys reading, mostly biographies, current events, and church topics, and writing? That Mary also loves cookie dough, date nights with Tom, and movie magazines but dislikes pizza, shopping, mornings, and flying on airplanes? That each consider their greatest accomplishment to be marrying the other?

If you include this feature, take extra care to make sure you feature *all* the members of the ward, and not just married couples. It is equally important that we get to know those who are single members, and single parents, old or young.

▶ Member Accomplishments

People love to see their names in print, and you can almost guarantee a loyal readership if you keep your newsletter focused on the lives of ward members. Chronicle the small and large achievements in the lives of people—not only church-related activities, but also those of a non-spiritual nature. It is especially important to focus on the youth, and praise them for their accomplishments in school, in athletics, and in the community. You may have to develop a network of ward sources to funnel you this type of information, but it will almost guarantee a successful newsletter if you do it well. When Kathy was a newsletter editor, one of her most popular features was a column called "The Snoop Sisters." The column was written and passed to her by unnamed leaders in the ward, and it contained details about achievements, honors, and sometimes hilarious experiences from the lives of ward members. Kathy used to call this a column of "positive gossip," because it highlighted the little acts of kindness and service that may not have been known through the standard sources. It also identified small opportunities for service in a way that would not embarrass those who needed the help.

▶ Member Artwork and Compositions

One idea that works quite well is to feature children's artwork on the cover of the newsletter each month. Not only does it regularly fill a page of the newsletter, but it also gives Primary children a chance to show their talents, and it gives their parents an opportunity to be proud of their little budding Picassos. Short compositions and poetry by both adults and children may also be appropriate. Please avoid the temptation to print similar material you find in copyrighted magazines or books.

▶ Member Birthdays

Another common feature of many newsletters is a listing of those members who will be having birthdays in the coming month. This gives them some recognition, and also reminds other ward members who may want to recognize certain birthdays with a card, present, or a phone call. Remember what we said earlier—the success of your newsletter will be directly proportional to the number of people you mention in every issue, and you can never mention too many names (although you should make sure you are not mentioning the same names in every issue). If you include a birthday list, make sure you work closely with the ward clerk to make sure your list is current and no one is omitted. It is not considered good taste to publish the birthday of a widow who died nearly a decade ago, but it has happened.

▶ Ward Changes

The ward newsletter is a perfect vehicle for disseminating information about the membership changes in the ward. Make sure to include the names of families who have recently moved in or out. Other information may include births, deaths, and important events such as baptisms, youth priesthood advancements, graduations from Primary, and other similar honors. For families that have moved out of the ward, list their new address in case ward members want to stay in touch with them. As new families move into the ward, it is important that they be contacted and made to feel welcome as soon as possible. You may assist in this process by helping ward leaders know the names, addresses, and phone numbers of such families in a timely manner.

▶ Other Church News

One function of a ward newsletter is to remind ward members of church events beyond the scope of the ward. This would include events at the stake level, as well as general church news relating to such events as general conference. Remind your readers of upcoming events, especially those events that alter your regular Sunday meeting schedule. Publicize stake events, such as temple trips and youth activities. Because each member who holds a temple recommend must have it renewed each year and signed by a member of the stake presidency, let members know the procedure for scheduling these interviews.

▶ Leader Roster

A certain portion of your readership will include new ward members, and others who have no idea of which members serve in leadership callings. Even active members may have this problem if you are in a ward with a lot of turnover. To help disseminate this information, many wards regularly print the names and phone numbers of those who serve in various ward callings. This usually includes the bishopric, the priesthood quorum leaders, and the leaders of each ward auxiliary. The roster may also include names of those who serve as clerks or executive secretaries. If you have full-time missionaries who serve in your ward, it is useful to list them as well.

▶ Editor Contact Information

Don't forget to include information as to how members can contact you, as well as the deadline date for your next issue. Include your name, phone number, fax number, and E-mail address if appropriate. Encourage members to submit any interesting information that would make for good news. The editor can't be everywhere in a ward, so it is critical that you develop reliable, accurate, and loyal sources to feed you news items each month.

▶ Missionary Information

It is important to mention the missionaries who are associated with your ward. For those ward members who are serving elsewhere, regularly list their names, mailing addresses, and the names of the missions where they are serving. This is always important, but is especially important just before the holidays so that ward members can be encouraged to write to them. Keep in contact with the family members of missionaries so that you have a current mailing address for each one. And it wouldn't hurt to occasionally print information about what is going on in the lives of those missionaries. The parents of those missionaries will be more than happy to feed tidbits to you.

For missionaries who live elsewhere but are currently serving in your ward, usually just listing their names and phone numbers is sufficient—although you may want to list other information you feel would help your members provide more support to the missionary effort.

▶ Games and Puzzles

It is a common feature of many newsletters to feature some type of game or puzzle. If you do this, make sure it has some kind of church-related or ward-related theme. Even though there are a number of LDS puzzle books on the market, you should not feel free to appropriate those in your newsletter, unless the book states that puzzles may be used freely for non-commercial purposes, or you have permission from the author or publisher to use them. If you do feature puzzles in your

Sneaky Secret
One thing we have mentioned several times in this section is the fact that you should not appropriate any kind of copyrighted material for your newsletter unless you obtain permission to use it. Granted, it is pretty unlikely that you would ever get caught if you didn't ask permission, but it does not set a good example of honesty for other ward members. Many will rationalize that this practice is acceptable if you are doing it for a good cause. This is not true, and you are still stealing the creative efforts of someone else. It is doubtful you would break into a home and steal money from the dresser drawers—even for a good cause—and yet stealing copyrighted material is the same thing.

newsletter, it is important that you recognize those who complete the puzzles or who make an effort to do them. This will generate more interest in future puzzles, as members will succumb to the spirit of competition in trying to get their name published in the next issue. Remember what we have mentioned numerous times—it is the names of the members that will make your newsletter interesting.

▶ Want Ads

In any ward you will find people who need to acquire items and people who are trying to dispose of them. If you can use your newsletter to bring these people together, you will be providing a great service to ward members. If you decide to use your newsletter for want ads, there is one cast-iron rule that you should *never* break: All items should be given away free of charge, with no exchange of money taking place. Your newsletter is not a vehicle for helping ward members obtain money from other members. If they want to make a profit, there are plenty of local want-ad papers that will run ads for a nominal fee. Part of becoming a united ward family is the common sharing of our excess goods, and expecting money for those goods flies in the face of that goal. In any case, if you are planning to have a section of want ads in your paper, allow members to publicize excess items they wish to give away, and allow other members to publicize their needs for the goods they are trying to acquire.

Once you have decided on what features to include in the newsletter, your next decisions will relate to the format of the paper and how it will be produced. Should it be several standard size sheets of paper stapled together at the top or side, or sheets folded over like a small book and stapled in the middle, or yet another format? Should you use colored paper or standard white? Many of these decisions will be governed by how you intend to print the newsletter. Will you copy it on the ward copy machine, or take it to a copy center, or do it on your own equipment and then be reimbursed for the costs? Based on budget factors, you can be pretty certain that whatever option is least expensive will be the one selected, so you may have to alter the appearance of your newsletter to work within those boundaries.

Another thing that you must decide is how often the newsletter will be produced. You would probably not want to produce a newsletter more often than once a month, and that may be too often. Once every other month or once each quarter might be more practical. That will keep the ward members entertained and looking forward to the next issue, but should not be too much work for you.

Another item that must be resolved is how the newsletter is going to be distributed to the ward. One option is to pass them out to the active members on Sundays, and then mail them to those who were not in church. Another option that works well is using the Deacons to pass out the newsletter while they are gathering fast offerings. Visiting teachers may find the ward newsletter to be a great tool that will give them an excuse to write to women who don't attend church. Look at all the alternatives for newsletter distribution and decide what will work best in your ward.

Once all these issues are resolved, it is time to set your first deadline and to notify other ward leaders of the publication schedule and what you expect from them. Based on our experience, some leaders will be quite faithful about submitting their news each month without a reminder. Others will miss deadlines no matter how often you remind them, and no matter how often they promise that they will do better. Don't get upset about this; just publish the newsletter with whatever news you have when the deadline arrives. After several months with no news from a particular organization, the leaders will either be shamed into writing something, or will delegate the assignment to a member of the organization who will be more faithful about filling the assignment.

Sneaky Secret

One thing that almost always guarantees a quick death for a ward newsletter is to decide that it will be produced on an irregular basis. Once this decision is made, you can almost guarantee you will never see more than one or two more issues until the newsletter goes into oblivion. With no fixed deadline, it is just too easy to postpone the next issue indefinitely. Select a reasonable deadline and then stick with it, even if you have to publish a two-page newsletter because nothing has happened and no ward leaders have submitted any articles.

The Sunday Bulletin

Although ward newsletters may not be as common as they used to be, just about every ward in the United States has a Sunday bulletin. Sunday bulletins are usually distributed by the ushers or by missionaries serving in the ward as members of the congregation enter the chapel for sacrament meeting.

The content and intent of the Sunday bulletin is quite similar to that of the ward newsletter, although there are important differences. One advantage of the bulletin is that it is published every week, so you can use it to provide more timely information. The main disadvantage of the bulletin is that your space is limited—usually only one sheet of paper folded in half—so that the articles it contains must be brief and to the point. Because the bulletin helps set the spiritual tone for sacrament meeting, it should also be more subdued than the ward newsletter.

For ideas as to what to put in the Sunday bulletin, make sure you have read the previous section on ward newsletters. Many of the same kinds of information can be included in the bulletin in a shorter and more formal format. Put special emphasis on calendar items and announcements that apply to the coming week. In addition to those ideas, here are some other ideas as to the kinds of information that are especially useful:

▶ Date and Ward Name

This seems pretty obvious, but you would be surprised at the number of bulletins that do not include this information. There is nothing more frustrating than to pick up a bulletin and find it is two months old. Put the name of your ward there as well, especially if you share the meetinghouse with one or more wards.

▶ Sacrament Meeting Program

This is the main purpose of the bulletin, so make sure you do it well. You will need to coordinate with the bishopric and other ward members to get all the information you need (often at 10 P.M. on a Saturday night, despite your best efforts to get it earlier). It is helpful to the members if you can list the title and number of each congregational hymn featured on the program. In most cases you can create a standard template program, and then fill in the holes as needed each week. On those Sundays with special programs (such as a Primary program or a Christmas program), you may have to throw away the template and start from scratch. For these special programs, consider forgoing the standard white paper stock for custom program stock that has appropriate artwork printed on the front cover.

▶ Primary Program

Many wards include the Primary opening or closing exercises as part of the Sunday bulletin. This recognizes the children who participate in the program, and also reminds parents that they may wish to put in an appearance to see their little darlings. As requested, other ward leaders may also ask you to include programs and announcements that apply to their organizations and auxiliaries.

▶ Leader Roster

Many bulletins list the names and phone numbers of the major ward leaders, including the bishopric, priesthood leaders, and auxiliary presidents. This is especially helpful for newer members in the ward who may not have a ward directory and who are unsure as to the leadership of the ward. If you include this in your program, make sure the roster is kept current. Because a roster of ward leaders takes so much valuable space, you may want to include it only on fast Sundays.

▶ Games and Puzzles

Even though they are a staple of ward newsletters, games and puzzles may not be as appropriate in the Sunday bulletin. If you use them, pick them carefully, and make sure they have a spiritual theme or that they are connected with the program or with other ward activities. Kent and Shannon have used puzzles quite effectively to encourage people to complete their weekly Sunday School reading assignments. The answers to the puzzle are all contained within the assigned scriptures, so members who want to solve the puzzle must first read the assignment.

Sneaky Secret

Make sure you keep a current ward directory close by to use when there is any question about how to spell the name of a ward member mentioned in the bulletin. Not only do you risk offending the member with spelling errors, but you also make the bishopric, the ward, and yourself look sloppy.

▶ **Editor Contact Information**

Your bulletin will only be as accurate as the information you receive, so you need to make it as easy as possible for members to contact you. In every bulletin, include your name and all possible ways of contacting you (phone, fax, E-mail). You may also wish to list your weekly deadline time, so that members will know the latest time they can get information to you and still have it appear in the next bulletin.

Funeral Dinners

As we were planning this section, some of us thought a jaunty title would be "The Final Activity." Good taste prevailed, and we ended up using the title you see above. But in the interest of full disclosure, we thought you should know the entire story.

If you belong to a ward that is top-heavy with old people, you may be able to plan a funeral in your sleep. But if your ward is a young ward, you may not ever come in contact with funeral etiquette until you're faced with a situation where you're in charge. This happened in our ward recently, when a death occurred, and some fairly new leaders were not quite sure how to proceed. You certainly don't want to be learning all this while dealing with a grieving family, so we will do you a favor and give you some funeral pointers ahead of time.

First of all, the funeral itself is considered to be a church service. All planning for that church service comes under the jurisdiction of the bishop or branch president, who will give the bereaved family a general outline of what should happen during the course of the program. If you don't know how to plan a funeral program, don't panic. It's almost a fill-in-the-blanks process, and the choices are all up to the family of the deceased. Survivors can even choose to wash their hands of the major decisions. If you don't want to do any planning whatsoever, turn it over to the bishop. He'll be glad to help.

After the Funeral

After the funeral service ends, the members take over. At least in the United States, it's traditional to have a sit-down luncheon or dinner for family members after the services are over. If you are in charge of a funeral dinner, the first thing you'll need to know is how the phrase "family members" is defined for the purposes of the funeral meal. The family does not just consist of the people who live under the same roof as the deceased. Nor does a family even consist of blood relatives. For the purposes of a funeral dinner, "family" is everyone who is close enough to the actual family members to be invited to the funeral dinner. This may range from anyone who takes part on the funeral program to close friends of the family who may even be fellow ward members. Before you start your planning, make sure to ask the survivors to give you a rough estimate of how many people you can expect to serve.

Here's a ballpark figure that may help you. The average funeral dinner probably serves fifty to sixty people. And this is for small families. If the deceased person had twelve brothers and sisters who have married and produced their own large families, you could be looking at twice that number of meals. *Do not panic.* This is not an insurmountable problem. It's easy to put together a funeral dinner if you know how to do it.

After getting a rough estimate of how many mouths you're going to feed, the first thing on your agenda should be to decide where the dinner should be held. The bereaved family should have a say in this decision, and the survivors will probably have very definite ideas of where the funeral dinner should be. Some people prefer to hold the dinner in the family home. Others prefer to have the dinner held in the ward cultural hall or Relief Society room. There are advantages to either location, so either decision should bring a smile to your face.

Funeral Dinners at Home

The big advantage of having a funeral dinner at the home of the bereaved family is that at-home dinners don't need to be served by ward members. Nor do ward members have to clean up afterwards. The food is placed attractively on a table, ready for the mourners to serve themselves and eat as soon as they return from the chapel or cemetery. When the mourners arrive, the meal coordinator and her committee members leave the premises, and the ward's job is over. This is a great incentive to have funeral meals in the home.

If the funeral dinner is held in the home, it is the job of the meal coordinator to have the food on site and ready to serve by the time the funeral is over. (If you can't make a ballpark time estimate on your own, you may want to speak to the funeral director to get an estimate.) The meal coordinator will need access to the home during the funeral, but that shouldn't be a problem. Somebody should be house-sitting the home of the bereaved family during the funeral anyway. If the meal coordinator also serves as the house-sitter, it will be easy for her to have the food ready to serve by the time the survivors descend on the home.

People who drop off food for a funeral dinner in a home should fully cook the food in their own kitchens. Warming may take place in the oven of the bereaved, but major cooking activity should be avoided. Bereaved families have enough on their minds without having to clean up after the people who are feeding them.

A family that is in mourning does not have the mental stamina to keep track of which ward member contributed what to the funeral dinner. As each item comes to the home, the house-sitter or meal coordinator should check to see that the serving dish is labeled with the name of the person who donated the food. That way serving dishes can be returned to the people who contributed, and the survivors will know whom to thank afterwards. If you're the meal coordinator or a house-sitter, go to the house with a roll of masking tape and a marking pen to mark those unlabeled dishes, as well as a pen and paper to write down the names of people who contributed food on disposable platters.

Because most households don't have enough dishes and cutlery to outfit the number of people who are served at a funeral dinner, funeral dinners that are served at home will probably require sturdy paper plates and napkins and plastic cups and utensils. Check with the family of the bereaved to see if they want to supply these things, or plan on bringing them with the food. The big advantage of disposable kitchenware is that it *is* disposable. This simplifies cleanup afterwards, and will be greatly appreciated by the family.

Funeral Dinners at Church

Although an in-home meal is coordinated by one person, a committee for a funeral dinner at church can consist of a half dozen or more people. People may be assigned to set and decorate the tables, to cook the entrée, to serve and replenish the buffet table, or to do cleanup after the event. Having a funeral meal at church means a lot more work for a lot more people, but it also results in a more polished presentation than an at-home dinner where people load their paper plates and eat standing up.

Another big advantage of having funeral dinners in the Relief Society room or cultural hall is that the kitchen is available and has sufficient oven space to warm food before the meal begins. This assures that the food is piping hot whenever the mourners arrive.

If a meetinghouse is equipped with plates, glasses, and flatware, a funeral dinner is greatly enhanced if these items are used. However, using reusable dishes requires a cleanup committee to wash those dishes afterwards. Take all these things into consideration when you're helping the bereaved family choose a site.

Planning the Menu

As with all ward activities, even unplanned ones such as funerals, your goal should be to follow the easiest and the least expensive course of action that produces acceptable results. For example, the ward or the Relief Society or a family friend may buy a spiral-sliced ham to serve as the main course. Spiral-sliced hams are cheap if you buy them at warehouse shopping stores, and they often come with a packet of cherry sauce or mustard sauce you can use to dress up the entrée and make the dinner look more expensive than it is.

Once you have your main course, everything else is easy. People eat less ham if you've got dinner rolls, mayonnaise, mustard, and lettuce to make ham sandwiches. Be sure to provide lots of dinner rolls, together with real butter, other condiments, and some sort of jam or jelly or cheese as inexpensive fillers.

If there's one thing you can count on that will be served at virtually every American funeral dinner you ever attend, it's the dish of all-purpose funeral potatoes. These potatoes come under many names, but the recipe is basically the same. Funeral potatoes are served because they're tasty and easy to prepare. One batch serves about sixteen hungry people, so you won't need many batches even for the largest funeral dinner. In addition, funeral potatoes are inexpensive—but they don't taste cheap. For those who do not have the recipe for funeral potatoes prominently displayed in your recipe book, here it is:

Funeral Potatoes

1 24-ounce bag frozen, shredded hash brown potatoes, thawed
2 10¾-oz. cans cream of chicken soup
2 cups sour cream
1 cup grated cheddar cheese
½ cup plus 2 tablespoons melted butter
⅓ cup chopped onion
2 cups crushed corn flakes cereal

Combine corn flakes with 2 tablespoons of the melted butter. Set aside. In a large mixing bowl, combine remaining ingredients. Blend well. Pour potato mixture in a large oblong pan. Sprinkle crushed corn flake mixture on top and bake at 350° F. for 30 minutes. Serve hot.

Recipe Notes: The potatoes must be thawed before you make the casserole or it won't work. Also, do not use low-fat sour cream or cheddar cheese, and do not use margarine instead of butter. Low-fat sour cream and cheddar cheese don't melt, and margarine has water in it.

Serves 16

Once you have a ham and the funeral potatoes and tons of dinner rolls, everything else will naturally fall together. Women in the ward are more than happy to help out with salads or sheet cakes. Sheet cakes go a long way, so you don't need too many of them. Salads are another issue, though. When assigning salads, be sure to get a variety. If everyone brings lime gelatin, the food won't go as far as it would if you added green salads, potato salad, pasta salad, coleslaw, or fruit salad to the mix. Vegetable sticks and dip also constitute salad. The more non-ham foods you have on hand, the further your ham will go and the cheaper your dinner will be.

Some Final Thoughts

If you've never attended a funeral dinner, you may be dreading a solemn event. On the contrary, a funeral dinner is often a festive occasion.

In the first place, American Saints tend to wait longer after death to bury their loved ones than do people who are outside the Church. Outside the Church, people are commonly buried the day after death, or at the most on the second day afterwards. Inside the Church, there's usually a three- to five-day mourning period before the funeral. This allows family members to travel to the funeral from across the country. It also allows funeral participants to practice their music, write their talks, or print the funeral programs—all things that are usually handled by the funeral director or the clergyman in non-LDS congregations. Although this extra time is necessary for the survivors to make all these preparations, five days is a long time for loved ones to suspend their lives and grieve before the closure of a funeral service. By the time the funeral is finally concluded, the survivors who gather for the funeral dinner are more than ready to get back to the business of living.

The other factor that may turn your funeral dinner into a party is that funerals draw friends and family from far away. When people get together who haven't seen one another for a decade or longer, a funeral dinner may serve as a family reunion as well as a time for mourning.

This is not to say your funeral dinner is guaranteed to be a funfest. People are different. The funeral dinner you attend may indeed be a somber occasion. But flexibility is the word of the day. If the survivors want to laugh and have fun at a funeral dinner, nobody should criticize them for doing so.

By the way, it's a rule of thumb that people eat like locusts at funeral dinners. After all, many of the people you'll be serving have been too distraught to eat for nearly a week. Plan on more food rather than less, and you'll come out just about right. You can always take leftover food to shut-ins or package it up for the bereaved family. Neither your effort nor your food will go to waste.

Unity-Building Activities

Do the members of your ward really know each other, or are they just strangers who happen to attend church in the same building? With the hectic pace of life these days, it is often difficult for ward members to slow down enough to get to know each other. If your ward needs some help in the unity department, here are some activities that might help.

Unlike some of the previous activities in this book, these are quite unstructured, and can be done by any number of people. They can be adapted for an entire ward, or for a smaller group. Some of these could even be done on an individual family level.

Flamingo Invasion

This is an activity that can start as a simple family home evening pastime within your own family, or within just a few families in the ward. If it catches fire, it will soon involve the entire ward and will produce a lot of fun and curiosity for those who participate.

First, go to a garden supply store and buy one of the tacky pink plastic flamingos that are so popular as garden decorations with some segments of the population. If you can't find them in your area, do an Internet search to find them or look in a novelty catalog. If you can't find a flamingo, use any kind of large and horrible object (such as a plastic frog), although you will need to modify the poem below if you don't use a flamingo.

Now you need to compose a little poem to attach to the flamingo. You can modify the one we used, or come up with your own:

Frederika Flamingo

I'm a flamingo—a long-legged beauty.
I'm not just an ornament; I have a duty.
This family home evening I nest in your yard,
Accompanied by goodies, from a friend in the ward.
Enjoy your goodies; keep me safe by and by.
And then, come next Monday, please help me to fly.
If you and your family will make some new treat,
And take it (and me!) to a whole different street.
And plant us both firmly in somebody's yard,
(making sure the new owner also lives in the ward),
Then you'll be a hero . . . you'll be helping spread cheer,
Among young folks and old, in homes far and near.

Print the poem on heavy paper and laminate it if possible so that it will be protected from the weather. Now just follow the instructions in the poem. Make a batch of cookies or some other edible treat, and put them in a disposable container that won't need to be returned. Take the goodies and the flamingo (complete with attached poem) to the house of someone in your ward. This is something that works better at night because you don't want to be seen. Place the flamingo in the yard near the front door, and place the goodies by the bird. Then just knock on the door and run. If the members of your ward have any spirit at all, they will continue the tradition and Frederika will be on her way to a different home each Monday night. To get even more people involved, buy several birds and start each of them on a separate adventure.

You'll find that excitement and participation in the flamingo exchange escalates when there's an official ward endorsement to the spreading of flamingoes. If you can get the bishop to announce the beginning of the program, or place tantalizing and cryptic announcements in your Sunday bulletins, you'll be more likely to have a successful project. Nevertheless, there are some people who just don't want to participate in this sort of thing. Put a note on the reverse side of the poem, asking people to return the flamingo to the bishop's office or to call a specific telephone number for pickup if they can't participate this week. That way you'll lose fewer flamingoes. But eventually you're going to lose your birds. Be sure to buy an extra flamingo or two, and don't be too discouraged if you lose one from time to time.

Book of Mormon Reading Marathon

We all know we're supposed to read the Book of Mormon on a regular basis, but sometimes we forget to do it. A Book of Mormon reading marathon was introduced in our ward Relief Society, and it was so successful that other ward members asked to participate the next time around.

The planning is simple. At the beginning of the reading period, pass out reading schedules to all who wish to participate. You may want to print them as bookmarks and laminate them so they can be used over and over again, but any printed schedule will do. This schedule should give members a plan for reading the Book of Mormon in three months. If you don't want to do the figuring yourself, a sample breakdown of chapters is included on the following page.

Once everyone has a reading schedule, let people read on their own throughout the reading period. It helps to make occasional announcements, encouraging people to continue with their reading—or to begin their reading if they haven't already.

At the end of the period, there should be an activity to cap off the reading marathon. An early-morning testimony meeting may work well, or you can try a party where participants in the program are each awarded some sort of small prize.

You may be surprised at how successful a group reading of the Book of Mormon can be. In our ward, active church members read the Book of Mormon who had never read the book in its entirety. They participated in the early-morning testimony meeting, too. In fact, the event was so successful that people began reading the book again the day after they'd finished it the first time, until finally the book was read as a ward three times during the course of the year.

BOOK OF MORMON READING SCHEDULE

DAY	ASSIGNMENT	DAY	ASSIGNMENT
Day 1	1 Nephi 1–3	Day 46	Alma 23–24
Day 2	1 Nephi 4–6	Day 47	Alma 25–27
Day 3	1 Nephi 7–10	Day 48	Alma 28–30
Day 4	1 Nephi 11–12	Day 49	Alma 31–32
Day 5	1 Nephi 13–14	Day 50	Alma 33–34
Day 6	1 Nephi 15–16	Day 51	Alma 35–36
Day 7	1 Nephi 17–18	Day 52	Alma 37–39
Day 8	1 Nephi 19–20	Day 53	Alma 40–42
Day 9	1 Nephi 21–22	Day 54	Alma 43–44
Day 10	2 Nephi 1–2	Day 55	Alma 45–46
Day 11	2 Nephi 3–4	Day 56	Alma 47–48
Day 12	2 Nephi 5–7	Day 57	Alma 49–50
Day 13	2 Nephi 8–9	Day 58	Alma 51–52
Day 14	2 Nephi 10–12	Day 59	Alma 53–55
Day 15	2 Nephi 13–18	Day 60	Alma 56–57
Day 16	2 Nephi 19–23	Day 61	Alma 58–60
Day 17	2 Nephi 24–25	Day 62	Alma 61–62
Day 18	2 Nephi 26–27	Day 63	Alma 63–Helaman 2
Day 19	2 Nephi 28–30	Day 64	Helaman 3–4
Day 20	2 Nephi 31–33	Day 65	Helaman 5–6
Day 21	Jacob 1–3	Day 66	Helaman 7–8
Day 22	Jacob 4–5	Day 67	Helaman 9–11
Day 23	Jacob 6–7	Day 68	Helaman 12–13
Day 24	Enos, Jarom, Omni	Day 69	Helaman 14–16
Day 25	Words of Mormon, Mosiah 1	Day 70	3 Nephi 1–3
Day 26	Mosiah 2–3	Day 71	3 Nephi 4–6
Day 27	Mosiah 4–5	Day 72	3 Nephi 7–9
Day 28	Mosiah 6–9	Day 73	3 Nephi 10–11
Day 29	Mosiah 10–12	Day 74	3 Nephi 12–15
Day 30	Mosiah 13–15	Day 75	3 Nephi 16–18
Day 31	Mosiah 16–18	Day 76	3 Nephi 19–20
Day 32	Mosiah 19–21	Day 77	3 Nephi 21–23
Day 33	Mosiah 22–24	Day 78	3 Nephi 24–27
Day 34	Mosiah 25–26	Day 79	3 Nephi 28–30
Day 35	Mosiah 27–29	Day 80	4 Nephi, Mormon 1–2
Day 36	Alma 1–2	Day 81	Mormon 3–5
Day 37	Alma 3–4	Day 82	Mormon 6–8
Day 38	Alma 5–6	Day 83	Mormon 9, Ether 1
Day 39	Alma 7–9	Day 84	Ether 2–5
Day 40	Alma 10–11	Day 85	Ether 6–8
Day 41	Alma 12–13	Day 86	Ether 9–11
Day 42	Alma 14–15	Day 87	Ether 12–13
Day 43	Alma 16–17	Day 88	Ether 14–15, Moroni 1–5
Day 44	Alma 18–19	Day 89	Moroni 6–7
Day 45	Alma 20–22	Day 90	Moroni 8–10

Secret Admirer

This activity is sometimes called Secret Santa, because it often takes place during the Christmas season. But it works just as well around Valentine's Day or at any time of year—with the possible exception of summer vacation. This activity can be used to serve your own family, or it can be adapted to work with larger groups such as classes of young men and young women. Like Christmas itself, this activity brings feelings of satisfaction to both the giver and the receiver.

The idea is to select a family or an individual and be that person's secret admirer for a week. If you're doing this as a family, select another family or individual in the ward or neighborhood, or perhaps have each family member choose an individual. If you're doing this as a group, have each member of the group select someone they wish to admire for a week. You may wish to encourage the selection of people who need a little more attention, rather than those who already have a lot of friends. When doing this with the youth, it is usually effective to help them choose some of the older members of the ward, particularly those who are widowed or single.

Once each person has someone to admire, he must devise a way to pay attention to that person every day for the next week. The attention could be as simple as a card or a small present that is left on the door. You may or may not choose for the admirers to be anonymous. If they are not anonymous, another idea is for an admirer to perform some type of service each day, such as mowing the lawn or washing the car.

Another option is to have some kind of final activity at the end of the week, where both the admirers and the admired are invited. If your admirers have remained anonymous, this might be a good time to reveal their names and introduce them to those they admired. If you have done this as a family activity, invite those being admired into your home for a small activity at the end of the week. This type of activity also works well as a missionary tool when working with neighbors who are not members of the Church, although you should be cautious not to be too aggressive with your proselytizing. Let your example convert them, not your words.

Linger Longer

This is an activity that has a variety of names, and is often held in singles' wards. The idea is to stay after the regular Sunday meeting block to visit together as ward members over a potluck lunch. A Linger Longer is similar to a Lunch Bunch, but is held on Sunday. The food should be simple, and attendance should be completely optional. It should last no longer than an hour, although those who wish to stay longer should not be discouraged unless there are conflicts with other wards that meet in the building.

Our ward (which is definitely not a singles' ward) tried this a couple of times and had great success with it. These activities provide a great vehicle for meeting new members or for catching up with old ones.

Some wards and stakes discourage nonessential meetings on Sunday, so be sure to get approval for this activity before you send out the announcements.

Teacher Recognition

This is an activity that provides a good community service, in addition to promoting goodwill and positive impressions of the Church in your community. It should probably be held just prior to the ending of the school year.

Have the youth leaders solicit nominations from the youth for outstanding schoolteachers. You can limit this to just high school, or it can also include the schools that teach younger children. Have each student compose a written nomination that includes things such as the teacher's name, school, and the subjects he teaches. The nomination should also include information about why the nominee is an exceptional teacher. If you have a lot of youth and a lot of nominations, you may wish to have some type of voting process to select the most popular choices.

Once the outstanding teachers have been selected, plan an event to recognize and honor them. You might want to invite the guests with a formal invitation from the bishop, followed up with a phone call from someone planning the activity. You will almost guarantee a higher rate of attendance if the teacher gets a personal visit or phone call in addition to the letter.

At the event, you might want to have a light dinner, followed by the program in which the awards are presented. You might want to read one or more of the nominations for that teacher, and then have them stand and accept some small gift. You might even let them give a small acceptance speech if you feel it is appropriate.

Several wards in our area have done this type of event with good success. The teachers are generally honored by the recognition, plus it gives them the opportunity to learn about us as well. This same type of event could be adapted to other individuals in the community or the neighborhood. For example, you could honor those who have been active in volunteer activities in the community.

Goals "R" Us

If you're like most people, all those noble resolutions you make in January will be broken and forgotten by the time March rolls around. But goals are easier if you work towards them as a group, especially if you can generate a little spirit of competition among the ward members. Consider implementing a goal program for your group. Those who participate will be able to improve their lives and develop good habits while having fun in the process.

Kathy has designed goal programs for a couple of different wards, and they have always been quite successful. The secret is to provide a lot of different options, and allow people to choose the ones they want to accomplish. On the following page is the goal sheet for a Relief Society goal program she did a few years ago. Notice that all these instructions will fit onto just one or two sheets of paper, so it is easy to reproduce and distribute to those who will participate in the program.

Obviously, the program could easily be adapted for any type of group by changing the goals to be relevant to your target audience. You could also separate the goals into different categories, such as spiritual improvement, cultural improvement, and physical improvement.

As the goal program runs throughout the year, continue to do things to remind participants about it, and to recognize those who achieve the 100-point goal.

At the end of the goal program, one way to wrap things up is to have a goal party. Just so there are no hurt feelings, invite all of those who participated in the program, even if they did not reach the target threshold of 100 points. Give special recognition to those who did well in accomplishing their goals. Recognize all of those who completed the program, and present them with some sort of award—even if it is just a certificate signed by the bishop. Also recognize those who went the extra mile or who had unusual experiences as they were accomplishing their goals. You might want to also recognize the two or three people with the highest number of goal points at the end of the program.

If you run your goal program correctly, it really will motivate members to reach their goals and to have fun in the process. Kathy is still being asked for copies of goal programs that were used nearly a decade ago.

Goals "R" Us

The Official 100-Point Relief Society Goal Program

If you can count to one hundred, you can compete in this year's goal program! This is a program you can customize to your own needs. The only requirement is that you complete enough goals to total 100 points.

To the right of each goal is the number of points you get for accomplishing that goal. If the number appears multiple times, you can get that many points each time you accomplish the goal. For example, you can accomplish the first goal up to five times and earn one point each time. Just circle each point value when the goal is complete, and periodically tally up the circled numbers to see how close you are to your target of 100 points. (Of course, you don't need to stop there.)

Good luck! Surprises await the women who achieve their 100-point goals—and a healthy sense of self-accomplishment is the reward for everyone who participates.

One-Point Goals

Read your Sunday School assignment: 1   1   1   1   1   Total: _____

Read a book: 1   1   1   1   1   Total: _____

Write and mail a letter: 1   1   1   1   1   Total: _____

Give up TV for a week: 1   1   1   1   1   Total: _____

Play on the floor with a child for an hour: 1   1   1   1   1   Total: _____

Watch a PBS special: 1   1   1   1   1   Total: _____

Say your prayers with your spouse: 1   1   1   1   1   Total: _____

Exercise three times in one week: 1   1   1   1   1   Total: _____

Do 100 percent of your visiting teaching: 1   1   1   1   1   Total: _____

Clean out a closet: 1   1   1   1   1   Total: _____

Visit a sick friend with food in hand: 1   1   1   1   1   Total: _____

Call somebody up on a birthday: 1   1   1   1   1   Total: _____

Take your spouse on a date: 1   1   1   1   1   Total: _____

Give a prayer in a church meeting: 1   1   1   1   1   Total: _____

Attend the temple: 1   1   1   1   1   Total: _____

Fast with a purpose: 1   1   1   1   1   Total: _____

Do a good deed in secret:	1	1	1	1	1	Total: _____
Bear your testimony in a church meeting:	1	1	1	1	1	Total: _____
Do a favor for a friend:	1	1	1	1	1	Total: _____
Try a new dish using your food storage:	1	1	1	1	1	Total: _____
Pray aloud morning and night:	1	1	1	1	1	Total: _____
Invite a family to dinner at your house:	1	1	1	1	1	Total: _____
Make a new friend in the ward:	1	1	1	1	1	Total: _____
Tell somebody you love him:	1	1	1	1	1	Total: _____
Write and mail a letter to a missionary:	1	1	1	1	1	Total: _____
Take food to a ward function:	1	1	1	1	1	Total: _____
Send a note of praise to a ward member:	1	1	1	1	1	Total: _____
Visit a place you've never been before:	1	1	1	1	1	Total: _____
Greet someone you don't know in church:	1	1	1	1	1	Total: _____
Help someone who is moving:	1	1	1	1	1	Total: _____
Supplement your food storage:	1	1	1	1	1	Total: _____
Listen to the prelude music on Sunday:	1	1	1	1	1	Total: _____
Take a morning to pamper yourself:	1	1	1	1	1	Total: _____
Check on someone you visit teach:	1	1	1	1	1	Total: _____
Go to lunch with a friend:	1	1	1	1	1	Total: _____
Think about the Savior during the sacrament:	1	1	1	1	1	Total: _____
Read the Relief Society lesson:	1	1	1	1	1	Total: _____
Comfort a friend:	1	1	1	1	1	Total: _____
Read and study your patriarchal blessing:	1	1	1	1	1	Total: _____

Five-Point Goals

Give a lesson in a church meeting:	5	5	5	5	5	Total: _____
Speak in sacrament meeting:	5	5	5	5	5	Total: _____
Give a nonmember the Book of Mormon:	5	5	5	5	5	Total: _____
Use a checklist every day for a week:	5	5	5	5	5	Total: _____
Host a missionary discussion:	5	5	5	5	5	Total: _____
Keep a food journal for a week:	5	5	5	5	5	Total: _____

Go on missionary exchanges:	5	5	5	5	5	Total: _____
Host a party for someone else:	5	5	5	5	5	Total: _____
Give up junk food for a week:	5	5	5	5	5	Total: _____
Submit family names for temple ordinances:	5	5	5	5	5	Total: _____
Do volunteer work for the community:	5	5	5	5	5	Total: _____
Develop a new hobby or interest:	5	5	5	5	5	Total: _____
Keep your temper when provoked:	5	5	5	5	5	Total: _____
Lose five pounds (can be the same ones!):	5	5	5	5	5	Total: _____
Keep your home clean for a week:	5	5	5	5	5	Total: _____
Remember the birthdays of those you visit teach:	5	5	5	5	5	Total: _____
Invite guests to family home evening:	5	5	5	5	5	Total: _____
Have the missionaries to dinner:	5	5	5	5	5	Total: _____
Participate in a ward temple trip:	5	5	5	5	5	Total: _____
Go on a Family History Center trip:	5	5	5	5	5	Total: _____
Help clean your ward meetinghouse:	5	5	5	5	5	Total: _____

Ten-Point Goals

Read the Book of Mormon from cover to cover	10	Total: _____
Read the entire Old Testament:	10	Total: _____
Read the entire New Testament:	10	Total: _____
Read the Doctrine and Covenants and Pearl of Great Price:	10	Total: _____
Introduce a friend or neighbor to the gospel:	10	Total: _____
Attend girls' camp as an adult leader:	10	Total: _____
Write in a journal every day for a month:	10	Total: _____
Finish a job that's been hanging over your head for ages:	10	Total: _____
Get a patriarchal blessing:	10	Total: _____
Do (yes, finish!) your spring cleaning:	10	Total: _____
Complete a 72-hour kit:	10	Total: _____
Participate in a ward or Relief Society service project:	10	Total: _____

Questions from the Clueless

? *What can be done with excess food after an activity?*

As you learned earlier in the chapter, you can sometimes recover some of your food costs by selling any excess food back to the members who attend. But that isn't always possible or practical. If there are full-time missionaries assigned to your ward, they are always grateful for tasty leftovers. Consider packaging the leftovers as individual portions so they can be easily frozen.

Your bishop or another ward leader may be able to identify individuals in your area who would appreciate the extra food. These could be either members of your ward or people who are not members of the Church. Be sensitive to the feelings of the recipients as you deliver the food so that they will not be embarrassed. After all, there are many reasons why someone may be chosen as a recipient. It could be a widow who can't leave her home, or someone who has the flu, or someone who needs a little extra food in the refrigerator. It is probably not a good idea to take your entire youth organization when you deliver the food.

Even if the recipient's cupboard is not bare, giving extra food to non-member neighbors provides a good opportunity to do some missionary work and get to know your neighbors better. You will want to do this when you have some really tasty leftovers, and not just a half bag of potato chip crumbs. Don't give away anything that you wouldn't want to eat yourself.

Most communities have soup kitchens or other facilities that feed the homeless, and many of these will accept donations of leftover food under certain conditions. Make sure you contact these organizations first before you arrive with a whole station wagon full of food. Ideally, contact these organizations well before the activity so that you will know whom to contact and what you must do so that the food will be in an acceptable condition.

? *How can I make our ward newsletter more interesting?*

The problem with many newsletters is that they simply pass along somewhat-dry announcements from each organization. The secret to a really interesting newsletter is to remember the phrase "names make news." Try to mention the names of as many ward members as you can.

Think up any excuse to get as many names in print as possible—even if you have to make up stories about people (okay, don't go that far.)

When mentioning names, make a point of including people who don't often get a lot of publicity. As you read through a typical newsletter, you will probably see the same names over and over—the "movers and shakers" who have leadership positions in the ward. There is nothing wrong with that, but your challenge as an editor should be to expand that vision to include every member if possible. You may have to develop some sources and dig for this information, because the people who typically go unnoticed in a ward are not big on self-promotion. But you can be sure their lives and their accomplishments are just as notable, even if they are not as vocal about their accomplishments.

The official title of your calling is probably "ward newspaper *editor.*" They call you an editor for a reason. You don't just throw information into a newsletter, but you edit what you're given to make it more interesting and understandable. You will find that some ward leaders have not written anything since they got out of school. They will give you the most boring and unimaginative articles ever to have crossed an editor's desk. Your job is to transform their words into an article that will interest people and hold their attention so they actually read every word. If you inform or amuse ward members in the process, so much the better. You are the editor, so wield your pen (or word processor) with boldness. Just make sure to use sensitivity as you do so. Don't ever make a joke at the expense of someone else, and be mindful of the feelings of the person whose information you're editing. Preserve enough of the original document so the author will recognize it as his own work. After all, you're hoping to get more information from the same ward member next month.

The bottom line is to build ward unity. Find good things to write about the people in your ward. Do all that you can to increase the feelings of friendship and concern among them. Promote the good things people do that often go unnoticed. If you see a ward member with a problem, try to publicize it in a way that will bring other members to their aid without causing them embarrassment. If you keep unity and friendship as your watchwords, you will almost certainly produce a result that will be interesting as well as informative.

? *What types of activities are not appropriate?*

Once you receive any kind of calling that involves the planning of activities, you can be sure it will only be a matter of time until people start contacting you with ideas for all kinds of activities they would like to see happen. Some of these people will probably have good ideas, and some of the ideas will seem to be more than a little strange. Sometimes an activity will not appeal to you just because of the theme. Some people love dances and athletic events, but an equal number of ward members would prefer to have dental surgery than to attend such an activity. You will probably have your share of activities that don't particularly appeal to you, but you'll hold them anyway because you know others like them.

But there are other activities you should avoid like the plague because they will cause nothing but trouble for you. First of all, the LDS Church has always maintained a position of strict political neutrality, and no church facilities should ever be used for any kind of activity that promotes a specific party or candidate. Breaking this rule will not only cause hard feelings, but it could also cause legal problems for the Church. Although it might be acceptable to use church facilities for some type of nonpartisan events, make sure you get the permission of your bishop before attempting this.

You should also be cautious of any kind of activity that asks members to donate money or buy items. Although this seems innocent enough on the surface, it can lead to problems. Be cautious even if the activity promotes a good cause, such as the storage of food. Such activities can be viewed as unfair competition by merchants, and could also cause legal problems for the Church.

There are some activities that seem innocent enough on the surface, but that can lead to hurt feelings if they are not handled correctly. Members will often hold going-away parties for popular families that move out of the ward. Although this is a nice idea, what does it say to those families who move out of the ward without any fanfare? If you hold these, be consistent and cautious of members' feelings. Perhaps you could hold a going-away party once or twice a year for all families that have left or will soon be leaving. If you hold the activity regularly, and you don't associate it with any particular family, you minimize the risk that someone will be overlooked and offended.

Another type of activity that can be abused is that of giving showers. Well-meaning Relief Society presidencies in many wards try to organize bridal showers or baby showers for selected new mothers or brides. This is a potentially disastrous situation. The hosts of these showers run the risk of offending people who aren't invited, plus the risk of placing a financial burden on those who are on the guest list. But that isn't all. Once the Relief Society gives one shower, it will have to give a shower for every new mother or new bride in the ward—even if it's a mother's eleventh child or the new bride has been married seventeen times. Otherwise, people in similar situations who are not similarly recognized will have their feelings hurt. Although it's fine for ward members to act independently and give showers for friends who live in the ward, these activities should never be sponsored as official ward activities. Not ever. No exceptions.

One practice that should be strictly forbidden is to restrict participation in any ward activity to the social elite. When Kathy served as editor of her ward's Sunday bulletin, she was asked to publicize the formation of dinner groups in the ward. It was only after she had publicized the event for several weeks that she learned that people who were not on the hostess's social A-list were being told that the groups were already filled. Thus an event that could have been a great unifying force in the ward turned into a disaster, with hurt feelings all around. There is no place in your ward—or in any ward—for members to be excluded because they aren't as rich or as pretty or as famous as others in the group. If you're an activities committee chairman, do not host such an event; if you're in a position to publicize events that are hosted by others, make sure before you publicize them that nobody will be excluded who wants to attend.

In fact, it is vital to your success as an event planner that all will feel welcome at the activities you plan. Consider the circumstances of all ward members, and ask yourself how each group will react to your proposed party or activity. If you have a "couples only" night, what can you do to let singles know that they are welcome also? And if singles do come, what can you do to make them feel a part of the group? What about daddy/daughter nights in a ward where not all daughters have daddies? Or mother/son events where some boys may be living with a divorced dad? The answers to these questions are not easy, but you should try your best to make every member feel totally welcome and comfortable at every event you plan. Remember—the slightest hurt feeling can be the stumbling block that drives a weak Saint away from the Church for the rest of his life.

In all cases, if you have questions about the appropriateness of an activity, direct those questions to the bishop or to the leader of your group. It is better to be safe and ask than to hold an activity that causes problems or hard feelings.

EPILOGUE
A Good Time Was Had by All

If you look in the *Encyclopedia of Mormonism* under the topic "Community," you will find the following observations: "The ward provides not only worship services but friends, economic assistance, and a support group that can be relied upon to provide the assistance any family might need, particularly in a society in which extended family members may not be nearby to provide such assistance. . . . One belongs in the community of Saints regardless of one's other affiliations or lack of them; one is welcome in the ward however outcast one may feel elsewhere" (Daniel H. Ludlow, ed. [New York: Macmillan Publishing Co., 1992], 1:301).

If you ask people outside the Church what they know about the Mormons, many will tell you about the sense of closeness and community that exists within the faith. Even those who are not yet ready to accept LDS doctrines will talk with some sense of envy about the feeling of belonging that exists within an LDS congregation.

But those feelings of community don't just happen; they have to be created. And this creation isn't just the job of the bishop, or the auxiliary leaders, or even the home and visiting teachers. Every individual within the framework of the ward is responsible for building the good feelings that lead to that sense of community.

No matter what other Church callings we may have, part of our duty as disciples of the Savior is to reach out to others in a spirit of friendship and kindness. The same feelings of love, acceptance, and forgiveness that we should find in our own immediate families need to spread out to encompass the extended family of "brothers and sisters" within our ward.

When you are asked to plan an activity for a group or for the entire ward, the logistics of that event often get in the way. It is common to focus on the type of food that will be served, and how it will be served. We try to figure out what decorations will be used, trying to get the most use out of our decoration budget. We worry about the format of the program, often changing our minds several times before we reach a final decision. We agonize whether children should be invited to this particular activity, and determine what accommodations will be made for them during the course of the event.

Although all these details are important, the issue that may be most important of all is the one we often overlook. That is the question of how your particular activity can and should foster the spirit of community within your ward. Perhaps there are games to play that will help people learn to know each other better. Maybe we can refine the theme of the activity so that it will appeal to ward members who rarely attend church. There may be a way to utilize the talents of those nonmember relatives or others who often find themselves on the fringes of an LDS community. There could also be some means of spotlighting members who are recent arrivals to the ward. Maybe you could use the activity to generate interest in a gospel principle, such as self-sufficiency or family history. There may be some activity or facet of your activity that would be particularly useful for the full-time missionaries working with investigators in the area. If you consider your activity from all angles, you can enhance it to meet the needs of those who will attend, fostering those feelings of acceptance and friendship that turn a congregation into a family.

If you plan your activity from the standpoint of ward unity, you'll realize that building a solid community of Saints is far more important than attending to the trivial details of the decorations or menu. A year from now, nobody will remember what food was served, or what was on the program, or whether the napkins at the table were white or blue. But there are other things that could happen that would be remembered for a lifetime:

- If your party becomes the turning point for activating a marginally active family, you could influence generations of church members.

- If your educational program inspires someone to start a hobby that lasts a lifetime and brings to pass much goodness, you can make changes that will be eternal in nature.

- If new families move into the area and decide after attending your ward activity that this is a place they can call home, they will immerse themselves in the life of the ward rather than looking for a sense of community in places that are outside the Church.

Don't ever underestimate the amount of goodwill that can be generated from a successful ward activity. You may be tempted to diminish your own role in this process, and think of the bishopric as the "big guns" when it comes to making a difference in people's lives. But people respond to different incentives, and some people will respond to an activity where they would not respond to a personal invitation to meet with the bishop.

Your calling is not just to create a pleasant diversion for ward members, but to help them grow spiritually and to inspire them to join together as a closely-knit ward family. You may be approaching this goal in a temporal way, but you are striving for the same result as the bishop, the Gospel Doctrine teacher, and the other leaders in the ward.

The fabric of the Lord's kingdom is woven out of many diverse souls. Each of us has a separate set of talents, and each of us strives to build the kingdom in his own particular way. We are different parts of the same body—different ingredients in the same batch of cookies. Just as the body isn't whole if one of its parts is missing, or a batch of cookies doesn't taste right if one of the ingredients is left out, the fabric of your ward will not be solid and strong unless every member is included.

As someone who plans activities, you may think of yourself as the "little toe" of your ward community. But don't minimize your importance in regards to the overall health of the body of your congregation. Anyone who thinks that the little toe is not important has never had a blister there!

Activities Index

Index